Student Engagement in the Language Classroom

PSYCHOLOGY OF LANGUAGE LEARNING AND TEACHING

Series Editors: **Sarah Mercer**, *Universität Graz, Austria* and **Stephen Ryan**, *Waseda University, Japan*

This international, interdisciplinary book series explores the exciting, emerging field of Psychology of Language Learning and Teaching. It is a series that aims to bring together works which address a diverse range of psychological constructs from a multitude of empirical and theoretical perspectives, but always with a clear focus on their applications within the domain of language learning and teaching. The field is one that integrates various areas of research that have been traditionally discussed as distinct entities, such as motivation, identity, beliefs, strategies and self-regulation, and it also explores other less familiar concepts for a language education audience, such as emotions, the self and positive psychology approaches. In theoretical terms, the new field represents a dynamic interface between psychology and foreign language education and books in the series draw on work from diverse branches of psychology, while remaining determinedly focused on their pedagogic value. In methodological terms, sociocultural and complexity perspectives have drawn attention to the relationships between individuals and their social worlds, leading to a field now marked by methodological pluralism. In view of this, books encompassing quantitative, qualitative and mixed methods studies are all welcomed.

All books in this series are externally peer-reviewed.

Full details of all the books in this series and of all our other publications can be found on http://www.multilingual-matters.com, or by writing to Multilingual Matters, St Nicholas House, 31–34 High Street, Bristol BS1 2AW, UK.

PSYCHOLOGY OF LANGUAGE LEARNING AND TEACHING: 11

Student Engagement in the Language Classroom

Edited by

Phil Hiver, Ali H. Al-Hoorie and Sarah Mercer

MULTILINGUAL MATTERS
Bristol • Blue Ridge Summit

DOI https://doi.org/10.21832/HIVER3606

Library of Congress Cataloging in Publication Data
A catalog record for this book is available from the Library of Congress.
Names: Hiver, Phil, 1984- editor. | Al-Hoorie, Ali H., 1982- editor. |
  Mercer, Sarah, editor.
Title: Student Engagement in the Language Classroom/Edited by Phil Hiver,
  Ali H. Al-Hoorie and Sarah Mercer.
Description: Bristol, UK; Blue Ridge Summit, PA : Multilingual Matters,
  2021. | Series: Psychology of Language Learning and Teaching: 11 |
  Includes bibliographical references and index. | Summary: "Through a mix of
  conceptual and empirical chapters, this book defines engagement for the field of
  language learning. It serves as an authoritative guide for anyone wishing to
  understand the unique insights engagement can give into language learning and
  teaching, or anyone conducting their own research on engagement within and
  beyond the classroom"—Provided by publisher.
Identifiers: LCCN 2020033226 (print) | LCCN 2020033227 (ebook) | ISBN
  9781788923590 (paperback) | ISBN 9781788923606 (hardback) | ISBN
  9781788923613 (pdf) | ISBN 9781788923620 (epub) | ISBN 9781788923637 (kindle
  edition)
Subjects: LCSH: Language and languages—Study and teaching—Psychological
  aspects. | Second language acquisition—Psychological aspects. |
  Motivation in education.
Classification: LCC P53.7 .S78 2021 (print) | LCC P53.7 (ebook) | DDC
  418.0071—dc23 LC record available at https://lccn.loc.gov/2020033226
LC ebook record available at https://lccn.loc.gov/2020033227

British Library Cataloguing in Publication Data
A catalogue entry for this book is available from the British Library.

ISBN-13: 978-1-78892-360-6 (hbk)
ISBN-13: 978-1-78892-359-0 (pbk)

Multilingual Matters
UK: St Nicholas House, 31-34 High Street, Bristol BS1 2AW, UK.
USA: NBN, Blue Ridge Summit, PA, USA.

Website: www.multilingual-matters.com
Twitter: Multi_Ling_Mat
Facebook: https://www.facebook.com/multilingualmatters
Blog: www.channelviewpublications.wordpress.com

The policy of Multilingual Matters/Channel View Publications is to use papers that
are natural, renewable and recyclable products, made from wood grown in
sustainable forests. In the manufacturing process of our books, and to further
support our policy, preference is given to printers that have FSC and PEFC Chain of
Custody certification. The FSC and/or PEFC logos will appear on those books
where full certification has been granted to the printer concerned.

Typeset by Nova Techset Private Limited, Bengaluru and Chennai, India.
Printed and bound in the UK by the CPI Books Group Ltd.
Printed and bound in the US by NBN.

Contents

External Reviewers   vii
Contributors   ix
Foreword   xv
Richard M. Ryan

1   Introduction   1
Phil Hiver, Sarah Mercer and Ali H. Al-Hoorie

Part 1: Conceptual Chapters

2   Engagement and Companion Constructs in Language
Learning: Conceptualizing Learners' Involvement in the L2
Classroom   17
Yuan Sang and Phil Hiver

3   Engagement with Language in Relation to Form-Focused
Versus Meaning-Focused Teaching and Learning   38
Agneta M-L Svalberg

4   Research on Learner Engagement with Written (Corrective)
Feedback: Insights and Issues   56
Ye Han and Xuesong (Andy) Gao

5   Measuring L2 Engagement: A Review of Issues and
Applications   75
Shiyao (Ashlee) Zhou, Phil Hiver and Ali H. Al-Hoorie

Part 2: Empirical Chapters

6   Exploring Connections between Classroom Environment
and Engagement in the Foreign Language Classroom   101
Giulia Sulis and Jenefer Philp

7   Examining Learner Engagement in Relationship to Learning
and Communication Mode   120
Carly Carver, Daniel Jung and Laura Gurzynski-Weiss

8   Fake or Real Engagement – Looks can be Deceiving   143
Sarah Mercer, Kyle R. Talbot and Isobel Kai-Hui Wang

9   The Effect of Choice on Affective Engagement: Implications
     for Task Design   163
     Linh Phung, Sachiko Nakamura and Hayo Reinders

10 How Ideal Classmates Priming Increases EFL Classroom
     Prosocial Engagement   182
     *Tetsuya Fukuda, Yoshifumi Fukada, Joseph Falout
        and Tim Murphey*

11 Engagement and Immersion in Virtual Reality Narratives   202
     Nicole Mills

12 Engagement Growth in Language Learning Classrooms:
     A Latent Growth Analysis of Engagement in Japanese
     Elementary Schools   224
     W.L. Quint Oga-Baldwin and Luke K. Fryer

13 Modeling the Relations Between Foreign Language
     Engagement, Emotions, Grit and Reading Achievement   241
     Gholam Hassan Khajavy

14 Conceptualizing Willingness to Engage in L2 Learning
     beyond the Classroom   260
     Isobel Kai-Hui Wang and Sarah Mercer

15 Engagement: The Active Verb between the Curriculum
     and Learning   280
     Phil Hiver, Sarah Mercer and Ali H. Al-Hoorie

     Index   288

External Reviewers

Scott Aubrey
Chinese University of Hong Kong, Hong Kong SAR

Ali Dincer
Erzincan Binali Yildirim University, Turkey

Alastair Henry
University West, Sweden

Gianna Hessel
Karl-Franzens-Universität Graz, Austria

Tae-Young Kim
Chung-Ang University, South Korea

Christine Muir
University of Nottingham, England

Richard Pinner
Sophia University, Japan

Mostafa Papi
Florida State University, USA

Masatoshi Sato
Universidad Andrés Bello, Chile

Alyssa Vuono
Florida State University, USA

Contributors

Ali H. Al-Hoorie is an Assistant Professor at the English Language and Preparatory Institute, Royal Commission for Jubail and Yanbu, Saudi Arabia. He completed his PhD degree at the University of Nottingham under the supervision of Professors Zoltán Dörnyei and Norbert Schmitt. He also holds an MA in Social Science Data Analysis from Essex University. His research interests include motivation theory, research methodology and complexity. His publications have appeared in a number of journals including *Language Learning, The Modern Language Journal, Studies in Second Language Acquisition, ELT J, Language Teaching Research* and *Learning and Individual Differences*. He is also the co-author (with Phil Hiver) of *Research Methods for Complexity in Applied Linguistics* and co-editor (with Peter D. MacIntyre) of *Contemporary Language Motivation Theory: 60 Years Since Gardner and Lambert (1959)*.

Carly Carver is an Assistant Professor of Hispanic Linguistics at Augusta University. She received her PhD from Indiana University. Her research focuses on the role of corrective feedback, technology-mediated task-based language teaching and learner individual differences in the second language acquisition of Spanish. She is particularly interested in how the timing, type, mode of provision and provider of corrective feedback interact with cognitive and affective individual differences to impact feedback efficacy and L2 development. She also conducts research on L2 and heritage oral proficiency. Her work appears in journals such as *Studies in Second Language Acquisition, The Modern Language Journal, Language Teaching Research,* and *Studies in Second Language Learning and Teaching* as well as in edited volumes including *Recent Perspectives on Task-based Language Teaching* (Ed. Ahmadian & García Mayo, de Gruyter, 2017).

Joseph Falout is an Associate Professor at Nihon University (Japan) and has authored or co-authored over 50 papers and book chapters about language learning psychology. He received awards for publications and presentations from the Japan Association for Language Teaching (JALT). He edits for JALT's *OnCUE Journal* and *Asian EFL Journal*. Collaborations include creating the theoretical and applied foundations of critical partici-patory looping, present communities of imagining and ideal classmates. Joseph teaches EAP and ESP to undergraduate and graduate students, and he conducts workshops for teachers at all educational levels. Previously he taught rhetoric and composition, public speaking and ESL at colleges in the USA.

Luke K. Fryer is an Associate Professor and Head of Program for faculty and research postgraduate student teaching and learning at the University of Hong Kong. His main area of research is the role of non-cognitive fac-tors like interest within teaching and learning.

Yoshifumi Fukada (EdD) is a Professor at Meisei University (Japan). His research interests include L2 learners' and users' dynamic identities, as in their agency in their English-learning and social interactions. He recently published 'An ethnographic case study of one Korean international stu-dent's TL-mediated socializing in affinity space of the host country' (*Internationalisation and Transnationalisation in Higher Education*, Peter Lang, 2018), 'Whole language approach' (*The TESOL Encyclopedia of English Language Teaching*, Wiley-Blackwell, 2018), and *L2 Learning During Study Abroad: The Creation of Affinity Spaces* (Springer, 2019).

Tetsuya Fukuda (PhD) is a Tenured Instructor at International Christian University in Tokyo, Japan, co-authored book chapters in *Psychology for Language Learning* (Palgrave McMillan), *Language Learning Motivation in Japan* (Multilingual Matters) and others. Tetsuya edits for proceedings including *JALT Pan-SIG Proceedings* and several in-house journals. His research interests include L2 motivation, school belonging, test analysis and program evaluation.

Xuesong (Andy) Gao is an Associate Professor in the School of Education at the University of New South Wales. His current research interests are in the areas of learner autonomy, language learning narratives, language education policy and language teacher education. He is co-editor of *System: An International Journal of Educational Technology and Applied Linguistics*.

Laura Gurzynski-Weiss is Associate Professor and Director of Undergraduate Studies in the Department of Spanish and Portuguese at Indiana University, USA. She investigates interaction- and task-based instructed second language acquisition, interlocutor and learner individ-ual difference, feedback use and perception, teacher cognition and emerg-ing bilingualism in elementary-aged children. Her research appears in journals such as *Studies in Second Language Acquisition, Language Learning, Applied Psycholinguistics, The Modern Language Journal,*

Language Teaching Research and *Hispania*. She is the editor of *Individual Difference Research in the Interaction Approach: Investigating Learners, Instructors, and Researchers* (John Benjamins, 2017) and *Cross-linguistic Examinations of Interlocutors and their Individual Differences* (John Benjamins, 2020), and co-author of *Introducción y aplicaciones contextualizadas a la lingüística hispánica* (with Manuel Díaz-Campos & Kimberly L. Geeslin; Wiley-Blackwell, 2018).

Ye Han is an Assistant Professor in the School of Humanities and Social Sciences at Harbin Institute of Technology, Shenzhen, China. Her research interests include written corrective feedback, writing conferences and the interface between cognition and emotion in second language writing.

Phil Hiver is an Assistant Professor of Foreign & Second Language Education at Florida State University. His published research takes a complex and dynamic view of individual differences in language learning and explores their interface with instructed language development and language pedagogy. He has also written on innovation and precision in research methods and the contribution of complexity theory/dynamic systems theory (CDST) to applied linguistics research. He is co-author (with Ali Al-Hoorie) of *Research Methods for Complexity Theory in Applied Linguistics* (Multilingual Matters). With Shaofeng Li and Ali Al-Hoorie, he edits the *Journal for the Psychology of Language Learning* (JPLL).

Daniel Jung is a PhD Candidate in Hispanic Linguistics at Indiana University, USA. His research focuses on the role of individual differences in foreign language and study abroad contexts. He is particularly interested in exploring how dynamic conceptualizations of individual differences can be incorporated to understand second language learning and achievement in the classroom. He has conducted research on the role of motivation and intensity of contact on speech act realization during short-term study abroad programs, and is part of a research group examining longitudinally the dynamic nature of motivation, cognitive styles, personality, working memory and learning strategies.

Gholam Hassan Khajavy is an Assistant Professor of foreign language education at University of Bojnord. His research interests include psychology of language education and research methodology. He has published in different international journals such as *TESOL Quarterly*, *Studies in Second Language Acquisition* and *Contemporary Educational Psychology*.

Sarah Mercer is Professor of Foreign Language Teaching at the University of Graz, Austria, where she is Head of ELT methodology. Her research interests include all aspects of the psychology surrounding the foreign language learning experience. She is the author, co-author and co-editor of several books in this area including *Towards an Understanding of Language Learner Self-Concept*, *Psychology for Language Learning*, *Multiple Perspectives on the Self in SLA*, *New Directions in Language Learning Psychology*, *Positive Psychology in SLA*, *Exploring Psychology for Language Teachers* (Winner of the IH Ben Warren Prize) and *Language Teacher Psychology*.

Nicole Mills is the Director of Language Programs (interim) in the Department of Romance Languages & Literatures at Harvard University. She teaches courses in French, language pedagogy and second language research and practice and serves as the advisor for Harvard's Certificate in Teaching Language and Culture. She has publications in various academic journals and edited volumes on various topics associated with virtual and simulated environments in language learning, global simulation, psychology of language learning and teaching, and language program evaluation. In 2015, she co-edited a volume entitled *Innovation and Accountability in Language Program Evaluation* (with John Norris) and her current book project, *Perspectives on Teaching Language and Content* (co-authored with Stacey Katz Bourns and Cheryl Krueger), will be published in 2020 with Yale University Press.

Tim Murphey (PhD Université de Neuchâtel, Switzerland) is TESOL's Professional Development in Language Education series editor, co-author with Dörnyei of *Group Dynamics in the Language Classroom* (CUP), author of *Music and Song* (OUP), *Language Hungry!* (Helbling), *The Tale that Wags* (Perceptia), *Teaching in Pursuit of Wow!* (Abax), and co-editor *Meaningful Action* (CUP). Semi-retired as of 2019, he is a visiting professor at Kanda University International Studies.

Sachiko Nakamura holds an MA in TESOL from Anaheim University and is a Doctoral candidate in Applied Linguistics at King Mongkut's University, Thailand. Her research areas include the psychology of language learning and self-regulated learning, with her current studies focusing on emotions of language learners and emotion regulation strategy instruction.

W.L. Quint Oga-Baldwin is a Professor in the School of Education at Waseda University, where he trains elementary and secondary school foreign language teachers. His research focuses on instructional methods, with an emphasis on teaching for engagement and motivation.

Jenefer Philp is a Senior Lecturer at Lancaster University in the UK. Her research and teaching interests include second language acquisition, learner engagement, language teaching and individual difference factors.

Her research focuses on the role of interaction in instructed language learning among adults and children. Her research interests spring from her experience as a teacher and teacher training in high schools, universities and informal settings in Australasia, South East Asia, US and the UK. Her three published books and varied journal articles focus on learner engagement, peer interaction and learning in the language classroom.

Linh Phung is Director of the English Language and Pathways Programs at Chatham University in Pittsburgh, Pennsylvania, USA. Her current research interests include engagement in task performance and language learning as well as international students' experience, language development, intercultural competence and global learning. She is also the founder and director of Eduling International Academy (www.eduling. com), which offers online English courses to kids all over the world.

Hayo Reinders (www.innovationinteaching.org) is Professor of Applied Linguistics at KMUTT in Thailand and TESOL Professor/Director of the doctoral program at Anaheim University in the USA. He is founder of the global Institute for Teacher Leadership (www.teacherleadership.ac). Hayo edits a book series for Palgrave Macmillan and is editor of the journal *Innovation in Language Learning and Teaching.*

Yuan Sang is a PhD Candidate in the Foreign and Second Language Education program (School of Teacher Education) at Florida State University. He earned his MS degree in Elementary Education from the same institution. His research interests include the language socialization of Chinese students learning English as an L2 and the contribution of language socialization to L2 instruction and English teacher education. His current work is focused on the language classroom phenomena of reticence and L2 avoidance.

Giulia Sulis is a post-doctoral fellow at the University of Graz. She graduated from the University of Groningen with a Master's in Applied Linguistics and pursued her PhD in Linguistics and English Language at Lancaster University. Alongside her PhD, she worked as Associate Lecturer in Literacy and Education and as a tutor of English for Academic Purposes (EAP) at Lancaster University. Her research interests lie in the psychology of language learning and teaching; she is currently focusing on teacher wellbeing, motivation, engagement and willingness to communicate (WTC).

Agneta M-L Svalberg teaches and supervises on Masters and Doctoral programs in Applied Linguistic & TESOL at the University of Leicester. She has a particular interest in researching the learning and teaching of grammar, and learners' engagement with language.

Kyle R. Talbot taught English as a Second Language at the University of Iowa in the United States before enrolling as a PhD student at the University of Graz in Austria. He holds an MA in TESOL/Applied Linguistics from the University of Northern Iowa, in Cedar Falls, IA. Currently, he is working as a researcher and pursuing his PhD. His research and teaching interests include the psychology of language teaching and learning, well-being, teacher stress and burnout, and complexity.

Isobel Kai-Hui Wang is a senior research fellow and teacher educator at the University of Graz, Austria. She obtained her MA in ELT and PhD in Applied Linguistics at the University of Warwick, UK. Her research interests lie in the areas of the teaching and learning of vocabulary, language learner strategies and intercultural communication. She is the author of *Learning Vocabulary Strategically in a Study Abroad Context* published by Palgrave Macmillan.

Shiyao (Ashlee) Zhou is a PhD Candidate in Foreign and Second Language Education at Florida State University. She earned her MA in Applied Linguistics from the University of Warwick (UK), and is also enrolled in the MS in Educational Measurement and Statistics in the Department of Ed. Psych. and Learning Systems at Florida State University. Her research focuses on individual differences in second language learning and teaching specifically on topics such as self-regulation, engagement and language learning strategies. Her current work investigates these issues in tertiary L2 writing classrooms in China.

Foreword

People are inherently social creatures, and in order to connect and regulate their social interactions, they must internalize their cultures. But cultures cannot be internalized without language. Indeed, language is the vehicle through which we learn about our social world, discover its rules and values, and express our personal natures, allowing us to connect with others, both in relationships of exchange and of caring.

Cultures themselves interact. As far back as the origins of human history, groups of individuals sharing a common culture and language made contact with other groups, each unified by their own shared tongue. Of great value was anyone who could ably facilitate those intergroup contacts – those people who were multilingual.

Today we humans exist in a globally interconnected world. We can transact with people from anywhere in seconds through the internet, or visit them through rapid means of travel, and in doing so experience a bit of their cultures. But others' cultures and experiences can only be deeply experienced when we share in the ways in which those others express themselves and connect with each other – when we can hear and speak with them in their own expressive forms. Being able to speak another's language is thus not just beneficial practically, for sharing knowledge or making economic transactions; it's also a gift of connectedness.

As useful and meaningful as sharing a language is, learning a second language is not easy. Although we have seemingly natural tools for learning languages during early development, adding new languages into our repertoire later comes only with work and effort. Nonetheless, it is not that uncommon. Approximately half of the world's population is bilingual, although many acquire those skills early on through exposure within their homes and families. Approximately 13% of people worldwide are also multilingual or polyglots, so clearly many people are motivated to learn others' tongues and those that do have richer lives indeed.

Because most of us do not have opportunity to pick up another language in our homes and early environments, in modern times the major way of acquiring this special gift is in classroom settings. That is, we tend to learn languages in formal school contexts, often with a classic format of a teacher who transmits this knowledge using the standard tools of educators – pedagogically determined instruction, textbooks, assignments, performances, tests and grades. This is in so many ways particularly unfortunate, because, sadly, schools are not always the most intrinsically motivating or engaging of environments. They tend to be characterized by social comparisons, extrinsic motivational strategies, winners and losers, with the resulting feelings of alienation, incompetence and failure for so many. My colleagues and I in self-determination theory have often bemoaned how the strategies applied to 'make' students learn are so often inadequate or even toxic in engendering engagement and satisfaction.

This is where this important volume comes into play. It concerns the why's and the how's of people acquiring a second language, and more specifically how we can make that engaging. *Engagement* is in fact the primary focus of all the papers included here. Important is that engagement is not treated herein simplistically, but rather in all its facets. Authors recognize that true engagement requires that the learner at least to some extent finds the process of learning a language intrinsically motivating – learners need to experience some joys and satisfactions in the activity itself. But it also means finding utility, purpose and meaning in the learning process. That sense of utility and purpose, of having a larger goal beyond just interest and enjoyment, is critical especially when it comes to the difficult part of learning languages, which are manifold. So, cultivating both intrinsic motivation and an autonomous or volitional extrinsic motivation is essential in catalyzing the attentiveness and disciplined actions entailed in truly engaged language learning. The editors and authors in this work also recognize that for language teachers inspiring such motivation is an especially complex and formidable task. This is because, for many students, a new language comes only with difficulty – it is truly foreign to them.

Chapters in this volume provide a treasure chest of resources for teachers and researchers who want to more deeply craft strategies for engagement. Indeed, they cover engagement in all its complexity. Chapters herein help define engagement (chapters by Sang & Hiver; Svalberg) and understand how we measure and evaluate it (Zhou, Hiver & Al-Hoorie). They address how feedback impacts leaners (Han & Gao) and the kinds of classrooms, and tasks and strategies that spawn or hinder engagement (Carver, Jung & Gurzynski-Weiss; Phung, Nakamura & Reinders) and positive emotional experiences (Khajavy). They describe the impact of modern tools and technologies used to facilitate learning (Mills). They also look at the experience of engagement from the eyes of learners (Mercer, Talbot & Wang), including the relationships between students and their teachers and peers which strongly impact engagement (Fukuda, Fukada, Falout & Murphey; Sulis & Philp). They address the nuances associated with learning at different stages of development (Oga-Baldwin & Fryer). Together they all help to understand how teachers can cultivate that true willingness to engage (Wang & Mercer) that is requisite to successfully mastering an additional language.

Speaking personally, it is only recently that I have come to be a student of engagement in the domain of language learning. As a long-time scholar in the field of motivation, however, I have been inspired by what I see emerging in this complex area of scholarship and practice. I thus found myself absorbed and engaged by these contributions. But more than such intrinsic motivation, I also felt a larger purpose here, one conveyed by a number of these authors. Yes, our world is shrinking in so many ways – becoming a global economy with increasing homogeneities and occupied with shared concerns, from pandemics to poverty to global warming. But, if there was ever a time for us to be investing in sharing and communicating it is now. If there was ever a time to enhance our students' engagement with what is 'foreign' to them, it is now. If there was ever a time to help people connect across human communities, it is now. As it has always been across history, language is the vehicle through which that is accomplished. I thus applaud this volume and the tasks undertaken by each of these author teams, which are all aimed at enhancing classroom engagement in L2 classrooms around the world. Our students need it, our schools need it, and more importantly our world needs it.

Richard M. Ryan
North Sydney, NSW, Australia

1 Introduction

Phil Hiver, Sarah Mercer and Ali H. Al-Hoorie

What is Engagement?

Although many educators or researchers have an intuitive sense of what engagement is, engagement is a notoriously slippery construct. It is widely accepted that engagement is multidimensional, although there remains some debate about its specific components (Reschly & Christenson, 2012). On closer examination, it becomes clear just how multifaceted engagement is and how difficult it is to empirically investigate in all its complexity (Hiver *et al.*, in preparation). For many scholars, engagement includes affective, cognitive and behavioral components. At the very least, all definitions tend to include some combination of psychological and behavioral components (Finn & Zimmer, 2012).

Compared to the field of educational psychology, the domain of language learning is still just beginning to understand engagement as it is manifested specifically in relation to learning diverse languages in a range of contexts. However, there is a considerable body of work in educational psychology that can be built upon and extended in domain-specific ways (Fredricks *et al.*, 2019). While there are differing perspectives and definitions of engagement, there is relative widespread agreement on several core characteristics.

One key characteristic of engagement is the notion of action. This feature of engagement as action is consistently reiterated across definitions and frameworks. Skinner and Pitzer (2012: 23) explain that 'Engagement is the active verb between the curriculum and actual learning.' Indeed, the role of action is key in distinguishing this construct from the related, and often confused, construct of motivation: 'motivation represents [initial] intention and engagement is [subsequent] action' (Reschly & Christenson, 2012: 14). Interestingly, many scholars refer to student engagement, but adopting an action perspective implies that it is the action, not the person, that is defining.

It is important to note that this focus on action does not imply that learners' intentions are unrelated to the material contingencies of the learning environment or that the ways in which learners engage in learning activities should be distanced from their initial desires and intent to participate in learning. Engagement refers to how actively involved a

1

student is in a learning activity (Christenson *et al.*, 2012). However, as the contributions to this volume show, student engagement extends beyond mere action because it is goal-directed and purpose-driven. Engagement has immediate appeal, too, because it is a construct that looks at teaching and learning together. As we and other contributors discuss throughout this volume, engagement is intertwined with many other individual and situational factors and relates to broad aspects of students' and teachers' functioning in school contexts.

Carefully specifying what engagement is, what it looks like, and what it does can help increase our fundamental understanding of how learners get involved in opportunities for language learning and use. The consensus is that motivation can be distinguished from engagement in the sense that the intensity and the quality of student involvement in the learning activity or environment (action) differs meaningfully from the forces that energize and direct that behavior (motivation) (Martin *et al.*, 2017). This is not to say that motivation ceases to exist when the action begins or that engagement does not in turn influence motivation. Throughout this volume, we have found it important to specify the boundaries of this construct, as educational research and the learning sciences do, for the sake of clarity.

Another characteristic, which has received differing degrees of attention and recognition in empirical work, is that engagement is situated and highly context-dependent across diverse timescales. It is in part a product of cultures, communities, families, schools, peers, classrooms and specific tasks and activities within those classrooms (e.g. Christenson *et al.*, 2012; Pianta *et al.*, 2012; Shernoff, 2013). Depending on the focus of investigation, particular contexts become more prominent and come into sharper focus. And, as with all nested systems, different contextual layers influence each other and extend their influence across various layers of engagement, all of which function across different timescales. For example, academic engagement in school settings is a long-term form of action that covers months or years, but within a specific classroom at school, there are task-level forms of engagement that function at a timescale of minutes or hours.

Engagement always has an object. We talk about being engaged with a topic, a person, a situation, or in an activity or task. This means that while definitions have often focused on the intrapersonal components of engagement, there must also be a commensurate understanding of its situated characteristic. A learner's engagement does not emerge in a vacuum, but is inherently situated in a spatiotemporal context. Reschly and Christenson (2012: 13) highlight the importance of understanding the 'person-environment fit' of learners in their learning contexts to fully appreciate the essence of learner engagement, how it works and how it can be enhanced. As such, engagement research must be clear about the contexts and the timescales of relevance to engagement and its development.

A final characteristic is that engagement is dynamic and malleable (Appleton *et al.*, 2008). Although at present, longitudinal research attempting to understand the trajectory of engagement for individuals and groups of learners remains rare (see e.g. Wylie & Hodgen, 2012), this characteristic provides great optimism for educators as it suggests that learners can become more engaged with the right kinds of intrapersonal and contextual conditions (Fredricks *et al.*, 2004: 61). It also indicates the potential for well-constructed interventions capitalizing on the dynamism of learning engagement on various timescales. As engagement varies, it can be conceived of as a quality measured on a continuum. Learners may find themselves at various points on this continuum. Then too, for some it is unclear what the extreme points represent – high and low engagement, or high engagement and disengagement. Disengagement may in fact be a qualitatively distinct construct running along a continuum of its own (Reschly & Christenson, 2012).

In this collection, we have encouraged authors to be explicit about their definitions and use of terms to try to reduce some of the ambiguity that accompanies many terms in use (Reschly & Christenson, 2012). From our work on this volume, we conclude that engagement is a dynamic, multidimensional construct comprising situated notions of cognition, affect and behaviors including social interactions in which action is a requisite component.

Why Engagement, and Why Now?

Engagement defines all learning. Learning requires learner action, and action is perhaps the defining characteristic of student engagement. Without engagement, meaningful learning is unlikely. An engaged learner is actively involved in and committed to their own learning. Specifically in language learning, the notion of learner action for learning is deeply embedded in the dominant pedagogical paradigms of communicative language teaching (e.g. TBLT), which sees interaction and language use as critical for language development. The predominant line of thinking in many theoretical understandings of language acquisition (e.g. cognitive-interactionist approaches, sociocultural theory and complexity/dynamic systems theory) is also that learning occurs through meaningful use of the language. As such, it is immediately apparent why learner engagement should be of particular interest to scholars and practitioners in the field of language learning.

The growing recognition for the importance of engagement in the 21st century has made it one of the most popular research topics in contemporary education, to the extent that it has been described as 'the holy grail of learning' (Sinatra *et al.*, 2015: 1). There are numerous, varied reasons for the growing interest in engagement, both in language learning and in educational research and practice more generally. One of the appeals of engagement as a construct is that it can provide a broad portrait of how students think, act and feel in instructional settings. High learner engagement has been linked to many positive outcomes in education (Fredricks *et al.*, 2019). These include high levels of academic persistence, effort and achievement (Chase *et al.*, 2014), high academic aspirations and increased mental health (Archambault *et al.*, 2009) and low dropout rates and reduced high-risk behaviors (Griffiths *et al.*, 2012).

There are also important policy implications of learner engagement. In formal education settings such as K-12 language classrooms, the emphasis on standards, outcomes and teacher accountability has intensified, and the progress and achievement of students faces greater scrutiny than ever. With so much dependent on their levels of success, students need to be engaged to actually take part in any meaningful learning. Socially and culturally in many educational systems, the makeup of the local communities which schools serve has become more diverse, pushing schools and teachers to manage a broader, more ambitious role in supporting their community. This is also perhaps why many educational systems keep close tabs on student engagement and disengagement to identify students who are struggling and could benefit from targeted interventions.

Engagement also resonates with practitioners because it is easily understood as an essential ingredient for learning and for quality instruction. Educators across the globe increasingly recognize the difficulties of keeping learners engaged and focused on their learning in the face of a myriad of distractions. As Barkley (2010: xi) explains, 'For many of us teaching today, competing for the attention of our students and engaging them in meaningful learning is a profound and ongoing challenge.' Although many language teachers will share a personal interest in motivating their learners, they will also recognize that even the most motivated learners can have their attention hijacked and their good intentions derailed (Mercer & Dörnyei, 2020). What many teachers witness in their daily classrooms are issues related to learner attention and action – problems of engagement. While understanding how to motivate learners remains a pressing concern, educators today need to know how to also engage learners – to help them focus on their learning with their heart, their mind and their actions. Studying engagement brings together teaching and learning perspectives, and for this reason it can help to identify the classroom and instructional conditions that shape learning outcomes and build engagement (Fredricks *et al.*, 2004).

Relating Engagement to the L2 Classroom

A number of second language acquisition (SLA) researchers have begun pushing the agenda and making notable contributions particular to our domain (see e.g. Oga-Baldwin, 2019; Philp & Duchesne, 2016; Svalberg, 2009 for topical overviews). They have raised a number of issues that are specific to language learning. One important dimension of this work has been a consideration of 'attention,' which is critical to engagement – that is, a learner must direct their attention to the task in order to be truly engaged. Attention itself is the gatekeeper of our working memory, and the ultimate currency of our classrooms. The field of language learning is notoriously divided regarding the role of deliberate attention and awareness in language acquisition (Rebuschat, 2015), yet as Philp and Duchesne (2016: 51) explain, 'Researchers of L2 [second language] acquisition have emphasized the need for L2 learners to pay attention to the connections between language form and its meanings in use.' This has led Philp and Duchesne (2016: 51) to define engagement as being 'a state of heightened attention and involvement, in which participation is reflected not only in the cognitive dimension, but in social, behavioral, and affective dimensions as well.' Because engagement is 'the major force of learning' (Ellis, 2019: 48), engagement research in second language learning raises critical questions about the link to implicit and explicit learning mechanisms and knowledge, and the elements that learners' attention is being directed to – including formal features of the language, the task, the content and/or the social interaction.

Focused attention is a core part of Svalberg's (2009) model of engagement with language (EWL), which she defines as comprising cognitive, affective and social components. She explains that engaged learners are those 'who are actively constructing their knowledge not only by mental processes but also equally by being socially active and taking initiatives' (Svalberg, 2009: 246). Given the typical format of language learning contexts, Svalberg (2009) stresses the social nature of engagement and the importance of peer, group and teacher–student relationships, as interaction is defining for language development. This emphasis on social engagement as distinct from behavioral engagement may be specific to models of engagement in language learning and reflects strongly the particular nature of language learning processes.

A further point that drives work on engagement for language learning is the object of the learner's attention and engagement. For Svalberg (2009: 247), the focus is clearly on the language itself: 'the learner is the agent and language is object (and sometimes vehicle)' (Svalberg, 2009: 247). This EWL gives rise to the critical notion of language awareness, which has been connected with language acquisition by some researchers (see Schmidt, 2001; Svalberg, 2007). Indeed, as several chapters in this collection show, much of the work in second language learning has focused on EWL itself (as the object being studied and the form of interaction in classroom tasks), and this has been the case in related areas of inquiry such as L2 interaction research using language-related episodes (LREs) (Storch, 2008; Swain & Lapkin, 1998). This focus on language in the process of learning and as the outcome of learning is especially pronounced in SLA research.

The focus on EWL itself also raises important questions about what is considered as an indicator or proxy of engagement. In a considerable number of studies looking at engagement in second language learning, the indicators of engagement have centered around the quantity, quality and form of discourse and interaction being used by the learners (Baralt *et al.*, 2016; Dörnyei & Kormos, 2000). However, there are likely to be other indicators of learner engagement, given the 'invisible' dimensions of engagement (cognition and affect). As such, the field will need to reflect on its choice of measures or indicators of engagement and, by extension, remain aware of what is not being considered. While readers will notice that we aim for definitional consensus in this volume in order to enhance coherence of this still new area of L2 research, this should not mask the reality that there is a healthy degree of variance and discussion across contributions to this volume in terms of what engagement means, and how it might be employed in research.

Finally, the vast majority of research examining engagement in second language learning has focused on task-level engagement (Philp & Duchesne, 2016). However, given its situated character, the context of engagement is also vital in defining the focus of study and level of granularity being investigated. Language engagement can be contextualized in a hierarchical way that ranges from engagement at the school level, to the subject level, the class level or the task level, and many educators may also be interested in understanding engagement in practical terms beyond individual tasks. In addition, how task-level engagement connects with other levels of engagement such as school-level and overall academic engagement will be important lines of inquiry to explore further. Engagement in second language learning will need to expand its foci and levels of granularity to gain a fuller picture of how such engagement is enacted and manifested in a range of contexts.

As it stands at present, there remain many questions and lines of inquiry open to further investigation across languages, ages of learners, levels of proficiency, cultures and learning contexts (formal and informal). There is little doubt that engagement is vitally important to understand for scholars and practitioners in light of the increasing difficulties educators face in capturing and maintaining learners' attention and focus on the learning tasks at hand. In the field of second language learning specifically, there is much work still to be done to add depth and breadth to our current understanding across theoretical, empirical and practical levels. The exploration of this potentially vast field of inquiry is only just beginning.

Our Motivation in Compiling this Volume

All three editors are educators and researchers, and both identities have played a significant role in our drive to bring this collection of papers together. As such, this book is part of a move to clarify understanding of the construct of engagement and ultimately to further enhance our teaching practice by reaching a greater appreciation of the conditions and factors which contribute to promoting and sustaining language learner engagement. We suspect that other L2 practitioners, whether primarily identifying as teachers or as researchers, will also find these issues of importance.

As researchers, we are excited by the potential of the construct and the relatively unchartered territory of engagement in language learning. As outlined above, although we do have a sound body of knowledge to build upon, our knowledge of engagement in the field of language learning is distinctly nascent compared to the depth and breadth of knowledge the field has with related constructs such as motivation. There remains theoretical, empirical and practical work to be done. First and foremost, we need to clarify definitional concerns, examine facets unique to the domain of language learning, and comprehend more fully how engagement connects to other aspects of the language learning and teaching processes in real and diverse settings (Hiver et al., in preparation).[1] We need to build frameworks and theoretical models that account for its complexity, situatedness and dynamism. Empirical work needs to be done with diverse types of learners in a range of linguistic, cultural and educational settings, across time and at varying and interconnected levels of granularity. In practical terms, we need to involve teachers and learners to understand their perspectives and experiences of engagement as it is lived and enacted in real classrooms.

For us, this edited collection marks the start of this initiative. Our hope for this collection is that we can draw attention to this highly important and topical construct and raise a call for more empirical and theoretical work as well as research that connects to actual classroom practice. We are grateful to the colleagues who came together with enthusiasm and passion to trigger thought-provoking and inspiring conversations about engagement in our field. There remains much work to be done and this book marks an early first step in that journey for us as teachers and scholars.

Outline of the Book

We have divided this volume into two parts. Part 1 is conceptual and comprises four chapters that explore definitional, theoretical and measurement issues around the construct of engagement. This is followed by Part 2, which includes a series of empirical studies showcasing novel research designs and setting out to further understand the nature of engagement and its contribution to learning and teaching in diverse L2 settings.

Yuan Sang and Phil Hiver open Part 1 by exploring definitions and dimensions of engagement. The chapter features a comparative review of the constructs of *engagement* and *investment*, with their areas of convergence to *interest* and *motivation*, teasing apart the nuances and commonalities between them for L2 learning. These detailed definitions contribute to a clearer picture of the ways and means through which L2 learners actively participate in learning opportunities. Sang and Hiver's stance is that engagement provides a key framework for conceptualizing L2 learners' meaningful involvement in learning opportunities over and above other notions or constructs in widespread use. Sang and Hiver end their chapter by proposing an ongoing agenda for L2 engagement research that will both inform practice and advance the field's understanding of the complex and dynamic processes that underlie learners' meaningful involvement in the L2 classroom.

Agneta Svalberg's chapter takes up the more specific notion of EWL (Svalberg, 2009, 2012), which she defines as learners thinking and talking about language, its forms, functions, and how it works. She begins by drawing an important distinction between motivation (what drives or underlies behavior) and engagement (the behavior itself and how an initial desire or intent manifests itself in action). Starting from her overview of this complex and dynamic process of EWL, Svalberg relates engagement to form- versus meaning-focused teaching, to consciousness-raising tasks, to learners' use of the first language (L1) in class, and to other affordances for learning in the communicative classroom. Throughout, Svalberg offers an extended discussion of the relation of EWL to other types of engagement (e.g. task engagement) and its implications for language teaching and learning.

Ye Han and Xuesong (Andy) Gao switch focus to issues surrounding learner engagement with written corrective feedback (WCF) in their synthesis of recent research on the topic. Their chapter highlights methodological and substantive insights from this area of research, and draws particular attention to consensus around the contextualized nature of feedback and to individual and temporal variability in engaging with and responding to WCF. Han and Gao discuss at length the situated nature of individuals' engagement with WCF at the micro-level of interactions between students, instructors, assignments and feedback as well as in a more macro-level setting. They summarize recent frameworks for understanding learner engagement with WCF and then offer a critical look at current research aims around this type of engagement. They end with forward-pointing advice on the issues and questions that remain to be explored and list concrete research avenues for doing so.

The final chapter in Part 1 by Ashlee Zhou, Phil Hiver and Ali Al-Hoorie examines the measurement of engagement. The authors define engagement as a 'meta-construct' and review prominent approaches to measuring student engagement. While discussing the strengths and limitations of each measurement approach for L2 researchers, Zhou *et al.* caution that there is still some fuzziness surrounding how engagement is operationalized and measured (see also Reschly & Christenson, 2012).

Their review also considers issues such as the variety of purposes for measuring L2 engagement, measuring general versus domain-specific L2 engagement (e.g. task- and skill-specific engagement), and differentiating between L2 engagement and related constructs. They extend this summary of currently available instruments for eliciting engagement data, and conclude by outlining future directions and developments for measuring engagement in the L2 classroom.

The empirical chapters in Part 2 begin with Giulia Sulis and Jenefer Philp's chapter investigating the interdependent nature of the learning environment and engagement in the language classroom. They report on a study of university learners of French as a foreign language designed to uncover the role of the learning environment in fostering or inhibiting learners' engagement. Drawing on a framework of *environmental complexity* (Shernoff *et al.*, 2016, 2017) in the classroom, their data revealed that both environmental challenge and support made available by the combined influence of peers, teacher and tasks played a key role in shaping learners' engagement at different levels. This study has important implications for capturing the interconnectedness of the different dimensions of learner engagement and for designing research in ways that do justice to its complex, dynamic and context-dependent reality.

Within a task-based paradigm, Carly Carver, Daniel Jung and Laura Gurzynski-Weiss's study looks at the role of interaction mode – occurring in face-to-face (FTF) versus synchronous computer mediated communication (SCMC) – on the cognitive, behavioral and affective engagement of L2 learners of Spanish. They set out to examine the effect differential levels of engagement have, as a function of interaction mode, on learning of task-essential L2 vocabulary and structures. This innovative combination of experimental conditions and outcomes of interest showed that meaningful differences exist in learners' engagement between these modes of interaction, and that learners' task-based interactions were facilitative of learning the task-essential vocabulary and structures regardless of engagement type or communication mode. The implications Carver *et al.* discuss are broad reaching when we consider the increasingly diverse learning modalities that feature in language classrooms worldwide.

Sarah Mercer, Kyle Talbot and Isobel (Kai-Hui) Wang's chapter reports an exploratory study of engagement, specifically from the learners' perspective. By conducting comprehensive focus group and follow-up probing interviews, the authors found that what you see is not always what you get when it comes to the quality and nature of learner engagement. Their data show that learners sometimes consciously manipulate their behaviors in order to feign engagement, comply procedurally, or otherwise project superficial outward displays of engagement. These manifestations that outwardly resemble engagement in learning may in fact be 'fake' or passive forms of behavior that are used for sophisticated reasons including to mask disengagement and to meet social expectations in the classroom. In discussing their findings, the authors offer cautionary implications for practice and for research, and note in particular the limits of over relying on observable classroom behaviors and assuming they are an unproblematic proxy for substantive engagement in learning.

Extending prior research that shows the positive effects of choice on learner engagement, Linh Phung, Sachiko Nakamura and Hayo Reinders conducted an in-depth analysis of data that indicates learners experience elevated levels of both negative and positive emotions while highly engaged in L2 classroom tasks. They explore various types of choice, in particular *action choice* and *options choice*, and highlight how the effects of choice on the affective dimension of engagement may be more complex than they appear at first glance. Their mixed-methods data illustrate that the type of choice provided by the task design (i.e. a +constraint vs. a −constraint task condition) resulted in varying configurations of emotional engagement, task focus and performance. Phung, Nakamura and Reinders conclude that teachers can develop and manipulate L2 task conditions to encourage active engagement – particularly emotional engagement.

Tetsuya Fukuda, Yoshifumi Fukada, Joseph Falout and Tim Murphey explore a novel type of engagement, *prosocial engagement*, defined as students' constructive participation in creating an ecology of learning that helps peers to learn better and more enjoyably. They propose that prosocial engagement is a key to combating the passivity, disinterest and unwillingness to engage that prevails in tertiary compulsory language classrooms. Using randomized assignment, the authors divided 21 class groups into two priming treatment conditions designed to target what they term 'mind–time frames of motivation' or the initial conditions which affect students' subsequent prosocial engagement. Fukuda *et al.* report on their longitudinal mixed-method data to show that these priming treatments can enhance students' in-class prosocial engagement. They further discuss particular ways students' mind–time frames are meaningfully related to visible actions manifested in prosocial engagement.

Nicole Mills' chapter is unique within this volume as it takes a theory-meets-practice approach and explores how immersion in digital virtual environments can target all dimensions of learner engagement. She describes the development of a virtual reality project in which the instructional aims are to recreate an authentic, experiential, inquiry-based and game-like environment that can facilitate collaboration and social interaction. Her chapter showcases how this deeply contextualized and culturally immersive platform and its accompanying teaching materials are aligned with engagement theory and research. She proposes that because engagement is both malleable and highly contextual, instructional design is an important way of constructing a pedagogy of engagement.

Quint Oga-Baldwin and Luke Fryer adopt a developmental perspective of learner engagement in their chapter and set out to identify how this construct grows or changes in instructed settings. They designed a study to follow a large sample of young English language learners from Japanese public schools over the first two years of classroom exposure to the language. By measuring these learners' levels of engagement at four-month intervals over the two-year time window, Oga-Baldwin and Fryer showed that learners beginning with lower initial engagement reported greater growth in all dimensions of engagement. Their results also reveal that all learners made significant gains in cognitive engagement in the language classroom, and that female students experienced stronger growth in behavioral engagement than male students did across the study. While their study does not explicitly investigate any intervention or manipulation of variables, there are numerous implications for similar contexts in which compulsory L2 learning over sustained periods often results in chronic disengagement and lower long-term interest.

Hassan Khajavy's chapter turns to expanding the reach of engagement research by relating engagement to positive and negative L2 classroom emotions and character strengths in the hope of examining its links to L2 reading comprehension outcomes. His study tests the hypothesis that such classroom emotions and character strengths (i.e. grit) are predictive of L2 engagement, and that L2 engagement is subsequently related to students' L2 reading comprehension. Khajavy discusses the implications of this new combination of variables for classroom engagement research and for practice.

In the final empirical chapter, Isobel (Kai-Hui) Wang and Sarah Mercer bridge many issues brought up by other contributors and tie numerous threads together as they extend learner engagement to language learning beyond the classroom. Through a longitudinal case study of a beginning learner of L2 German, Wang and Mercer propose that one's willingness to engage (WTE) is a necessary antecedent state that emerges prior to learners' actual engagement. They discuss the many ways that out-of-classroom learning experiences provide rich affordances for language learning and use and make the case that, perhaps even more so than in traditional classroom contexts, success in language learning beyond the classroom depends largely on the proactivity and engagement of the individual learner. They show how individual, social and contextual variables interact on different timescales to create a state in which learners are more (or less) likely to engage with opportunities for language learning and use.

In sum, the papers in this collection offer an enlightening introduction to the construct of engagement in language learning. They tackle some of the thorny issues surrounding definitional and measurement concerns and they offer concrete empirical examples of innovative and diverse research designs for engagement in language learning, opening up new lines of thinking and directions for research. It is our hope that these papers will serve as further inspiration for more extensive work in the field. In the final chapter, we look ahead to the future of research on this topic and outline some ideas of the directions that development could take. To our readers, L2 practitioners, language learning researchers, established engagement scholars and newcomers to the topic alike, we hope you find the collection useful for your own work and that it will further contribute to the growth of this exciting area of research.

Note

(1) As our synthesis of over 350 self-labeled L2 engagement studies published in 22 field-specific journals shows, fewer than 20% featured a clear definition and/or operationalization of the construct itself – a genuinely puzzling state of affairs, and one which requires immediate attention if further work is to contribute substantively to this domain.

References

Appleton, J.J., Christenson, S.L. and Furlong, M.J. (2008) Student engagement with school: Critical conceptual and methodological issues of the construct. *Psychology in the Schools* 45, 369–386.

Archambault, I., Janosz, M., Fallu, J.-S. and Pagani, L.S. (2009) Student engagement and its relationship with early high school dropout. *Journal of Adolescence* 32, 651–670.

Baralt, M., Gurzynski-Weiss, L. and Kim, Y. (2016) The effects of task complexity and classroom environment on learners' engagement with the language. In M. Sato and S. Ballinger (eds) *Peer Interaction and Second Language Learning: Pedagogical Potential and Research Agenda* (pp. 209–240). Philadephia, PA: John Benjamins.

Barkley, E. (2010) *Student Engagement Techniques: A Handbook for College Faculty.* San Francisco, CA: Jossey-Bass.

Chase, P.A., Hilliard, L.J., Geldhof, G.J., Warren, D.J.A. and Lerner, R.M. (2014) Academic achievement in the high school years: The changing role of school engagement. *Journal of Youth Adolescence* 43, 884–896.

Christenson, S.L., Reschly, A.L. and Wylie, C. (eds) (2012) *Handbook of Research on Student Engagement.* New York: Springer.

Dörnyei, Z. and Kormos, J. (2000) The role of individual and social variables in oral task performance. *Language Teaching Research* 4, 275–300.

Ellis, N.C. (2019) Essentials of a theory of language cognition. *The Modern Language Journal* 103 (S1), 39–60.

Finn, J.D. and Zimmer, K.S. (2012) Student engagement: What is it? Why does it matter? In S.L. Christenson, A.L. Reschly and C. Wylie (eds) *Handbook of Research on Student Engagement* (pp. 97–131). New York: Springer.

Fredricks, J., Blumenfeld, P. and Paris, A. (2004) School engagement: Potential of the concept, state of the evidence. *Review of Educational Research* 74 (1), 59–109.

Fredricks, J., Reschly, A.L. and Christenson, S.L. (2019) Interventions for student engagement: Overview and state of the field. In J. Fredricks, A.L. Reschly and S.L. Christenson (eds) *Handbook of Student Engagement Interventions: Working with Disengaged Students* (pp. 1–11). San Diego, CA: Academic Press.

Griffiths, A.-J., Lilles, E., Furlong, M.J. and Sidhwa, J. (2012) The relations of adolescent student engagement with troubling and high-risk behaviors. In S.L. Christenson, A.L. Reschly and C. Wylie (eds) *Handbook of Research on Student Engagement* (pp. 563–584). New York: Springer.

Hiver, P., Al-Hoorie, A.H., Vitta, J. and Wu, J. (in preparation) *A Systematic Review of 20 Years of L2 Engagement Research.*

Martin, A.J., Ginns, P. and Papworth, B. (2017) Motivation and engagement: Same or different? Does it matter? *Learning and Individual Differences* 55, 150–162.

Mercer, S. and Dörnyei, Z. (2020) *Engaging Language Learners in Contemporary Classrooms.* New York: Routledge.

Oga-Baldwin, W.L.Q. (2019) Acting, thinking, feeling, making: The engagement process in language education. *System* 86, 102–120.

Philp, J. and Duchesne, S. (2016) Exploring engagement in tasks in the language classroom. *Annual Review of Applied Linguistics* 36, 50–72.

Pianta, R.C., Hamre, B.K. and Allen, J.P. (2012) Teacher-student relationships and engagement: Conceptualizing, measuring, and improving the capacity of classroom interactions. In S.L. Christenson, A.L. Reschly and C. Wylie (eds) *Handbook of Research on Student Engagement* (pp. 365–386). New York: Springer.

Rebuschat, P. (ed.) (2015) *Implicit and Explicit Learning of Languages.* Philadelphia, PA: John Benjamins.

Reschly, A.L. and Christenson, S.L. (2012) Jingle, jangle, and conceptual haziness: Evolution and future directions of the engagement construct. In S.L. Christenson, A.L. Reschly and C. Wylie (eds) *Handbook of Research on Student Engagement* (pp. 3–19). New York: Springer.

Schmidt, R. (2001) Attention. In P. Robinson (ed.) *Cognition and Second Language Instruction* (pp. 3–32). Cambridge: Cambridge University Press.

Shernoff, D.J. (2013) *Optimal Learning Environments to Promote Student Engagement.* New York: Springer.

Shernoff, D.J., Kelly, S., Tonks, S., Anderson, B., Cavanagh, R., Sinha, S. and Abdi, B. (2016) Student engagement as a function of environmental complexity in high school classrooms. *Learning and Instruction* 43, 52–60.

Shernoff, D.J., Ruzek, E.A. and Sinha, S. (2017) The influence of the high school classroom environment on learning as mediated by student engagement. *School Psychology International* 38, 201–218.

Sinatra, G.M., Heddy, B.C. and Lombardi, D. (2015) The challenges of defining and measuring student engagement in science. *Educational Psychology* 50, 1–13.

Skinner, E.A. and Pitzer, J.R. (2012) Developmental dynamics of student engagement, coping, and everyday resilience. In S.L. Christenson, A.L. Reschly and C. Wylie (eds) *Handbook of Research on Student Engagement* (pp. 21–44). New York: Springer.

Storch, N. (2008) Metatalk in a pair work activity: Level of engagement and implications for language development. *Language Awareness* 17, 95–114.

Svalberg, A.M.L. (2007) Language awareness and language learning. *Language Teaching* 40, 287–308.

Svalberg, A.M.L. (2009) Engagement with language: Interrogating a construct. *Language Awareness* 18, 242–258.

Svalberg, A.M.L. (2012) Thinking allowed: Language awareness in language learning and teaching: A research agenda. *Language Teaching* 45, 376–388.

Swain, M. and Lapkin, S. (1998) Interaction and second language learning: Two adolescent French immersion students working together. *The Modern Language Journal* 82, 320–337.

Wylie, C. and Hodgen, E. (2012) Trajectories and patterns of student engagement: Evidence from a longitudinal study. In S.L. Christenson, A.L. Reschly and C. Wylie (eds) *Handbook of Research on Student Engagement* (pp. 585–599). New York: Springer.

Part 1

Conceptual Chapters

2 Engagement and Companion Constructs in Language Learning: Conceptualizing Learners' Involvement in the L2 Classroom

Yuan Sang and Phil Hiver

Introduction

Language learning is a long and sometimes arduous journey that requires devoted effort to the process of learning. As the contributions to this volume attest, researchers in the field of second and foreign language (L2) education are uniquely concerned with the ways and means by which learners actively devote effort and attention to L2 learning. This is because learners' interest and desire to immerse themselves in learning opportunities, and their expenditure of effort while learning, are crucial conditions for L2 development. Ideally, L2 learning is not merely a process whereby learners go through the motions of learning (Philp & Duchesne, 2016); instead, it should involve active participation in the learning tasks, thinking and concentration on the intellectual work, and the development of positive emotions throughout. In other words, if they are going to spend time on it at all, language learners ought to be *engaged* in L2 learning.

The term 'engaged' is frequently used in a generic way to describe L2 learners who exhibit heightened involvement in language learning (Dörnyei & Kormos, 2000). As evidenced by engagement's close relation to its companion constructs, it is a concept that provides a key framework for conceptualizing L2 learners' meaningful involvement and expenditure of effort, as a corollary to deliberate attention and active participation in learning (Platt & Brooks, 2002). Rooted in educational psychology and the learning sciences, engagement refers to 'a state of heightened attention and involvement, in which participation is reflected' in cognitive, social, behavioral and affective dimensions (Philp & Duchesne, 2016: 3). Therefore, cognitive, social, behavioral and affective engagement are the focus of our discussion of engagement in this chapter, in addition to task engagement, which also has captured the interest of scholars in L2 education. Recent years have witnessed more deliberate use of this term in the field of language learning and teaching, and the body of evidence lends support to the notion that engagement is a crucial condition for optimal learning (Mercer, 2019). By exploring definitions and dimensions of engagement, our objective in this chapter is to contribute to a fuller picture of the ways and means through which learners actively engage with learning opportunities.

We explore other related notions as points of comparison. For instance, the notion of *investment* in language learning is grounded in poststructuralist social theories and the accompanying perspectives of language and identity. Though also conceptualizing learners' expenditure of effort and discussing concepts such as motivation, investment emphasizes the coordinated 'relationship between language learner identity and language learning commitment' (Norton, 2012: 343). This chapter provides a comparative review of the constructs of engagement and investment, with their connections to interest and motivation, and highlights their uniquenesses and commonalities for L2 learning. We end this chapter by proposing an agenda for L2 engagement research that will advance the field's understanding of the complex and dynamic makeup and processes that underlie learners' meaningful involvement in the L2 classroom.

Defining Engagement

While differing in approach, scholars agree on one definitional aspect of engagement: Engagement refers to action (Lawson & Lawson, 2013). This action dimension is believed to be the most important characteristic of engagement, distinguishing it from other related constructs such as motivation, which relates more closely to desire or intent (Mercer, 2019). This idea is embraced by Skinner *et al.* (2009), who describe engagement as 'energized, directed, and sustained actions' (2009: 225). Under this rubric of energy in action, in classroom settings specifically engagement is conceived of as 'constructive, enthusiastic, willing, emotionally positive and cognitively focused participation with learning activities' (Skinner & Pitzer, 2012: 22). Language learning scholars too, such as Bygate and Samuda (2009) construe engagement as the extent to which learners understand the objectives and content of a learning task, as well as gather and utilize resources to complete it. This resonates also with Reeve's (2012) definition of engagement as 'the extent of a student's active involvement in a learning activity' (2012: 150), a definition grounded in Wellborn's (1991) pioneering work.

While there is a connection between engagement and motivation in learning contexts, motivation is most often thought of as an antecedent or precursor of engagement (Reschly & Christenson, 2012), while engagement is the subsequent step in which learners convert this pro-active drive into action to complete specific learning goals. In other words, a learner may be fully motivated (i.e. desire or intend to act) but still not engaged in learning, unless they subsequently apply the energy of motivation and proactively get involved through engagement. Definitions of engagement also point clearly to the fact that it is not a monolithic or static individual difference. Instead engagement is multifaceted and closely related to the demands of particular tasks (see also Chapter 9 by Phung *et al.*, this volume) and learning contexts (see also Chapter 14 by Wang & Mercer, this volume). As Reeve (2012) argues, 'it almost does not make sense to refer to "student" engagement because it cannot be separated or disentangled from the social context in which it occurs' (2012: 152). Järvelä and Renninger (2014) also sound off on this issue and affirm that '[engagement] is not a psychological variable, per se', but connected more to learners' relationships and responses to the learning environment (2014: 673). Below, we delve further into some of these dimensions of engagement.

Dimensions of Engagement

Scholars posit at least three (though sometimes four or more) core dimensions within engagement. Among early work that explores the specific dimensions of engagement, Fredricks *et al.* (2004), for instance, refer to three central dimensions of engagement: (a) a behavioral dimension, which refers to individuals' qualitative behavioral choices in learning; (b) an affective dimension, including learners' emotional connections and responses to the learning tasks and peers; and (c) a cognitive dimension, which relates to learners' mental activity in the learning process. In contexts of language learning and use, Larsen-Freeman and Cameron (2008: 201–204) rightly contend that how individuals engage shapes how their engagement develops and that researchers should carefully examine the complex interdependent relationships among various dimensions of learners' engagement. Mercer (2019) takes this one step further in proposing that 'true engagement necessitates all three components' (2019: 4). In real-life learning, it is possible that students are only partially engaged in learning (e.g. they are behaviorally engaged and on-task but are merely going through the motions to look busy), whereas they lack cognitive and emotional involvement in the learning (see Chapter 8 by Mercer *et al.*, this volume). In relation to this, Nystrand and Gamoran (1991) underscore the difference between procedural engagement and substantive engagement. The former refers to learners complying and following instructions for the purpose of going through the motions of learning – a sort of superficial, pseudo-engagement. The latter refers to an authentic, intrinsic, and sustained commitment to learning. An example of students engaged procedurally in a content domain can be seen in students following instructions to solve math problems step-by-step. Though ultimately reaching the correct answers, they may not develop deeper knowledge or thinking in that domain. Comparatively, students' sensemaking develops more deeply when they are substantively engaged, and they may even discover new ways to solve the math problems.

In the domain of language learning, Svalberg (2009) proposes that the social dimension is a crucial additional component of engagement as 'social engagement [is] essentially linked to interaction and to learners' initiation and maintenance (or not) of it' (2009: 252). This idea has been embraced by scholars focusing on the role of engagement in language learning. For example, Philp and Duchesne (2016) define engagement as 'a state of heighted attention and involvement, in which participation is reflected not only in the cognitive dimension, but in social, behavioral, and affective dimensions as well' (2016: 51). In more recent years, the concept of engagement has gone beyond the purely learner-internal psychological conceptualization of its early days and come to be used in descriptions of learners' active connections to the learning environment (Järvelä & Renninger, 2014). Engagement is, thus, understood to include socioemotional and cognitive relationships to the learning environment (Reschly & Christenson, 2012).

The multidimensionality of engagement is even more apparent in its application to language learning. Among scholars with an interest in engagement in language learning, Agneta Svalberg has contributed greatly to the understanding of engagement by theorizing a domain-specific type of engagement: 'engagement with language' (Svalberg, 2009). Engagement with language is defined as 'a cognitive, and/or affective, and/or social state and a process in which the learner is the agent and the language is the object and may be the vehicle (means of communication)' (Svalberg, 2009: 244). Based on this admittedly broad definition she distinguishes cognitive, affective and social dimensions within the construct of engagement, and also identifies differences between engagement and other similar concepts, such as involvement, commitment and motivation (Svalberg, 2009). In her recent work, Svalberg (2017) also discusses the connections between 'engagement with language' and other related topics in language learning, specifically task engagement; all of which we turn to in more detail below.

Behavioral engagement

Scholars think of behavioral engagement in different ways, but often around the notions of effort and initiative. Early work viewed behavioral engagement dichotomously, describing students as either behaviorally engaged and 'on-task' in learning, or disengaged and 'off-task' (Anderson,

1975). Summaries of school-based research show that academic time on task or the amount of time that students are actually involved in learning is often the chief measure of behavioral engagement (Gettinger & Walter, 2012). Some early L2 research similarly operationalizes behavioral engagement by measuring word counts (Bygate & Samuda, 2009) and turn counts (Dörnyei & Kormos, 2000). Examples of behavioral engagement in L2 learners include their voluntary involvement in speaking and their interactional initiative. Drawing on this tradition, Philp and Duchesne (2016) see behavioral engagement as students' active involvement 'in terms of time on task or participation' (2016: 55). Thus, in classroom settings, behavioral engagement can be measured through observation of students' active participation in learning.

Of course, this highlights the difficulty of disentangling behavioral engagement from cognitive, affective and social engagement, given that all dimensions of engagement entail active student participation and involvement. One possibility is that behavioral engagement may refer to amount of effortful involvement while other dimensions of engagement may capture the precise nature of involvement. Human action, we should not forget, is clearly multidimensional, and the limitation of a dichotomous standpoint lies in its neglect of other dimensions of engagement: When students are thought to be solely behaviorally engaged, no concern is given for whether and to what extent they might be cognitively, affectively, or socially engaged. As a way of distinguishing between the dimensions of engagement, which all involve some degree of action, more recent studies consider behavioral engagement as students' continuous performance in learning as determined by their expenditure of effort on learning tasks, the quality of their participation, and their degree of active involvement in the learning process (e.g. Finn & Zimmer, 2012; Mahatmya *et al.*, 2012). This newer perspective of behavioral engagement transcends the conventional dichotomous perception, and opens the possibility for researchers to link behavioral engagement to other dimensions.

Cognitive engagement

Cognitive engagement refers to learners' mental effort in the process of learning. Learners are cognitively engaged when they exhibit deliberate, sustained attention and expend mental effort to achieve learning goals (Helme & Clarke, 2001; Reeve, 2012). Cognitive engagement is also believed to be connected to learners' observable alertness and attention to a given task or goal (Svalberg, 2009). Others see cognitive engagement as involving learners' 'focused attention to [language] form, direction of cognitive resources and problem solving' (Baralt *et al.*, 2016: 213).

As a proxy for the internal mechanisms, cognitive engagement research relies on external evidence of mental effort. For example, students' suggestions, reasoning, hesitations and repetitions in verbal communications with the teacher and peers have been used to demonstrate their cognitive engagement in learning (Reschly & Christenson, 2012). Additionally, evidence of cognitive engagement can be gathered from learners' collaborative work during learning, such as the exchange of ideas, developing explanations, evaluating opinions and materials, and providing further information (Helme & Clarke, 2001). Learners' private speech is another useful source of evidence for demonstrating cognitive engagement (Mercer & Hodgkinson, 2008). In addition to the more obvious verbal cues in communication, it is also possible to study cognitive engagement through nonverbal cues such as body language, facial expressions, eye movements and body positioning; however, more research is needed on these aspects as certain nonverbal indicators may be poor proxies for cognitive engagement while others might be highly informative (Fredricks & McColskey, 2012).

Affective engagement

Definitions of affective engagement (see also: emotional engagement) differ depending on the research purpose. With the aim of examining learners' school (i.e. institutional) engagement, Yazzie-Mintz (2009) defines affective engagement as 'students' feelings of connection to (or disconnection from) their school [or] how students feel about where they are in school, the ways and workings of the school, and the people within their school' (2009: 16). In their study investigating affective engagement in a classroom context, Skinner *et al.* (2009) described affective engagement as learners' positively motivated participation in learning tasks and activities. Overall, expressions of positive emotions such as enjoyment, enthusiasm and anticipation are thought to be representations of students' affective engagement, whereas negative emotions such as anxiety, boredom, frustration and anger demonstrate emotional disengagement or disaffection (Reeve, 2012). Students' positive feelings of their relationships with teachers and peers in classroom learning are also subsumed under affective engagement (Mercer, 2015). In language learning, Svalberg (2009) proposes that students are affectively engaged in learning when they hold a 'positive, purposeful, willing, and autonomous disposition' toward the target language (2009: 247). Affective engagement is, therefore, related to learners' attitudes toward learning contexts, the members in those contexts, the learning tasks, and their own participation in learning.

The interconnections among the dimensions of engagement are particularly salient when affective engagement is considered (Philp & Duchesne, 2016). As Baralt *et al.* (2016) report, positive interactions among peers, such as encouragement and active listening, can raise affective engagement, which primes and further shapes learners' cognitive, behavioral and social engagement. Conversely, the negative emotions that can arise during group work may cause participatory exclusion, which leads to cognitive, behavioral and social disengagement. In light of this, scholars note that emotion is intrinsic to engagement, and that emotions can either activate or deactivate engagement (Pekrun & Linnenbrink-Garcia, 2012).

Social engagement

The social dimension of engagement is unique to some definitions (see also Chapter 5 by Zhou *et al.*, this volume). However, social aspects of learning and their association with other dimensions of engagement are widely recognized. Learning, many scholars agree, is situated and context-dependent, as cognitions, emotions and behavior are all relational and embedded in a social environment (Mercer, 2019; Reeve, 2012). Social engagement is a key dimension of engagement in language learning research and can be distinguished from other forms of engagement when considering that it is explicitly relational in nature and that its purpose is interaction with and support of others. Social engagement relates particularly to the relations between interlocutors and how they work together. One notable illustration of social engagement within a broader framework is Svalberg's (2009) work to develop the notion of 'engagement with language,' used to specifically frame how engagement influences language learning as a social endeavor and is entwined with language awareness – a capacity which is believed to 'engender engagement with language and [to be] constructed through it' (Svalberg, 2007: 302). Language awareness is a resource that facilitates learners' engagement with language socially in instructional settings as learners use their language knowledge to interact with peers and other interlocutors. Additionally, learners' engagement with language can in turn increase their language knowledge and, in social settings, can enhance their language awareness.

When language learners are genuinely engaged with language, Svalberg (2009) notes that language learning usually involves a combination of cognitive, affective and social aspects of engagement. Social engagement, specifically, refers to 'interaction [in language learning] and to learners' initiation and maintenance (or not) of it' (2009: 252). Learners are thought to be socially engaged in language learning when they demonstrate readiness to interact behaviorally, maintain that interaction, and respond positively to interlocutors during the course of interaction. Examples of this might be when students actively listen to each other's opinions, backchannel, provide reciprocal feedback and share equally distributed turns in conversation (Storch, 2002).

Research has demonstrated the importance of the social dimension of engagement because it can facilitate overall engagement (Svalberg, 2009). This is because, when socially engaged, learners need to activate and use cognitive resources, be affectively connected and behaviorally involved in learning. Philp and Duchesne (2016) also suggest that social engagement and affective engagement are closely linked to each other, especially among young children and adolescents who are eager to develop social affiliation with community members and for whom peers are an important condition for learning. A number of other recent studies show that language learning can be more effective if learners are socially engaged in a positive manner (e.g. Moranski & Toth, 2016; Sato & Ballinger, 2012; Toth *et al.*, 2013).

Task engagement

The majority of recent engagement research in language learning has been concentrated on task engagement, that is students' participation in concrete L2 learning tasks (Mercer, 2019). Task engagement occurs 'when learners display through either private or social speech their own structuring of the task, say, to establish goals as they feel necessary to move from mere compliance with the task itself to actual engagement with it' (Platt & Brooks, 2002: 373). In the field of L2 education, task engagement can be considered more a mode of engagement rather than a dimension of engagement (Svalberg, 2017). A useful distinction to draw here is one between language-related engagement and task (-related) engagement. The former refers to language learners practicing and responding to linguistic data or formal features of the language, while the latter is about students learning language through the achievement and completion of tasks (Platt & Brooks, 2002).

Task engagement should be recognized as an important condition for language learning 'because it is considered a primary pathway by which motivational processes contribute to learning and development' (Furrer & Skinner, 2003: 149). In an early study, Dörnyei and Kormos (2000) operationalized task engagement as the degree of students' participation in language learning tasks, thus suggesting that task engagement should be measured through actual language output instead of learners' self-report. Task engagement has also been measured by evaluating learners' time on task in addition to non-functional behavior (e.g. pencil tapping, head scratching) (Svalberg, 2017). In addition, some recent studies have examined learners' behavioral, affective and social engagement while engaged in task-based language learning, thus using various means to measure the multiple dimensions of the construct (e.g. Dao & McDonough, 2018; Lambert *et al.*, 2017; Phung, 2017).

An intriguing line of work examines the relationship between task engagement and task design in language learning. Studies have demonstrated that some features of task design, such as task familiarity, task repetition and the level of challenge are associated with learners' task engagement. Decades ago, Maehr (1984) demonstrated that L2 learners are more motivated and more likely to engage in learning tasks if they find that tasks are achievable. Others have similarly discovered that the challenge inherent in tasks influences learners' behavioral engagement and that L2 learners engage more actively in familiar learning tasks and tend to respond negatively to unfamiliar tasks (Dao, 2019; Phung, 2017; Qiu & Lo, 2017). Task repetition, for its part, returns mixed findings. For example, Lambert *et al.* (2016) reported that L2 learners recognize the usefulness of task repetition, whereas Kim (2013) concludes that L2 learners are less interested, motivated and engaged when the same task is repeated multiple times. As would be expected, additional research is needed to explore the relationship between task engagement and task design, particularly in different educational contexts, with varying participant groups, and using various types of tasks for language learning.

Other Ways of Conceptualizing Learner Engagement

Investment

The emergence of the notion of investment in second language acquisition (SLA) originates in Norton's research on migrant women in Canada (Norton Peirce, 1995; Norton, 2000), where she discovered subtle inconsistencies between the ways participants engaged in or resisted L2 learning and what would normally be predicted by theories of motivation in SLA.

Motivation, from the Latin '*movere*' signals the desire to move – to choose, initiate and sustain a course of action. A motivated individual is typically thought of as being in a 'state of wanting to perform a specific activity in a given situation' (Schiefele, 2009: 197); one example of this is being goal-directed. L2 learning is often seen as an individual endeavor and motivation is thought of as one characteristic that shapes language learners' behavior. Studies of motivation usually anticipate positive language learning results from motivated learners and, conversely, explain lack of success in L2 learning under conditions of adequate exposure as due to a lack of motivation or sufficiently strong desire to learn the target language. However, Norton reports in her research that L2 learners with strong motivation may not necessarily fully participate, or 'invest', in language learning, and that such resistance on their part may be related to the unequal power relations between the L2 learners and the native speakers of the target language (Norton Peirce, 1995; Norton, 2000).

Norton's development of investment borrows from Bourdieu's research on 'cultural capital'. As Bourdieu and Passeron (1977) propose, people in all societies are differentiated into classes and communities based on their cultural capital, which refers to the knowledge, credentials, and ideas held by different groups of people. Building on this metaphor, Norton (2012) underscores how L2 learners invest in language learning at particular times and in particular settings is a function of their desire to acquire certain symbolic and material resources, presenting a socially grounded choice architecture of sorts. That is, L2 learners are driven to acquire knowledge and develop proficiency in the target language; they anticipate that by doing so they can increase the value of their cultural capital, which will further strengthen the learners' perceptions of themselves and help realize their desires in the future (Norton & Toohey, 2011).

The notion of investment holds that a language learner has 'a complex identity, changing across time and space, and reproduced in social interaction' (Norton, 2012: 343). This conceptualization, thus, signifies a symbiotic relationship between L2 learners' commitment to language learning and who they are seen as by others – their social identity. L2 learners' investment in opportunities for language learning and use is accompanied by identity formation because learners' relational hopes and desires are implicated in the process of language learning. These hopes and desires can originate from complex collections of memories, or be based on learners' projections of their potential future positions in imagined communities. While it may be possible that learners' hopes and desires are at times too immaterial to be clearly articulated, investment and L2 learners' social identity capture neatly the 'socially and historically constructed relationship of learners to the target language and their sometimes ambivalent desire to learn and practice it' (Norton & Toohey, 2011: 420).

The construct of investment has inspired a number of studies in the field of SLA to investigate the relationships between L2 learners' desire, identity and commitment in language learning (Cummins, 2006). For instance, studies suggest that the concept of motivation may be insufficient to explain the intricate learning experiences of participants (Skilton-Sylvester, 2002), that an understanding of learners' social identities is critical to explaining their investment in language classes (Kinginger, 2004), and that an individual's investment must correspond with the objectives of a language training program in order for those learners to achieve the expected language learning results (Potowski, 2007).

Although investment and engagement differ, they share common theoretical concerns and empirical emphases. These commonalities and uniquenesses are examined in more detail later in this chapter.

Interest

Interest too is often studied under the umbrella of motivation science as an initial condition for an individual's meaningful involvement and voluntary participation in desired behaviors (Renninger & Hidi, 2016). Yet, unlike many motivational notions such as goal-orientations, motives, needs and self-concepts, a key characteristic of interest is that it is always linked to a specific target – a subject area, a task, domain or topic. This notion of interest as relational (i.e. existing as the quality of a relation between an individual and an object) was first highlighted by Krapp (2002). Interest is always motivating and engaging. As such, it can be seen as an antecedent of motivation and engagement. This has also been true of its appearance in conceptual work in L2 motivation (e.g. Crookes &

Schmidt, 1991; Dörnyei, 1994; Williams & Burden, 1997). Additionally, motivation that results in subsequent engagement in a given task can in turn generate further or more enduring interest in a topical domain or with a given task. Interest in learning content, classroom tasks and academic topics affects engagement positively because interested learners are more likely to participate fully in learning, pay closer attention, expend greater effort, process information more effectively, become more involved, perform better and take advantage of further learning opportunities (Hidi & Harackiewicz, 2000). In language learning too, it is not farfetched to imagine one's meaningful involvement, effort and attention resulting in potential benefits to the quantity and quality of their interest in that domain. Conversely, it is also plausible that requiring individuals to become and stay involved or engaged despite a lack of interest in a given domain or activity will require atypically high levels of executive function capacity (inhibitory control, emotion regulation, etc.) and may not lead to much learning or development.

Although not the first or the only scholars to explore this area, research and theorizing on interest is most closely associated with the work of Suzanne Hidi and K. Ann Renninger (Hidi, 1990; Renninger *et al.*, 1992). These and other scholars have proposed several major dimensions or conceptions of interest. When we think of the essence or nature of the thing we call 'interest,' we can think first of an affective dimension (Ainley, 2006). *Affective interest* has to do with feelings such as enthusiasm, excitement, anticipation, stimulation and in-the-moment enjoyment that an individual experiences or expects to experience from certain content or from a learning activity (Hidi *et al.*, 2004). In everyday life, a friend asking, 'Are you interested in seeing the new movie opening this weekend?' closely approximates a layperson understanding about what stimulates interest. Another aspect of interest, often implicated in learning situations, is when a student genuinely values the learning content, the subject matter or the learning processes – this sense of deep value and utility is referred to as *cognitive interest* (Ainley, 2012). Here, we could imagine someone saying, 'I'm really interested in illuminated Medieval manuscripts' in reference to their close interest in these decorative texts. Cognitive interest such as this develops when the individual has both some knowledge of a topic and the desire to understand the topic more fully; that is, they recognize its value and utility personally. In this sense, it has broad parallels with identified regulation[1] from self-determination theory. To summarize so far, then, interest is essentially a motivational concept that combines affective and cognitive functioning (Hidi, 2006).

With regard to the temporal stability of interest, scholars propose a duality between an individual's momentary experience of being captivated by an object, on the one hand, and the more lasting feelings that the object is enjoyable and worth further exploration on the other (Renninger & Hidi, 2011). The first of these, closer in essence to a dynamic psychological state, is referred to as *situational interest* (Renninger & Hidi, 2016). In learning settings, situational interest is triggered in the moment by features of a text or activity (e.g. surprise, humor, or novelty), instructional conditions, interaction with group members and the learning environment (Rotgans & Schmidt, 2014). This means it links closely, though not exclusively, to affective interest. Once it is triggered, situational interest can be maintained through task meaningfulness, personal involvement and social support, which sustain engagement in the activity (Durik & Harackiewicz, 2007). Due to its characteristics, there is some evidence that stimulating situational interest can promote learning and lead to the development of other more sustained forms of interest (Brophy, 2008). The second and more enduring predisposition to engage with particular objects, content, or activities as opportunities arise is what has been called *individual interest*. For instance, studies have found that as an individual begins to value opportunities for learning and starts to better regulate her own involvement in these tasks, individual interest begins to emerge (Fryer & Ainley, 2019; Hidi & Ainley, 2008). A well-developed individual interest can blossom once an individual finds spending time on the topic or activity rewarding and begins to recognize its relevance or utility for their goals. It can also come about through opportunities to demonstrate competence and extend knowledge (Harackiewicz & Hulleman, 2010). In addition, while individual interest usually becomes increasingly cognitive when compared with its more temporary and affective counterpart situational interest, we should also remember that 'being in a state of interest means that affective reactions, perceived value, and cognitive functioning intertwine, [with the result] that attention and learning feel effortless' (Harackiewicz *et al.*, 2016: 221). In this sense, interest also appears to closely mirror the Gardnerian concept of integrativeness which encompasses interest in foreign languages and attitudes toward the L2 community, also reflecting the 'individual's willingness and interest in social interaction with members of other groups' (Gardner & MacIntyre, 1993: 159).

Commonalities and Uniquenesses

As with interest and motivation, engagement is a construct that originates from the field of educational psychology and the learning sciences. As we have noted earlier in this chapter, motivation refers to the forces that drive and direct individuals to select and initiate a course of action, while engagement is the energized action and behavior itself (e.g. Mercer, 2019; Skinner *et al.*, 2009). This connective tissue between the two is why engagement and motivation function in close relation and are thought to be inseparable from each other in comprehensive phenomenological descriptions of learning behavior.

The construct of engagement also has connections to the notion of investment. As Svalberg (2009) notes, '[engagement's] affective-state quality, "positive readiness", is related to motivation, while "behavioral readiness", a social-state feature, is perhaps closer to aspects of investment' (2009: 256). First and foremost, both of these constructs are concerned with individuals' action – the L2 learners' behavioral endeavors (or lack thereof). An important difference between engagement and its psychological antecedents (e.g. interest and motivation) is that engagement emphasizes L2 learners' actual observable learning activity and performance. Motivation has more to do with desire and intent than proactivity, and interest is much more a measure of the relational bond between an individual and a target topic or object. Even for dimensions of engagement that appear to be more related to learners' internal functioning, such as cognitive and affective engagement, the investigation of such types of engagement still relies on students' qualitative behavioral practices, such as focused attention, meaningful questioning, explaining and elaborating one's ideas, evaluating opinions and private speech for cognitive engagement, and positive body language, active listening, back channeling and openness to interaction with others for affective and social engagement. Similarly, investment research also focuses on L2 learners' learning practices in the target language. For instance, students are considered to be investing in L2 learning when they demonstrate commitment to learning practice, stay on task in classroom learning, actively participate in target activities, remain persistent in their attendance, take initiative and utilize resources for L2 learning.

Engagement and investment also focus on L2 learners' connection to and actions within the learning context, while motivation is often related to an outcome or a process (e.g. a learner may be motivated to reach a goal or achieve an objective). Interest, as we have explored, may be triggered situationally, but is eventually anchored to the personal utility and value for an object or topical domain (e.g. a learner may be interested in phonological features of the target language as these will help distinguish their proficiency in the language). As discussed previously, the social dimension is thought to be a key aspect of the construct of engagement, and is seen as closely related to the behavioral, cognitive and affective dimensions. Learners are socially engaged in L2 learning when they interact with teachers and peers in positive ways, such as maintaining interactive communication, actively listening to others' opinions, and providing reciprocal feedback during social interactions. Investment, too, stresses the role of the social context in any L2 learning. In fact, the social environment is one of the most important aspects of the notion of investment because L2 learners' social identities, relations of power and positions are fluid and changeable in different contexts, and thus their practices of L2 learning also shift in shape under various conditions and in different environments.

Apart from their commonalities, these constructs also differ in important ways. The notion of investment was developed to complement the

field's understanding of motivation by drawing insights from the poststructuralist theories of language and identity (Norton & Toohey, 2011).
Investment itself is a sociological construct, rather than a psychological one,
that 'explores how relations of power impact human relationships' (Norton,
2012: 343). Interest research looks for links between features of particular
situations (e.g. novelty, ambiguity, surprise) that catch individuals' attention, how these features are associated with initial interest development,
and how meaningful involvement in tasks that the learner perceives as valuable and enjoyable can develop into a more enduring individual interest so
that the individual seeks opportunities to reengage when subsequent learning opportunities or tasks present themselves (Harackiewicz *et al.*, 2008;
Hidi & Renninger, 2006; Renninger & Hidi, 2016).

Engagement and investment, for their part, tend to be researched in
different ways. One example of key differences is reflected in research
questions related to the two concepts. For instance, an engagement study
might investigate questions such as, 'To what extent are the learners
engaged in learning the L2?' and 'How do changes in learners' engagement lead to respective learning outcomes?' To answer these questions,
data may need to be elicited relating to the learners' in-class learning
behavior, task-performance and interaction patterns, in addition to relevant processes of language development through time. Comparatively in
an investment study, researchers might be interested in a question such as
'In what ways are learners invested in the language practices of this classroom?' (Norton & Toohey, 2011: 421). One area of divergence may be that
although the learners are behaviorally engaged in L2 learning, they may
not, at a more macro level, be investing in it, because the students' identities and beliefs may conflict with the values of the learning context (e.g.
an immigrant L1-user of Spanish who is studying English in a setting characterized by anti-immigrant rhetoric that devalues and marginalizes such
individuals). We should note that genuine engagement (featuring a combination of all dimensions of engagement) is also likely to link conceptually to learners' investment, though this notion has yet to be investigated
empirically. Therefore, an investment study has potential to demonstrate
separate findings of L2 learners' experiences which may be tangential to
or wider in scope than engagement research proper.

Toward a Research Agenda for L2 Engagement

In this chapter, we have reflected on engagement and several of its
companion constructs in order to bring greater definition to the enterprise
of studying how L2 learners engage with learning opportunities and
actively devote effort and attention to L2 learning. We turn now to several
recommendations for current and future L2 engagement research. While
not intended to be comprehensive, we feel that these are central to the task
of advancing the field's understanding of the landscape of L2 learners'

meaningful involvement and active participation in learning as well as strengthening its utility for practice.

Focus on capturing the nature of engagement

As our review of definitions, subtypes and strands of engagement research above illustrates, there is still a need for greater consistency and clarity in operationalizing and measuring engagement. The definitions discussed in this chapter may be helpful for understanding the nature of engagement. Since L2 engagement research is still in its infancy, the return on investment for such fundamental work in establishing clear operational definitions and measurement tools will be substantial. Although it is likely that 'consensus across scholars regarding theoretical models, measurement, and definitions may not be possible, or even desirable' (Christenson et al., 2012: 814), ideally, some empirical agreement is possible about the impact engagement has on L2 learning and developmental outcomes. In addition to valid and reliable field-specific measures of engagement that will push research forward, other issues that may need sorting out include, for example, how the various dimensions of engagement interact with one another, whether there are phenomenological differences in how individuals experience engagement, whether engagement is separate from disengagement, whether levels of engagement are linear in the sense that more engagement is better for L2 learning and whether there are thresholds of disengagement at which learners no longer benefit from instruction.

Focus on the necessary conditions for engagement

There is an increasing awareness throughout much of our field of the complex systems that comprise L2 learners, classrooms, schools and language communities (Hiver & Al-Hoorie, 2016, 2020; Larsen-Freeman & Cameron, 2008). Within these complex systems, research is needed to identify what makes language learning engaging for students both inside and outside of classroom settings, what conditions are part of an engaging instructional context, what makes for engaging language learning tasks and how engaging contexts differ across groups of diverse learners with varied levels and learning objectives. If engagement is thought of as the organizing mechanism for greater involvement and higher quality participation in opportunities for language learning, then amplifying the necessary conditions for it to thrive can help teachers attend to these multiple dimensions of students' participation. In addition to establishing a person–environment fit and identifying disaffected learners, identifying disengaging learning environments may shed light on the policies, practices and contextual influences that have little 'holding' power or that provide a disincentive for active learner involvement and meaningful participation (Christenson et al., 2012: 816).

Focus on the development of engagement over time

Student engagement is not static or immutable – it can change (Mercer, 2019). How it is dynamic, under what conditions and for whom remains unclear. Often student engagement is conceptualized as a desired outcome, and this is a sound design choice in many instances that we have no issue with. With just a modicum of creativity, however, it is possible to take more explicit temporal considerations into account, for example, by investigating the role of teachers, peers and learning tasks on engagement over time (i.e. through developmental transitions), and examining how classroom learning opportunities, assessments and extramural interests and experiences influence learners' engagement. There are also other means through which engagement can be studied to foreground the ways in which it is dynamic and emergent. Engagement can be studied as the process or activity through which development occurs (e.g. what happens to the learner cognitively, emotionally, etc. as they are engaging?), as a system input embedded in thinking about what the learners might achieve (e.g. how does engaging provide a vehicle for bridging learners' current performance or competencies with their future goals?), or as a mediator in the mechanisms of learning and development (e.g. what are the ways in which engaging in learning tasks impacts what learners can expect to gain from those instances of participation and involvement?).

Focus on re-engaging disengaged and disaffected students

Research shows that engaged learners reach higher levels of learning achievement and benefit from many desirable 'side-effects' such as deeper interest, greater motivation, stronger self-efficacy and persistence (Reschly & Christenson, 2012). By comparison, developmental problems will occur if students are disengaged from learning. The effects of chronic disengagement and lack of interest in learning activities extend beyond passivity and into maladaptive feelings of alienation from other members in learning contexts, dispersed and wasted attention and effort for learning, and poor persistence and commitment to learning more broadly (Shernoff, 2013). Genuinely engaging in an activity often generates further engagement, and this 'Matthew effect' (i.e. positive feedback loop) of engagement highlights the importance of targeted interventions that can help disengaged learners, of which we suspect there are no shortage, recapture their energy for action and rediscover their appetite for meaningful involvement in language learning. Doing so must include an appropriate focus on student voices and perspectives and encourage an upward trajectory toward personal investment in language learning.

Engagement is a kind of 'hands-on' and 'heads-on' energy for learning (Skinner et al., 2009: 227) characterized by enthusiasm, willingness, effortful exertion, interest and concentrated attention directed toward understanding, learning, or mastering the knowledge and skills necessary to be a competent language user. For purposes of language pedagogy and policy, research on this concept suggests that specific interventions and teaching strategies can enhance learners' engagement (see e.g. Harbour *et al.*, 2015). Teaching does not cause learning. At its best, it creates the conditions necessary for learning to occur by engaging and involving L2 learners in compelling tasks, interactions, and opportunities for development. Given the complexity of what transpires in L2 classrooms, engaging learners can be seen as a key part of building L2 classroom environments that are thoughtful, demanding, and supportive of learners' development. We believe that L2 pedagogy can have strong relevance for learners and their development provided that engaging language learners in the complex dynamic classrooms of the 21st century is at its core.

Note

(1) An individual with identified regulation engages in an activity because they highly value and identify with the behavior, and recognize its usefulness.

References

Ainley, M. (2006) Connecting with learning: Motivation, affect and cognition in interest processes. *Educational Psychology Review* 18, 391–405.

Ainley, M. (2012) Students' interest and engagement in classroom activities. In S.L. Christenson, A.L. Reschly and C. Wylie (eds) *Handbook of Research on Student Engagement* (pp. 283–302). New York: Springer.

Anderson, L.W. (1975) Student involvement in learning and school achievement. *California Journal of Educational Research* 26, 53–62.

Baralt, M., Gurzynski-Weiss, L. and Kim, Y. (2016) Engagement with language: How examining learners' affective and social engagement explains successful learner-generated attention to form. In M. Sato and S. Ballinger (eds) *Peer Interaction and Second Language Learning: Pedagogical Potential and Research Agenda* (pp. 209–240). Amsterdam: John Benjamins.

Bourdieu, P. and Passeron, J. (1977) *Reproduction in Education, Society, and Culture.* London: SAGE.

Brophy, J. (2008) Developing students' appreciation for what is taught in school. *Educational Psychologist* 43, 132–141.

Bygate, M. and Samuda, V. (2009) Creating pressure in task pedagogy: The joint roles of field, purpose, and engagement within the interaction approaches. In A. Mackey and C. Polio (eds) *Multiple Perspectives on Interaction: Second Language Research in Honour of Susan M. Gass* (pp. 90–116). New York: Routledge.

Christenson, S.L., Reschly, A.L. and Wylie, C. (eds) (2012) *Handbook of Research on Student Engagement.* New York: Springer.

Crookes, G. and Schmidt, R. (1991) Motivation: Reopening the research agenda. *Language Learning* 41, 469–512.

Cummins, J. (2006) Identity texts: The imaginative construction of self through multiliteracies pedagogy. In O. García, T. Skutnabb-Kangas and M. Torres-Guzmán (eds) *Imagining Multilingual Schools: Languages in Education and Glocalization* (pp. 51–68). Clevedon: Multilingual Matters.

Dao, P. (2019) Effects of task goal orientation on learner engagement in task performance. *International Review of Applied Linguistics in Language Teaching*. Advance online access. doi:10.1515/iral-2018-0188

Dao, P. and McDonough, K. (2018) Effect of proficiency on Vietnamese EFL learners' engagement in peer interaction. *International Journal of Education Research* 88, 60–72.

Dörnyei, Z. (1994) Understanding L2 motivation: On with the challenge! *The Modern Language Journal* 78, 515–523.

Dörnyei, Z. and Kormos, J. (2000) The role of individual and social variables in oral task performance. *Language Teaching Research* 4, 275–300.

Durik, A.M. and Harackiewicz, J.M. (2007) Different strokes for different folks: How individual interest moderates the effects of situational factors on task interest. *Journal of Educational Psychology* 99, 597–610.

Finn, J.D. and Zimmer, K.S. (2012) Student engagement: What is it? Why does it matter? In S.L. Christenson, A.L. Reschly and C. Wylie (eds) *Handbook of Research on Student Engagement* (pp. 97–132). New York: Springer.

Fredricks, J.A., Blumenfeld, P.C. and Paris, A.H. (2004) School engagement: Potential of the concept, state of the evidence. *Review of Educational Research* 74, 59–109.

Fredricks, J.A. and McColskey, W. (2012) The measurement of student engagement: A comparative analysis of various methods and student self-report instruments. In S.L. Christenson, A.L. Reschly and C. Wylie (eds) *Handbook of Research on Student Engagement* (pp. 763–782). New York: Springer.

Fryer, L. and Ainley, M. (2019) Supporting interest in a study domain: A longitudinal test of the interplay between interest, utility-value, and competence beliefs. *Learning and Instruction* 60, 252–262.

Furrer, C.J. and Skinner, E.A. (2003) Sense of relatedness as a factor in children's academic engagement and performance. *Journal of Educational Psychology* 95, 148–162.

Gardner, R.C. and MacIntyre, P.D. (1993) On the measurement of affective variables in second language learning. *Language Learning* 43, 157–194.

Gettinger, M. and Walter, M.J. (2012) Classroom strategies to enhance academic engaged time. In S.L. Christenson, A.L. Reschly and C. Wylie (eds) *Handbook of Research on Student Engagement* (pp. 653–673). New York: Springer.

Harackiewicz, J.M., Durik, A.M., Barron, K.E., Linnenbrink-Garcia, L. and Tauer, J.M. (2008) The role of achievement goals in the development of interest: Reciprocal relations between achievement goals, interest, and performance. *Journal of Educational Psychology* 100, 105–122.

Harackiewicz, J.M. and Hulleman, C.S. (2010) The importance of interest: The role of achievement goals and task values in promoting the development of interest. *Social and Personality Psychology Compass* 4, 42–52.

Harackiewicz, J.M., Smith, J.L. and Priniski, S.J. (2016) Interest matters: The importance of promoting interest in education. *Policy Insights from the Behavioral and Brain Sciences* 3, 220–227.

Harbour, K.E., Evanovich, L.L., Sweigart, C.A. and Hughes, L.E. (2015) A brief review of effective teaching practices that maximize student engagement. *Preventing School Failure* 59, 5–13.

Helme, S. and Clarke, D. (2001) Identifying cognitive engagement in the mathematics classroom. *Mathematics Education Research Journal* 13, 133–153.

Hidi, S. (1990) Interest and its contribution as a mental resource for learning. *Review of Educational Research* 60, 549–571.

Hidi, S. (2006) Interest: A unique motivational variable. *Educational Research Review* 1, 69–82.

Hidi, S. and Ainley, M. (2008) Interest and self-regulation: Relationships between two variables that influence learning. In D.H. Schunk and B.J. Zimmerman (eds) *Motivation and Self-regulated Learning: Theory, Research and Applications* (pp. 77–109). New York: Lawrence Erlbaum.

Hidi, S. and Harackiewicz, J.M. (2000) Motivating the academically unmotivated: A critical issue for the 21st century. *Review of Educational Research* 79, 151–179.

Hidi, S. and Renninger, K.A. (2006) The four-phase model of interest development. *Educational Psychologist* 41, 111–127.

Hidi, S., Renninger, K.A. and Krapp, A. (2004) Interest, a motivational variable that combines affective and cognitive functioning. In D.Y. Dai and R.J. Sternberg (eds) *Motivation, Emotion, and Cognition: Integrative Perspectives on Intellectual Functioning and Development* (pp. 89–115). Mahwah, NJ: Lawrence Erlbaum.

Hiver, P. and Al-Hoorie, A.H. (2016) A 'dynamic ensemble' for second language research: Putting complexity theory into practice. *The Modern Language Journal* 100, 741–756.

Hiver, P. and Al-Hoorie, A.H. (2020) *Research Methods for Complexity Theory in Applied Linguistics*. Bristol: Multilingual Matters.

Järvelä, S. and Renninger, K.A. (2014) Designing for learning: Interest, motivation, and engagement. In K. Sawyer (ed.) *The Cambridge Handbook of the Learning Sciences* (pp. 668–685). Cambridge: Cambridge University Press.

Kim, Y. (2013) Promoting attention to form through task repetition in a Korean EFL context. In K. McDonough and A. Mackey (eds) *Second Language Interaction in Diverse Educational Settings* (pp. 3–24). Amsterdam: John Benjamins.

Kinginger, C. (2004) Alice doesn't live here anymore: Foreign language learning and identity construction. In A. Pavlenko and A. Blackledge (eds) *Negotiation of Identities in Multilingual Contexts* (pp. 219–242). Clevedon: Multilingual Matters.

Krapp, A. (2002) Structural and dynamic aspects of interest development: Theoretical considerations from an ontogenetic perspective. *Learning and Instruction* 12, 383–409.

Lambert, C., Kormos, J. and Minn, D. (2016) Task repetition and second language speech processing. *Studies in Second Language Acquisition* 39, 167–196.

Lambert, C., Philp, J. and Nakamura, S. (2017) Learner-generated content and engagement in second language task performance. *Language Teacher Research* 21 (6), 665–680.

Larsen-Freeman, D. and Cameron, L. (2008) *Complex Systems and Applied Linguistics*. Oxford: Oxford University Press.

Lawson, M.A. and Lawson, H.A. (2013) New conceptual frameworks for student engagement research, policy, and practice. *Review of Educational Research* 83, 432–479.

Maehr, M.L. (1984) Meaning and motivation: Toward a theory of personal investment. In R.E. Ames and C. Ames (eds) *Motivation in Education: Student Motivation* (Vol. 1) (pp. 115–144). San Diego, CA: Academic Press.

Mahatmya, D., Lohman, B.J., Matjasko, J.L. and Feldman Farb, A. (2012) Engagement across developmental periods. In S.L. Christenson, A.L. Reschly and C. Wylie (eds) *Handbook of Research on Student Engagement* (pp. 45–64). New York: Springer.

Mercer, N. and Hodgkinson, S. (eds) (2008) *Exploring Talk in School*. London: SAGE.

Mercer, S. (2015) Learner agency and engagement: Believing you can, wanting to and knowing how to. *Humanising Language Teaching* 17 (4), 1–19.

Mercer, S. (2019) Language learner engagement: Setting the scene. In X. Gao (ed.) *Second Handbook of English Language Teaching* (pp. 1–19). Basel: Springer.

Moranski, K. and Toth, P. (2016) Small-group meta-analytic talk and Spanish L2 development. In M. Sato and S. Ballinger (eds) *Peer Interaction and Second Language Learning: Pedagogical Potential and Research Agenda* (pp. 291–319). Amsterdam: John Benjamins.

Norton Peirce, B. (1995) Social identity, investment, and language learning. *TESOL Quarterly* 29, 9–31.

Norton, B. (2000) *Identity and Language Learning: Gender, Ethnicity, and Educational Change* (1st edn). Harlow: Pearson.

Norton, B. (2012) Investment. In P. Robinson (ed.) *The Routledge Encyclopedia of Second Language Acquisition* (pp. 343–344). New York: Routledge.

Norton, B. and Toohey, K. (2011) Identity, language learning, and social change. *Language Teaching* 44, 412–446.

Nystrand, M. and Gamoran, A. (1991) Instructional discourse, student engagement, and literature achievements. *Research in the Teaching of English* 25, 261–290.

Pekrun, R. and Linnenbrink-Garcia, L. (2012) Academic emotions and student engagement. In S.L. Christenson, A.L. Reschly and C. Wylie (eds) *Handbook of Research on Student Engagement* (pp. 259–282). New York: Springer.

Philp, J. and Duchesne, S. (2016) Exploring engagement in tasks in the language classroom. *Annual Review of Applied Linguistics* 36, 50–72.

Phung, L. (2017) Task preference, affective response, and engagement in L2 use in a US university context. *Language Teaching Research* 21, 751–766.

Platt, E. and Brooks, F.B. (2002) Task engagement: A turning point in foreign language development. *Language Learning* 52, 365–400.

Potowski, K. (2007) *Language and Identity in a Dual Immersion School*. Clevedon: Multilingual Matters.

Qiu, X. and Lo, Y.Y. (2017) Content familiarity, task repetition and Chinese EFL learners' engagement in second language use. *Language Teaching Research* 21, 681–698.

Reeve, J. (2012) A self-determination theory perspective on student engagement. In S.L. Christenson, A.L. Reschly and C. Wylie (eds) *Handbook of Research on Student Engagement* (pp. 149–172). New York: Springer.

Renninger, K.A. and Hidi, S. (2011) Revisiting the conceptualization, measurement, and generation of interest. *Educational Psychologist* 46, 168–184.

Renninger, K.A. and Hidi, S. (2016) *The Power of Interest for Motivation and Engagement*. New York: Routledge.

Renninger, K.A., Hidi, S. and Krapp, A. (eds) (1992) *The Role of Interest in Learning and Development*. Hilsdale, NJ: Lawrence Erlbaum.

Reschly, A.L. and Christenson, S.L. (2012) Jingle, jangle, and conceptual haziness: Evolution and future directions of the engagement construct. In S.L. Christenson, A.L. Reschly and C. Wylie (eds) *Handbook of Research on Student Engagement* (pp. 3–20). New York: Springer.

Rotgans, J.I. and Schmidt, H.G. (2014) Situational interest and learning: Thirst for knowledge. *Learning and Instruction* 32, 37–50.

Sato, M. and Ballinger, S. (2012) Raising language awareness in peer interaction: A cross-context, cross-method examination. *Language Awareness* 21 (1–2), 157–179.

Schiefele, U. (2009) Situational and individual interest. In K.R. Wentzel and A. Wigfield (eds) *Handbook of Motivation at School* (pp. 197–223). New York: Routledge.

Shernoff, D.J. (2013) *Optimal Learning Environment to Promote Student Engagement*. Dordrecht: Springer.

Skilton-Sylvester, E. (2002) Should I stay or should I go? Investigating Cambodian women's participation and investment in adult ESL programs. *Adult Education Quarterly* 53, 9–26.

Skinner, E.A., Kindermann, T.A., Connell, J.P. and Wellborn, J.G. (2009) Engagement and disaffection as organizational constructs in the dynamics of motivational development. In K.R. Wentzel and A. Wigfield (eds) *Handbook of Motivation at School* (pp. 223–245). New York: Routledge.

Skinner, E.A., Kindermann, T.A. and Furrer, C. (2009) A motivational perspective on engagement and disaffection: Conceptualization and assessment of children's behavioral and emotional participation in academic activities in the classroom. *Educational and Psychological Measurement* 69, 493–525.

Skinner, E.A. and Pitzer, J.R. (2012) Developmental dynamics of engagement, coping, and everyday resilience. In S.L. Christenson, A.L. Reschly and C. Wylie (eds) *Handbook of Research on Student Engagement* (pp. 21–44). New York: Springer.

Storch, N. (2002) Patterns of interaction in ESL pair work. *Language Learning* 52, 119–158.

Svalberg, A.M.L. (2007) Language awareness and language learning. *Language Teaching* 40, 287–308.

Svalberg, A.M.L. (2009) Engagement with language: Interrogating a construct. *Language Awareness* 18 (3–4), 242–258.

Svalberg. A.M.L. (2017) Researching language engagement: Current trends and future directions. *Language Awareness* 27 (1–2), 21–39.

Toth, P.D., Wagner, E. and Moranski, K. (2013) 'Co-constructing' explicit L2 knowledge with high school Spanish learners through guided induction. *Applied Linguistics* 34, 255–278.

Wellborn, J.G. (1991) Engaged and disaffected action: The conceptualization and measurement of motivation in the academic domain. Unpublished doctoral dissertation, University of Rochester, Rochester.

Williams, M. and Burden, R.L. (1997) *Psychology for Language Teachers*. Cambridge: Cambridge University Press.

Yazzie-Mintz, E. (2009) *Engaging the Voices of Students: A Report on the 2007 & 2008 High School Survey of Student Engagement*. Bloomington, IN: Center for Evaluation and Education Policy.

3 Engagement with Language in Relation to Form-Focused Versus Meaning-Focused Teaching and Learning

Agneta M-L Svalberg

Introduction

Learner engagement has attracted increased researcher attention in the past couple of decades, some focusing on general school engagement (Skinner & Pitzer, 2012), or learners' engagement in specific school subjects (e.g. Ainley, 2000; Ainley *et al.*, 2006). A smaller more specialized body of work explicitly theorizes and investigates learners' engagement in language learning settings (Ellis, 2010; Han & Hyland, 2015; Storch, 2008; Svalberg, 2009, 2012), sometimes indirectly by using terms other than engagement such as 'language-related episodes' (LREs) (Storch, 2008; Swain & Lapkin, 1995, 2001), 'collaborative dialogue' (Swain & Lapkin, 2001) or subsuming engagement into task-based interaction (Seedhaus & Almutairi, 2009). As other chapters in this section of the present volume show, a fairly comprehensive view of the wider engagement field is provided by Christenson *et al.*'s (2012) edited volume; a review of research on engagement in language learning and elsewhere can be found in Philp and Duchesne (2016).

It is now widely agreed that while implicit learning may account for most language development, conscious engagement is also needed for efficient learning (e.g. Ellis, 2015). Noticing of and attention to language features increases the likelihood of learning (Schmidt, 1990, 2001) and may indeed be necessary for acquisition of some more complex, or less frequent, features. But what do researchers mean by engagement? The authors explain:

> Engagement is the term frequently employed to talk broadly about learners' interest and participation in an activity. To date, however, in applied linguistics research there is little principled understanding of this overused term although there is a shared intuitive recognition of 'engagement' as optimal for learning. (Philp & Duchesne, 2016: 50)

The current chapter focuses on the more specific notion of engagement with language (EWL; Svalberg, 2009, 2012), its relation to other types of engagement and its implications for language teaching and learning. Below, different definitions of engagement will be considered, followed by discussions of EWL in classroom settings, how opportunities for it arise, and what form it might take. The remaining sections consider how EWL relates to form- versus meaning-focused teaching; consciousness-raising (CR) tasks; the use of the first language (L1); and EWL in the communicative classroom. The chapter closes with a brief summary and some conclusions.

Defining Engagement

To understand EWL it is useful to first consider the contrasting notions of academic engagement (school engagement) and task engagement (TE) (Svalberg, 2017). In a study involving over 1000 UK school pupils, Skinner *et al.* (2009: 494) explain that academic engagement 'refers to the quality of a student's connection or involvement with the endeavour of schooling and hence with the people, activities goals, values and place that compose it'. The authors focus on observable behavior, and some affective engagement is included, e.g. enthusiasm or boredom. Academic engagement can perhaps be described as the behavioral manifestation of the learner's motivation (i.e. intent or desire) to be in education generally, and in their particular school environment.

A narrower construct, TE, was investigated in an early study by Platt and Brooks (2002). Any teacher who uses tasks, be it in languages or any other subject, will be familiar with TE, or its absence. It is often evident in written or spoken outputs but also in body language, facial expressions, speech features (loudness, intonation, silence etc.), peer interaction or the lack of it (Platt & Brooks, 2002).

EWL, in contrast, is defined as 'a cognitive, and/or affective, and/or social process in which the learner is the agent and language is object (and sometimes vehicle)' (Svalberg, 2009: 2). In other words, EWL is learners thinking and talking about language, its forms, functions and how it works. Experienced teachers are likely to intuitively notice learners' engagement, or lack of it. Researchers, however, need explicit criteria. Figure 3.1 (where L stands for 'learner') suggests how EWL might be identified by teachers or researchers.

Cognitive	Affective	Social
How alert is the learner? Does the learner (L) seem energetic or lethargic? Does L seem to notice language/interaction features? How focused? Is L's attention on the language or not? Does L's mind seem to wander? How reflective? Does L notice and reflect on the language, or simply react? How critical/ analytical? Is L's reasoning inductive or memory/ imitation based? With regard to the target language, does L compare, ask questions, infer/draw conclusions?	How willing is L to engage with language? Is L withdrawn or eager to participate? How purposefully does L explore the language? Does L seem bored or not focused on the task, or to be focused? How autonomous is L in their EWL? Is L's behavior dependent or independent?	How interactive? Does L interact, verbally or otherwise, with others to learn about the language? How supportive of others? (e.g. by verbal or other behaviors?) Does L engage in negotiation and scaffolding to investigate the language? Leader or follower? Are L's language focused interactions reactive or initiating? L = the learner

Figure 3.1 Criteria for identifying engagement with language (adapted from Svalberg, 2009: 247)

As shown in the figure, there are three types of EWL (cognitive, affective and social), characterized by certain behaviors and attitudes (Svalberg, 2009). While engaging with the language, a cognitively engaged individual 'is alert, pays focused attention and constructs their own knowledge' about the language; affective engagement is characterized by 'a positive, purposeful, willing and autonomous disposition' toward the language and what it represents; and a socially engaged individual, finally, is 'interactive and initiating' (Svalberg, 2009: 247).

TE and EWL are illustrated below with extracts from a project discussed in Svalberg and Askham (2014, 2016) and Svalberg (2015). The participants were international MA students on a grammar course for English teachers at a UK university. Following lecture style input, the students carried out collaborative CR tasks. In the following example of TE, four learners are doing a verb identification and classification task in two parts, A and B. The group are deciding in what order to do the two parts of the task.

Extract 1

1.	Isabelle	Ok – are we doing A and B or just A – or see how time goes?
2.	Emily	I think see how time goes
3.	Isabelle	I found B quite difficult so – if we can't start B then
4.	Harry	We leave it
5.	Isabelle	Yes
6.	Harry	Shall we {...} verb one by one or?
7.	Emily	Yes I think we should
8.	Isabelle	Yes – let's find the verb and also try and classify them at the same time

(Svalberg & Askham, 2014[1])

There is no EWL at this stage. The second episode, below, is an example of EWL by another group of four in the same class (Svalberg & Askham, 2016: 187–188). Their main focus here is on the verbs underlined in the following sentence: 'I did not say this to Mahjoub, though I wish I had done so, for he was intelligent; in my conceit I was afraid he would not understand.'[2] Their task is to analyze the tense and time reference of the verbs.

Extract 2

1.	Amelia	You can understand like *I wish* definitely is – for the speaker is at present – *I wish* – and *I had done* – er – just leave that alone – look the end of sentence – *in my conceit I was afraid he – I was afraid – was afraid* – is at past then at past right?
2.	Mia	Yeah
3.	Amelia	Then at past then – what's before the past is *I have done* something
4.	Jack	But *I didn't say – I had - I should be* – but he didn't do that
5.	Amelia	Yes so it's before the *I was afraid*
6.	Mia	Yeah so it's er before past
7.	Jessica	What about *I wish*? You know we should follow by the er object –
8.	Jack	There's a phrase – yeah – for example I say *I wish I could do something* but before the present time – maybe it's a past but not now – maybe I didn't do that as well – I'm just – I'm regret about something
9.	Mia	Oh yes yes
10.	Amelia	Yes
11.	Jessica	Oh all right I understand ok ok ok
12.	Mia	Yes it's for the situation is different with the
13.	Jessica	Ah – *I wish I hadn't do done that*
14.	Amelia	Yes

Amelia confidently asserts that 'I wish' refers to the speaker's present (1). She skips the next verb, perhaps because its time reference is less clear to her, and directs her group's attention to 'I was afraid', which clearly refers to the past. This is followed by a discussion about the sequence of events as the learners are developing their understanding of how tense can express regret. In (8) Jack is struggling to express his view, first voiced in (5), that 'had done' refers to a past event which did not happen, and hence expresses regret. The others seem to agree, and Jessica (13) makes the connection between 'I wish' and regret explicit. The learners are clearly cognitively engaged with language, noticing and reflecting on it although to varying degrees. By discussing what they have noticed, they are also socially engaged. Affective engagement is not explicit in the wording but the discussion is animated indicating willingness.

Some engagement researchers consider a fourth distinction, 'behavioral engagement'. Philp and Duchesne (2016), for example, define engagement as 'a state of heightened attention and involvement' including cognitive, affective, social and behavioral engagement (2016: 51). Behavioral engagement, according to the authors, includes listening to others, actively collaborating, completing the task, multiple readings, time on task and number of turns. The category is apparently trying to capture duration, amount, frequency, repetition and, perhaps, also degree (intensity) of engagement, but does not seem internally coherent. Some behavioral aspects could instead be classified as TE (time on task and completing the task), others would seem to indicate cognitive engagement (multiple readings), or social engagement (actively collaborating, number of turns). As several other chapters in this volume highlight, all dimensions of engagement are manifested behaviorally. Below, what has been called 'behavioral engagement' will therefore be subsumed under cognitive, affective or social EWL, and (when appropriate) TE.

The knowledge constructed through EWL is declarative, i.e. it is knowledge *about* language, also called language awareness (Association for Language Awareness n.d.). It might relate to cultural, sociolinguistic or pronunciation issues, text structure, or any other aspect of the use and understanding of language. In this chapter, the concern is learners' construction of declarative knowledge about the target language (TL) grammar.

EWL in the Classroom

The criteria in Figure 3.1 have proved useful as an analytical framework in a number of EWL studies (Ahn, 2016; Baralt *et al.*, 2016; Kearney & Ahn, 2014; Kearney & Barbour, 2015) and have been applied to different ages and contexts. Ahn (2016) employed them to investigate the ludic language play of Korean 11–15-year-olds, and Kearney and Ahn (2014) and Kearney and Barbour (2015) to study even younger learners' language socialization.

Baralt *et al.* (2016) investigated the engagement of 40 learners of Spanish in the US, working in dyads to retell a story either with online partners or face-to-face in a traditional classroom. They analyzed three sets of data: transcripts of university students completing a language task in face-to-face interaction, chat logs for other students doing the same task online, and post-task questionnaires for all participants. The coding scheme used was an adapted version of Figure 3.1. No explicit distinction was made by the researchers between EWL and TE, but the analysis sheet included three criteria headings for each of the three EWL dimensions, with space for coder comments. Relevant comments from the questionnaire were also included for triangulation. The findings from this study will be discussed further below.

The criteria in Svalberg (2012) were the basis also for Kearney and Ahn's (2014) analysis of 3–5-year-old children's normal classroom activities in World Languages classes. EWL episodes were identified in over 13 hours of video recordings and fieldnotes. The study showed that even children this young can and do engage with language. It provided an understanding of how and why they do so, which could potentially shape pedagogy and teacher training to encourage EWL in young learners.

It is useful to distinguish EWL from other types of engagement. As shown above, cognitive EWL refers to how the learner applies their cognitive resources to a language problem, and affective EWL to how the learner feels while they are investigating the language. Social EWL is concerned with how the learner interacts with others during, and for the purposes of, such language investigation. *Use* of language does not constitute EWL unless what is talked about is language. Thus, a learner saying '*I wish I hadn't done that*' to a peer could simply be interacting socially by communicating her regret. In Extract 2 above, however, when Jessica (13) says this she is not expressing regret but instead reflecting on its grammar and meaning, i.e. it forms part of her cognitive and social EWL. Having said that, non-linguistic engagement and EWL may overlap and interact. For example, general alertness, a positive attitude and an orientation toward interaction at school or task level are likely to contribute positively to cognitive, affective, and social EWL.

The fact that affective EWL is characterized by an initial willingness to engage might make it resemble motivation by a different name. Nevertheless, in the research literature there tend to be two important differences: focus and time span. MacIntyre and Serroul (2015) offer the following general definition of motivation as 'the force that gives behavior its energy and direction' (2015: 109). Underlying factors such as the need for competence, autonomy and relatedness (Niemiec & Ryan, 2009), or learners' conception of their own ideal, future self and their ought-to self (Dörnyei, 2009) have been the focus of L2 motivation studies. In contrast, engagement researchers are typically concerned with how engagement manifests, as discussed earlier and operationalized in behavioral terms for EWL in Figure 3.1. This is an important distinction made equally by other chapters in this first part of the current volume (see e.g. Chapter 2 by Sang & Hiver; Chapter 5 by Zhou *et al.*, this volume). Motivation research is thus usually concerned with what drives behavior, while engagement research tends to focus on the behavior itself.

The second difference is time span. MacIntyre and Serroul (2015: 109) state that most motivation theories adopt 'a time scale of months and years' (e.g. Dörnyei, 2009; Gardner, 1985; Muir & Dörnyei, 2013). Willingness to engage (one possible way of seeing affective engagement) operates at the micro level in that it can change from one moment to another, much like willingness to communicate (MacIntyre, 2012; though see also Chapter 14 by Wang & Mercer, this volume). These are, however, tendencies rather than absolutes. For example, MacIntyre and Serroul (2015) take a micro-analytical approach in their own motivation research.

The engagement perspective has the advantage of explicitly addressing the interaction between cognitive, affective and social aspects. Swain (2013) recently argued that the role of emotions in language learning has been greatly underestimated. In regard to EWL, they are central in that cognitive and/or social engagement is unlikely to take place unless there is some willingness to engage to start with, and willingness can also result in persistence. Conversely, the interaction and interdependency in the system is three-way as positive experiences of cognitive and/or social engagement can further boost willingness to engage.

An important affective factor is learners' perception of meaningfulness (Kearney & Ahn, 2014). In Svalberg (2017), it was argued that meaningfulness can enhance willingness to engage. A perception of a task as purposeful, having utility (Ainley, 2000), or giving pleasure, is likely to render it meaningful at a linguistic, social or individual level. The study by Ahn (2016), for example, shows how children's humoristic play with TL words can render them both linguistically and socially meaningful.

EWL is clearly influenced by contextual factors. In Baralt et al.'s (2016) study, the online partners did not know each other, and some did not like each other. As a result, there was little engagement of any kind and little collaboration. One of the online students described her disengagement by saying that she 'mentally checked out' while her partner retold the story (Baralt et al., 2016: 233). The face-to-face pairs, in contrast, enjoyed working together and engaged more, cognitively, affectively and socially. The authors explain that 'those who reported feeling happy, having fun, and who saw their partners as friends engaged in more social scaffolding that led to greater instances of cognitive engagement' (Baralt et al., 2016: 233). The online pairs seem to have failed to find the tasks socially meaningful and consequently failed to engage. Conversely, face-to-face helped create friendly relationships, which in turn facilitated engagement (see also Chapter 7 by Carver et al., this volume).

Affordances

There is interdependence and constant interaction between EWL, other types of engagement, and contextual variables. In other words, like other socially embedded systems, including language (Beckner et al., 2009; Ellis & Larsen-Freeman, 2009), EWL is complex and dynamic. Hence, learners' EWL is not caused by any one factor but emerges from the interaction of numerous factors. A situation which facilitates such emergence can be called an EWL 'affordance'.

An affordance in this context is a learning opportunity. Factors related to the task design, the teacher, and the learners themselves are the most immediate contributors. Affordances can be unplanned, or planned by the teacher or task designer. Any affordance is, however, only *potential* unless and until it is recognized as an affordance by the learner who exercises their agency (Mercer, 2011) by making use of it. An example already mentioned is Ahn's (2016) study where the children noticed and then joked about similarities of English and Korean words. Hence, affordances are ultimately realized by learners (Larsen-Freeman & Cameron, 2008).

From this perspective, communicative tasks are those that aim to achieve implicit learning by offering multiple affordances for (as far as possible) spontaneous, purposeful language use, while form-focused CR tasks aim to present maximum affordances for explicit learning through EWL. The latter not only encourage metatalk, they require it. Consequently, research on EWL often involves form-focused CR tasks (Eckerth, 2008; Fotos, 1994; Scott & De La Fuente, 2008; Storch, 2002, 2008). A CR task generates EWL by presenting learners with language data (a text, or examples) and a problem to solve. Figure 3.2 shows an example task which requires the learners to formulate a rule based on the data they have been given (key in Appendix 3.1).

Other types of CR tasks are, for example, text editing and text reconstruction (including dictogloss) (Thornbury, 1997). They all promote learners' noticing and talking about the language. The purpose of CR is not to enable immediate mastery of the target feature in output. Rather, it is to raise learners' awareness of the feature, making them more likely to notice and understand it in subsequent meaningful input (Ellis, 2009; Fotos, 1994). Hence, CR tasks have the potential to create affordances for continued learning.

CR TASK

In the interview text below,

- *underline all the verbs*
- *highlight the tensed verbs only (If necessary, test by changing the tense of the sentence, from past to present, or from present to past. Verbs that change are tensed.)*
- *then complete the rule*

B: Can you tell me a little bit about yourself and your job?

A: I am near retirement now, but I first came to Britain as a child. We all studied.

B: What did you want to be?

A: I wanted to be a barrister, and for some years I was self-employed in the home improvement business, but the recessions of the 80s and 90s put a stop to that.

B: And how long have you been a taxi driver?

A: I've been driving a minicab for 10 years. I wanted to be self-employed and I like talking to people. But now the novelty has worn off and I do not like this job. You work long hours and you earn a pittance.

RULE: Tense is marked on _____ verb in the VGr only.

Figure 3.2 A form-focused consciousness-raising task[3]

Learners' subjective perceptions of tasks are central to EWL, its quality and eventual effect. In Svalberg and Askham's (2014) study, the collaborative CR tasks participants completed were similar to but more advanced than the one in Figure 3.2. Interviews revealed their attitudes to and views of the experience. In the following two extracts, two of the participants whose interactions were discussed above (Extract 1), express their views.

Extract 3

Emily: Well – erm – I think the most helpful way is to listening to others – because erm – […] well – listening to other people you can know what you didn't know before – but – well – I have to say that speaking – erm – expressing your own ideas is also very helpful but you are just suing [showing] what you already known – but getting other peoples' ideas is a kind of learn – is a kind of learning opportunity – because you are learning something new. (2014: 127)

Emily perceived the 'listening to others' aspect of social EWL as an affordance for cognitive EWL; listening allowed her to construct new knowledge. The speaking aspect of social EWL was also 'very helpful' but perhaps to consolidate knowledge rather than create it. For Isabelle (below), an awareness of her own limitations and the greater expertise of her peers together created EWL affordances (Svalberg & Askham, 2014[1]).

Extract 4

1.	Interviewer	And what do you think were the factors that helped you to engage with the tasks?
2.	Isabelle	There was a task to be completed and grammar is my weak point and there's probably – most of the other students on the course – particularly those - the non-native students – it is probably their strongest point so
3.	Interviewer	So your awareness that this was something you needed sort of spurred you on
4.	Isabelle	Yes – I am quite a – I like problem-solving – to me if there is a problem to be solved and I can
5.	Interviewer	A puzzle
6.	Isabelle	Yes – a puzzle

The situation created in her a willingness to engage and hence affordances for social and cognitive engagement. The problem-solving aspect of the tasks, which she enjoyed, further increased her affective EWL.

For some less proficient learners, however, doing the CR tasks in English presented an obstacle, as exemplified by this quote from an interview with Mia (Svalberg & Askham, 2016[1]).

Extract 5

1.	Mia	Sometimes maybe I – I have the knowledge or I have some opinions about it but cause we teach – we are taught grammar in Chinese – so sometimes I don't know how to use English – I mean the
2.	Interviewer	The correct terminology
3.	Mia	The terminology to – express it

The metalanguage was a stumbling block for Mia, inhibiting her social EWL, and possibly creating anxiety. Unless learning the TL terminology is itself an aim of the CR task, minimizing the need for it can avoid blocking affordances for social and cognitive engagement.

Language-Related Episodes as a Manifestation of EWL

One important form of EWL in instructed contexts is the LRE (Swain & Lapkin, 1995, 2001; Storch, 2008) which, as mentioned above, is also referred to as collaborative dialogue (Swain & Lapkin, 2001). LREs show learners collaborating by correcting, negotiating and scaffolding to reach some kind of solution to a problem. Extract 2 above showed an LRE in the context of a form focused task. In Swain and Lapkin (2001), learners carried out either a form-focused task (dictogloss) or a meaning-focused task (jigsaw) after watching a mini-lesson on pronominal verbs. Contrary to the researchers' expectations, the learners engaged with form to the same extent in both tasks. In Extract 6 below (Swain & Lapkin, 2001: 108), the English-speaking students are engaged in the jigsaw task using the TL, French. They each have four pictures, which together make up a story. Without looking at each other's pictures, they have to agree on the story and then write it down.

Extract 6

(Class J, Pair 4)

1.	B	Yvonne va a l'ecole. (**Yvonne goes to school.**)
2.	A	Se part a l'ecole. (**Yvonne leaves [uses non-existent pronominal form] for school.**)
3.	B	Oui. Elle … se marche (**She walks [uses non-existent pronominal form]**)
4.	A	Se part, parce que … (**Leaves [uses non-existent pronominal form], because**)
5.	A	Est-ce que c'est part ou se part? (**Is it leaves or leaves [in the non-existent pronominal form]**)
6.	B	Part. (**Leaves.**)

The learners' intellectual effort (cognitive engagement) and collective problem solving (social engagement) are evident in this extract. They use non-existent pronominal forms (2–4) but in (5) A spots the problem, and B confirms (6) that '*part*' does not take a reflexive pronoun. Although the task was designed to be meaning-focused, the students did not merely *use* the TL but also engaged with its grammar. The authors suggest that the mini-lesson had the effect of priming the learners to subsequently notice the target feature.

EWL does not always manifest as LREs. A solitary individual can engage on their own, reflecting on and investigating the language by means of private speech or internal dialogue. A learner, who seems inactive, may be engaged by listening attentively to others and reflecting on what they hear. Young learners' EWL, finally, is likely to result in briefer and less explicit verbal exchanges than those of adults, making it essential to also consider their non-verbal behaviors (e.g. Kearney & Ahn, 2014).

The learning effect of LREs depends in part on the quality of the EWL. In Storch (2008), international English as a Second Language (ESL) students participated in two text re-construction tasks: one in pairs, the second individually. The pair work was recorded, the output from both tasks collected, and the second task used to establish any learning effect. Analyzing the students' task-based LREs, the author found instances of 'limited' and 'elaborate' engagement.

> LREs, where the participants deliberated over the language items, sought and provided confirmation and explanations, and alternatives, were coded as showing evidence of elaborate engagement (E). LREs, where participants simply stated the linguistic item without further deliberation, were coded as showing limited engagement (L). (Storch, 2008: 100)

Limited engagement often failed to result in learning but when it did, the person learning was usually the one suggesting the solution rather than a partner who had repeated or agreed to it. In contrast, Storch found that elaborate engagement was highly likely to lead to language development, usually for both learners in a dyad.

The Form-Focused, Meaning-Focused Dilemma

The discussion at the beginning of the chapter implied that to be effective, language learning needs to be both deliberate, *and* incidental; both conscious *and* unconscious; and to have both a form-focus *and* a focus on meaning. Hence, teachers and researchers have tried to find efficient and effective ways of facilitating explicit learning of form within a communicative classroom environment (Fotos, 1994; Long, 2015).

A presentation–practice–production (PPP) approach (Harmer, 2007) might seem able to combine an explicit grammar focus (presentation and practice) with communicative tasks at the production stage. It also has the advantage that it is easy for novice teachers to understand and use (Anderson, 2016), but in terms of EWL it fails to deliver. The presentation stage normally consists of teacher delivered explanations and examples, with little involvement by the learners. Nor does the practice stage usually require any elaborate EWL. Grafting a communicative component onto an essentially teacher centered approach is clearly not the answer.

In Long's (2015) classification, PPP is a *focus-on-forms* approach as the teaching of grammar is pre-planned by a syllabus or textbook. He argues that this is incompatible with a *focus on meaning* approach in its pure form (e.g. the Natural Approach, Krashen & Terrell, 1983) and that the ability of either to result in effective learning is unsupported by research findings. One of the problems he identifies with focus-on-forms is the assumption that learners learn what they are taught, and in the order it is taught, which has been shown to be false (e.g. Eckerth, 2008). Instead he advocates an overall focus on meaning but with teacher input on grammar as and when the need becomes apparent in learners' communicative interaction (this he calls *focus-on-form* – without a plural -s). Long's argument is that this reactive approach works in harmony with the learners' interlanguage so that they receive input from the teacher when they are ready for it and in a meaning-focused context. It is, however, unlikely to provide affordances for the elaborate conscious noticing of and reflection on language form likely to lead to learning. Neither PPP nor focus-on-form are therefore likely to contribute sufficient affordances for elaborate EWL.

CR Tasks in a Meaning-Focused Classroom

The effects of EWL on language development can be difficult to ascertain but some research has shown significant gains (e.g. Eckerth, 2008; Storch, 2002, 2008). In Eckerth (2008), German as a second language students carried out CR tasks (text reconstruction and text editing) in pairs and showed learning gains on both targeted and untargeted features. The untargeted features had been identified in the students' EWL during the CR tasks, and then tested, showing the ability of CR to generate useful EWL and for EWL to lead to language development.

Some may, however, question whether CR tasks are really tasks. To Ellis, a task is meaning-focused, and 'requires the participants to function primarily as language users' (2003: 3). Hence, form-focused CR tasks, by this metric, do not seem to be tasks. The same author, however, states later that tasks should present an information gap of some kind, to be filled by the learners using their own prior knowledge and abilities, to achieve a specific outcome (Ellis, 2009). This accurately describes collaborative CR tasks, which he concedes can 'double up' as communicative tasks if they are conducted in TL.

In contexts where the learners share an L1, CR tasks, however, tend to be completed mostly in this language. For this reason, and to add purpose to the CR task, it is important to combine it with opportunities to use the new knowledge communicatively. The first stage can be a CR task of the type shown above (Figure 3.2), on a grammar feature chosen by the teacher, followed by a 'confirmation' stage, where the teacher brings the class together and elicits answers to the CR task, checking that all have understood, explaining or answering questions if necessary. The final stage can then be a communicative task related to the CR task, e.g., in the overall topic, vocabulary and/or grammar needed to complete it. This results in a task package consisting of: CR task + Confirmation + Comm unicative task (Svalberg & Askham, 2018).

For example, a communicative task to accompany the CR task example in Figure 3.2 might have the following instructions: 'Work in pairs. One person interviews the other about themselves, and then you swap. Ask each other 3–4 questions and listen to the answers. Then each person tells someone else in the class what they learnt about their friend.' Having just worked through the taxi-driver interview extract, the students would tend to ask similar questions, thus re-using grammar and vocabulary from the CR stage.

The assumption is that a combination of affordances for both explicit and implicit learning facilitates learning, as supported both by theory (Anderson *et al.*, 2004) and empirical research (Khatib & Nikouee, 2012). The aim is (1) to offer affordances for conscious construction of declarative knowledge, through EWL (at the CR stage) *and* opportunities for meaningful interaction where the new knowledge might be used (at the communicative stage) and (2) to do it in a way that makes the form-focused and meaning-focused stages a coherent, meaningful whole. While Ellis (2009) recommends CR after a communicative task, to introduce a form-focus into task-based language teaching (TBLT), in this approach the form-focus instead precedes and is made more purposeful by the communicative task.

Should L1 Engagement with Language be Encouraged in the Communicative Classroom?

Maximizing TL use among learners who share an L1 can be challenging. Fotos (1994) carried out a study comparing CR grammar tasks, traditional teacher-fronted grammar explanation, and communicative tasks without an explicit focus on grammar. The overall aim was to find a way of 'integrating grammar instruction with the provision of opportunities for meaning focused use of the TL' (Fotos, 1994: 325). The participants were non-English major university students of English in Japan. Some of the learners' negotiations (i.e. EWL) were carried out in the L1 but only TL negotiations were considered in the analysis. The author found that grammar CR tasks engendered similar amounts of TL talk as communicative, meaning-focused tasks while also promoting learning of the targeted structures and could be recommended as a way of teaching grammar in communicative classrooms. This implies, however, that CR tasks should not be used unless the students are sufficiently proficient to do them mostly in the TL. The assumption seems to be that they would otherwise take up valuable time better used for meaning-focused tasks (e.g. Ellis, 2009; Long, 2015; Storch, 2008).

Educational psychology, however, suggests that L1 use plays an important positive role in all learning (Mercer, 2013). In the second language acquisition (SLA) field, Scott and De La Fuente (2008) investigated French and Spanish learners' L1 English use in a form-focused CR task, and the effect on EWL if L1 was prohibited. The dyadic task-interaction was video recorded and followed by stimulated recall interviews. The authors found that L1 facilitated problem solving and enhanced collaboration while the use of TL-only meant that little collaboration took place. Collaboration in the L1 tended to be coherent and balanced, whereas TL collaboration was fragmented and one-sided. L1, but not the TL, enabled the students to use metalanguage to facilitate interaction. Reading-thinking-talking were sequential in the TL, each needing separate attention, but integrated in L1. Silence, or looking away, indicated that the learners sometimes thought in their L1 first and then translated into the TL. Overall, the exclusion of L1 use created a number of obstacles to learning and very few affordances for communicative TL interaction. Scott and De La Fuente reached the conclusion that 'current pedagogy does not recognize the potential role of the L1 in the task-based FL classroom' (2008: 103).

In an interview study by Carless (2008), the author points out that using the L1 in CR tasks can facilitate the development of hypotheses and explicit grammar awareness but suggests teachers need clearer advice. 'Is it possible, for example, to distinguish between communicative tasks (when TL use is mandatory) and language analysis tasks where the use of [L1] is accepted or even encouraged?' (Carless, 2008: 36).

In summary, among the arguments for allowing the use of the L1 to talk about the TL, are that it facilitates thinking, including collective thinking (Mercer, 2013), hypothesis formation, problem solving, interaction and learning generally. Not allowing the L1 in form-focused tasks is likely to result in less and poorer quality collaboration, and thinking in L1 with subsequent translation. Crucially, it could exclude lower level learners from CR tasks.

Summary and Conclusions

This chapter has attempted to put learners' task-based EWL into context. Throughout, I have made the case that achieving the learning objective (e.g. acquisition of a particular grammar feature) requires affordances for a focus on both form and meaning. It was shown above that learners can notice form in a communicative task if they have been primed to by prior EWL. It was also argued that learners' social relationships and their perceptions of tasks as meaningful can facilitate their task interaction and engagement. EWL should thus be seen as a part of a greater whole – in the first instance the classroom environment.

Both academic and practitioner led research into EWL is needed. For example, the effects of EWL on language development are not sufficiently well understood. Also, teachers can use the criteria in Figure 3.1 to observe and understand their learners' EWL, or might wish to try out and evaluate the CR+ approach in their own classrooms using the CR task + Confirm ation + Communicative task combination suggested above.

Acknowledgments

I am grateful to my colleague Dr Jim Askham for permission to use previously unpublished data extracts from our joint research, and to the School of Arts, University of Leicester for a period of research leave which facilitated the completion of this chapter.

Notes

(1) Extracts from the data for Svalberg and Askham's study but not included in the (2014, 2016) papers.
(2) Extract from Salih, T. (1991) *Season of Migration to the North.* Oxford: Heinemann.
(3) Text adapted from The Guardian, 6 March, 2009 'You let a stranger into your life' https://www.theguardian.com/uk/2009/mar/07/cabbies-taxi-stories-work

References

Ahn, S.-Y. (2016) Exploring language awareness through students' engagement in language play. *Language Awareness* 25 (1–2), 40–54.
Ainley, J. (2000) Constructing purposeful mathematical activity in primary classrooms. In C. Tikly and A. Wolf (eds) *The Maths We Need Now* (pp. 138–153). London: Institute of Education, Bedford Way Papers.
Ainley, J., Pratt, D. and Hansen, A. (2006) Connecting engagement and focus in pedagogic task design. *British Educational Research Journal* 32 (1), 23–38.
Anderson, J. (2016) Why practice makes perfect sense: The past, present and potential future of the PPP paradigm in language teacher education. *ELTED* 19, 14–22.
Anderson, J.R., Bothell, D., Byrne, M.D., Douglass, S., Lebiere, C. and Qin, Y. (2004) An integrated theory of the mind. *Psychological Review* 111 (4), 1036–1060.
Association for Language Awareness (n.d.) See https://www.languageawareness.org/?page_id=48 (accessed 24 May 2019).
Baralt, M., Gurzynski-Weiss, L. and Kim, Y.-J. (2016) Engagement with the language. How examining learners' affective and social engagement explains successful learner-generated attention to form. In M. Sato and S. Ballinger (eds) *Peer Interaction and Second Language Learning: Pedagogical Potential and Research Agenda* (pp. 209–240). Amsterdam: John Benjamins.
Beckner, C., Blythe, R., Bybee, J., Christiansen, M.H., Croft, W., Ellis, N.C., Holland, J., Ke, J., Larsen-Freeman, D. and Schoenemann, T. (2009) Language is a complex adaptive system: Position paper. *Language Learning* 59 (1), 1–26.
Carless, D. (2008) Student use of the mother tongue in the task-based classroom. *ELT Journal* 62 (4), 331–338.

Christenson, S.L., Reschly, A.L. and Wylie, C. (eds) (2012) *Handbook of Research on Student Engagement*. New York: Springer.

Dörnyei, Z. (2009) The L2 motivational self system. In Z. Dörnyei and E. Ushioda (eds) *Motivation, Language Identity and the L2 Self* (pp. 9–42). Bristol: Multilingual Matters.

Eckerth J. (2008) Investigating consciousness-raising tasks: Pedagogically targeted and non-targeted learning gains. *International Journal of Applied Linguistics* 18 (2), 119–145.

Ellis, N. (2015) Implicit and explicit language learning: Their dynamic interface and complexity. In P. Rebuschat (ed.) *Implicit and Explicit Learning of Languages* (pp. 3–24) Amsterdam: John Benjamins.

Ellis, N.C. and Larsen-Freeman, D. (eds) (2009) *Language as a Complex Adaptive System*. Chichester: Wiley-Blackwell.

Ellis, R. (2003) *Task-based Language Learning and Teaching*. Oxford: Oxford University Press.

Ellis, R. (2009) Task-based language teaching: Sorting out the misunderstandings. *International Journal of Applied Linguistics* 19 (3), 221–246.

Ellis, R. (2010) A framework for investigating oral and written corrective feedback. *Studies in Second Language Acquisition* 32, 335–349.

Fotos, S. (1994) Integrating grammar instruction and communicative language use through grammar consciousness raising tasks. *TESOL Quarterly* 28 (2), 323–351.

Gardner, R.C. (1985) *Social Psychology and Second Language Learning: The Role of Attitudes and Motivation*. London: Edward Arnold Publishers.

Han, Y. and Hyland, F. (2015) Exploring learner engagement with written corrective feedback. *Journal of Second Language Writing* 30, 31–44.

Harmer, J. (2007) *The Practice of English Language Teaching*. Harlow: Longman.

Kearney, E. and Ahn, S.-Y. (2014) Preschool world language learners' engagement with language: What are the possibilities? *Language Awareness* 23 (4), 319–333.

Kearney, E. and Barbour, A. (2015) Embracing, contesting and negotiating new languages: Young children's early socialization into foreign language learning. *Linguistics and Education* 31, 159–173.

Khatib, M. and Nikouee, M. (2012) Planned focus on form: Automatization of procedural knowledge. *RELC Journal* 43 (2), 187–201.

Krashen, S.D. and Terrell, T.D. (1983) *The Natural Approach: Language Acquisition in the Classroom*. Oxford: Pergamon.

Larsen-Freeman, D. and Cameron, L. (2008) Research methodology on language development from a complex systems perspective. *The Modern Language Journal* 92 (2), 200–213.

Long, M. (2015) *Second Language Acquisition and Task Based Language Teaching*. Chichester: Wiley Blackwell.

MacIntyre, P.D. (2012) The idiodynamic method: A closer look at the dynamics of communication traits. *Communication Research Reports* 29 (4), 361–367.

MacIntyre P.D. and Serroul, A. (2015) Motivation on a per-second timescale: Examining approach avoidance motivation during L2 task performance. In Z. Dörnyei, P.D. MacIntyre and A. Henry (eds) *Motivational Dynamics in Language Learning* (pp. 109–138). Bristol: Multilingual Matters.

Mercer, N. (2013) The social brain, language, and goal-directed collective thinking: A social conception of cognition and its implications for understanding how we think, teach, and learn. *Educational Psychologist* 48 (3), 148–168.

Mercer, S. (2011) Understanding learner agency as a complex dynamic system. *System* 39 (4), 427–436.

Muir, C. and Dörnyei, Z. (2013) Directed motivational currents: Using vision to create effective motivational pathways. *Studies in Second Language Learning and Teaching* 3, 357–375.

Niemiec, C. and Ryan, R.M. (2009) Autonomy, competence, and relatedness in the class-
room. Applying self-determination theory to educational practice. *Theory and Research in Education* 7 (2), 133–144.

Philp, J. and Duchesne, S. (2016) Exploring engagement in tasks in the language classroom. *Annual Review of Applied Linguistics* 36, 50–72.

Platt, E. and Brooks, F.B. (2002) Task engagement: A turning point in foreign language development. *Language Learning* 52 (2), 365–400.

Schmidt, R. (1990) The role of consciousness in second language learning. *Applied Linguistics* 11 (2), 129–158.

Schmidt, R. (2001) Attention. In P. Robinson (ed.) *Cognition and Second Language Instruction* (pp. 3–32). Cambridge: Cambridge University Press.

Scott, V.M. and De La Fuente, M.J. (2008) What's the problem? L2 learners' use of the L1 during consciousness-raising, form-focused tasks. *The Modern Language Journal* 92 (1), 100–113.

Seedhaus, P. and Almutairi, S. (2009) A holistic approach to task-based interaction. *International Journal of Applied Linguistics* 19 (3), 311–338.

Skinner, E.A. and Pitzer, J.R. (2012) Developmental dynamics of engagement, coping, and everyday resilience. In S.L. Christenson, A.L. Reschly and C. Wylie (eds) *Handbook of Research on Student Engagement* (pp. 21–44). New York: Springer.

Skinner, E.A., Kindermann, T.A. and Furrer, C. (2009) A motivational perspective on engagement and disaffection: Conceptualization and assessment of children's behavioral and emotional participation in academic activities in the classroom. *Educational and Psychological Measurement* 69, 493–525.

Storch, N. (2002) Patterns of interaction in ESL pair work. *Language Learning* 52 (1), 119–158.

Storch, N. (2008) Metatalk in a pair work activity: Level of engagement and implications for language development. *Language Awareness* 17 (2), 95–114.

Svalberg, A.M.L. (2009) Engagement with language: Interrogating a construct. *Language Awareness* 18 (3–4), 242–258.

Svalberg, A.M.L. (2012) Language awareness in language learning and teaching: A research agenda. *Language Teaching* 45 (3), 376–388.

Svalberg, A.M.L. (2015) Understanding the complex processes in developing student teachers' knowledge about grammar. *The Modern Language Journal* 99 (3), 529–545.

Svalberg, A.M.L. (2017) Researching language engagement; current trends and future directions. *Language Awareness* 27 (1–2), 21–39.

Svalberg, A.M.L. and Askham, J. (2014) Student teachers' collaborative construction of Grammar Awareness: The case of a highly competent learner. *Language Awareness* 23 (1–2), 122–136.

Svalberg, A.M.L. and Askham, J. (2016) A dynamic perspective on student language teachers' different learning pathways in a collaborative context. In J. King (ed.) *The Dynamic Interplay between Context and the Language Learner* (pp. 172–193). London: Palgrave Macmillan.

Svalberg, A.M.L. and Askham, J. (2018) Adult foreign language learners' engagement with Arabic. *14th International Language Awareness Conference: Towards Language Aware Citizenship.* Vrije Universiteit, 4–7 July. Amsterdam: Association for Language Awareness.

Swain, M. (2013) The inseparability of cognition and emotion in second language learning. *Language Teaching* 46 (2), 195–207.

Swain, M. and Lapkin, S. (1995) Problems in output and the cognitive processes they generate: A step towards second language learning. *Applied Linguistics* 16 (3), 371–391.

Swain, M. and Lapkin, S. (2001) Focus on form through collaborative dialogue: Exploring task effects. In M. Bygate, P. Skehan and M. Swain (eds) *Researching Pedagogic Tasks: Second Language Learning, Teaching and Testing* (pp. 99–118). London: Longman.

Thornbury, S. (1997) Tasks that promote noticing: Reformulation and reconstruction. *ELT Journal* 51 (4), 326–335.

Appendix 3.1

TASK KEY

B	Can you tell me a little bit about yourself and your job?
A	I am near retirement now, but I first came to Britain as a child. We all studied.
B	What did you want to be?
A	I wanted to be a barrister, and for some years I was self-employed in the home improvement business, but the recessions of the 80s and 90s put a stop to that.
B	And how long have you been a taxi driver?
A	I've been driving a minicab for 10 years. I wanted to be self-employed and I like talking to people. But now the novelty has worn off and I do not like this job. You work long hours and you earn a pittance.

RULE   Tense is marked *on the first* verb in the Verb Group only.

4 Research on Learner Engagement with Written (Corrective) Feedback: Insights and Issues

Ye Han and Xuesong (Andy) Gao

Introduction

One of the most widely researched topics in second language (L2) writing research is feedback, specifically written feedback, i.e. comments on student writing in the written form. In general, language teachers provide written feedback to address various issues, including content and language use. In the last two decades, written corrective feedback (WCF), which specifically focuses on linguistic accuracy, has drawn considerable attention in research (e.g. Ferris *et al.*, 2013), due to its controversial role in the development of L2 learners' writing ability and general L2 competence (e.g. Ferris, 1999; Truscott, 1996). Most studies on WCF from the 1990s to the early 2010s investigated learning outcomes of WCF through repeated measures in controlled settings, making 'the pendulum [swing] too far towards experimental studies' (Storch, 2010: 29). Qualitative, contextualized inquiries into learner engagement with WCF, or written feedback in general, were under-represented in L2 writing research, although consistent endeavors have been made in this body of work to understand individual learners' perceptions of and revisions elicited by feedback. Empirical studies have recently begun to use a variety of frameworks, including Ellis's (2010a) componential framework, to conceptualize learner engagement with written feedback. This burgeoning research area has not only fostered interdisciplinary interactions between L2 writing, instructed second language acquisition (SLA) and educational research, but also revealed the multifaceted, contextualized, temporal and individual-based nature of learner engagement with feedback (e.g. Y. Han & F. Hyland, 2015; Zhang & K. Hyland, 2018; Zheng & Yu, 2018).

This chapter[1] presents a critical review of recent research on learner engagement with written feedback. We first sort out the lines of research that have informed research endeavors on the topic, followed by a synthesis of findings from published studies. We will then problematize the results before concluding the chapter with directions for future research.

Major Lines of Research on Learner Engagement with Written Feedback

L2 writing research on written feedback

Recent research on learner engagement with written feedback, especially WCF, has been informed by L2 writing research, SLA research and educational research. Researchers in L2 writing have a longstanding interest in student writers' responses to written feedback, and initially explored the topic quantitatively. Research following A. Cohen's (1987) pioneering use of questionnaires revealed that learners attended more to WCF by employing learning strategies such as making a mental note and reading again (Cohen, 1987; Saito, 1994) and consulting others and reference books (Cohen & Cavalcanti, 1990; Ferris, 1995). Research also found that learner attention to feedback depended on the stage of writing (e.g. Ferris, 1995) and the characteristics of feedback (e.g. Saito, 1994). Furthermore, these studies collectively reported L2 student writers' positive attitudes and beliefs about teacher feedback, particularly WCF (e.g. Cohen, 1987; Cohen & Cavalcanti, 1990; Ferris, 1995; Saito, 1994).

Along with these survey findings, in-depth, thick descriptions of individual L2 student writers explored how feedback is processed and used (Conrad & Goldstein, 1999; Goldstein, 2006; Ferris *et al.*, 2013; Hyland, 1998, 2000, 2003; Hyland & Hyland, 2001; Hyland & Hyland, 2006a). These studies offered two prominent, interlocking insights: the contextualized nature of feedback and individual variations in responding to feedback. Corresponding to Ferris (1995) and Saito (1994), case narratives revealed that L2 student writers' processing, use and perceptions of feedback are often shaped by both local and broader contexts (e.g. Goldstein, 2006; Hyland & Hyland, 2006a). Lee's (1997, 2004, 2008a, 2008b) survey studies on WCF practices in Hong Kong secondary schools also provided rich accounts of the social, cultural and political dimensions of the settings that dictate teachers' WCF strategies and shape the learners' responses to WCF.

Case narratives also found that L2 student writers exercised agency in selecting what feedback to attend to, how to process it, what sources to consult, and how to deal with problematic texts within complex contextual conditions. Their engagement with feedback is often contingent upon their L2 proficiency, prior L2 learning and L2 writing experience, beliefs, motivation, goals and other characteristics (e.g. Ferris *et al.*, 2013;

Goldstein, 2006; Hyland, 1998, 2003). In other words, these studies consistently showed that individual learners responded to feedback differently under the influences of writer-related factors and contextual factors (see the review by Bitchener, 2012a, 2012b; Bitchener & Ferris, 2012; Ellis, 2010a, 2010b; Ferris, 2010; Hyland & Hyland, 2006b). Although this body of research was far outstripped by quantitative intervention studies on the effects of WCF at the time they were published, retrospectively, the insights are far-reaching and inform ongoing research on L2 writers' engagement with feedback.

These case studies differentiate themselves from early survey studies by adopting different theoretical perspectives and methodological approaches. For instance, the studies conducted by F. Hyland (1998, 2000, 2003) drew on concepts such as goals and agency to explain how the gaps between teacher and student agenda mediate students' responses to feedback. Individual L2 student writers processed and used feedback according to their own goals, which could mismatch with the teacher's. In this case, L2 student writers tended to ignore, discard or misunderstand feedback and even misconstrue the teacher's character, resulting in mistrust and demoralization (Goldstein, 2006; Hyland, 1998, 2000).

Methodologically, these investigations have a few common features, which have been followed in recent studies on L2 student writers' engagement with feedback:

(a) using a multiple-case study approach in naturalistic settings;
(b) collecting and triangulating data from multiple sources using various instruments, including interviews, verbal reports, journals, observations, sometimes combined with surveys;
(c) employing verbal reports to investigate L2 student writers' cognitive processing of feedback; and
(d) conducting text analysis to examine revisions and conducting thematic content analysis to understand L2 student writers' processing and perceptions of feedback.

SLA research on cognitive processing of WCF

Another line of research contributing to our understanding of learner engagement with WCF is instructed SLA research (Bitchener, 2019; Bitchener & Ferris, 2012). Informed by Skill Learning Theory and interrelated theories under the umbrella term Focus on Form (Noticing Hypothesis, Output Hypothesis, Interaction Hypothesis), research has argued that WCF directs L2 learners' attention to the gaps in their interlanguage, helps them test their hypotheses about L2, and facilitates their uptake and internalization of target forms (Bitchener, 2019; Bitchener & Ferris, 2012; Bitchener & Storch, 2016; Ferris, 2010). Provided certain conditions are satisfied, WCF eventually triggers the restructuring of their

L2 knowledge system and increases their control over the accurate use of target forms.

Closely related to learner engagement are investigations of L2 learners' quality of noticing, also termed depth of processing (originally from Craik & Lockhart, 1972), in written feedback situations. Influenced by Schmidt's Noticing Hypothesis on SLA research, researchers have endeavored to examine the attentional resources allocated to written feedback. Qi and Lapkin's (2001) experimental study on two English as a second language (ESL) learners with different L2 proficiency levels employed think-aloud protocols and found two levels of processing: perfunctory noticing (noticing without providing a reason) versus substantive noticing (noticing with a reason). Sachs and Polio (2007) found that concurrent verbalization is reactive and discussed the inferential nature of coding and classifying learners' depth of processing. Multiple variables were identified to have possibly influenced verbal protocols, including the complexity of errors, one's prior knowledge and the lack of availability of awareness for verbalization. The interaction between error types and feedback types in mediating depth of processing was also reported by Kim and Bowles (2019). Their participants receiving direct WCF attended to a wider scope of errors than those receiving reformulations, but at the cost of the depth of processing. Storch and Wigglesworth (2010) studied language-related episodes (LREs) in L2 learners' pair talk as they were comparing reformulations with original drafts that were generated collaboratively. The more extensive LREs were, the greater the cognitive engagement that was said to have occurred. Storch and Wigglesworth's (2010) research was, in fact, framed within the sociocultural framework. Converging with F. Hyland's (1998) findings, they also reported the importance of learners' goals and beliefs: some participants ignored reformulations when this type of feedback deviated from their beliefs.

Research on learner strategies and self-regulated learning also explored learner engagement with written feedback, especially given that written feedback is delayed, offline and permanent, providing L2 learners with more time to process, use and study it (Williams, 2012). In fact, the outlet that published A. Cohen's (1987) pioneering study was an edited volume on L2 learning strategies, and his study was initially devised to capture L2 learners' strategies in response to teachers' written feedback. Oxford's (2011) model of self-regulation, particularly the taxonomy of meta-strategies and strategies along cognitive, social and affective dimensions, also provided a useful framework for researchers to describe and categorize metacognitive and cognitive strategies captured by self-reported data or through observation.

Moreover, inspired by the social turn of SLA research, sociocultural perspectives on L2 learning have informed the exploration of learner engagement. As an example, Aljaafreh and Lantolf (1994) reconceptualized feedback as scaffolding provided within individual learner's zone of proximal development (ZPD), and Coughlan and Duff (1994) interpreted the differences between learners' engagement with activities versus tasks under the framework of Activity Theory. In short, sociocultural perspectives have enabled researchers to consider not only the appropriateness of written feedback for individual learners, but also the emergent, changing nature of appropriateness itself. Recent research on learner engagement with written feedback has been open to more than one theoretical lens (e.g. Y. Han, 2017, 2019) and positioned more toward a broad sociocognitive perspective, as suggested by Ellis (2010b).

Educational research on learner engagement

While learner engagement seems to be a novel topic in the areas of L2 writing and SLA, the construct in the form of *student engagement* has been widely explored in educational research. In a broad sense, student engagement concerns students' identification, sense of belonging and participation in an institution or a community (Krause & Coats, 2008). A narrower definition of this construct (see also Chapter 2 by Sang & Hiver, this volume) focuses on students' engagement or actions within a specific activity, such as a writing assignment (Handley *et al.*, 2011). Fredricks *et al.*'s (2004) study pinned down three facets of engagement: the cognitive, the behavioral, and the affective. This framework has been adapted to account for activity-level engagement, i.e. learner engagement with written feedback (Zhang, 2017; Zhang & K. Hyland, 2018). According to Fredricks *et al.* (2004), cognitive engagement involves mindfulness and willingness to make mental effort (Fredricks *et al.*, 2004: 60). Mindfulness was later interpreted as involving the use of cognitive strategies (Davis *et al.*, 2010) and metacognitive strategies to regulate effort (Walker *et al.*, 2006). However, willingness as part of cognitive engagement is debatable, as willingness is more accurately part of motivation and is akin to Handley *et al.*'s (2011: 550–551) notion of 'students' readiness to engage', rather than 'active engagement' itself, i.e., students' thoughts and actions taking place as they actively participate in an activity. To enhance conceptual clarity, we suggest that Fredricks *et al.*'s (2004) original conceptualization of cognitive engagement be narrowed down to cognitive and metacognitive processes during students' active participation. Another important dimension is affective engagement, defined as students' affective reactions including interest, boredom, happiness, sadness and anxiety (Fredricks *et al.*, 2004), although educational psychology research may differentiate between affective engagement (e.g. curiosity, excitement and joy) and affective disengagement (e.g. boredom and disaffect).

In addition to the multifaceted nature of engagement, these studies, in parallel with L2 writing research, highlight contextual influences on the evolving processes of learner engagement. Handley *et al.* (2011) have stressed that learner engagement with assessment feedback is situated within both situational and temporal contexts. They further argued that learner engagement should be recognized as embedded in the micro-level of interactions between students/tutors/assignments/feedback and the macro-level contexts including 'biographical, social and course-related; institutional and disciplinary; and wider social, political and economic' settings (Handley *et al.*, 2011: 550). With regard to the temporal changes of engagement, Handley *et al.* (2011) have also contended that a student's previous experiences of engaging with feedback, their own expectations, and those of the teacher and other persons could profoundly influence their process of making sense of feedback. Similarly, Fredricks *et al.* (2004) have also pointed out the malleability of student engagement in specific contexts.

Educational literature, in comparison with L2 writing research and SLA research, has particularly illuminated the issues of students' feedback-related emotional experiences, thanks to a proliferation of educational psychology research into emotions (e.g. Pekrun *et al.*, 2002). Emotions emerging in academic contexts, especially those relate to students' achievements, have been intensively researched through surveys (e.g. Goetz *et al.*, 2006). Qualitative studies employing semi-structured interviews have also been carried out to understand and categorize particular emotional reactions to teacher feedback in higher education (e.g. Rowe *et al.*, 2014). This bulk of research has generated valuable insights into feedback-related emotions: (a) emotion can be classified as state emotions and trait emotions (Pekrun & Linnenbrink-Garcia, 2012); (b) emotion is fluid and can be regulated (Pekrun, 2006); (c) emotions are triggered by a specific object focus (Pekrun & Linnenbrink-Garcia, 2012), (d) emotion can be categorized as discrete emotions, but also categorized along dimensions such as valence and activation (Pekrun & Linnenbrink-Garcia, 2012); and (e) linear relationships between emotion, cognition and behaviors are unlikely to exist (Barrett, 2017; Pekrun *et al.*, 2002).

Recent Research on Learner Engagement with Written Feedback

The tripartite framework of learner engagement with written feedback

F. Hyland (2003) was one of the first L2 writing researchers to explore L2 learners' engagement with WCF, but the notion of learner engagement with feedback has been popularized through Ellis's (2010a) effort to theorize a componential framework of learner engagement with oral feedback and WCF. He defines language learners' feedback engagement as having cognitive, behavioral and affective dimensions. Cognitive engagement is conceived of as depth of processing (Qi & Lapkin, 2001; Sachs & Polio, 2007). Behavioral engagement mainly involves uptake (e.g. revisions in the context of writing). Affective engagement includes language learners' attitudes toward and emotions related to feedback. This tripartite framework has been adapted to explore learner engagement with WCF (Y. Han & F. Hyland, 2015), by identifying and specifying subconstructs in each dimension of engagement. Table 4.1 shows a comparison between the original framework and the revised.

The adapted framework has been used in studies on engagement with written feedback since 2015. For instance, Zhang and K. Hyland (2018) included length of time and numbers of submissions in behavioral engagement with automated writing evaluation (AWE) feedback, as the program can conveniently record the amount of time spent on revising and allows students to submit as many times as they wish. Yu *et al.* (2018) also included self-editing, i.e., revisions unsolicited by feedback, in this dimension of engagement. While Zhang (2017) positioned his case study as inspired by Fredricks *et al.*'s (2004) conceptualization of engagement rather than Ellis's (2010a) or Y. Han and F. Hyland's (2015) research, engagement was operationalized in parallel to the tripartite framework presented in Table 4.1. In other words, the framework provides a systematic and comprehensive way to understand learner engagement with teacher written feedback on both content and language, AWE feedback and peer feedback.

In addition to extending the tripartite framework, studies have also uncovered the asymmetrical relationship between the three dimensions of engagement (Y. Han & F. Hyland, 2015; Yu *et al.*, 2018; Zhang & K. Hyland, 2018). Even when individual learners exert considerable cognitive effort, make extensive revisions, employ learning strategies and regulate emotions (e.g. Ying in Y. Han & F. Hyland, 2015; Jack in Yu *et al.*, 2018), they do not necessarily engage with written feedback at the same depth across the three dimensions. Some learners may be affectively engaged with WCF (e.g. responding with strong emotions) but cognitively and behaviorally less engaged (reluctant to make revision efforts)

Table 4.1 Ellis's (2010a) framework and Y. Han and F. Hyland's (2015) framework for understanding learner engagement with WCF

	Ellis (2010a)	Y. Han and F. Hyland (2015)
Cognitive engagement	How learners attend to CF (a) noticing (b) understanding	(a) depth of processing of WCF (b) metacognitive operations (c) cognitive operations
Behavioral engagement	In what ways do learners revise their written texts	(a) revisions elicited by WCF (b) observable strategies taken to improve drafts, future writing, and overall L2 competence
Affective engagement	How learners affectively respond to CF, such as anxiety and dislike	(d) immediate emotional reactions upon the receipt of WCF and changes in these emotions over the revision process (e) attitudinal responses toward WCF

(Yu *et al.*, 2018). Others may be actively incorporating overt corrections with minimal understanding (Y. Han & F. Hyland, 2015, 2019), whereas some learners are still able and willing to undertake revisions albeit with negative emotions (Y. Han & Xu, 2019). This sharp contrast resonates with Nystrand and Gamoran's (1991) distinction between procedural engagement, characterized by compliance with classroom rules and protocols, and substantive engagement, which involves genuine commitment to academic activities.

L2 learners' affective engagement with written feedback

While recent explorations provided a comprehensive account of L2 learners' engagement with written feedback, several studies focused specifically on the most under-researched dimension of engagement with feedback (Ellis, 2010a) – affective engagement. Recent studies have paid increasing attention to L2 learners' emotions associated with written feedback. Mahfoodh (2017) challenged the simplistic presumption of the connection between written feedback, negative emotions and the lack of revisions, by showing that (a) the relationship between feedback and emotions can be non-linear, mediated by contextual factors; and (b) some negative emotions (*frustration* and *disappointment*) about revisions were more likely to lead to successful revisions rather than rejection or ineffective revisions. Inspired by research by Pekrun and his colleagues (e.g. Pekrun *et al.*, 2002; Pekrun & Linnenbrink-Garcia, 2012) on academic emotions, as well as Prior and Kasper's (2016) research on emotion using conversation analysis, Y. Han and F. Hyland (2019) explored two learners' emotional experiences related to WCF in a Chinese university. They adopted a dual approach to coding and analyzing emotions: first, like Mahfoodh (2017), discrete emotions were understood based on individual participants' descriptions of their affective experiences; second, following Pekrun and Linnebrink-Garcia's (2012) taxonomy of academic emotions, a dimensional approach of emotions was also used to understand valence (positive–negative), activation (activating–deactivating) and the object foci of emotions (epistemic emotions, achievement emotions and social emotions). To understand the activation of the learners' emotions, they coded the tone, rate and volume of speech, as well as facial expressions and body language. The study provided a microscopic view into the complexity of individual learners' emotional reactions to WCF. The findings suggest that the learners displayed mixed emotions upon receiving WCF, and their emotions often evolved throughout the revision process, from a more highly activated state to a neutral state. Also, echoing Mahfoodh's (2017) results, Y. Han and F. Hyland (2019) reported that negative emotions do not necessarily hinder engagement, as the activating–deactivating dimension of emotions should be considered along with the positive–negative dimension.

Individual variations

Most research on learner engagement with written feedback has adopted qualitative case studies as the methodological approach. The qualitative narratives, collectively, have uncovered a variety of L2 learners' experiences with written feedback, which can be grouped into five profiles shown in Table 4.2.

Factors mediating learner engagement with written feedback

Research has consistently reported a wide range of learner-related and contextual factors contributing to variations in learner engagement (Ellis, 2010a; Y. Han, 2019; Y. Han & F. Hyland, 2015; Murphy & Roca de Larios, 2010; Zhang & K. Hyland, 2018). These learner-related factors include L2 proficiency (Zheng & Yu, 2018), learner beliefs (Y. Han, 2017; Storch & Wigglesworth, 2010a), motivation, metalinguistic knowledge and prior knowledge of particular types of written feedback (Y. Han, 2019). Y. Han and Xu (2019: 3) economically integrated multiple learner factors under the umbrella term 'student feedback literacy,' defined as 'the cognitive capacity, socio-affective capacity (the ability to manage affect positively), and socio-affective disposition (motivation, beliefs, and attitudes) that prepares them for engaging with WCF'.

Contextual factors, as Goldstein (2006) suggested, encompass layers of situational contexts and can be grouped into four levels – textual level factors, interpersonal and interactional level factors, instructional level factors and sociocultural level factors – interconnected to one another (Y. Han, 2019). The impact of textual factors (e.g. types of errors, types of WCF, etc.) and interpersonal and interaction level factors (e.g. availability and quality of teacher follow-up oral feedback, and teacher–student interpersonal relationship) on L2 learners' cognitive processing and uptake of WCF has been widely investigated, whereas instructional factors and sociocultural factors have received less attention. In fact, L2 learners often voluntarily draw connections between WCF and teacher instruction. Lee (2019) also highlighted the importance of situating and integrating WCF into L2 instruction through pre-writing form-focused instruction and activities, as well as post-writing form-focused consolidations.

While these factors influence individual learners' engagement with feedback, learner factors that are socially constructed and dynamically shaped (e.g. motivation and beliefs, Y. Han, 2017), as well as local contextual factors (e.g. the ways that feedback is provided), may also be influenced in turn. This dynamic relationship between engagement and mediating factors is illustrated in Figure 4.1.

Taking a step further, Y. Han (2019) endeavored to explain how learner factors and contextual factors jointly mediate learner engagement with WCF in the light of van Lier's (2000) ecological perspective on

Table 4.2 Profiles/portraits of different types of student writers/feedback receivers

Categories	Example cases	Engagement profiles
Active learner: Deeply engaged	Jack in Yu *et al.* (2018); Ying in Y. Han and F. Hyland (2015); Rose in Zhang (2017); Du in Y. Han and F. Hyland (2019)	Beliefs: – one should shoulder one's own responsibility as a learner – positive attitudes toward feedback and its provider(s) (teachers, peers, etc.) Cognitive: – deep understanding of feedback – metacognitive strategies, self-regulating mental efforts that foster learning Behavioral: – using (multiple) external resources – making extensive revisions and unsolicited revisions Affective: – remaining calm or being able to regulate emotions and attitudes
Pessimistic ruminator: relatively engaged but emotionally annoyed	Jia in Y. Han and Xu (2019)	Beliefs: – errors can only be revised but prior products cannot be fundamentally changed – one cannot undo his or her mistakes/errors Cognitive: – deep understanding of feedback – metacognitive strategies, self-regulating mental efforts that foster learning Behavioral: – using external resources – making extensive revisions and unsolicited Affective: – immersed in guilt and disappointment
Obedient performer: Seemingly active, but superficially engaged	Isabel in Yu *et al.* (2018); Dai in Y. Han and F. Hyland (2015); Liu and Feng in Y. Han (2019); Yu in Y. Han and Xu (2019)	Beliefs: – positive attitudes toward feedback and its provider(s) – a learner should always follow the teacher and other authorities without questioning them – the teacher is the ultimate assessor/evaluator of one's learning Cognitive: – partial understanding of written feedback – using some metacognitive strategies to regulate mental effort with limited intention to pursue the issue further Behavioral: – making revisions in response to feedback but with minimal self-editing effort – playing safe and avoiding problematic texts by substitution and deletion – using external resources but mostly just seeking ready-made answers Affective: – prone to experience activated negative emotions upon the receipt of written feedback – quickly relieved if the problems are easily solved or can be avoided – feeling overwhelmed easily and hoping there would have been less feedback

| Resistor: Defending oneself from negative feedback | Alice in Yu *et al.* (2018); Song in Y. Han and F. Hyland (2015) | Beliefs:
– having doubts about the value of feedback or about the feedback from a particular group/person
– having a sense of learner autonomy
Cognitive:
– partially understanding feedback
– focusing much more on defending one's own idea/texts than on understanding what might be the problem/issue, being reluctant to consider alternative perspectives/solutions
Behavioral:
– making revisions selectively
– may rely on avoidance strategies despite disagreeing with the feedback provider
– may use other external resources to look for evidence and information to defend oneself
– doing self-editing sparingly
Affective:
– unwilling to negotiate with the feedback provider and constructing the provider as being hostile, unapproachable, or unreasonable
– feeling nervous, offended, wronged, loss of trust and even angry
– negative emotions may be alleviated as time goes by but usually do not disappear |
| Bystander: Disengaged, and indifferent | Lin in Y. Han and K. Hyland (2015); Hong in Y. Han and F. Hyland (2019) | Beliefs:
– identifying oneself as an underachiever with little aspiration and low self-efficacy beliefs
– having no genuine interest in L2 writing or learning an L2
– strategies could be used to get by in the courses without making genuine effort
Cognitive:
– little understanding of feedback or writing problems
– exerting minimal cognitive effort to make sense of feedback or figure out revisions
Behavioral:
– only responding to overt corrections
– seeking ready-made answers from external resources, and even 'outsourcing' the revision task
– ignoring and discarding content feedback or feedback with a higher demand on cognitive processing
Affective:
– completely lacking curiosity or interest and feeling indifferent or alienated
– feeling relieved or even pleased about the absence of feedback
– seeming calm but actually feeling somewhat bored and even hopeless |

language learning. Deep engagement was reconceptualized as learners' perceptions and use of learning opportunities embedded in layers of contexts in which feedback practices are situated. When the learning opportunities embedded in feedback are noticed and seen as worth taking, deep engagement will take place. For instance, Liu only concentrated on coded

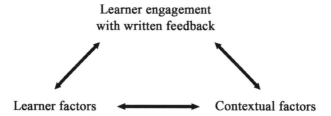

Figure 4.1 Interactions between learner engagement with written feedback, learner factors and contextual factors

WCF and ignored indirect WCF, holding the belief that that coded WCF was only provided to errors of greater severity. Her failure to appreciate the learning potential of indirect WCF limited her engagement. Another participant, Feng, chose not to follow his teacher's instruction to take notes after receiving feedback because he strongly believed in his own memory capacity. These findings suggest that deep engagement hinges on an alignment between individual factors and the contextual factors. In addition, we need to highlight that learner factors and contextual factors are non-static and subject to change, especially when temporal dimension of context is taken into consideration. Y. Han and Xu (2019), for instance, found that a student cross-referenced several pieces of WCF on the same type of error (a redundant definite article) and even identified an error token without WCF. She would have failed to do so if without being repeatedly exposed to WCF in the preceding paragraphs. This finding reveals the fluidity of context (also see King, 2016), in which students engage with feedback, even within such as short period of time.

To summarize, research efforts over the past decade have improved our understanding of learner engagement with written feedback. A number of recurring themes have emerged across studies, across contexts and across individual learners, which should be considered as fundamental to advancing our knowledge about this construct:

(a) learner engagement with written feedback incorporates multiple dimensions including (but perhaps not limited to) cognitive, behavioral and affective aspects;
(b) each dimension incorporates multiple subconstructs;
(c) these dimensions relate to one another in a non-linear, dynamic way;
(d) each dimension may change over time;
(e) learner engagement with written feedback varies across individuals;
(f) learner engagement with written feedback is mediated by both learner factors and contextual factors, and these factors themselves can also be dynamic rather than static;
(g) learner engagement with written feedback emerges once the learners are willing and able to perceive and use the learning opportunities embedded in the written feedback and related learning resources.

Problematizing Current Research on Learner Engagement with Written Feedback

Despite the valuable insights summarized above, some issues persist as barriers to our efforts to expand the knowledge about learner engagement with written feedback. We believe the prominent issues are the dominance of descriptive research, homogeneity of research methods and contexts, as well as the elusive nature of affective engagement.

Dominance of descriptive research aims

Recent studies into this matter often share similar research aims: to capture, explore and describe learner engagement with feedback. Taking an emic perspective to reflect the nuances of learners' lived experiences, these studies have generated thick, comprehensive and contextualized accounts of learner engagement and present a collection of portraits of learners.

However, little research has pursued the crux of the matter – the underlying mechanisms of engagement – and sought answers to research questions of *how* and *why*. Although various mediating factors were identified, the impact(s) of a single factor or of multiple factors as a synergy have not been investigated in greater depth. One may easily notice some high-frequency words such as *complex, dynamic, multifaceted, contextualized* and *interrelated* recurring in papers on engagement with written feedback. However, merely reporting the complexity and dynamicity of these processes will only turn these words into clichés without pushing the boundaries further. This under-representation of explanatory research aims may also weaken the connection between the current scholarship of learner engagement with written feedback and broader instructed SLA research, as the latter keenly seeks to design and devise feedback to enhance learners' meaningful engagement with the L2; and answering *how* and *why* questions is a prerequisite for achieving this goal.

Highly similar research methods, participants and contexts

Under the influence of L2 writing research on feedback (e.g. Conrad & Goldstein, 1999; Hyland, 1998; Ferris *et al.*, 2013), most of the published studies on learner engagement with written feedback are single or multiple case studies. In these studies, researchers followed one or several participants (and often their teachers too) for varied lengths of time and collected data mainly from written texts, interviews and sometimes concurrent or retrospective verbal reports. These studies relied heavily on (a) text analysis of student writing and feedback and (b) thematic content analysis of verbal reports, field notes and interview transcripts. Conversation analysis has been used but only occasionally (Y. Han &

F. Hyland, 2019), and so have reflective accounts/journals (Y. Han & F. Hyland, 2015).

While case studies have significantly enriched our knowledge about engagement, two problems have also emerged. First, case study findings have limited generalizability (Bitchener, 2012b; Cohen *et al.*, 2007). Second, given the repetitive, cliché-like findings as summarized earlier, using case studies alone may not allow us to continue expanding our understanding of engagement with feedback. Future research will need to adopt more sophisticated methods (Hiver & Al-Hoorie, 2020), such as the idiodynamic method (MacIntyre & Legatto, 2011), Q methodology, longitudinal cluster analysis and the trajectory equifinality model (Ortega & Z. Han, 2017) to explore and explain the complexity and dynamicity of learner engagement beyond a conceptual level. For instance, quantitative methods with large-size samples would be a welcome addition (Yu, Jiang & Zhou, 2020), although it is necessary to acknowledge that researchers have struggled with ways to quantify or measure engagement with feedback, except in terms of depth of processing (Qi & Lapkin, 2001) and length of time spent revising and times of submission in AWE feedback scenarios (Zhang, 2017; Zhang & K. Hyland, 2018).

The homogeneity of recent studies is also reflected in the highly similar participants and research contexts. Most of the participants are Chinese or Asian EFL university students, and most of them wrote five-paragraph essays rather than more challenging, either academic or professional, writing tasks (except Yu *et al.*, 2018). These students, in contrast to the Generation 1.5 students in Ferris *et al.* (2013), had received formal L2 instructions for years, but most of them had only achieved an intermediate proficiency level or even lower (e.g. Zheng & Yu, 2018). While motivation, beliefs, and prior knowledge can vary across individuals, they are still similar in comparison to their ESL counterparts or those who study foreign languages other than English. Also, since most case studies have taken place in east Asia, particularly in China, it is possible that some factors may be so deeply rooted in the sociocultural and sociopolitical context that they have been taken for granted or barely noted.

Elusive affective engagement with written feedback

Affective engagement with written feedback has sometimes been brought to the fore (Mahfoodh, 2017; Y. Han & F. Hyland, 2019). However, probably due to the elusive nature of emotions, it is still challenging, if not daunting, to investigate this dimension of engagement. Researchers have not reached a consensus about the indicators of emotional reactions to WCF, how to code emotions, and how to track learners' emotional experiences over time with minimal intrusion. For instance, Yu *et al.* (2018: 54) suggest that neutral emotional experiences ('no mood swings') indicate that a learner, Jack, was affectively 'disengaged', whereas research on academic emotions has revealed that disengagement would be more likely to be reflected in feeling bored and indifferent, since anxiety would in fact have ambivalent effects on learning (e.g. Pekrun *et al.*, 2002). Also, when interviews, verbal reports and reflective accounts are conducted in the participants' native language, it is difficult to faithfully translate their emotional responses into English. Another issue is that describing, coding and interpreting emotional reactions to feedback should consider sociocultural influences, which places a very high demand on the reflexivity of researchers. Additionally, little research has investigated positive emotions elicited by WCF and revision, which is arguably surprising given the fast-growing SLA research taking a positive psychology perspective (e.g. Li *et al.*, 2018; MacIntyre *et al.*, 2019).

Directions for Future Research

To extend current research on learner engagement with written feedback and particularly address the lingering issues, researchers may consider the following directions.

First, more explanatory research is needed to deepen our understanding of individual variations in engagement with written feedback. We should not be satisfied with simply describing and labeling the complexity and dynamicity of learner engagement, but delve more deeply into the issue of how and why particular learner factors and contextual factors mediate learner engagement. The interrelations between learner factors, contextual factors and learner engagement could be further explored from various theoretical perspectives as well. Explanatory research that provides insights into L2 development mechanisms triggered by written feedback or WCF would do well to generate more immediate implications for instructed SLA researchers and practitioners, and to encourage interactions between SLA and L2 writing research.

Second, more diverse research paradigms and research instruments should be used. Drawing upon the insights gained through extant case studies, researchers can explore ways to operationalize learner engagement and even measure this construct quantitatively. Mixed-method and multi-method research integrating qualitative and quantitative methodologies would be a valuable addition to this field. In terms of research design and instruments, questionnaires, intervention studies, action research, as well as other less frequently used qualitative methods including narrative inquiry, conversation analysis and multi-modal analysis, may also be adopted.

Future research should continue investigating affective engagement with written feedback, both to understand this dimension in its own right and also to investigate its relationship with the cognitive and the behavioral dimensions of engagement. Explorations of affective engagement would benefit enormously from interdisciplinary perspectives by bringing insights both from (a) educational research on emotions and (b) research on emotions involved L2 teaching and learning to bear on research on L2 writing.

Finally, research should be expanded from a narrow focus on EFL university students to include other participants in diverse linguistic, sociocultural and sociopolitical contexts, such as multilingual students in school settings, online adult education programs, graduate schools or professional training programs. Feedback delivered through computer technologies, such as AWE feedback, teacher/peer feedback provided synchronically/asynchronically, or combined with portfolio assessment, can contribute to the current understanding of engagement with written feedback.

Note

(1) This work was supported by China National Social Science Fund [grant number 19CYY052]. The second author's writing is supported by an internal project grant at the School of Education, the University of New South Wales.

References

Aljaafreh, A. and Lantolf, J.P. (1994) Negative feedback as regulation and second language learning in the zone of proximal development. *The Modern Language Journal* 78, 465–483.

Barrett, L.F. (2017) The theory of constructed emotion: an active inference account of interoception and categorization. *Social Cognitive and Affective Neuroscience* 12, 1–23.

Bitchener, J. (2019) The interaction between SLA and feedback research. In K. Hyland and F. Hyland (eds) *Feedback in Second Language Writing: Contexts and Issues* (2nd edn) (pp. 85–105). New York: Cambridge University Press.

Bitchener, J. (2012a) A reflection on 'the language learning potential' of written CF. *Journal of Second Language Writing* 21, 348–363.

Bitchener, J. (2012b) Written corrective feedback for L2 development: Current knowledge and future research. *TESOL Quarterly* 46, 855–860.

Bitchener, J. and Ferris, D. (2012) *Written Corrective Feedback in Second Language Acquisition and Writing.* New York: Routledge.

Bitchener, J. and Storch, N. (2016) *Written Corrective Feedback for L2 Development.* Bristol: Multilingual Matters.

Cohen, A.D. (1987) Student processing of feedback on their composition. In A.L. Wenden and J. Rubin (eds) *Learner Strategies in Language Learning* (pp. 57–69). Englewood Cliffs, NJ: Prentice-Hall.

Cohen, A.D. and Cavalcanti, M.C. (1990) Feedback on compositions: Teacher and student verbal reports. In B. Kroll (ed.) *Second Language Writing: Research Insights for the Classroom* (pp. 155–177). Cambridge: Cambridge University Press.

Cohen, L., Manion, L. and Morrison, K. (2007) *Research Methods in Education* (6th edn). New York: Routledge.

Conrad, S. and Goldstein, L. (1999) ESL student revision after teacher written comments: Texts, contexts and individuals. *Journal of Second Language Writing* 8, 147–180.

Coughlan, P. and Duff, P. (1994) Same task, different activities: Analysis of a SLA task from an activity theory perspective. In J. Lantolf and G. Appel (eds) *Vygotskian*

Approaches to Second Language Research (pp. 173–194). Norwood, NJ: Ablex Publishing Corporation.

Craik, F.I.M. and Lockhart, R.S. (1972) Levels of processing: A framework for memory research. *Journal of Verbal Learning and Verbal Behavior* 11, 671–684.

Davis, H.A., Chang, M-L., Andrzejewski, C.E. and Poirier, R.R. (2010) Examining behavioral, relational, and cognitive engagement in smaller learning communities: A case study of reform in one suburban district. *Journal of Educational Change* 11, 345–401.

Ellis, R. (2010a) A framework for investigating oral and written corrective feedback. *Studies in Second Language Acquisition* 32, 335–349.

Ellis, R. (2010b) Cognitive, social, and psychological dimensions of corrective feedback. In R. Batstone (ed.) *Sociocognitive Perspectives on Language Use and Language Learning* (pp. 151–165). Oxford: Oxford University Press.

Ferris, D.R. (1995) Student reactions to teacher response in multiple-draft composition classrooms. *TESOL Quarterly* 29, 33–54.

Ferris, D.R. (1999) The case for grammar correction in L2 writing classes: A response to Truscott (1996). *Journal of Second Language Writing* 8, 1–10.

Ferris, D.R. (2010) Second language writing research and written corrective feedback in SLA. *Studies in Second Language Acquisition* 32, 181–201.

Ferris, D.R., Liu, H., Sinha, A. and Senna, M. (2013) Written corrective feedback for individual L2 writers. *Journal of Second Language Writing* 22, 307–329.

Fredricks, J.A., Blumenfeld, P.C. and Paris, A.H. (2004) School engagement: Potential of the concept, state of the evidence. *Review of Educational Research* 74, 59–109.

Goetz, T., Pekrun, R., Hall, N. and Haag, L. (2006) Academic emotions from a social-cognitive perspective: Antecedents and domain specificity of students' affect in the context of Latin instruction. *British Journal of Educational Psychology* 76, 298–308.

Goldstein, L. (2006) Feedback and revision in second language writing: Contextual, teacher, and student variables. In K. Hyland and F. Hyland (eds) *Feedback in Second Language Writing: Contexts and Issues* (pp. 185–205). New York: Cambridge University Press.

Han, Y. (2017) Mediating and being mediated: Learner beliefs and learner engagement with written corrective feedback. *System* 69, 133–142.

Han, Y. (2019) Written corrective feedback from an ecological perspective: The interaction between the context and individual students. *System* 80, 288–303.

Han, Y. and Hyland, F. (2015) Exploring learner engagement with written corrective feedback in a Chinese tertiary EFL classroom. *Journal of Second Language Writing* 30, 31–44.

Han, Y. and Hyland, F. (2019) Academic emotions in written corrective feedback situations. *Journal of English for Academic Purposes* 38, 1–13.

Han, Y. and Xu, Y. (2019) Student feedback literacy and engagement with feedback: A case study of Chinese undergraduate students. *Teaching in Higher Education.* Advance online access. doi:10.1080/13562517.2019.1648410

Handley, K., Price, M. and Millar, J. (2011) Beyond 'doing time': Investigating the concept of student engagement with feedback. *Oxford Review of Education* 37, 543–560.

Hiver, P. and Al-Hoorie, A. (2020) *Research Methods for Complexity Theory in Applied Linguistics.* Bristol: Multilingual Matters.

Hyland, F. (1998) The impact of teacher written feedback on individual writers. *Journal of Second Language Writing* 7, 255–286.

Hyland, F. (2000) ESL writers and feedback: Giving more autonomy to students. *Language Teaching Research* 4, 33–54.

Hyland, F. (2003) Focus on form: Student engagement with teacher feedback. *System* 31, 217–230.

Hyland, F. and Hyland, K. (2001) Sugaring the pill: Praise and criticism in written feedback. *Journal of Second Language Writing* 10, 185–212.

Hyland, K. and Hyland, F. (2006a) Contexts and issues in feedback on L2 writing: An introduction. In K. Hyland and F. Hyland (eds) *Feedback in Second Language Writing: Contexts and Issues* (pp. 1–19). New York: Cambridge University Press.

Hyland, K. and Hyland, F. (2006b) Feedback on second language students' writing. *Language Teaching* 39, 77–95.

Kim, H.R. and Bowles, M. (2019) How deeply do second language learners process written corrective feedback? Insights gained from think-alouds. *TESOL Quarterly* 53, 913–938.

King, J. (2016) Introduction to the dynamic interplay between context and the language learner. In J. King (ed.) *The Dynamic Interplay between Context and the Language Learner* (pp. 1–10). New York: Palgrave Macmillan.

Krause, K. and Coats, H. (2008) Students' engagement in first-year university. *Assessment & Evaluation in Higher Education* 33, 493–505.

Lee, I. (1997) ESL learners' performance in error correction in writing. *System* 25, 465–477.

Lee, I. (2004) Error correction in L2 secondary writing classrooms: The case of Hong Kong. *Journal of Second Language Writing* 13, 285–312.

Lee, I. (2008a) Understanding teachers' written feedback practices in Hong Kong secondary classrooms. *Journal of Second Language Writing* 17, 69–85.

Lee, I. (2008b) Student reactions to teacher feedback in two Hong Kong secondary classrooms. *Journal of Second Language Writing* 17, 144–164.

Lee, I. (2019) Teacher written corrective feedback: Less is more. *Language Teaching* 52, 524–536.

Li, C., Jiang, G. and Dewaele, J-M. (2018) Understanding Chinese high school students' foreign language enjoyment: Validation of the Chinese version of the foreign language enjoyment scale. *System* 76, 183–196.

MacIntyre, P.D., Gregersen, T. and Mercer, S. (2019) Setting an agenda for positive psychology in SLA: Theory, practice, and research. *The Modern Language Journal* 103, 262–274.

MacIntyre, P.D. and Legatto, J.J. (2011) A dynamic system approach to willingness to communicate: Developing an idiodynamic method to capture rapidly changing affect. *Applied Linguistics* 32, 149–171.

Mahfoodh, O.H.A. (2017) 'I feel disappointed': EFL university students' emotional responses towards teacher written feedback. *Assessing Writing* 31, 53–72.

Murphy, L. and Roca de Larios, J. (2010) Feedback in second language writing: An introduction. *International Journal of English Studies* 10, i–xv.

Nystrand, M. and Gamoran, A. (1991) Instructional discourse, student engagement, and literature achievement. *Research in the Teaching of English* 25, 261–290.

Ortega, L. and Han, Z.H. (eds) (2017) *Complexity Theory and Language Development: In Celebration of Diane Larsen-Freeman*. Amsterdam/Philadelphia, PA: John Benjamins.

Oxford, R.L. (2011) *Teaching and Researching: Language Learning Strategies*. Harlow: Pearson.

Pekrun, R. (2006) The control-value theory of achievement emotions: Assumptions, corollaries, and implications. *Educational Psychology Review* 18, 31–341.

Pekrun, R., Goetz, T., Titz, W. and Perry, R.P. (2002) Academic emotions in students' self-regulated learning and achievement: A program of qualitative and quantitative research. *Educational Psychologist* 37, 91–105.

Pekrun, R. and Linnenbrink-Garcia, L. (2012) Academic emotions and student engagement. In S.L. Christenson, A.L. Reschly and C. Wylie (eds) *The Handbook of Research on Student Engagement* (pp. 259–282). New York: Springer.

Prior, M.T. and Kasper, G. (eds) (2016) *Emotion in Multilingual Interaction*. Amsterdam: Benjamins.

Qi, D.S. and Lapkin, S. (2001) Exploring the role of noticing in a three-stage second language writing task. *Journal of Second Language Writing* 10, 277–303.

Rowe, A.D., Fitness, J. and Wood, L.N. (2014) The role and functionality of emotions in feedback at university: A qualitative study. *The Australia Educational Researcher* 41, 283–309.

Sachs, R. and Polio, C. (2007) Learners' uses of two types of written feedback on a L2 writing revision task. *Studies in Second Language Acquisition* 29, 67–100.

Saito, H. (1994) Teachers' practices and students' preferences for feedback on second language writing: A case study of adult ESL learners. *TESL Canada Journal* 11, 46–70.

Storch, N. (2010) Critical feedback on written corrective feedback research. *International Journals of English Studies* 10, 29–46.

Storch, N. and Wigglesworth, G. (2010) Learners' processing, uptake, and retention of corrective feedback on writing. *Studies in Second Language Acquisition* 32, 303–334.

Truscott, J. (1996) The case against grammar correction in L2 writing classes. *Language Learning* 46, 327–369.

Van Lier, L. (2000) From input to affordance: Social-interactive learning from an ecological perspective. In J.P. Lantolf (ed.) *Sociocultural Theory and Second Language Learning: Recent Advances* (pp. 245–259). Oxford: Oxford University Press.

Walker, C.O., Greene, B.A. and Mansell, R.A. (2006) Identification with academics, intrinsic/extrinsic motivation, and self-efficacy as predictors of cognitive engagement. *Learning and Individual Differences* 16, 1–12.

Williams, J. (2012) The potential role(s) of writing in second language development. *Journal of Second Language Writing* 21, 321–331.

Yu, S., Jiang, L. and Zhou, N. (2020) Investigating what feedback practices contribute to students' writing motivation and engagement in Chinese EFL context: A large scale study. *Assessing Writing 44*. Advance online access. doi:10.1016/j.asw.2020.100451

Yu, S., Zhang, Y., Zheng, Y., Yuan, K. and Zhang, L. (2018) Understanding student engagement with peer feedback on master's theses: A Macau study. *Assessment & Evaluation in Higher Education* 44, 50–65.

Zhang, Z. (2017) Student engagement with computer-generated feedback: A case study. *ELT Journal* 71, 317–328.

Zhang, Z. and Hyland, K. (2018) Student engagement with teacher and automated feedback on L2 writing. *Assessing Writing* 36, 90–102.

Zheng, Y. and Yu, S. (2018) Student engagement with teacher written corrective feedback in EFL writing: A case study of Chinese lower-proficiency students. *Assessing Writing* 37, 13–24.

5 Measuring L2 Engagement: A Review of Issues and Applications

Shiyao (Ashlee) Zhou, Phil Hiver and
Ali H. Al-Hoorie

Introduction

Engagement is considered a 'new kid on the block' (Reschly & Christenson, 2012: 4), particularly compared with other more mature and established constructs such as motivation. Yet, despite the relatively short history of engagement research, it has received an exponential increase in popularity (Sinatra *et al.*, 2015). Many stakeholders would agree that engagement is a leading indicator of performance and ultimate attainment, and thus a key contribution classroom instruction can make to students' ultimate learning is enhancing their engagement (Mercer, 2019; Philp & Duchesne, 2016).

Engagement has achieved this popularity with researchers, policy-makers and practitioners for several reasons. First, engagement plays a critical role in educational outcomes and in learning success (Hattie, 2009). Second, the nature of engagement as a 'meta-construct' combining observable behaviors, internal cognitions, emotions and sociocultural interactions (Fredricks *et al.*, 2016) makes it appealing to many scholars. Third, practitioners seem to both recognize and readily grasp the phenomenological manifestations of engagement and disengagement, given their clear behavioral dimensions (although see Chapter 8 by Mercer *et al.*, this volume). Finally, its potential as a target for interventions remains strong. The idea that engagement may be malleable and responsive to intervention draws attention from all sides as evidence builds for promoting engagement across social and academic contexts (Appleton *et al.*, 2008).

In educational psychology, studies on engagement have centered around four broad contexts: community, school, classrooms and learning activity (Skinner & Pitzer, 2012). In the community, engagement concerns learners' degree of participation and active membership in school and other community organizations. At the school level, outcomes of engagement are routinely measured through attendance, dropout or retention rates (Finn, 1989). In foreign and second language (L2) classroom settings, relevant indicators of engagement are associated with interaction, involvement or participation in class and with outcomes related to language use and development (Philp & Duchesne, 2016). Within a learning activity, engagement refers to the quality and intensity of learners' contribution to completing a specific task during class time. Because engagement can occur in these and other settings, a point further illustrated by the various empirical chapters of this volume, definitions and operationalizations of engagement are rich and varied (Reschly & Christenson, 2012). Consensus in the academic literature is that student engagement is a multifaceted construct with multiple, at times interwoven, dimensions (see also Chapter 2 by Sang & Hiver, this volume). Empirical studies of engagement might focus on the cognitive, emotional, social or behavioral facets that lead to effective learning (Philp & Duchesne, 2016). Additionally, because of the important role engagement appears to play in the student learning process across contexts and within numerous learning subdomains, the need for reliable, valid and domain-specific measures of student engagement is imperative (Anderson, 2017).

In this chapter, our objective is to explore the past, present and future of measuring the construct of engagement. We first introduce some of the more prominent approaches to measuring student engagement from general education, including student self-report, experience sampling, teacher ratings of students, interviews and observations (Hofkens & Ruzek, 2019). We describe how each approach has been applied to measuring engagement, examine their validity and reliability and discuss the strengths and weakness of each measurement approach for L2 researchers. We also examine several widely used self-report measures in student engagement research with reference to their operational definitions, use, samples and psychometric properties. We elaborate on considerations related to the measurement of engagement in L2 learning, such as the differentiation between L2 engagement and related constructs, the variety of purposes for measuring L2 engagement, and measuring general versus domain-specific L2 engagement (e.g. task- and skill-specific engagement). Finally, we summarize the limitations of currently available instruments for eliciting engagement data and discuss directions for future development in the field.

Defining the Meta-construct of Engagement

Engagement is action ('energy in action' according to Lawson & Lawson, 2013: 435). Previous work has proposed that engagement is manifested not only in its behavioral facet (e.g. active participation), but also in demonstrations of action through the cognitive (e.g. tracking a speaker for attention) and social dimensions (e.g. back channeling in interaction), as well as in students' emotional responses to learning activities and subjective perceptions (Baralt *et al.*, 2016; Henry & Thorsen, 2018; Lambert *et al.*, 2017).

Cognitive engagement refers to mental processes such as the deliberate allocation and maintenance of attention and intellectual effort (Helme & Clarke, 2001). This cognitive dimension also implicates the active use of relevant self-regulated strategies that facilitate these mental processes (Philp & Duchesne, 2016). In L2 classroom settings, research on cognitive engagement has focused primarily on verbal manifestations, including peer interactions, asking questions, volunteering answers, exchanging ideas, offering feedback, providing direction, informing and explaining (Helme & Clarke, 2001). Non-verbal communication, private speech and exploratory talk (i.e. learner discourse that occurs as they attempt to make sense of learning) are also seen by some as further indicators of this dimension (see e.g. Mercer & Hodgkinson, 2008).

Behavioral engagement corresponds with the amount and quality of learners' in-class participation and time spent on task (Reschly & Christenson, 2012). For their part, Philp and Duchesne (2016) propose that learners' degree of effort, persistence and active involvement are leading indicators of behavioral engagement. Action is key, and the degree and quality of time students spend in active participation repeatedly appears as a positive predictor of academic achievement (Gettinger & Walter, 2012). Of course, even with this clear link between behavioral engagement and desired learning outcomes, the true potential of engagement lies in the interaction of its different facets, not on any one dimension in isolation (see also Chapter 6 by Sulis & Philp, this volume; Chapter 7 by Carver *et al.*, this volume).

Definitions of emotional engagement vary with the focus of research, from school level to specific learning activity (Skinner & Pitzer, 2012). In most instances, emotional engagement refers to the affective character of learners' involvement (see also Chapter 9 by Phung *et al.*, this volume). Enthusiasm, interest and enjoyment – essentially markers of one's affective involvement during class time – have been identified as critical indicators of emotional engagement in the classroom (Skinner *et al.*, 2009). Perhaps unsurprisingly, these emotions – both positive (e.g. enthusiasm, interest) and negative (e.g. anxiety, hopelessness) – that are elicited by the learning context, by peers and by instructional tasks and activities are assumed to play a key role in learners' effort (Pekrun & Linnenbrink-Garcia, 2012).

Although the social dimension is not included in all models of engagement, an increasing number of scholars agree that social interactions play an essential role in the types of engagement that foster student learning (Fredricks *et al.*, 2016). This aspect of engagement is defined in light of the social forms of activity and involvement that are prevalent in communities of language learning and use (see also Chapter 10 by Fukuda *et al.*, this volume), including participation and interaction with interlocutors, and the quality of such social interactions (Linnenbrink-Garcia *et al.*, 2011). The social dimension is clearly prominent both within and outside of language classrooms (Philp & Duchesne, 2016), and this dimension may be distinguished from other forms of engagement when considering that it is explicitly relational in nature and its purpose is interaction with and support of others.

One domain-specific type of engagement has been prominent in the work of Agneta Svalberg (see Chapter 3). Svalberg (2009) has described engagement with language (EWL) as the process through which *Language Awareness* is developed. In her work on the topic, she offers the following definition:

> In the context of language learning and use, Engagement with Language is a cognitive, affective, and/or social process in which the learner is the agent and language is the object (and sometimes vehicle). The learner is engaged:
>
> - Cognitively: the engaged individual is alert, pays focused attention and constructs their own knowledge.
> - Affectively: the engaged individual has a positive, purposeful, willing and autonomous disposition towards the language and/or what it represents.
> - Socially: the engaged individual is interactive and initiating. (Svalberg, 2009: 247; see also Svalberg, 2012)

Related to this, but developed in separate lines of research is the notion of engagement in task-based interaction (Dao, 2019; Lambert *et al.*, 2017). Within language learning research, the level of granularity is at times narrower even than the classroom and often focused more precisely on meaning- or language-focused classroom tasks. Task engagement, within these settings, has been described as the degree to which language learners identify with the objectives of the task, relate to its content, and make effective use of the sources available to carry out it (e.g. Bygate & Samuda, 2009). Put differently, task engagement is learners' energy in action observable during the course of exchanging ideas and information with an interlocutor or while completing a language-related task.

Given these multiple dimensions and the diverse topical areas of concern that engagement touches on (Philp & Duchesne, 2016; Svalberg, 2009), engagement can be positioned as a meta-construct that unites many separate lines of research within the field.

Researching Engagement

Let us now segue to considerations regarding how these definitions are used for engagement research. The educational research community has witnessed a burst of interest and activity around the construct of engagement over the last two decades. This points to a clear desire to probe the nature of engagement, capture the necessary conditions for engagement, explore the development of engagement over time, maintain and sustain learners' engagement as well as re-engage disaffected students. However, several unsettled issues that would facilitate this program of research have yet to be resolved. The first and foremost of these is related to the fuzziness surrounding how engagement is operationalized. Reschly and Christenson (2012) caution that engagement still suffers from a *jingle* (i.e. different terms being used to refer to identical notions or constructs) and *jangle* (i.e. the same terminology being used to describe distinct notions and constructs) in the way it is defined and operationalized. This state of affairs is no different in our field (Hiver *et al.*, in preparation). Given the variety of operational definitions used across studies it is not uncommon to discover, for instance, that one researcher's conceptualization of cognitive engagement is used as another's measurement of behavioral engagement (Christenson *et al.*, 2012). Some see engagement as an outcome that predicts learning, while others see it as a resource progressively built during the process of learning (e.g. Janosz, 2012). This state of affairs is puzzling to an observer and may be due to the broad conceptual definitions of engagement, the overlap of its dimensions and the theoretical starting point and perspectives of various scholars. The consequence of this lack of clarity is that the unique contribution of engagement to student learning and development has yet to reach its full potential (Eccles & Wang, 2012).

In addition to these operational issues, a number of methodological challenges related to eliciting, measuring and analyzing this multidimensional construct remain. As experts have argued, 'one of the challenges with research on student engagement is the large variation in the measurement of this construct, which has made it challenging to compare findings across studies' (Fredricks & McColskey, 2012: 763). To date, the most frequently used approach in evaluating engagement is indirect self-reports. However, as some reviews of designs and measurement techniques for engagement show, very few valid and psychometrically sound measures of student engagement exist with which to assess the multidimensional nature of engagement (Hofkens & Ruzek, 2019). Exacerbating matters, similarly worded items (e.g. *I work hard and contribute to class*) in some of the most widely used instruments are featured inconsistently or included throughout behavioral, emotional, cognitive and social engagement scales. To assess engagement across these dimensions as accurately as possible, it is essential to take stock of existing tools for measuring engagement and to evaluate the most commonly used data collection methods. This may be the first step to developing more systematic and better integrated quantitative and qualitative methods (Glanville & Wildhagen, 2007) that can also accommodate scholars who wish to assess longer-term engagement and variations across learning tasks and conditions, as well as engagement in both individual and group settings (see e.g. Hiver & Al-Hoorie, 2020, for an extended discussion on such designs).

Data Collection Methods in Engagement Research

Various approaches to measuring student engagement are found throughout education and the learning sciences more broadly. These include surveys and questionnaires, direct observations, expert (e.g. teacher, caretaker) ratings, interviews and experience sampling methods. Each of these approaches to measuring student engagement comes with its own strengths and limitations. In this section, we examine each approach in turn. Table 5.1 provides a helpful summary of these.

Engagement surveys and questionnaires

Self-report surveys and questionnaires are the most frequently used methods for measuring student engagement. In this type of measurement, students are presented with items describing different facets of engagement and are directed to choose the response from a range of possibilities that best describes them. Anchors might include the degree of agreement (i.e. 'strongly agree/disagree'), or the extent to which an item describes the respondent (i.e. 'very much/not at all like me) or is true of them (i.e. 'very true/untrue of me'). Surveys and questionnaires can be used to assess various domains of engagement. To date there is no single instrument that is accepted for use across contexts – just as there is none that is accepted as a field-specific measure of engagement. Yet, the state of affairs in educational psychology and the learning sciences is striking when considering that surveys and questionnaires (some administered to over 350,000 students!) continue to be used as a main source of data. Fredricks and McColskey's (2012) review provides a comprehensive introduction to such instruments.

Although there are a small number of such instruments that are content- or domain-specific, such as math engagement (Kong *et al.*, 2003), science (Sinatra *et al.*, 2015) or reading engagement (Wigfield *et al.*, 2008), the majority of these surveys assess learning engagement in a domain-general way. In second language acquisition (SLA) specifically, recently, Hiver *et al.* (2020) developed and piloted a set of survey scales to assess learners' engagement in the language classroom across the cognitive, affective, behavioral and social domains (see Appendix 5.1). More recently, this questionnaire has been used in a sequence of studies investigating the role of learners' ($N > 400$, from both China and Colombia) engagement and persistence on their task performance (i.e. their syntactic and lexical complexity, rate and amount of language production, accuracy, time on task) under various task conditions.

Table 5.1 Commonly employed approaches to eliciting engagement data

Student engagement measure	Advantages	Disadvantages	Sample studies
surveys and questionnaires	Suitable for psychometric testing and validation (e.g. item analysis, factor analysis and item response theory); Simple and straightforward administration; Measures can be standardized	Limited to self-report; Lack of real-time data collection; Participant bias and other drawbacks of self-report	Wang et al. (2016): 4-scale survey of students' math and science engagement and its psychometric properties Wang et al. (2019): domain-general survey of secondary school learners' (N = 3632) engagement and disengagement Hiver et al. (2020): 3-scale survey (adapted from Wang et al., 2016) of learners' language learning engagement. Translated into multiple languages
observations and expert ratings	Spans quantitative or qualitative techniques; Results are detailed and descriptive; Able to capture real-time data; Can link contextual factors to student engagement levels; Measures can be standardized	Results in individual or small samples at a time; Time-consuming to assess; Not easily generalizable without large-N; Lacks ability to clearly measure affective and/or cognitive aspects of engagement	Järvelä et al. (2016): Classroom observations (84 hours) of collaborative engagement and self-regulated learning in different task conditions Baralt et al. (2016): Expert ratings of L2 learners' (N = 40) engagement in face to face and online task-based interaction Lambert et al. (2017): Expert ratings of L2 students' (N = 32) cognitive, behavioral and social engagement on learner-generated vs teacher-generated tasks

(Continued)

Table 5.1 *Continued.*

Student engagement measure	Advantages	Disadvantages	Sample studies
interviews	Good for collecting cognitive processing data; Identifies contextual and background factors of student engagement; Able to collect in-depth information on student engagement	One interview at a time; Time-consuming to assess; Socially desirable responses; Interviewer training dependent; Difficult to generalize idiosyncratic findings to a population	Fredricks et al. (2016): In-depth interviews with math and science students ($N = 106$) to explore multiple dimensions of their engagement Han and Hyland (2015): Interviews (one of multiple data sources) examining L2 students' ($N = 4$) cognitive, behavioral and affective engagement with teacher written corrective feedback (WCF) Hiver et al., 2019: Longitudinal life-story interviews of whether, how and why L2 learners ($N = 8$) engaged in opportunities for language learning and use
experience sampling	Real-time engagement ratings; Tracks length and intensity of engagement; Observations recorded without interference from an observer; Multiple students' data collected simultaneously; Many data points over time able to trace changes in development	Time-consuming and resource-intensive; Quality of data depends on participation of student respondents; Struggle to include range of items that represent multidimensional nature of constructs in each sampling moment; Not suitable for younger children, student participants	Salmela-Aro et al. (2016): Signal-contingent study of situational demands and resources associations with students' ($N = 487$) emotional engagement Shernoff et al. (2016): Signal-contingent study of associations between quality of the learning environment and student ($N = 108$) engagement in six subject areas Schmidt et al. (2018): Signal-contingent study of relations between students' ($N = 244$) momentary engagement and science learning activities/choices

Source: Adapted from Anderson, 2017: 23–24

The strengths of these self-report designs for measuring engagement relate to the practicality of administering them and the modest investment of resources needed for data elicitation purposes. First, multi-item response scales present far fewer practical challenges than other methods when administering such instruments in classroom settings (Dörnyei & Taguchi, 2010). Such surveys can be administered to large and diverse samples of students simultaneously, particularly using online distribution methods, with a relatively low expenditure of time and effort. This makes it possible to collect data across various levels, at multiple time points, and compare results from different institutions with broad geographic representations. In addition, the quantitative feature of surveys and questionnaires readily lend themselves to necessary psychometric testing and validation through, for example, reliability and validity testing (Anderson, 2017).

Another reason why self-report instruments may highlight important information is that, in contrast to the purely objective data on behavioral indicators such as tardiness, instances of active participation, or percentage of assignment completion that are features of measurement at the school engagement level, self-report can be useful to elicit data from students' viewpoint and acknowledge the inherent subjectivity of engagement (Appleton *et al.*, 2006; Garcia & Pintrich, 1996). Self-report methods are especially useful for measuring emotional and cognitive engagement, which tend to be elusive and less easily observable or inferred from external behaviors.

Despite the advantages of surveys and questionnaires highlighted in the literature, there are still some concerns about this approach to measuring engagement. These include, among other things, the very nature of self-report that risks participant bias and may skew results by drawing a less accurate picture of student engagement than desired, and the lack of real-time data given that such response-scales are typically retrospective in their time reference and are situation-general rather than context/domain specific (Fredricks & McColskey, 2012).

Observations and expert ratings of engagement

Observations and teacher or caretaker ratings of engagement are useful for eliciting data at both the individual and whole classroom levels. The data elicited from such observations and expert ratings can be quantitative, qualitative or a mixture of the two. For instance, some observational measures evaluate individual students' on- and off-task behavior (e.g. attentiveness, note-taking, body-language) as an individual-level indicator of behavioral engagement (Volpe *et al.*, 2005). These data might result in dichotomous ratings (i.e. whether a learner is on task or not), percentages (i.e. time spent on-task), ordinal scales (i.e. the extent to which a learner is on task) or descriptively detailed summaries (i.e. details of how a learner exhibited on-task behavior). The point of entry for many scholars who have adopted observations and expert ratings to examine student engagement is some form of predetermined categories of behaviors that encompass either engagement or disengagement (Fredricks & McColskey, 2012). A more interpretivist tradition of engagement research drawing on observations tends to employ chiefly qualitative methods to collect descriptive and narrative data that assess student engagement (Anderson, 2017). When compared with data elicited exclusively from observations, expert rating methods are used primarily to measure behavioral and emotional engagement (Finn *et al.*, 1991; Wigfield *et al.*, 2008).

Observations and expert ratings of language learners' on-task performance or qualitative aspects of classroom discourse (e.g. language-related episodes (LREs)) have been the primary source of L2-specific measurements of engagement. This is particularly the case in research adopting Svalberg's (2009, 2012) EWL model as a framework for engagement in the classroom. For example, Baralt *et al.* (2016) draw on expert ratings of L2 learners' engagement in face-to-face and online task-based interaction in various task conditions. Lambert *et al.* (2017) also use expert ratings of L2 students' cognitive, behavioral and social engagement to examine differences in task performance on learner-generated versus teacher-generated tasks.

The principal strength of observations and expert ratings is its ability to capture contextual factors that are intertwined with indicators of student engagement (Fredricks & McColskey, 2012). For instance, it would be important to know if learner engagement wanes toward the end of a learning task, how distractions can interfere with maintaining engagement, or whether engagement peaks during certain interactional events in a classroom – observation allows the researcher to record such aspects. Observation and expert ratings can also be used to triangulate and verify data collected from self-report methods such as surveys and interviews.

Although observations and expert ratings work well when linking contextual factors or specific instructional events with student engagement levels, neither observations nor ratings can capture a complete picture of student engagement. The limitations of both methods for data elicitation is that they are subject to observer or rater biases, and are often dependent on applying clear observation schemes or rater codes – an issue particularly when such data collection is done by third-party observers or raters. In addition, participant bias may be a concern in instances when students are aware of being observed (Fredricks & McColskey, 2012). There is also the question of whether observations and ratings are capable of documenting engagement levels and behaviors for more than one specific student or classroom at a time (see also Chapter 8 by Mercer *et al.*, this volume) even with very recent advances in video recording technology. These drawbacks, while minor in nature, make this data elicitation method time-consuming and the data that results from it not easily generalizable.

Engagement interviews

Interviews are another common data collection technique used to assess student engagement. As with most interviewing techniques, interviews that examine student engagement vary, from tightly structured questions to more open-ended question types. These serve as a flexible tool with the capability to collect in-depth information regarding both emotional and cognitive engagement. In the field of language learning, such interviews have been used to examine learners' engagement with WCF (e.g. Han & Hyland, 2015). They have also been used to examine which contextual factors appear to connect to student engagement, how these factors are situated in time and place, and to elicit meaningful episodes or instances demonstrating how engagement relates to student learning experiences (Hiver *et al.*, 2019). Another strength of examining engagement through interviews, particularly stimulated recall interviews, is that this data can provide a window into learners' cognitive processing and thus shed light on the cognitive component of engagement (Reschly & Christenson, 2012).

As a way of tapping into engagement, interviews have some limitations as well. The interviewing technique of the interviewer has a major influence on the data elicited and the outcome of interviews. For example, if the interviewer appears to be an authority figure interrogating the participants, there may be a tendency for interviewees to respond in socially desirable ways when confronted with the interview questions rather than with more factual and transparent answers about their engagement. Existing concerns about the objectivity of what people say about themselves all apply to this data elicitation method. After all, how individuals portray and speak about themselves and their engagement to others is susceptible to social desirability and selective self-censoring (Al-Hoorie, 2016a, 2016b). In addition, interviews as a data collection technique seem to work best when conducted with a small population of respondents, and even so, are likely to result in large amounts of textual data that require judicious and systematic analysis in order for any meaningful conclusions about engagement to be drawn. This obviously decreases the generalizability of the results.

Real-time sampling methods for engagement

The experience sampling method (ESM) originates in studies of flow, which could itself be seen as a special, intense instance of engagement that occurs while an individual is so immersed in an activity that they lose consciousness of time and space (Hektner *et al.*, 2007). When used as a data elicitation tool, ESM treats the tangible experience of engagement as complex, emerging through interconnections between the individual and the learning environment, and as structurally dynamic, undergoing adaptive change (for a more detailed overview, see Hiver & Al-Hoorie, 2020).

The characteristic feature of using ESM to assess engagement is that individuals are prompted to respond to data elicitation stimuli at regular intervals (e.g. to indicate their affective state, expenditure of effort or level of alertness throughout a learning episode each time they are signaled to do so) (Reis & Gable, 2000). ESM data are elicited by asking individuals to provide systematic self-reports either at regular intervals (e.g. interval-contingent sampling), when they are signaled (i.e. signal-contingent sampling), or following a particular event of interest such as after every task ends (i.e. event-contingent sampling) (Goetz *et al.*, 2016). In the most commonly used technique, individuals provide a response to these stimuli whenever a signaling device prompts them to respond. In previous decades, this was done through electronic beepers or pagers; however, such signals can now be fully automated and sent to any one of the latest smart devices or wearables (see Kubiak & Krog, 2012, for one review). The signal is a cue to complete the data elicitation measures at that precise moment, and intervals can be scheduled as regularly or infrequently as desired. Some variations include every 5 or 10 minutes in an hour-long class, between every stand-alone activity in a group meeting or project, every two hours over a day-long period, or three times a day over a week.

While no L2-specific study has investigated engagement using an ESM template, owing perhaps to the time- and resource-intensive nature of this method, a new wave of studies in educational psychology use ESM as a primary method for examining the association between qualities of the learning environment and student engagement and learning behavior (e.g. Salmela-Aro *et al.*, 2016; Schmidt *et al.*, 2018; Shernoff *et al.*, 2016).

One advantage of employing ESM in studies of learner engagement is that ESM frees the researcher from the need to be directly involved or physically present during any data elicitation. It also addresses a limitation of observational methods that rely on data from single individuals or single classrooms. ESM allows the tracking of many individuals' engagement levels simultaneously, over time, and across situations (Shernoff *et al.*, 2003; Shernoff & Schmidt, 2008). Compared to other self-report methods that are retrospective, ESM taps into the ways in which individuals actually experience those activities and contexts in real time. Unlike most traditional self-report techniques, it does not rely on a single assessment moment but gathers repeated measurements across many occasions. By doing this, ESM combines the ecological validity of naturalistic behavioral observation with the nonintrusive nature of diaries and the rigor and precision of psychometric techniques (Csikszentmihalyi, 2014: 23).

Of course, ESM studies of engagement must also grapple with practical implementation issues (Goetz *et al.*, 2016). One major drawback is the question of obtrusiveness, that is whether the repeated measurement procedure has an excessively disruptive influence on learners' engagement in the moment (Shiffman *et al.*, 2008). Perhaps the biggest challenge is the heavy demand that such regular responses to the data elicitation stimuli (i.e. the questions or items) impose on respondents. This can be a factor that discourages potential participants, lowers overall completion rates and causes data quality to deteriorate as time passes.

Measuring Engagement in Language Learning

Research measuring language-specific engagement in instructional settings has existed for at least two decades (e.g. Dörnyei & Kormos, 2000; Platt & Brooks, 2002). This early work relied heavily on observation as a tool for data collection. These measures included, for instance, total counts (i.e. the quantity) of talk or interaction among language learners (Bygate & Samuda, 2009; Dörnyei & Kormos, 2000). This type of 'instance' measurement, like measures of on-task versus off-task behavior, has, of course, been limited to capturing episodes of behavioral engagement and is silent on the quality of that engagement. In more recent literature (e.g. Baralt *et al.*, 2016; Dobao, 2016; García Mayo & Azkarai, 2016; Svalberg, 2012), LREs (Kowal & Swain, 1994) have been employed as the major unit of analysis for engagement in the language class as they show the appropriateness and quality of effort in completing a classroom task. Storch (2008), for instance, proposes that the dialogue and peer correction that occur during LREs demonstrate the degree to which language learners are addressing the features of interest in the given task, and, therefore, serve as a measure of cognitive engagement in the language classroom. Others have focused more on the quality of involvement in task-related behavior (e.g. Henry & Thorsen, 2018; Lambert *et al.*, 2017). Here we examine these more closely in relation to the multiple dimensions of engagement.

The cognitive dimension

In language classrooms, both verbal interaction and nonverbal markers of interactional involvement (e.g. facial gestures) have been considered appropriate indicators of cognitive engagement. For example, Philp and Duchesne (2016) propose that private speech and exploratory talk – expressions such as 'I believe', causal sequencing phrases such as 'because', references to previous sentences through questioning or agreement, or argument that includes reasoning and exemplification – are markers of such deliberate, selective and sustained attention. In addition to such negotiating of meaning, or 'any part of the dialogue in which students talk about the language they are producing, question their language use, or other- or self-correct' (Swain, 1998: 70), others see LREs as fitting indicators of cognitive engagement (e.g. Baralt *et al.*, 2016; Svalberg, 2009).

One illustrative example of this is a study by Lambert *et al.* (2017) comparing student engagement in learner-generated content as opposed to teacher-generated content. In their study, Lambert *et al.* (2017)

operationalized learners' attention and mental effort while they repeated a sequence of tasks as being (a) *invested in task content*, measured by the number of clauses which served to expand on the semantic content of the narrative (i.e. suggestions, propositions, elaborations, reasons and opinions); and (b) *devoted to clarifying meaning* (whether receptive or productive), measured by the number of moves connected with the negotiation of meaning (i.e. corrective feedback, modified output, co-constructions, confirmation checks, clarification requests and metalinguistic exchanges). Results demonstrated that students engaged more with all aspects of L2 use during class time when involved in learner-generated activities than for teacher-generated activities.

The behavioral dimension

In language learning research, much like domain-general studies, indicators of behavioral engagement include students' active participation, persistence and expenditure of effort in the instructional setting (Philp & Duchesne, 2016). As with classroom studies outside our field, behavioral engagement is commonly measured by time on task (Gettinger & Walter, 2012) and word counts or turn-taking instances (Bygate & Samuda, 2009; Dörnyei & Kormos, 2000). Lambert *et al.* (2017) measured another dimension of engagement in their study. This was one of the more meticulous operationalizations of the behavioral dimension of language learner engagement through actual language use as measured by (a) how much semantic content learners produced while on task (i.e. the number of words produced in pruned discourse[1]); and (b) persistence or how long learners sustained the task without the need for support or direction (i.e. the amount of time invested in performance). In this regard, these scholars found that when students worked on tasks with learner-generated content (as opposed to teacher-generated tasks), their behavioral engagement increased in terms of the contributions they made to the task, the time they spent on tasks, the degree to which task content was embellished and discussed, and overall responsiveness when performing a task.

The emotional dimension

In classroom settings, emotional involvement is often manifested in learners' personal affective reactions as they participate in target language-related activities or tasks. Emotionally engaged learners are characterized as having a 'positive, purposeful, willing, and autonomous disposition' toward language and associated learning tasks (Svalberg, 2009: 247). Emotional engagement is considered to have a key impact on other dimensions of engagement because the subjective attitudes or perceptions learners carry with them in a class or through language-related tasks are fundamental to the other dimensions of engagement (Henry &

Thorsen, 2018; Swain, 2013). On close scrutiny, however, it is not clear how Svalberg's (2009) description qualifies as exclusively emotional. Additionally, when cross-referenced with definitions from mainstream education, it is apparent that very little work has been done on affective engagement in SLA. The commonly used method to measure emotional or affective engagement in L2 includes questionnaires or surveys including items pertaining to student attitudes or feelings in classroom settings or in particular tasks, and interviews with stimulated recalls. As with the other dimensions, self-report measures such as journals, interviews, questionnaires and experience sampling can be used to tap into affective engagement through attitudes and feelings toward learning contexts, individuals in that context, learning tasks, and their own participation in those settings (Baralt *et al.*, 2016; Fredricks & McColskey, 2012). One study in particular (Dao, 2019) explores quite explicitly how emotional engagement during peer interaction predicted low-proficiency learners' question development. He operationalized emotional engagement as laugh episodes and post-task questionnaire ratings and comments. Given these measures, his results showed that although there was a positive association between emotional engagement and L2 question development, emotional engagement could not significantly predict L2 question development for low-proficiency learners. Only cognitive engagement was found to significantly predict L2 question development in this study.

The social dimension

Because much of language learning and use is relational and serves important social functions, social engagement occupies a central place in language learning (Philp & Duchesne, 2008). Social engagement underlies the connections among learners in terms of the learner's affiliation with peers in the language classroom or community, and the extent of his/her willingness to take part in interactional episodes and learning activities with others. This dimension of engagement is linked also to phenomena such as reciprocity and mutuality (Storch, 2008) as manifested in learners' willingness to listen to one another or pay attention to the teacher's talk. For instance, a useful metric for social engagement may be the number of backchannels[2] produced in language learning tasks (Lambert *et al.*, 2017). Besides backchannels, turn taking with an interlocutor and developing topics in interaction, other prosocial expressions of affiliation such as empathetic discourse moves and responsive laughter are also considered to be indicators worth investigating in social engagement. With the help of data such as stimulated recalls or videos and interviews, it is possible to examine the extent to which such actions contribute to language-related task completion.

What is also clear from the above is that none of the dimensions of engagement are fully coherent when separated and should instead be considered together. In essence, examining the interacting and overlapping processes of the combined components of engagement, and their connections to learning, must be the default instead of focusing on one or two dimensions separately. One way of doing this may be to integrate quantitative analyses that can deal with high-dimensional aggregated data on engagement at a larger level of granularity or temporal window, with qualitative analyses of specific dimension of engagement at a smaller grain size.

The Future of Engagement Measures

In this final section, we turn to measurement issues that seem to hold potential in advancing the measurement of engagement and depth of insights obtained from learning activities. More specifically, we focus on *indirect measures* of engagement, but we also see value in the use of skill-specific measures and in ways that the dynamics of engagement (e.g. how it is sustained and how it deteriorates) could be made more prominent. We highlight the role technology could play, the potential contribution of implicit measures and the relevance of biological markers.

Starting with technology, there currently seems to be an exponential increase in interest in investigating the role of technology in learning in general and in L2 learning in particular (Al-Hoorie, 2017). This is understandable considering the easy access and ubiquity of technology in many language educational settings and the potential it has in facilitating learning. A substantial amount of research has looked at the value of flipped learning, an instructional design in which students study the material outside of class (a task which is made more feasible with technology) and then come to class not to learn the material but to practice it, ask question and help struggling peers.

A number of platforms can be utilized by the teacher to prepare activities and tasks for learners. Examples include Coursera, Khan Academy, EdX, Udemy and other MOOC providers. When used for research purposes, such platforms usually offer the investigator a useful function, namely, the ability to follow the progress of each individual learner. The investigator can obtain detailed engagement-related statistics such as:

- which videos or lectures are watched and for how long;
- which readings are done and for how long;
- which exercises and tasks are attempted (un)successfully;
- which parts of the material attract the more/less attention from learners;
- which tasks seem more easy/difficult with more (in)correct attempts made;
- which learners seem to be particularly struggling and thus need special attention from the teacher;

- which learners seem to be doing particularly well and thus may benefit from more advanced material.

With the use of technology, engagement researchers can easily obtain a large (perhaps overwhelming) amount of data about engagement of learners in different task- and skill-specific activities over a course. This is real-time, authentic data that can be used to test hypotheses and the effectiveness of different interventions.

Even without these platforms, there has been some interest in the use of social media (or Web 2.0) for L2 learning (see Al-Hoorie, 2017). One example is the use of private Facebook groups. Here, engagement in writing, reading, viewing and listening activities can be easily stimulated and measured through various indicators such as the number of reads, 'likes' and comments. Emotional responses are indicated by the use of emojis and emoticons. These can be content-specific or time-specific and as such reflect the situated and dynamic nature of engagement. Analysis of comments and discussions is not limited to quantitative approaches but can also be analyzed qualitatively, revealing, for example, intensity and quality of engagement.

Admittedly using social media, though convenient for any teacher with internet access, may not capture as deep insights on engagement as other specialized platforms. Teachers may only have access to relatively 'superficial' indicators of engagement such as a 'like' or number of 'reads,' let alone the multitude of potential distractions that students may encounter while trying to learn on social media. In some contexts, this may also lead to attentional concerns related to classroom management, especially with younger learners. Nevertheless, the use of social media in education is booming (Manca & Ranieri, 2017).

Another indirect approach that may be useful to measuring attitudes toward different tasks is the use of implicit measures. Implicit measures are typically computerized experiments that focus on reaction time (Al-Hoorie, 2016a, 2016b). Depending on the exact type of the implicit measure, the participant may be asked to respond to stimuli appearing on the screen as quickly as possible (e.g. to classify them to the right or left of the screen; see Al-Hoorie, 2020). Many participants realize that they have 'implicit' associations in that they cannot control how well they perform in certain tasks. Such implicit associations may reveal implicit attitudes about the certain tasks (positive or negative) that may or may not coincide with explicit, self-reported attitudes.

Neuroscientific research has shown that implicit and explicit attitudes correlate with different areas in the brain. While explicit attitudes correlate with activation in the frontal cortex – which is responsible for control and self-regulation – implicit attitudes correlate with activation in the amygdala (Cunningham *et al.*, 2003, 2004; Phelps *et al.*, 2000). Considering that the amygdala is the area in the brain responsible for emotions, Dasgupta *et al.* (2003: 241) have argued that implicit attitudes are not cold cognition but may be 'capturing something warm and affect-laden'. Indirect measures that can tap into the subconscious side of engagement have potential to open entirely novel avenues of research that would tie in with the parts of instructed language learning research where implicit processes are 'a stable topic of investigation' (Al-Hoorie, 2017: 5).

Finally, L2 researchers should engage more seriously with physiological markers of engagement. While there is some research has been done on the neuroscientific underpinnings of L2 learning, far less has been done on other biological markers. However, such investigation has the potential to reveal interesting insights into learner engagement. For example, one critical factor influencing engagement is how the task is perceived and the amount of stress and anxiety it generates (Pekrun & Linnenbrink-Garcia, 2012). Stress is associated with a host of biological reactions, activating neuroendocrine, catecholamine and opioid systems, as well as more familiar markers such as heart rate and blood pressure. Research has shown that such biological markers interact with psychological states, and the ways they are interpreted plays an important role in their influence on motivation, stress and anxiety (see Bandura, 1997).

L2 engagement researchers will certainly benefit from incorporating such measures. Researchers will obtain a more fine-tuned, micro-level view of how their participants react in different situations and how their reactions fluctuate within a single situation. Merely asking the participant to provide self-report responses at regular intervals assumes that all processes of interest are consciously reportable, while some biological measures might be too subtle or imperceptible by the individual. Furthermore, asking the participant to provide responses at regular intervals can be intrusive and may interfere with the task at hand. For this reason, some measures, such as the idiodynamic method (Hiver & Al-Hoorie, 2020; MacIntyre, 2012), have been devised to provide retrospective accounts to avoid interfering with the task. However, as long as these methods make the participant the ultimate arbiter of the inner workings of their learning, they can be richly complemented with a biological vantage point.

Conclusion

Engagement holds substantial promise as a future direction for the psychology of language learning and teaching. However, it is crucial that our field employs a selection of measures to capture the different dimensions of this complex construct. In this chapter, we set out to explore the past, present and future of measuring engagement. We reviewed operational definitions of engagement and then explained various domain-general and language-specific aspects that have been measured. We then provided an overview of instruments that have been used to measure the different aspects of engagement both in general learning sciences and in L2 learning more specifically. We highlighted a caveat to this program of measuring engagement: at times, different terms are used to refer to the same notions, while at other times the same terms are used to refer to distinct notions. We then ended the chapter by discussing some novel approaches to measuring engagement that might be useful for future research. Given the array of topical areas in language learning and teaching for which the study of engagement has untapped potential, attention to conceptual and operational clarity is crucial to ensure robust methods and designs are adopted. By investing in the development and refining of measures for engagement in the L2 classroom, researchers can rest assured that subsequent analysis and reporting will be on firm ground. This will go far in advancing an agenda of innovation and rigor in language learning research.

Notes

(1) A method used in discourse analysis that redacts disfluencies such as hesitations, fillers, false starts, etc. from a text as a way of reducing clutter and making the underlying message easier to understand.
(2) Verbal or non-verbal expressions or responses directed toward a speaker that serve a meta-conversational purpose, such as signifying the listener's attention, understanding or agreement.

References

Al-Hoorie, A.H. (2016a) Unconscious motivation. Part I: Implicit attitudes toward L2 speakers. *Studies in Second Language Learning and Teaching* 6 (3), 423–454.
Al-Hoorie, A.H. (2016b) Unconscious motivation. Part II: Implicit attitudes and L2 achievement. *Studies in Second Language Learning and Teaching* 6 (4), 619–649.
Al-Hoorie, A.H. (2017) Sixty years of language motivation research: Looking back and looking forward. *SAGE Open* 1-11. doi:10.1177/2158244017701976
Al-Hoorie, A.H. (2020) Motivation and the unconscious. In M. Lamb, K. Csizér, A. Henry and S. Ryan (eds) *Handbook of Motivation for Language Learning*. Palgrave Macmillan.
Anderson, E. (2017) Measurement of online student engagement: Utilization of continuous online student behaviors as items in a partial credit Rasch model (Unpublished doctoral dissertation). University of Denver, Denver, CO.
Appleton, J.J., Christenson, S.L. and Furlong, M.J. (2008) Student engagement with school: critical conceptual and methodological issues of the construct. *Psychology in the Schools* 45, 369–386.
Appleton, J.J., Christenson, S.L., Kim, D. and Reschly, A.L. (2006) Measuring cognitive and psychological engagement: Validation of the Student Engagement Instrument. *Journal of School Psychology* 44, 427–445.
Bandura, A. (1997) *Self-Efficacy: The Exercise of Control*. New York: Freeman.
Baralt, M., Gurzynski-Weiss, L. and Kim, Y. (2016) Engagement with language: How examining learners' affective and social engagement explains successful learner-generated attention to form. In M. Sato and S. Ballinger (eds) *Peer Interaction and Second Language Learning: Pedagogical Potential and Research Agenda* (pp. 209–240). Amsterdam: John Benjamins.

Bygate, M. and Samuda, V. (2009) Creating pressure in task pedagogy: The joint roles of field, purpose, and engagement within the interaction approaches. In A. Mackey and C. Polio (eds) *Multiple Perspectives on Interaction: Second Language Research in Honour of Susan M. Gass* (pp. 90–116). New York: Routledge.

Csikszentmihalyi, M. (ed.) (2014) *Flow and the Foundations of Positive Psychology: The collected works of Mihaly Csikszentmihalyi.* New York: Springer.

Cunningham, W.A., Johnson, M.K., Gatenby, J.C., Gore, J.C. and Banaji, M.R. (2003) Neural components of social evaluation. *Journal of Personality and Social Psychology* 85 (4), 639–349.

Cunningham, W.A., Johnson, M.K., Raye, C.L., Gatenby, J.C., Gore, J.C. and Banaji, M.R. (2004) Separable neural components in the processing of black and white faces. *Psychological Science* 15 (12), 806–813.

Dao, P. (2019) Effects of task goal orientation on learner engagement in task performance. *International Review of Applied Linguistics in Language Teaching.* Advance online access. doi:10.1515/iral-2018-0188

Dasgupta, N., Greenwald, A.G. and Banaji, M.R. (2003) The first ontological challenge to the IAT: Attitude or mere familiarity? *Psychological Inquiry* 14 (3–4), 238–243.

Dobao, A.F. (2016) Peer interaction and learning: A focus on the silent learner. In M. Sato and S. Ballinger (eds) *Peer Interaction and Second Language Learning: Pedagogical Potential and Research Agenda* (pp. 33–62). Amsterdam: John Benjamins.

Dörnyei, Z. and Kormos, J. (2000) The role of individual and social variables in oral task performance. *Language Teaching Research* 4, 275–300.

Dörnyei, Z. and Taguchi, T. (2010) *Questionnaires in Second Language Research: Construction, Administration, and Processing* (2nd edn). New York: Routledge.

Eccles, J. and Wang, M.-T. (2012) So what is student engagement anyway? In S.L. Christenson, A.L. Reschly and C. Wylie (eds) *Handbook of Research on Student Engagement* (pp. 133–148). New York: Springer.

Finn, J.D. (1989) Withdrawing from school. *Review of Educational Research* 59, 117–142.

Finn, J.D., Folger, J. and Cox, D. (1991) Measuring participation among elementary grade students. *Educational and Psychological Measurement* 51, 393–402.

Fredricks, J.A., Filsecker, M.K. and Lawson, M.A. (2016) Student engagement, context, and adjustment: Addressing definitional, measurement, and methodological issues. *Learning and Instruction* 40, 1–4.

Fredricks, J.A., Wang, M., Schall, J., Hofkens, T., Parr, A. and Snug, H. (2016) Using qualitative methods to develop a measure of math and science engagement. *Learning and Instruction* 43, 5–15.

Fredricks, J.A. and McColskey, W. (2012) The measurement of student engagement: A comparative analysis of various methods and student self-report instruments. In S.L. Christenson, A.L. Reschly and C. Wylie (eds) *Handbook of Research on Student Engagement* (pp. 763–782). New York: Springer.

García Mayo, M.P. and Azkarai, A. (2016) EFL task-based interaction: Does task modality impact on language-related episodes? In M. Sato and S. Ballinger (eds) *Peer Interaction and Second Language Learning: Pedagogical Potential and Research Agenda* (pp. 241–266). Amsterdam: John Benjamins.

Garcia, T. and Pintrich, P. (1996) Assessing students' motivation and learning strategies in the classroom context: The motivation and strategies in learning questionnaire. In M. Birenbaum and F.J. Dochy (eds) *Alternatives in Assessment of Achievements, Learning Processes, and Prior Knowledge* (pp. 319–339). New York: Kluwer.

Gettinger, M. and Walter, M.J. (2012) Classroom strategies to enhance academic engaged time. In S.L. Christenson, A.L. Reschly and C. Wylie (eds) *Handbook of Research on Student Engagement* (pp. 653–673). New York: Springer.

Glanville, J.L. and Wildhagen, T. (2007) The measurement of school engagement: Assessing dimensionality and measurement invariance across race and ethnicity. *Educational and Psychological Measurement* 67, 1019–1041.

Goetz, T., Bieg, M. and Hall, N. (2016) Assessing academic emotions via the experience sampling method. In M. Zembylas and P.A. Shutz (eds) *Methodological Advances in Research on Emotion and Education* (pp. 244–258). New York: Springer.

Han, Y. and Hyland, F. (2015) Exploring learner engagement with written corrective feedback in a Chinese tertiary EFL classroom. *Journal of Second Language Writing* 30, 31–44.

Hattie, J. (2009) *Visible Learning: A Synthesis of over 800 Meta-analyses Related to Achievement*. New York: Routledge.

Hektner, J.M., Schmidt, J.A. and Csikszentmihalyi, M. (2007) *Experience Sampling Method: Measuring the Quality of Everyday Life*. Thousand Oaks, CA: SAGE.

Helme, S. and Clarke, D. (2001) Identifying cognitive engagement in the mathematics classroom. *Mathematics Education Research Journal* 13 (2), 133–153.

Henry, A. and Thorsen, C. (2018) Disaffection and agentic engagement: 'Redesigning' activities to enable authentic self-expression. *Language Teaching Research*. Advance online access. doi:10.1177/1362168818795976

Hiver, P. and Al-Hoorie, A.H. (2020) *Research Methods for Complexity Theory in Applied Linguistics*. Bristol: Multilingual Matters.

Hiver, P., Al-Hoorie, A.H., Vitta, J. and Wu, J. (in preparation) *A Systematic Review of 20 years of L2 Engagement Research*.

Hiver, P., Obando, G., Sang, Y., Tahmouresi, S., Zhou, A. and Zhou, Y. (2019) Reframing the L2 learning experience as narrative reconstructions of classroom learning. *Studies in Second Language Learning and Teaching* 9, 85–118.

Hiver, P., Zhou, A., Tahmouresi, S., Sang, Y. and Papi, M. (2020) Why stories matter: Exploring learner engagement and metacognition through narratives of the L2 learning experience. *System* 91, 1–12.

Hofkens, T.L. and Ruzek, E. (2019) Measuring student engagement to inform effective interventions in schools. In J. Fredricks, A.L. Reschly and S.L. Christenson (eds) *Handbook of Student Engagement Interventions: Working with Disengaged Students* (pp. 309–324). San Diego, CA: Academic Press.

Janosz, M. (2012) Outcomes of engagement and engagement as an outcome: Some consensus, divergences, and unanswered questions. In S.L. Christenson, A.L. Reschly and C. Wylie (eds) *Handbook of Research on Student Engagement* (pp. 695–703). New York: Springer.

Järvelä, S., Järvenoja, H., Malmberg, J., Isohätälä, J. and Sobocinski, M. (2016) How do types of interaction and phases of self-regulated learning set a stage for collaborative engagement? *Learning and Instruction* 43, 39–51.

Kong, Q., Wong, N. and Lam, C. (2003) Student engagement in mathematics: Development of instrument and validation of a construct. *Mathematics Education Research Journal* 54, 4–21.

Kowal, M. and Swain, M. (1994) Using collaborative language production tasks to promote students' language awareness. *Language Awareness* 3 (2), 73–93.

Kubiak, T. and Krog, K. (2012) Computerized sampling of experiences and behavior. In M.R. Mehl and T.S. Conner (eds) *Handbook of Research Methods for Studying Daily Life* (pp. 124–143). New York: Guilford Press.

Lambert, C., Philp, J. and Nakamura, S. (2017) Learner-generated content and engagement in second language task performance. *Language Teaching Research* 21, 665–680.

Lawson, M.A. and Lawson, H.A. (2013) New conceptual frameworks for student engagement research, policy, and practice. *Review of Educational Research* 83, 432–479.

Linnenbrink-Garcia, L., Rogat, T. and Koskey, K. (2011) Affect and engagement during small group instruction. *Contemporary Educational Psychology* 36, 13–24.

MacIntyre, P.D. (2012) The idiodynamic method: A closer look at the dynamics of communication traits. *Communication Research Reports* 29 (4), 361–367.

Manca, S. and Ranieri, M. (2017) Implications of social network sites for teaching and learning. Where we are and where we want to go. *Education and Information Technology* 22, 605–622.

Mercer, N. and Hodgkinson, S. (eds) (2008) *Exploring Talk in School*. London: SAGE.

Mercer, S. (2019) Language learner engagement: Setting the scene. In X. Gao (ed.) *Second Handbook of English Language Teaching* (pp. 1–19). Basel: Springer.

Platt, E. and Brooks, F.B. (2002) Task engagement: A turning point in foreign language development. *Language Learning* 52, 365–400.

Pekrun, R. and Linnenbrink-Garcia, L. (2012) Academic emotions and student engagement. In S.L. Christenson, A.L. Reschly and C. Wylie (eds) *Handbook of Research on Student Engagement* (pp. 259–282). New York: Springer.

Philp, J. and Duchesne, S. (2008) When the gate opens: The interaction between social and linguistic goals in child second language development. In J. Philp, R. Oliver and A. Mackey (eds) *Child's Play? Second Language Acquisition and the Young Learner* (pp. 83–104). Amsterdam: John Benjamins.

Philp, J. and Duchesne, S. (2016) Exploring engagement in tasks in the language classroom. *Annual Review of Applied Linguistics* 36, 50–72.

Phelps, E.A., O'Connor, K.J., Cunningham, W.A., Funayama, E.S., Gatenby, J.C., Gore, J.C. and Banaji, M.R. (2000) Performance on indirect measures of race evaluation predicts amygdala activation. *Journal of Cognitive Neuroscience* 12 (5), 729–738.

Reis, H.T. and Gable, S.L. (2000) Event-sampling and other methods for studying everyday experience. In H.T. Reis and C.M. Judd (eds) *Handbook of Research Methods in Social and Personality Psychology* (pp. 190–222). New York: Cambridge University Press.

Reschly, A.L. and Christenson, S.L. (2012) Jingle, jangle, and conceptual haziness: Evolution and future directions of the engagement construct. In S.L. Christenson, A.L. Reschly and C. Wylie (eds) *Handbook of Research on Student Engagement* (pp. 3–19). New York: Springer.

Salmela-Aro, K., Moeller, J., Schneider, B., Spicer, J. and Lavonen, J. (2016) Integrating the light and dark sides of student engagement using person-oriented and situation-specific approaches. *Learning and Instruction* 43, 61–70.

Schmidt, J., Rosenberg, J. and Beymer, P. (2018) A person-in-context approach to student engagement in science: Examining learning activities and choice. *Journal of Research in Science Teaching* 55 (1), 19–43.

Shernoff, D.J., Kelly, S., Tonks, S., Anderson, B., Cavanagh, R. … and Abdi, B. (2016) Student engagement as a function of environmental complexity in high school classrooms. *Learning and Instruction* 43, 52–60.

Shernoff, D.J., Csikszentmihalyi, M., Schneider, B. and Shernoff, E.S. (2003) Student engagement in high school classrooms from the perspective of flow theory. *School Psychology Quarterly* 18, 158–176.

Shernoff, D.J. and Schmidt, J.A. (2008) Further evidence of the engagement-achievement paradox among U.S. high school students. *Journal of Youth and Adolescence* 5, 564–580.

Shiffman, S., Stone, A.A. and Hufford, M.R. (2008) Ecological momentary assessment. *Annual Review of Clinical Psychology* 4, 1–32.

Sinatra, G.M., Heddy, B.C. and Lombardi, D. (2015) The challenges of defining and measuring student engagement in science. *Educational Psychology* 50, 1–13.

Skinner, E.A. and Pitzer, J.R. (2012) Developmental dynamics of student engagement, coping, and everyday resilience. In S.L. Christenson, A.L. Reschly and C. Wylie (eds) *Handbook of Research on Student Engagement* (pp. 21–44). New York: Springer.

Skinner, E.A., Kindermann, T.A. and Furrer, C. (2009) A motivational perspective on engagement and disaffection: Conceptualization and assessment of children's behavioral and emotional participation in academic activities in the classroom. *Educational and Psychological Measurement* 69, 493–525.

Storch, N. (2008) Metatalk in a pair work activity: Level of engagement and implications for language development. *Language Awareness* 17, 95–114.

Svalberg, A.M.L. (2009) Engagement with language: Interrogating a construct. *Language Awareness* 18, 242–258.

Svalberg, A.M.L. (2012) Thinking allowed: Language awareness in language learning and teaching: A research agenda. *Language Teaching* 45, 376–388.

Swain, M. (1998) Focus on form through conscious reflection. In C. Doughty and J. Williams (eds) *Focus on Form in Classroom Second Language Acquisition* (pp. 471–484). Cambridge: Cambridge University Press.

Swain, M. (2013) The inseparability of cognition and emotion in second language learning. *Language Teaching* 46, 195–207.

Volpe, R.J., DiPerna, J.C., Hintze, J.M. and Shapiro, E.S. (2005) Observing students in classroom settings: A review of seven coding schemes. *School Psychology Review* 34, 454–474.

Wang, M.-T., Fredricks, J.A., Ye, F., Hofkens, T.L. and Linn, J.S. (2016) The math and science engagement scales: Scale development, validation, and psychometric properties. *Learning and Instruction* 43, 16–26.

Wang, M.-T., Fredricks, J.A., Ye, F., Hofkens, T.L. and Linn, J.S. (2019) Conceptualization and assessment of adolescents' engagement and disengagement in school: A multidimensional school engagement scale. *European Journal of Psychological Assessment* 35 (4), 592–606.

Wigfield, A., Guthrie, J., Perenchevich, K., Taboala, A., Klanda, S., McCrae, A. and Barbosa, P. (2008) Role of reading engagement in mediating effects of reading comprehension instruction on reading outcomes. *Psychology in the Schools* 45, 432–445.

Appendix 5.1

(In my language class today/this week…)

Behavioral engagement

I stayed focused even when it was difficult to understand.
I participated in all the activities.
I kept trying my best even when it was hard.
I continued working until I completed my work.
I just pretended like I was working. (R)
I didn't participate much in class. (R)
I did other things when I was supposed to be paying attention. (R)
I paid attention and listened carefully.

Emotional engagement

I looked forward to the next class.
I enjoyed learning new things.

I wanted to understand what I was learning.
I felt good while I was in the class.
I felt frustrated while I was in the class. (R)
I found it boring to be in the class. (R)
I didn't want to be in the class. (R)
I felt that I didn't care about learning. (R)

Cognitive engagement

I went through my work carefully to make sure it was done right.
I thought about different ways to solve problems in my work.
I tried to connect new learning to the things I already learned before.
I tried to understand my mistakes when I got something wrong.
I preferred to be told the answer than do the work. (R)
I didn't think too hard while I was doing the work. (R)
I only studied the easy parts because the class was hard. (R)
I did just enough to get by. (R)

Part 2

Empirical Chapters

6 Exploring Connections between Classroom Environment and Engagement in the Foreign Language Classroom

Giulia Sulis and Jenefer Philp

Introduction

While educational psychologists recognize the importance of the classroom environment in learning (e.g. Hattie, 2012; Shernoff, 2013; Shernoff *et al.*, 2016, 2017), it is not commonly discussed in relation to engagement in foreign language classrooms (see Oga-Baldwin, 2019; Philp & Duchesne, 2016 as exceptions). Within applied linguistics, to some degree this has been due to a lack of a clear operationalization of the constructs *classroom environment* and *engagement*. Drawing on constructs derived from work in the educational psychology and applied linguistics literature (Philp & Duchesne, 2016; Shernoff *et al.*, 2016), we explore the connections between the classroom environment and learner engagement in undergraduate foreign language classrooms at beginner and advanced levels. Regarding the learning environment, we draw on Shernoff's (2013) binary model which describes it as comprising both challenge and support, operationalized as environmental complexity (Shernoff *et al.*, 2016). Based on their research in high school classrooms, including final-year Spanish classes, we found Shernoff *et al.*'s (2016) construct relevant to identifying potential strengths and limitations of the learning environment with regard to learners' engagement in university undergraduate French and Spanish classes. Regarding engagement, we draw on Philp and Duchesne (2016) who conceptualize it as a multidimensional construct made up of behavioral, cognitive, emotional and social components. Specifically, we identify three main factors which are optimal for a successful learning environment and engagement. These comprise: teachers' provision of calibrated levels of support; challenging and interesting tasks requiring active involvement; and positive teacher and peer relations.

Engagement in the Foreign Language Classroom

Increasing attention within the field of educational psychology on learner engagement is reflected in a handbook on engagement (Christenson *et al.*, 2012) and, more recently, within applied linguistics, as a special issue on engagement in the journal *Language Teaching Research* (2017).

This body of research associates student engagement with positive academic outcomes such as higher grades in the short term, greater persistence and higher school-completion rates over the long term (Christenson *et al.*, 2012; Reschly & Christenson, 2012). There is widespread agreement in terms of the positive impact of engagement on academic development and success (Fredricks *et al.*, 2016). Researchers also agree that learner engagement is malleable and mutable, thus variable in response to the learning environment (Shernoff *et al.*, 2016; Skinner *et al.*, 2009). That is, engagement can be shaped through intervention (e.g. Martin, 2012; Menzies *et al.*, 2017). Drawing on Russell *et al.* (2005), we view motivation and engagement as distinct yet interrelated constructs, where motivation represents intent and engagement is action (see also chapters in Part 1 of this volume for more detailed exposition on this issue).

Within applied linguistics, earlier conceptualizations of the construct of engagement have simply acknowledged one or more components – behavioral engagement, operationalized in terms of quantity of talk among learners (e.g. Bygate & Samuda, 2009; Dörnyei & Kormos, 2000) and cognitive engagement, in terms of language-related episodes (LREs; e.g. Storch, 2008). However, more recent research (e.g. Baralt *et al.*, 2016; Lambert *et al.*, 2017; Philp & Duchesne, 2016; Svalberg, 2009, 2012) recognizes a more complex operationalization of this construct, as made up of multiple interrelated components (i.e. behavioral, cognitive, social and emotional).

In this study, we identify engagement as 'a state of heightened attention and involvement, in which participation is reflected not only in the cognitive dimension, but in social, behavioral, and affective dimensions as well' (Philp & Duchesne, 2016: 3). Based on this work, operationalization of the components of engagement is summarized below in Table 6.1.

Learning Environment

In order to operationalize the learning environment in language classrooms, we draw on research from educational psychology. Shernoff's work

Table 6.1 Operationalization of engagement

Dimension of engagement	Operationalization
Cognitive engagement	Concentration, task-specific reasoning, strategic thinking, self-regulation (Cleary & Zimmerman, 2012; Helme & Clarke, 2001; Pintrich & De Groot, 1990).
Behavioral engagement	Effort, participation, initiative-taking, persistence (Skinner *et al.*, 2008, 2009).
Emotional engagement	Positive and negative affective reactions toward learning activities (e.g. interest, enjoyment, enthusiasm, anxiety, boredom, frustration; Connell & Wellborn, 1991; Skinner *et al.*, 2008, 2009).
Social engagement	Interactiveness, supportiveness (Philp & Duchesne, 2016; Svalberg, 2009).

cited above describes the construct of *environmental complexity* comprising *environmental challenge* and *environmental support* (Shernoff *et al.*, 2016). *Environmental challenges* are 'reflected in the challenges, tasks, activities, goals and, expectations intended to guide student action or thinking' (Shernoff *et al.*, 2016: 52). Translated to the language classroom, tasks should push learners to move further in their ability range, both conceptually and in language development. For example, students are challenged through questions that require higher-order thinking and use of the target language to carry out specific activities. Ideally, outcomes and teacher expectations are clear and align with interest and ability level of students (Csikszentmihalyi, 1990; Hattie, 2012; Shernoff *et al.*, 2016).

Similar to Hattie's research (2012), Shernoff *et al.* (2016) identify *environmental support* as vital to meet the challenges, including providing tasks that match students' own interests and contribute to their intrinsic motivation, sense of competence and autonomy. The social dimension of engagement is fostered through development of respective and supportive relationships between teacher and students and between peers; that is, a sense of mutual regard and cooperation or a *collaborative mindset* (Sato & Ballinger, 2012, 2016). Support is also offered through tasks that require active involvement and meaningful interaction between students as well as the opportunity for learners to evaluate their own learning (Hattie, 2012; Shernoff *et al.*, 2016). Hattie's (2012) work, synthesizing 800 meta-analyses of classroom research, showed that of all factors a positive classroom environment itself was a strong determiner of successful learning. This included positive relationships between class members; teachers matching their high expectations with appropriate support to motivate and sustain students' effort to learn; and tasks aligning with students' interests, needs and proficiency.

Within applied linguistics, Dörnyei (2019) conceptualizes the *L2 Learning Experience* as the perceived quality of a learner's engagement with specific components of the learning environment, including the school, the syllabus, the tasks, peers and teachers.

Regarding the relationship between the learning environment and engagement, the empirical research to date has mainly focused on specific dimensions of behavioral or emotional engagement. Clément *et al.* (1994), for instance, found a relationship between students' evaluation of the learning environment and their L2 achievement, attitudes and effort, thus focusing on the behavioral dimension of engagement. Dewaele and MacIntyre (2014) demonstrated the key role played by the combined influence of classroom activities, teacher and classmates on enjoyment (relating to emotional engagement). Khajavy *et al.* (2018) also highlight the role of a positive learning environment, defined in terms of teachers' support, students' cohesiveness and task orientation, in fostering both enjoyment and willingness to communicate (WTC) in secondary school Iranian students. In sum, while previous studies have highlighted the crucial role of the classroom environment on different aspects of learning and on specific facets of engagement (e.g. behavioral and emotional), more empirical research is needed to determine the interconnections between the learning environment and behavioral, cognitive, emotional and social dimensions of engagement in the foreign language classroom.

There is very little research that investigates engagement in the foreign language classroom, and even less that explores the role of the learning environment in fostering or inhibiting engagement. This study seeks to research the ways in which students perceive the challenges and support they receive from teachers, peers, and tasks and how this influences engagement (emotional, cognitive, behavioral and social). Specifically, this study explores the following research question:

(1) To what extent do students' perceptions of the learning environment interconnect with their engagement in the foreign language university classroom?
   (a) How do students' perceptions of environmental challenges interconnect with engagement?
   (b) How do students' perceptions of environmental support interconnect with engagement?

Method

Participants

The research comprises a subset of data drawn from a larger dataset gathered by the first author. The data were collected from a first year French Beginner class (FR1) ($n = 14$) and a second-year French Advanced class (FR2) ($n = 16$) in a British university. Both classes were taught by the same experienced French tutor. Focal students were four beginners and nine advanced students who volunteered to participate and completed at least three of four data collection sessions. Based on the full set of all data collected, these 13 students appeared representative of the two classes as a whole, manifesting a cross-section of proficiency levels, motivation and self-confidence. That is, it was not only the most proficient, motivated or confident students who volunteered to take part, but also those who were less confident and less competent. The classes observed were compulsory modules that were part of the students' French Language degree. With one exception, all students in the second-year advanced class were majoring in French. First-year students were yet to decide on French as their major or minor at the point of data collection.

Research context

French One (FR1)

FR1 was a first-year class for students with very little or no knowledge of French. The majority of the activities carried out during the lessons were based on the coursebook and consisted of grammar, listening, reading and writing exercises. The topics in the coursebooks related to everyday situations (e.g. getting around town, going to the pharmacy). In addition to these, each class included interactive peer work in pairs or small groups often based on dialogues in the coursebook. Other times, students created dialogues, scripting it themselves. Teacher-fronted time was substantial, including grammar or lexical explanations, either in English or French.

French Two (FR2)

FR2 was an advanced class for second-year students of French. The majority of students had previously studied French at A-level (matriculation). Lessons were mainly based on debate and discussion activities relating to content from texts or videos prepared before class. Typically, debates were carried out as a whole class activity, after preparatory discussion in small groups or pairs before the actual debate. One of the investigated lessons (WK8) involved students' presentations. The teacher acted as a mediator during the debates and provided corrective feedback when needed. The topics mainly focused on the culture and society of Francophone countries. French was predominantly used in class.

Instruments and procedures

The lessons

The data are drawn from eight French lessons in total: four lessons in each of the two classes across the academic year, respectively in Week 8 (December 2017), Week 12 (January 2018), Week 16 (February 2018) and Week 20 (March 2018). The lessons were 50 to 55 minutes. To ensure consistency and validity, over the year, a variety of lessons within intact classes were selected to ensure learning environment and engagement were representative of classroom conditions.

Classroom observations and video/audio recording

In order to obtain a grounded understanding of the classroom dynamics and to examine the visible manifestations of students' engagement in the classroom context, the selected lessons were observed and video-audio recorded. Detailed handwritten observation notes were taken of the classroom activities, observable indicators of engagement and teachers' behaviors and interactions with students. The video-audio recordings captured classroom discourse and enabled triangulation alongside observation notes. This caught any details overlooked by the researchers and strengthened the validity of our findings. Students in both classes gave consent to the study being carried out in the classroom. They were given varied options: (a) full participation, (b) consent to being filmed [without participation], and (c) not being within the camera range. In keeping with the ethical requirements of the university, all students in each class and the teacher were given an information sheet. Those who wished to be participants signed a consent form for inclusion in the study.

Semi-structured interviews

Within 48 hours of an observed lesson, the participants took part in an audio-taped semi-structured interview (interviews concerning the Friday evening lessons, however, were occasionally conducted the following Monday). The interview data for this study derive from a much larger dataset for a PhD study aimed at investigating the dynamics of motivation and engagement in the classroom. Here we draw exclusively on interview data relating to engagement. Additional questions aimed to elicit learner perceptions about their cognitive, behavioral, emotional and social engagement in the classroom, both in general and at specific points during the lesson. Table 6.2 provides an overview of the sample interview questions concerning engagement.

Table 6.2 Interview questions on engagement

Dimension of engagement	Interview questions
Cognitive engagement	• Did you feel constantly focused during the lesson and during each task today? • When something in class is difficult – how do you manage it? Can you give me an example from today? • Did you have any specific objective for today's lesson/tasks?
Behavioral engagement	• How much do you feel you have to really work hard in class? Can you give me an example from today? • How much effort did you put into each task today?
Emotional engagement	• What part of the lesson/tasks did you enjoy the most today? • What part of the lesson/tasks did you enjoy the least today?
Social engagement	• How did your team work together (during group activities)? • What was the classroom atmosphere?

Analysis

Following transcription and removal of hesitations and repetitions, data analysis drew on Braun and Clarke's (2006) six-step process of thematic analysis. Both literature-based and emergent codes were developed to label data extracts systematically across the data set. All statements falling within each code were then examined multiple times. Codes were grouped together to create overarching themes. The themes identified were then reviewed, and detailed notes of the ideas expressed by each theme were taken. The findings from the interviews were then compared with those from the classroom observations and video/audio recordings with the purpose of data triangulation, and re-examined in light of our research questions and relative literature.

Findings

The process of thematic analysis revealed the emergence of three interdependent macro-themes with regards to the impact of the learning environment on engagement: the peer group, the teacher, and the tasks. These themes and related subthemes are explored in the following sections.

Peer group

Mutual aid and encouragement in the face of academic challenges

The quality of social interactions within the classroom environment was reported by the majority of students to influence their emotional, behavioral and social engagement in tasks. Supportive and cooperative peer relationships positively impacted learners' enjoyment, persistence, and interactiveness as well as proactive contributions through volunteering and asking questions. Twelve of thirteen participants mentioned mutual aid as key to tackling complex tasks. Four students highlighted peers' mutual aid and encouragement as positively contributing to intrinsic enjoyment of the task or lesson at hand. Olivia, for instance, reported that helping each other during task completion could make the French class inherently enjoyable:

> I really like coming [to the class] because I like how it's a small group so you all kind of know each other so you can just like say, if I need help, I'll say 'oh I don't understand' [...] I think it's nice to help each other when you're working together so that it's motivating to see that if you help someone then they understand it better (FR1, WK8).

Four participants underscored the crucial role played by peer encouragement on the motivation to persist with the task at hand. Hannah reports on mutual encouragement during a collaborative task:

We worked very well [...] I feel like we did work together and if one person was struggling, then we did help them as well and we tried to motivate each other as well and encourage each other to go on (FR2, WK16).

Non-judgmental and friendly peer group

About half of the participating students mentioned a connection between the sense of support provided by a friendly, non-judgmental peer group and their behavioral engagement, especially in terms of participation and initiative-taking. Alice's reflection suggests that a supportive environment promoted greater participation over the year:

When I ask a question it's just like with my friends [...] there's no threat, no like 'oh, she asked a stupid question'. It's just nice and it makes me engage more and I think you can see [...] how more confident I am, more like speaking in the class, it's just a nice environment to be in (FR1, WK20).

Alice noted a gradual familiarization over the year: 'now it's more like [...] a community [...] when you're surrounded by people like that, you feel like you can engage more and then you can learn better, it's not hostile or intimidating' (FR1, WK20).

Observation data suggest Alice's behavioral engagement underwent a substantial change over the year: while initially she neither volunteered nor dared ask questions in class, from Week 16, she progressively took initiative during whole class activities. Similarly, Amy noted herself a change in the classroom atmosphere over two years, reporting:

It is a class I enjoy coming to. Definitely more so than last year because I know everybody in it and like I said, it's a very friendly environment [...] you can kind of be friendly with everyone and not have to worry too much about getting things wrong. You can just ask questions (FR2, WK16).

Teacher

Equal opportunities for participation and understanding

All students recognized the teacher as being an important source of support and success: providing opportunities for deeper understanding, equal participation in class and for creating a pressure-free classroom atmosphere in which students could contribute and interact with each other without being afraid of making mistakes. Five students highlighted the role of the teacher in supporting both cognitive and behavioral engagement in class, ensuring all students' understanding and participation in the class activities, as evident from student interviews: '[the teacher] does a really good job of making sure that everyone's [...] participating in the lesson. I feel that does really help' (Leah, FR2, WK7). Chloe reported on the teacher's support for understanding: 'he [the teacher] will ask for every students(sic) if you understand it. If you don't understand it, we can spare some time to talk about it so in this class we have enough time to deal with different people's problems' (FR1, WK20).

The teacher's commitment to all students' understanding and participation in the class was corroborated by the observation data. In both classes, the teacher ensured that each student had spoken at least once during the lesson, and frequently encouraged participation from those showing less initiative. This suggests the importance of the teacher's ability to provide all students with both challenge and support in classroom tasks. This might include the teacher providing encouragement to take an active part in the class.

Monitoring and one-to-one help

Nine students reported that they particularly enjoyed and valued the teacher's monitoring of small group work, providing opportunities to ask questions, receive one-to-one help and immediate feedback. This support appeared crucial for those who found asking questions in front of the whole class daunting, as Lily notes: 'I think we become more engaged and motivated when the teacher like speaks to us or aids us [...] I'm scared to [...] talk in front of the class, and I like when he comes over and we just have a chat about the stuff and we can ask him questions' (Lily, F100, WK12). Similarly, Alice, one of the quietest students up until the middle of the second term, also preferred one-to-one help and feedback from the teacher, reporting: 'I enjoyed it when the teacher was walking around, so if I asked a question I could just ask it to him rather than in front of the whole class [...] that would help, [...] if we learned a new thing and then he'd walk around and see if we got it' (Alice, FR1, WK12).

Feedback on performance

Eight of the participating students reported that feedback contributed to their sense of competence and motivation, helped them track progress and determine how much effort they would invest in subsequent tasks. Emily's comment provides an example of how the teacher's feedback identifies areas for consolidation and future improvement: 'I think positive feedback [...] from teachers would help [...] because then I'd know where I'm going wrong, or what I could do to improve [...] you sort of need that constant reassurance, that would help me' (Emily, FR2, WK16). Students also saw the teacher's feedback as beneficial to move forward onto the next activities: 'I want to try and practice as much as possible, and then when I get engagement back and when I'm getting feedback and everything, that helps me move forward' (Lily FR1, WK12).

A pressure-free and pleasant classroom atmosphere

Five of the participating students commented on the emotional support and encouragement offered by the teacher. Three participants highlighted the teacher role in lowering anxiety and creating a positive classroom environment where they were comfortable to participate without feeling discouraged or intimidated. For example, Sam noted: 'he's like really nice [...] so that makes you feel more at ease, then you kind of don't dread going to it as much' (Sam, FR2, WK20). Chloe reported that she felt more inclined to participate because she knew her peers and teacher would not negatively judge her for her mistakes and offered her motivational support:

> When you answer some question and you make some mistakes, if the teacher or like the classmates, they laugh at you, it will lose your confidence so you won't raise your hand to say anything [...] all of the classmates and the teacher are really good, they are really kind, they help me a lot [...] they won't laugh at me and they will like encourage me to the final answer so I think it will motivate myself (FR1, WK16).

Three students recognized a link between the fun and light-hearted classroom atmosphere shaped by the teacher and their emotional well-being in the French class. Lily, for instance, reported that the teacher being funny contributed to her enjoyment of the class, motivation and learning:

> I always like coming to French. I guess it's because of the atmosphere the teachers provide. They make it fun, [...] I was more motivated when the... yeah, when the teacher was a bit funny and I guess the information goes in a bit easier and it's much better to understand (FR1, WK8).

Tasks

Tasks matching learner abilities and proficiency

Interview data revealed that the demands posed by the classroom learning activities had a large impact on learners' behavioral and cognitive effort, as well as their emotional engagement. Seven learners reported higher effort and focus when the task at hand was perceived as challenging their abilities. Ellie invested higher effort when the teacher asked difficult questions to the class: 'when he asks questions to you in front of everyone, that's when you have to, I have to work the most hard because... yeah, usually they're quite difficult ones [...] so it makes me work hard' (FR2, WK16).

Five students reported feeling overwhelmed by activities perceived as too demanding. This led them to abandon the task altogether, as reported by Emily:

> I think when it's difficult I end up going very shy and don't really want to talk [...] unless he specifically asks me, in which case I'll just try my best to answer, but my usual reaction as in the video is just to sort of not say anything and probably put my head down (FR2, WK16).

Two students also mentioned that tasks deemed too simple were not worth the investment of effort and focus or were simply considered as less enjoyable compared to more challenging tasks. Asked about the tasks she enjoyed the least in her French class, Lily replied: 'I think it was in pairs that we had to do [...] like describe the action of the person using the vocab we just learned. It was too simple for me, I think, so I didn't like it as much' (FR1, WK16). This suggests that a balance between the sense of challenge posed by the task and learners' ability to accomplish it was required to guarantee both behavioral and cognitive engagement in the learning activity as well as intrinsic enjoyment of the task. The need for this balance was explained by Alice: 'it's kind of hit or miss sometimes in my writing classes, whether it's like too difficult and I shut down or it's like the perfect amount of like difficult and interesting where it pushes my motivation' (FR1, WK20). Our findings appear consistent with research on flow (Csikszentmihalyi, 1990); as in flow experiences, to reach a state of intense concentration and absorption in the activity at hand, a balance between the challenge posed by the task and the learner's actual skills were required. Furthermore, this topical area highlights the role of structuring the task in alignment with a learner's zone of proximal development (ZPD), understood as the difference between what an individual can do independently and what they are able to do with mediation (Vygotsky, 1987).

Interesting and relatable task topics

Student interviews revealed that topic interest and relatedness contributed to fostering their enjoyment, active involvement and focus on the task at hand. Interest and relatedness were supported through the provision of activities or topics which triggered their curiosity or were connected to their own lives (see also Chapter 2 by Sang & Hiver, this volume). Five students reported that topic familiarity was crucial to their participation in discussion task, as it simply determined how much they could contribute to it. When learners were unfamiliar with a given topic, they would not have much to say even in their L1, as reported for instance by Rosie:

> It definitely depends on the topic, like as much as I try and talk about something in a class, if it was a discussion about football, I really wouldn't have much to say in English so it'd be hard for me to think of something to say in French (FR2, WK12).

Rosie also underscored the impact of topic familiarity on the general classroom atmosphere and her peers' lack of participation in a whole class discussion activity:

> So, I think it depends really on what we're talking about on, maybe that's why people weren't engaging because they genuinely didn't have anything to say or didn't know what to say about that topic so yeah, I think it is quite dependent on what we're talking about in the session (Rosie, F200, WK12).

In addition to topic familiarity, the provision of tasks fostering interest development or matching learners' prior interests also appeared as a crucial determinant of intrinsic motivation and subsequent engagement, as reported by almost the totality of students. Students' interest was supported through topics that were current, non-specialized and connected to learners' own lives. Two students underscored the role played by topic interest on their focus, four on their enjoyment and seven on their participation to the activity at hand. An example of the effect of topic interest on participation was provided by Leah; she mentioned:

> The topics that we do are quite interesting. They're very current [...] if we do a topic that I don't have a lot of interest, like I'm not really politically inclined so if we do a big heavy political topic, I tend to find that not as inclined to share in the lesson whereas if we're doing a topic that I'm interested in, it's like 'oh actually I know a bit about this', I will talk about this (FR2, WK7).

Tasks relevant to learning goals and needs

The support provided through tasks perceived as both important and relevant to their own learning played a vital role in shaping engagement at different levels. Eight students reported higher enjoyment when the learning activity was seen as a means to meet specific learning needs or useful for their learning in general. Hannah, for instance, recognized the importance of the French class to meet her learning goal of acquiring oral proficiency, and acknowledged a connection between her enjoyment of the class and its perceived usefulness to meet this goal:

> I do enjoy it [the French class] because it's a chance that I get to actually speak French because I'm obviously doing a French degree I need to practice it as much as possible and for speaking the only place you can really do it is within a French speaking lesson so it is the perfect opportunity to do that and I come out enjoying it because I know that I've spoken some French and it's improving slowly (FR2, WK12).

Not only did the perceived importance and relevance of the activity affect emotional engagement, but it also appeared to have an impact on behavioral and cognitive engagement. Four learners reported investing higher effort, greater active involvement and being more focused when the activity at hand was seen as useful in terms of enhancing their L2 competence and meeting their learning goals directly relevant to upcoming assessments. The latter case was described by Amy with reference to a lesson where learners could practice for the upcoming assessed debate: 'it was obviously a really important lesson to go to, [I was] just making sure that I took everything in [...] and then in the actual tasks, making sure that I was 100% sure of what you had to do' (FR2, WK16). Interestingly, in this case the perceived importance of the task had a stronger effect on Amy's effort than her enjoyment of it, as she reported: 'even if it wasn't necessarily enjoyable, I was focused because I knew it was important' (FR2, WK12).

Opportunities for active involvement and interaction

Interview data from all 13 students revealed that both their own and their peers' degree of participation and interactiveness in learning activities had a large effect on other dimensions of engagement, including effort (behavioral), attention (cognitive) and enjoyment (emotional). Nine students mentioned that activities requiring active participation and interaction contributed to keep them focused and effortfully involved in the task. Learners reported small group activities, as opposed to whole class and textbook activities, tended to promote equal participation, and were also seen as more beneficial for learning as they provided opportunities for speaking practice. Hannah exemplifies this:

> Things that make me engaged the most are doing smaller tasks [...] with two or three people maybe, because that really forces you to speak [...] you've got to do it. So, I am most engaged when I am made to do a task because I've got to use my skills, there's no option. You've got to listen to the other person and you've got to speak yourself and it's really when you improve the most as a French speaker (FR2, WK20).

Emily explained that during whole class activities learners tended to contribute less, in comparison with small group tasks. When the same students always tended to volunteer, the rest of the class appeared reticent to get involved in whole class activities, showing the impact of the general classroom dynamics on individual participation. She noted: 'everyone tends to remain quiet because you've got those couple of dominant people which can make it more difficult for the quiet people because then they're really really reluctant to speak so that's the usual feeling' (FR2, WK12).

Sam highlighted the impact of the task at hand on his cognitive engagement. He reported lower focus during whole class activities as opposed to interactive tasks, since it required less mental effort:

> When somebody else is answering a question, I don't need to be thinking, I mean, I should be listening and paying attention and stuff, but I don't need to be, which is maybe sometimes why people lose focus, because they don't have to be. But if everyone is in individual groups and having to interact and work and being observed then that makes you even more motivated (FR2, WK7).

Active involvement in the classroom activities not only contributed to shaping behavioral and cognitive engagement but also to learners' affective reactions toward the task at hand, showing the reciprocal interconnections between different facets of engagement. Four students recognized a link between the degree of involvement required by the task and their enjoyment of it. George reflected on his experience in small group work: 'I feel like I'm more involved in that whereas when it's just like asking individual people questions and they talk at everyone else, it's a little less enjoyable' (FR2, WK12). Five learners also noted a preference for interactive activities as these require spontaneous language use in authentic communicative contexts, thus providing opportunities for speaking practice, as opposed to textbook exercises. Rosie mentioned that her favorite task during the lesson was small group discussion, as she felt it encouraged her and her peers to use French in an authentic way: 'it's a bit more, like, relaxed and a bit more, like, real life, I guess, like, how you'd chat with somebody normally in French' (FR2, WK12).

Discussion

When analyzing students' perceptions of the *environmental complexity* in these two foreign language classrooms, we see a balance between *environmental challenge* and *environmental support*, in line with Shernoff and colleagues (Shernoff *et al.*, 2016, 2017). That is, tasks were seen as sufficiently challenging, and matched by a supportive learning environment. For example, where there was alignment between tasks, interest and learning objectives, learners were engaged and willing to try making use of the target language. Importantly, environmental challenges encouraged and pushed learners to move further in their ability range where it was matched by appropriate support from teachers or peers.

Four elements stand out in the data: firstly, where support matched learning needs and interests, students perceived higher-order thinking tasks as cognitively and emotionally engaging, particularly in small-group peer settings. Yet, those who found tasks too challenging or too simple reported feeling confused and/or disengaged. While this mismatch may seem intuitive for practitioners, even with the volume of work on L2 task complexity there is surprisingly little empirical evidence that substantiates this phenomenon in the context of L2 learners' task-work. These findings underline the importance of matching interest, ability, objectives and support consistently with previous literature (e.g. Clément *et al.*, 1994; Dewaele & MacIntyre, 2014; Hattie, 2012; Khajavy *et al.*, 2018; Shernoff *et al.*, 2017; Wu, 2003). Our findings also suggest the importance of providing scaffolded support to students in order for them to meet academic challenges and learn within their ZPD (Vygotsky, 1987).

What stands out is also the value of positive relationships between peers, and between teachers and students (see Philp & Mackey, 2010; Philp *et al.*, 2010; for similar findings in a tertiary French classroom). Peers' willingness to interact and cooperate cohesively in the task contributed to influence one's decision to take part in the learning activity at hand, corroborating earlier findings from Choi and Iwashita (2016). This highlights the impact of a *collaborative mindset* (Sato & Ballinger, 2012,

2016) on individual participation, as well as the mutual interdependence between social and behavioral engagement. While the classroom environment contributed to shape individual engagement, both individual and peer behavioral and social engagement contributed, in turn, to the creation of an active, supportive and cohesive learning environment, showing the reciprocal interconnections between engagement and learning environment.

Furthermore, students' perception of the peer group as being friendly and non-judgmental also contributed to shape their sense of initiative in the classroom. This underscores the role played by *psychological safety* (Edmondson, 1999), namely the 'shared belief that the team is safe for interpersonal risktaking' (1999: 354). That is, when learners felt that their peers would not react negatively to potential risk-taking behaviors, such as asking for help or admitting mistakes, they would feel more confident to take the initiative and speak up in class.

This study also suggests it is vital to recognize the part played by the teacher in providing both opportunities for challenges and the support to meet these. Learners were challenged through the provision of tasks pushing them forward in their ability range and requiring substantial behavioral and cognitive engagement. The teacher was perceived as supportive when encouraging equal participation in the learning activities, ensuring understanding, monitoring peer group and providing personalized feedback. This support was reported by learners as key to their participation and enjoyment of the class. The teacher was also seen to play a particularly vital role in fostering supportive relationships within the class, especially through the provision of tasks requiring interaction and collaboration. This is consistent with earlier work on *classroom climate* (Ryan & Patrick, 2001; Patrick & Ryan, 2005; Joe *et al.*, 2017), especially in terms of the role played by students' perceptions of the teacher as invested in their learning, offering both emotional and academic support, in conjunction with encouragement and mutual respect from peers.

One further element standing out from the data was the dynamic and mutual interconnection between different dimensions of engagement, consistent with Philp and Duchesne (2016). Tasks requiring behavioral, cognitive and social engagement appeared to trigger more positive emotional responses from students, especially in terms of enjoyment. In turn, a learner's interest in a topic was reported as influencing concentration and effort expenditure throughout the activity at hand. The degree of peers' social engagement in the task, manifested through interactiveness, supportiveness and willingness to cooperate, was reported as key to individual participation and initiative-taking. Furthermore, when the task required constant interaction in a small-group setting, it was seen by learners as fostering higher and more sustained task participation and cognitive effort in comparison with teacher-led or whole-class activities.

Summary of Findings and Conclusions

The aim of this study was to investigate the interconnections between the learning environment and engagement in two foreign language classrooms. The data collected through classroom observations and student interviews over the course of two academic terms revealed the complex and interdependent nature of the learning environment and engagement in the language classroom. Both environmental challenge and support made available by the combined influence of peers, teacher and tasks played a key role in shaping learners' engagement at different levels. This suggests *environmental complexity* (Shernoff *et al.*, 2016) can be a fruitful approach to better understanding this multifaceted construct. Students' and teacher's own engagement and interactions, in turn, contributed to shape the learning environment, highlighting the mutual influence between the environment and engagement.

With regards to the impact of environmental challenges on engagement in the foreign language classroom, we found that the opportunities learners were offered to develop their reasoning and communicative skills, relevant to their learning goals and needs, and matching their abilities and proficiency were reported as influencing not only the cognitive and behavioral effort invested in the task at hand and class participation but also the task enjoyment and degree of interactiveness.

As for the interconnections between environmental support and engagement, the development of a supportive, lively and low anxiety classroom atmosphere as shaped by both the teacher and the students seemed to influence their behavioral, social, emotional and cognitive engagement in the classroom, specifically in terms of initiative-taking, cognitive and behavioral effort, participation, enjoyment, and both initiation and maintenance of interaction. At a group level, the support, encouragement and mutual aid offered by peers during challenging tasks fostered persistence, enjoyment and interactiveness. In turn, the degree of peer engagement and perceived enthusiasm in a given task could contribute to changes in individual participation and initiative-taking. The teacher's support also played a key role in promoting initiative-taking and class participation, through the provision of equal opportunities for active involvement in the lesson and one-to-one help during group tasks. Furthermore, through the feedback provided by the teacher during the lesson or via assessments, learners could evaluate their competence and regulate the effort to be exerted in the following classroom activities. Finally, interactive tasks requiring constant involvement and authentic L2 communication, matching students' own interests and fostering their autonomy positively contributed to the degree of effort invested in them, participation, focus, enjoyment as well as mutual aid and support.

Limitations and Implications for L2 Teaching Practice

This study has a series of limitations. The first limitation relates to the small sample size of our study, both in terms of the students and the teacher. Both participating classes were also instructed by the same teacher. Future research could compare classes taught by different teachers to provide further insights into the role of the teacher in shaping the learning environment and engagement. Another limitation relates to the small number of lessons observed: investigating a wider variety of instructional episodes could have offered a more in-depth view of the role of tasks in fostering or hindering engagement in the classroom.

Notwithstanding its limitations, the results of our study offer several implications for L2 teaching practice. Engagement can be fostered through the provision of tasks slightly above learners' own capabilities, thus guiding them to move higher in their ability range. Furthermore, engagement can be encouraged through the provision of clearly set tasks requiring high involvement and interaction in the L2, which are relevant to students' own needs and goals, and which allow learners to produce their own input and to work independently. In order to guarantee both learners' participation and emotional well-being in the classroom, the quality of the teacher's presence is vital in the classroom – giving feedback, monitoring students' understanding, ensuring equal involvement in the classroom activities and creating a positive, safe and supportive classroom atmosphere where learners feel free to take the initiative and interact without being afraid of making mistakes.

References

Baralt, M., Gurzynski-Weiss, L. and Kim, Y. (2016) Engagement with language: How examining learners' affective and social engagement explains successful learner-generated attention to form. In M. Sato and S. Ballinger (eds) *Peer Interaction and Second Language Learning: Pedagogical Potential and Research Agenda* (pp. 209–240). Amsterdam: John Benjamins.

Braun, V. and Clarke, V. (2006) Using thematic analysis in psychology. *Qualitative Research in Psychology* 3 (2), 77–101.

Bygate, M. and Samuda, V. (2009) Creating pressure in task pedagogy: The joint roles of field, purpose, and engagement within the interaction approach. In A. Mackey and C. Polio (eds) *Multiple Perspectives on Interaction: Second Language Research in Honour of Susan M. Gass* (pp. 90–116). New York: Routledge.

Choi, H. and Iwashita, N. (2016) Interactional behaviours of low-proficiency learners in small group work. In M. Sato and S. Ballinger (eds) *Peer Interaction and Second Language Learning: Pedagogical Potential and Research Agenda* (pp. 113–134). Amsterdam: John Benjamins.

Christenson, S., Reschly, A. and Wylie, C. (eds) (2012) *Handbook of Research on Student Engagement*. New York: Springer.

Cleary, T. and Zimmerman, B. (2012) A cyclical self-regulatory account of student engagement: Theoretical foundations and applications. In S.L. Christenson, A.L. Reschly and C. Wylie (eds) *Handbook of Research on Student Engagement* (pp. 237–258). New York: Springer.

Clément, R., Dörnyei, Z. and Noels, K.A. (1994) Motivation, self-confidence and group cohesion in the foreign language classroom. *Language Learning* 44 (3), 417–448.

Connell, J.P. and Wellborn, J.G. (1991) Competence, autonomy, and relatedness: A motivational analysis of self-system processes. In M.R. Gunnar and L.A. Sroufe (eds) *Self-processes and Development* (pp. 43–77). Hillsdale, NJ: Lawrence Erlbaum.

Csikszentmihalyi, M. (1990) *Flow: The Psychology of Optimal Experience*. New York: Harper Perennial.

Dewaele, J.-M. and MacIntyre, P.D. (2014) The two faces of Janus? Anxiety and enjoyment in the foreign language classroom. *Studies in Second Language Learning and Teaching* 4 (2), 237–274.

Dörnyei, Z. (2019) Towards a better understanding of the L2 learning experience, the Cinderella of the L2 motivational self system. *Studies in Second Language Learning and Teaching* 9 (1), 19–30.

Dörnyei, Z. and Kormos, J. (2000) The role of individual and social variables in oral task performance. *Language Teaching Research* 4 (3), 275–300.

Dörnyei, Z. and Muir, C. (2019) Creating a motivating classroom environment. In X. Gao (ed.) *Second Handbook of English Language Teaching*. New York: Springer.

Edmondson, A. (1999) Psychological safety and learning behavior in work teams. *Administrative Science Quarterly* 44 (2), 350–383.

Fredricks, J.A., Filsecker, M. and Lawson, M.A. (2016) Student engagement, context, and adjustment: Addressing definitional, measurement, and methodological issues. *Learning and Instruction* 43, 1–4.

Hattie, J.A.C. (2012) *Visible Learning for Teachers*. London: Routledge.

Helme, S. and Clarke, D. (2001) Identifying cognitive engagement in the mathematics classroom. *Mathematics Education Research Journal* 13 (2), 133–153.

Joe, H., Hiver, P. and Al-Hoorie, A. (2017) Classroom social climate, self-determined motivation, willingness to communicate, and achievement: A study of structural relationships in instructed second language settings. *Learning and Individual Differences* 53, 133–144.

Khajavy, G.H., MacIntyre, P.D. and Barabadi, E. (2018) Role of the emotions and classroom environment in willingness to communicate: Applying doubly latent multilevel analysis in second language acquisition research. *Studies in Second Language Acquisition* 40 (3), 605–624.

Lambert, C., Philp, J. and Nakamura, S. (2017) Learner-generated content and engagement in second language task performance. *Language Teaching Research* 21 (6), 665–680.

Lambert, C. (ed.) (2017) Affective factors in second language task design and performance [Special issue]. *Language Teaching Research* 21 (6).

Martin, A.J. (2012) Part II commentary: Motivation and engagement: Conceptual, operational, and empirical clarity. In S.L. Christenson, A.L. Reschly and C. Wylie (eds) *Handbook of Research on Student Engagement* (pp. 303–313). New York: Springer.

Menzies, H.K., Lane, K., Oakes, W. and Ennis, P. (2017) Increasing students' opportunities to respond: A strategy for supporting engagement. *Intervention in School and Clinic* 52 (4), 204–209.

Oga-Baldwin, W.L.Q. (2019) Acting, thinking, feeling, making, collaborating: The engagement process in foreign language learning. *System* 86, 102–128.

Patrick, H. and Ryan, A.M. (2005) Identifying adaptive classrooms: Dimensions of the classroom social environment. In K.A. Moore and L.H. Lippman (eds) *What do Children Need to Flourish?* (pp. 271–287). New York: Springer.

Philp, J. and Duchesne, S. (2016) Exploring engagement in tasks in the language classroom. *Annual Review of Applied Linguistics* 36, 50–72.

Philp, J. and Mackey, A. (2010) What can socially informed approaches offer to cognitive (and vice versa)? In R. Batstone (ed.) *Sociocognitive Perspectives on Language Use and Language Learning* (pp. 210–228). Oxford: Oxford University Press.

Philp, J., Walter, S. and Basturkmen, H. (2010) Peer interaction in the foreign language classroom: What factors foster a focus on form? *Language Awareness* 19 (4), 261–279.

Pintrich, P. and De Groot, E. (1990) Motivational and self-regulated learning components of classroom academic performance. *Journal of Educational Psychology* 82, 33–40.

Reschly, A.L. and Christenson, S.L. (2012) Jingle, jangle, and conceptual haziness: Evolution and future directions of the engagement construct. In S.L. Christenson, A.L. Reschly and C. Wylie (eds) *Handbook of Research on Student Engagement* (pp. 3–19). New York: Springer.

Russell, J., Ainley, M. and Frydenberg, E. (2005) *Student Motivation and Engagement*. Canberra, Australia: Department of Education and Training.

Ryan, A.M. and Patrick, H. (2001) The classroom social environment and changes in adolescents' motivation and engagement during middle school. *American Educational Research Journal* 38, 437–460.

Sato, M. and Ballinger, S. (2012) Raising language awareness in peer interaction: A cross context, cross-methodology examination. *Language Awareness* 21 (1-2), 157–179.

Sato, M. and Ballinger, S. (eds) (2016) *Peer Interaction and Second Language Learning: Pedagogical Potential and Research Agenda*. Amsterdam: John Benjamins.

Shernoff, D.J. (2013) *Optimal Learning Environments to Promote Student Engagement*. New York: Springer.

Shernoff, D.J., Kelly, S., Tonks, S., Anderson, B., Cavanagh, R., Sinha, S. and Abdi, B. (2016) Student engagement as a function of environmental complexity in high school classrooms. *Learning and Instruction* 43, 52–60.

Shernoff, D.J., Ruzek, E.A. and Sinha, S. (2017) The influence of the high school class-room environment on learning as mediated by student engagement. *School Psychology International* 38 (2), 201–218.

Skinner, E.A., Furrer, C., Marchand, G. and Kindermann, T.A. (2008) Engagement and disaffection in the classroom: Part of a larger motivational dynamic? *Journal of Educational Psychology* 100 (4), 765–781.

Skinner, E.A., Kindermann, T.A., Connell, J.P. and Wellborn, J.G. (2009) Engagement as an organizational construct in the dynamics of motivational development. In K. Wentzel and A. Wigfield (eds) *Handbook of Motivation in School* (pp. 223–245). Mawah, NJ: Erlbaum.

Storch, N. (2008) Metatalk in a pair work activity: Level of engagement and implications for language development. *Language Awareness* 17, 95–114.

Svalberg, A.M.L. (2009) Engagement with language: Developing a construct. *Language Awareness* 18 (3-4), 242–258.

Svalberg, A.M.L. (2012) Language awareness in language learning and teaching: A research agenda. *Language Teaching* 45 (3), 376–388.

Wu, X. (2003) Intrinsic motivation and young language learners: The impact of the class-room environment. *System* 31 (4), 501–517.

Vygotsky, L.S. (1987) Thinking and speech (N. Minick, Trans.). In R.W. Rieber and A.S. Carton (eds) *The Collected Works of L.S. Vygotsky: Vol. 1. Problems of General Psychology* (pp. 39–285). New York: Plenum Press. (Original work published 1934).

7 Examining Learner Engagement in Relationship to Learning and Communication Mode[1]

Carly Carver, Daniel Jung and
Laura Gurzynski-Weiss

Introduction

Among the myriad factors examined in relation to the processes and outcomes of second language (L2) acquisition (e.g. Dörnyei & Ryan, 2015), learner engagement has received little attention. This is despite arguments that engagement 'requires energy and effort, [and is what] drives learning' (Christenson *et al.*, 2012: 817), and calls by scholars to examine how engagement relates to L2 learning (Dörnyei, 2019; Philp & Duchesne, 2016).

Learner engagement has received much attention in educational psychology (e.g. Christenson *et al.*, 2012). While early conceptualizations centered on the amount of time learners engaged with academic tasks (e.g. Mosher & McGowan, 1985), engagement is now conceptualized as a multifaceted construct, involving behavioral components such as participation, and aspects of emotion and cognition (Fredricks *et al.*, 2004), with the ability to explain important outcomes of interest (Balfanz *et al.*, 2007; Reschly & Christenson, 2012).

Despite the demonstrated significance of learner engagement, only recently has the construct been investigated by L2 researchers, where outcomes are traditionally measured by language use and/or development, although other recent work takes a broader approach to achievement and development (e.g. Henry & Thorsen, 2019). The current study continues this research, examining whether cognitive, affective and behavioral engagement among learners of Spanish, engaging in task-based interaction in face-to-face (FTF) and computer-mediated contexts, predicts learning of three linguistic structures. As rightly pointed out by a reviewer,

120

our study is an initial one attempting to bridge the gap between the afore-mentioned empirical research that has demonstrated the benefits of engagement, while attempting to operationalize a more holistic construct more representative of the dynamic nature of learner individual differences.

Literature Review

The role of cognitive engagement in L2 learning: Language-related episodes and beyond

L2 research has largely limited its scope of engagement to cognitive indices of learners' attention to, or awareness of, language. Whether operationalized as noticing (Leow, 1997; Schmidt, 2001), negotiation for meaning (Long, 1996), or output production and hypothesis testing (Swain, 2005), learner's attention to, interaction with, and awareness of the L2 has related to L2 learning (see Mackey *et al.*, 2012, for an overview). L2 researchers have measured cognitive constructs using language-related episodes (LREs): 'any part of a dialogue where the students talk about the language they are producing, question their language use, or correct themselves or others' (Swain & Lapkin, 1998: 326).

Some of this research reports a facilitative role for LREs in L2 development (e.g. Baralt, 2014; Kim, 2012; Révész, 2011; Swain & Lapkin, 1998; Williams, 2001). For example, Storch (2008) defined LREs during interme-diate-level English as a second language (ESL) peer interaction as either elaborate (deliberation/explanation of forms) or limited (stating a form) engagement. On a text reconstruction task, elaborate engagement pro-moted the most target-like use of new or already acquired morphosyntactic forms. Similarly, in their examination of engagement with teacher feed-back on collaborative, peer writing tasks, Storch and Wigglesworth (2010) found extensive (deliberating/discussing feedback) – rather than limited (acknowledging/repeating feedback) – engagement led to more learning of morphosyntactic and lexical forms. Learning did not occur when learners felt the feedback did not align with their beliefs about good writing.

However, other research reports more nuanced relationships between cognitive engagement (LREs) and L2 learning. For instance, Wigglesworth and Storch (2012) found that high and low engagement (multiple vs. single-turn LREs, respectively) did not mediate the facilitative role of teacher feedback on advanced ESL students' grammatical accuracy and syntactic complexity in collaborative writing tasks. They do argue, however, that affective factors such as learner attitudes, desires and beliefs about receiv-ing and engaging with feedback may have mediated these outcomes.

Other research shows the relationship between LREs and learning depends on interaction mode (FTF or computer-mediated). McDonough and Sunitham (2009) found first-year English as a foreign language (EFL) learners interacting in FTF but completing self-accessed computer tasks correctly resolved LREs, but only one third of grammatical forms and less than half of lexical forms discussed in the LREs were correctly recalled later. The authors suggest the dissimilarity between the computer tasks and the learners' typical FTF classroom tasks may have led to learners perceiving the computer tasks as irrelevant to learning, decreasing their incentive to remember and subsequently use the forms.

Similarly, Baralt (2014) found more LREs and morphosyntactic learning in FTF, while neither occurred in synchronous computer-mediated communication (SCMC) (text-chat). Baralt suggests the FTF learners felt more accustomed to interaction and talking about language given these actions are often encouraged in their FTF classrooms, while the SCMC groups may have not viewed the online setting as a natural place to focus on form. Thus, it will be important for researchers to assess the extent to which different interaction modes allow for LREs to occur in general before investigating their relation to learning across these different modes. Baralt also argues learners may have felt less comfortable and competent to provide elements of LREs (e.g. feedback) to a peer versus an expert interlocutor.

The aforementioned studies explored how learners attend to language through cognitive measures (LREs) which some (e.g. Storch, 2008) have referred to as engagement and have explored with a dual focus (amount and quality). Findings are mixed regarding how cognitive engagement influences learning and point to affective and social factors, and communication mode, as potentially mediating this relationship. Thus, while cognitive engagement may contribute to L2 learning, other ways learners engage with language may provide a more complete picture, an approach advocated by Dörnyei (2019: 55), who argues the focus on cognitive variables in research comes at the expense of motivational or attitudinal variables, which limits the validity of findings for the classroom, where 'student cooperation cannot be taken for granted,' to the extend that researchers may take it for granted in a laboratory context. Acknowledging the limitations of a solely cognitive view of engagement echoes the 'dynamic turn' (de Bot, 2015) of second language acquisition (SLA). Given the interconnected nature between aspects of learning including the cognitive, affective, behavioral, and social dimensions (e.g. Lantolf, 2012), L2 scholars have begun expanding engagement beyond cognitive dimensions.

Expanding the construct of engagement in L2 research

Svalberg (2009: 247) proposed engagement with language to be a 'cognitive, and/or affective, and/or social state and a process in which the learner is the agent and language is the object (and sometimes vehicle).' Examining engagement beyond the cognitive recognizes the complexity of how learners perceive and interact with language (Philp & Duchesne,

2016), including emotionally. These dimensions have been argued as inseparable from cognition, capable of rendering learning opportunities more salient and mediating learning over time (Swain, 2013), and able to 'support effective learning' (Philp & Duchesne, 2016: 52) in the classroom. In Svalberg's (2009, 2012) definition, cognitive engagement refers to focusing attention on form, utilizing and directing cognitive resources, and solving problems (e.g. do learners ask questions, compare and make hypotheses regarding their use of the L2?). Affective engagement refers to attitudes about the task, the interlocutor and task participation (e.g. is the learner focused or bored? Does the learner experience anxiety? Is the learner willing and eager to participate?). Social engagement refers to initiating and maintaining interaction (e.g. does the learner participate in scaffolding?).

Baralt *et al.* (2016) were the first to implement Svalberg's (2009) operationalization of engagement. Examining peer interaction between intermediate learners of Spanish in FTF and SCMC, Baralt and colleagues found more cognitive engagement (e.g. reflection/experimentation with forms) in FTF vs. SCMC, where learners in SCMC simply stated linguistic information in one word (e.g. 'irregular'). There was also greater affective engagement in FTF where learners viewed the task as 'helpful, enjoyable, and fun' (Baralt *et al.*, 2016: 323), and learners with high affective (e.g. viewed the task as fun/were eager to participate) and social (e.g. reported feeling supported/included in the task) engagement demonstrated more cognitive engagement, i.e. attention to form. FTF learners reported that willingness to interact (i.e. affective engagement, often due to feelings of a shared focus with their partner on task completion) influenced their task performance. SCMC participants, however, expressed feelings of tension and anxiety due to lack of partner familiarity. Thus, interacting online impacted learners' affective and social engagement, which in turn affected cognitive engagement and thereby attention to form. These results reveal the interrelated nature of engagement dimensions beyond the cognitive and their ability to provide a deeper understanding of how and why learners do (or do not) attend to form during interaction, along with the role of communication mode.

An additional facet of engagement borrowed from educational psychology and considered recently in L2 research is *behavioral* engagement (Philp & Duchesne, 2016),[2] often defined as time on task or participation including word or turn counts (e.g. Dörnyei & Kormos, 2000; Lambert *et al.*, 2017; Phung, 2017). Education researchers argue academic engaged time predicts achievement and directly links to learning outcomes (Gettinger & Walter, 2012). L2 researchers (e.g. Dörnyei & Kormos, 2000) have argued a lack of task involvement and insufficient language production (e.g. number of turns) may inhibit the cognitive and linguistic processes necessary for L2 development, but this has not been examined empirically. Although scholars have investigated how cognitive, affective, social, and behavioral engagement components impact outcomes such as task content (e.g. Lambert *et al.*, 2017; Phung, 2017) and attention to form (Baralt *et al.*, 2016), their impact on L2 learning has been minimally investigated, despite calls for it by L2 researchers (e.g. Philp & Duchesne, 2016).

Dao (2017) has explored how cognitive, emotional (affective) and social engagement during peer interaction predicted L2 learning, specifically, EFL question development (Mackey, 1999) by low-proficiency learners. Cognitive engagement was measured using LREs, and question and answer idea units (an information segment/comment/idea about a theme being discussed). Emotional engagement was operationalized as laugh episodes and post-task questionnaire ratings and comments. Social engagement consisted of instances of responsiveness (commenting/adding to/repeating a partner's ideas and mutual encouragement). Results revealed only cognitive engagement (question idea units) predicted learning, which one may argue was due to the similarity between the cognitive engagement indices and measures of learning. Indeed, Dao (2017: 61) acknowledges a potential argument that question idea units simply reflect question production practice which may have been what drove learning.

Interaction and engagement in FTF and SCMC

Examining how learners engage with and learn language in computer-mediated contexts is practically and theoretically relevant given the increasing number of language programs offering or planning to offer classes online, as well as the posited (Smith, 2004) and empirically attested L2 benefits of interaction in SCMC (text-chat) (e.g. Gurzynski-Weiss & Baralt, 2014; Yilmaz, 2012; Ziegler, 2016). These include additional processing time (Lai & Zhao, 2006), permanency of the text allowing learners to return to/potentially use forms (Gurzynski-Weiss & Baralt, 2014) and the written modality potentially increasing form salience (Long, 2007; Smith, 2004) and attention to form (Salaberry, 2000; Warschauer, 1997). Research also demonstrates mode effects on L2 learning including advantages of SCMC over FTF (e.g. Payne & Whitney, 2002; Yilmaz, 2012) and vice versa (e.g. De la Fuente, 2003).

While one mode comparison study reports more cognitive engagement (e.g. awareness of negotiation for meaning and self-corrections: Lai & Zhao, 2006) in SCMC, others (Baralt, 2014; Baralt *et al.*, 2016) report less. Regarding affective engagement, some studies (e.g. Baralt, 2014; Baralt *et al.*, 2016) found more in FTF vs. SCMC while others report no mode differences (e.g. anxiety: Baralt & Gurzynski-Weiss, 2011). Concerning behavioral engagement, some research reports more turns in FTF vs. SCMC (e.g. Baralt *et al.*, 2016), while others report the opposite (e.g. Lai & Zhao, 2006).

In summary, research points to a role for engagement and communication mode in attention to language but no study has examined how cognitive, affective and behavioral engagement relate to learning in both FTF and SCMC. This study addresses this gap; its findings may enrich our understanding of how these three types of engagement may mediate the effect of communication mode on L2 development, which may deepen our understanding of why some modes prove more effective for learning than others, as found in the mode comparison literature.[3] This study will also further our understanding of the predictive power of engagement more broadly, regarding learning three linguistic structures (of varying salience) measured by open and guided production. Thus, the design of this study addresses questions of not only *whether* engagement influences L2 learning, but also *how* – given the study also examines how learning plays out according to different engagement dimensions, across different modes and with different linguistic structures and types of learning outcomes. This reflects the field's interest in examining related constructs in more complex and dynamic ways. This study was guided by two research questions:

(1) Are there significant differences between FTF and SCMC regarding presence of behavioral, cognitive, and affective engagement?
(2) Is there a significant change over time for L2 learning of Spanish vocabulary, copula, and preposition use? If so, to what extent does cognitive, affective, and behavioral engagement predict this development? Are patterns similar in both modes?

Method

Participants

Sixteen learners (4 male and 12 female) enrolled in a FTF third-year Hispanic Linguistics course at a US Midwestern university during summer of 2015 participated in this study in exchange for extra credit. Participants' typical interaction mode in Spanish was FTF and they reported using technology on average 31.5 hours per week including 3.3 hours in Spanish. Three learners studied other languages (French, Arabic and Italian) for less than two semesters.

Target structures

The three structures examined in this study were Spanish vocabulary, copula and prepositions, selected due to their task-essential nature (Loschky & Bley-Vroman, 1993). Research shows FTF (e.g. De la Fuente, 2002, 2003) and SCMC interaction (Blake, 2000; De la Fuente, 2003) foster L2 vocabulary development, as does greater motivational and cognitive involvement with a word (e.g. Hulstijn & Laufer, 2001; Laufer & Hulstijn, 2001). However, less is known about how cognitive, affective, and behavioral engagement as often operationalized in L2 research may mediate vocabulary development in both modes.

The second structure examined was Spanish locative copula (*estar* 'to be') used to locate people or objects (e.g. *El jabón está* al lado del fregadero 'The soap is next to the sink'). Locative *estar* has been argued to occur in later stages of acquisition, (Gunterman, 1992; Ryan & Lafford, 1992). While also task-essential in this study, copula choice is arguably less communicatively salient than vocabulary, although it entails semantic and pragmatic dimensions and native-speaker variation (Geeslin, 2003).

Finally, Spanish locative prepositions were targeted. According to Huddleston (1984), prepositions may entail grammatical use with little room for variation (e.g. *Tim gave the book **to** Annie*), or a full lexical meaning (*Patricia lives **behind/in front of** the bank*). The Spanish locatives targeted in the present study were those with full lexical meaning, e.g. *detrás de* ('behind'); *a la izquierda de* ('to/on the left of'); *debajo de* ('below'), etc. Locative prepositions have received minimal attention in L2 Spanish (e.g. Gunterman, 1992; Lafford & Ryan, 1995), thus, this study contributes to understanding how Spanish learners acquire lexical uses of locative prepositions and whether interaction and engagement may influence its acquisition, along with that of Spanish vocabulary and copula.

Treatment tasks

The treatment tasks were two information-gap tasks used in previous studies (Gurzynski-Weiss & Baralt, 2014, 2015; Gurzynski-Weiss *et al.*, 2018, available on www.iris-database.org and the TBLT Language Learning Task Bank, tblt.indiana.edu). Learners were given either a living room or kitchen scene with 12 furniture or appliance items highlighted. They were told their interlocutor had the same picture, but was missing the items. Participants described the location of each item so their partner could correctly place cut outs they had of each so the two pictures matched. This interaction constituted the treatment in this study during which corrective feedback was provided on a variety of error types (including the three target structures) as felt natural by the interlocutor (see Gurzynski-Weiss & Baralt, 2014, 2015). No glossing techniques, nor formal pre- or post-task attention was given to the three linguistic targets (or any other language features).

Learning assessments

The pretests and posttests were open and guided oral production tasks. In the open production task, learners viewed a living room and kitchen scene and were asked to describe the location of seven furniture items or appliances that appeared in the treatment to elicit targeted vocabulary, locative copula, and locative prepositions. In the guided production task, learners viewed several pictures of a mouse and were asked to describe its location in relation to other objects to elicit copula and prepositions.

Post-task questionnaire

After the two treatments, participants completed a questionnaire (Appendix 7.1) containing information about demographics, experience and motivation for studying Spanish, technology use in English and Spanish, and perceptions regarding practicing Spanish in the two communication modes.

Procedure

This study largely replicated the methodology employed by Gurzynski-Weiss and Baralt (2014, 2015). Learners first completed the pretests online (open followed by guided oral production) which were audio recorded. In a counterbalanced design, learners then completed one treatment task in FTF and the other in SCMC, interacting individually with a near-native speaker of Spanish. FTF interactions were video recorded and SCMC interactions were carried out in separate rooms using Skype and screen recorded using iShowU software. After each interaction, learners completed the posttests online followed by the paper post-task questionnaire.

Coding

Transcribed FTF treatment and assessment recordings were coded for cognitive and behavioral engagement and the three questionnaire adjectives were coded for affective engagement. Cognitive engagement was coded as instances of LREs, modified output after feedback, self-correction, and hand motions used to support language use in FTF, or instances of learners scrolling up to view previously used forms in SCMC. These elements were selected as indicating learners' reflecting on, questioning their own attempts at, and asking about language, thus showing their attention on language as an object/medium (Svalberg, 2009). Research operationalizing cognitive engagement has used similar indices (e.g. Baralt *et al.*, 2016; Dao, 2017; Lambert *et al.*, 2016; Phung, 2017). A sum was then taken of all cognitive engagement instances and divided by total number of turns produced by each participant, yielding a percentage serving as a cognitive engagement score for each participant. Examples of cognitive engagement in FTF and SCMC can be found in Appendix 7.2.

Following previous operationalizations (e.g. Phung, 2017) and arguments that turn-taking indicates student involvement (Dörnyei & Kormos, 2000), behavioral engagement was operationalized as number of turns produced per participant. A turn was defined as a 'string of utterances produced by a single speaker and bounded by other speakers' turns' (Gumperz & Berenz, 1993: 95) and was tallied in each mode after removing fillers (e.g. *um*).

Regarding affective engagement, two of the post-task questionnaire items asked learners to provide three adjectives describing their experience completing the task in each communication mode. These adjectives were used to measure affective engagement. Research operationalizing affective engagement has used the same (e.g. Baralt *et al.*, 2016; Dao, 2017) or similar (e.g. interviews in Phung, 2017) open-ended indices where learners generate their own perceptions. Learners' perceptions (vs. observational data) were used as the primary data source for understanding affective engagement. This was done to avoid the limitations of using observational measures to capture a subjective construct (see Fredricks & McColskey, 2012) such as researcher bias (e.g. attempting to interpret a smile or laugh as positive engagement where it could in fact be a sign of nervousness; see Baralt *et al.*, 2016: 227). Each learner was then assigned an average affective engagement score based on the positive adjectives they generated. This score was calculated as a percentage by dividing the number of positive adjectives by 3 (total possible adjectives) and scores ranged from 0 to 100. Such coding allowed for the gradient nature of engagement to be captured. Examples of adjectives coded as positive across both modes included 'educational,' 'relaxing' and 'creative,' while negative adjectives included 'isolated,' 'stressful' and 'tedious.'

Finally, for L2 learning, assessment transcriptions were coded and 'correct uses of each linguistic structure' was divided by 'total attempts to use the structure', resulting in a percentage score for each participant on each of the five outcome measures (open production scores for all three target structures and guided production for copula and prepositions).

Results and Discussion

The independent variables in this study were the three engagement types and the dependent variables were pretest and posttest scores on both production tasks; all variables were continuous. Statistical analyses were conducted using Statistical Analysis System (SAS) 9.4.

Research question 1: Engagement according to interaction mode

The first research question explored potential differences between FTF and SCMC modes in terms of behavioral, cognitive and affective engagement. The descriptive statistics for these analyses are presented in Table 7.1.

Overall, participants were more engaged during FTF compared to SCMC. To determine if these differences were significant, paired-samples *t*-tests were run, comparing engagement types in both modes. These tests revealed a non-significant difference for behavioral engagement according to mode, with a small to medium effect size;[4] $t(15) = 1.91$, $p = 0.075$,

Table 7.1 Descriptive statistics of engagement across both modes

Mode	Engagement	M	SD	Min	Max
FTF	Behavioral	43.31	9.63	28.00	59.00
	Cognitive	0.34	0.19	0.00	0.93
	Affective	0.73	0.22	0.33	1.00
SCMC	Behavioral	36.19	11.19	22.00	67.00
	Cognitive	0.14	0.08	0.00	0.32
	Affective	0.40	0.36	0.00	1.00

$d = 0.63$. Cognitive engagement was significantly different across modes; $t(15) = 4.45$, $p < 0.001$, $d = 1.37$, as was affective engagement; $t(14) = 2.62$, $p = 0.02$, $d = 1.11$, both exhibiting large effect sizes.

Thus, we answer our first research question affirmatively: there are significant mode differences for the presence of cognitive and affective engagement, but not behavioral. The greater cognitive and affective engagement in FTF vs. SCMC echoes findings by Baralt (2014) and Baralt et al. (2016). It is important to mention that these studies argue that social factors inhibited affective and cognitive engagement in SCMC, e.g. students feeling their partner was not invested in completing the task (Baralt et al., 2016) and their dissatisfaction with not being corrected by their partner (Baralt, 2014). Though social engagement was not examined in our study and our interlocutor was an expert, rather than a peer-interactor, who did provide feedback, we still found less cognitive and affective engagement in SCMC.

This may point to a potential uniqueness of the FTF mode itself that fosters more engagement vs. SCMC, such as non-verbal expression and a view of FTF as a superior way to practice Spanish as it involves speaking – two themes emergent from our learner questionnaire comments. Future research would do well to explore learners' mode perceptions further to understand what else unique to the FTF mode might promote more engagement vs. SCMC.

However, rather than a mode difference, the greater cognitive and affective engagement in FTF reported here may be (as one anonymous reviewer suggested) because learners were simply more accustomed to FTF interaction. This is a valid point, particularly considering that these learners' typical interaction mode was FTF and scholars (e.g. Baralt, 2014; McDonough & Sunitham, 2009) have argued similarly. However, recall Baralt et al. (2016) found learners enrolled in online courses (thus arguably accustomed to the SCMC mode) still exhibited lower levels of engagement in SCMC vs. FTF, highlighting the potential of other factors at work.

One factor Baralt et al. (2016) argue for is a social factor, specifically, interlocutor familiarity, and in fact, our study may disentangle the role of interlocutor familiarity from *type* of interlocutor (peer vs. expert). Lack of interlocutor familiarity has resulted in less cognitive and affective engagement in SCMC (Baralt, 2014; Baralt *et al.*, 2016; this study where our expert interlocutor was unknown to participants). Conversely, given the greater engagement and learning in SCMC found in the current study as compared to prior studies (e.g. Baralt, 2014 who found no engagement and no learning), interacting with an expert vs. a peer may increase cognitive and affective engagement in SCMC itself, even if not surpassing FTF. This may also explain why learning still occurred in SCMC in this study but not in Baralt (2014) where no engagement occurred – highlighting the need for research delving into different types of engagement and engagement patterns to explain learning differences reported in the L2 communication mode comparison literature. A final point to mention is the laboratory setting of this study (vs. previous work), which may have increased cognitive engagement overall. Indeed, Dörnyei (2019) argues laboratories presuppose a certain amount of cognitive engagement as participant attendance is typically voluntary and learners likely know they are participating in a study on language learning.

Lastly, turning to behavioral engagement, we found that number of turns was not significantly different in the two modes, diverging from previous research reporting more turns in either FTF (e.g. Baralt *et al.*, 2016) or SCMC peer interaction (e.g. Lai & Zhao, 2006). Perhaps the interlocutor also played a role concerning this result; interacting with an expert rather than a peer rendered production more uniform across modes; a factor to be explored in future research.

The previous discussion points to several factors (absolute mode differences, mode familiarity, social relationships between interlocutors, any combination of the aforementioned, etc.) potentially impacting engagement in different communication modes and reinforces arguments (e.g. González-Lloret & Ortega, 2014) that one cannot simply take a FTF task and carry it out online without considering the uniqueness of the two modes; this appears to extend to engagement, as well. Future research, taking a more situated approach, is needed to examine how these, and other factors (e.g. task-type) influence the development of affective and social dispositions (e.g. Henry & Thorsen, 2019). This will additionally increase the ecological validity of engagement studies and their classroom generalizability (Dörnyei, 2019), including online contexts.

Research question 2: Evidence of learning and the potentially predictive power of engagement

The second research question investigated if learning occurred and, if so, whether engagement predicted learning. Table 7.2 presents the descriptive statistics of pre-posttest improvement for the five learning measures (vocabulary, copula and prepositions on the open production tests, and copula and prepositions on guided production). Overall, mean posttest

Table 7.2 Descriptive statistics of the learning measures

Measure	Pretest				Posttest				Gain scores			
	M	SD	Min	Max	M	SD	Min	Max	M	SD	Min	Max
OPCop	48.5	41.1	0	100	73.4	33.9	5.8	100	24.9	30.6	−23.1	85.1
OPPrep	75.3	20.9	11.1	100	87.9	8.97	68.4	100	12.4	23.6	−14.3	81.2
OPVocab	37.6	22.8	0	93.3	78.9	17.0	47.3	100	41.3	24.3	6.7	85.5
GPCop	50.8	47.1	0	100	72.1	38.8	0	100	21.3	42.1	−60.0	100
GPPrep	67.5	23.8	0	100	82.2	16.0	42.9	100	14.8	30.1	−28.5	100

Note: OP = open production; GP = guided production.

scores are higher than pretest scores on all measures, although examining the gain scores indicates some learners exhibited lower posttest vs. pretest scores; 12 gain scores across seven learners were negative.

To determine if learners scored significantly better at the posttest and if engagement predicted posttest scores, a repeated-measures analysis of variance (ANOVA) was performed, including time (pre, post), and six engagement variables (FTF cognitive, SCMC cognitive, FTF affective, SCMC affective, FTF behavioral and SCMC behavioral). Results showed significant pre-posttest improvement for three of the five learning measures: copula in open production (OPCop) with a small to medium effect size ($F(1, 22) = 4.7$, $p = 0.05$, $d = 0.66$), prepositions in guided production (GPPrep) with a medium effect size ($F(1, 22) = 5.41$, $p = 0.03$, $d = 0.73$) and vocabulary in open production (OPVocab) with a very large effect size ($F(1,22) = 28.72$, $p < 0.001$, $d = 2.1$). No significant improvement occurred for copula in guided production (GPCop), with a small to medium effect size ($F(1, 22) = 2.08$, $p = 0.17$, $d = 0.49$), or for prepositions in open production (OPPrep), with a medium to large effect size ($F(1,22) = 3.19$, $p = 0.10$, $d = 0.77$).

Thus, we can say that, overall, learners' task-based interactions were facilitative of learning all three structures, regardless of engagement type or communication mode, aligning with previous research reporting a facilitative role for interaction in L2 learning. These results demonstrate the tasks were successful in promoting learning; learners exhibited the most improvement in vocabulary, followed by prepositions and copula. This is in keeping with the expected difficulty of these linguistic structures arguably due, in part, to their differences in communicative salience. Our interest becomes, then, the potentially nuanced patterns within this learning: Does engagement predict learning? If so, what types of engagement might predict learning more than others? And, are patterns limited to one mode? This is addressed in the latter part of our second research question.

The aforementioned ANOVA included the six engagement variables according to mode, and we found only affective engagement in FTF predicted one measure of learning, copula in open production: ($F(1,22) = 8.2$,

$p <. 001).^5$ This finding aligns with arguments that affective factors may influence (Swain, 2013) and facilitate (Philp & Duchesne, 2016: 52) L2 learning. This result also concords with Baralt *et al.* (2016) who showed affective engagement in FTF facilitated attention to form, which has been argued as a pre-cursor to learning. Interestingly, in our study, affective engagement in FTF predicted copula improvement in open production, arguably the most difficult structure (due to low communicative salience) in the more difficult learning measure (open production). That is, open oral production required learners to retrieve vocabulary as well as locate it in relation to other objects. Conversely, guided production may have been less taxing; learners were given the word for mouse (*ratón*) and simply had to state its location relative to only one or two objects. Therefore, affective engagement in FTF interaction appeared to be the most important factor when learning this challenging structure required for use in this difficult task.

Our findings regarding a link between affective, but not cognitive engagement, and learning is similar to what Wigglesworth and Storch (2012) found – no effect for cognitive engagement (LREs) on learning after feedback, but a likely role for affective factors. An important question in our study then, becomes why affective engagement in FTF predicted learning, but cognitive engagement (also higher in FTF) did not?

It may be that learners' more positive disposition toward the task in FTF vs. SCMC (evidenced by significantly higher affective engagement in FTF and student descriptions of the FTF task as 'engaging' and 'educational'), influenced other cognitive processes (e.g. memorization strategies: Wigglesworth & Storch, 2012) not captured by the measures of cognitive engagement employed in this study. This would align with the argument by Wigglesworth and Storch (2012) that LREs, as one example, may not provide the whole picture of cognitive engagement. Therefore, our learners may have 'silently engaged' (Wigglesworth & Storch, 2012: 91) and done so more in FTF, which may have contributed to the learning we found. Other elements of cognitive engagement not captured in our study may have been concentrated effort, thinking, or other learning strategies which Philp and Duchesne (2016) argue are likely driven by affective engagement dimensions such as learners viewing the task as interesting or exciting, the precise adjectives used by many of our learners and used to measure affective engagement in our study. Storch and Wigglesworth (2010) and Wigglesworth and Storch (2012) likewise argue that varying student interest levels impact whether and how they engage with elements of language, e.g. corrective feedback – feedback being an element of cognitive engagement. Future studies would do well to add retrospective measures of learner perceptions such as stimulated recalls (see Gurzynski-Weiss & Baralt, 2014, 2015) to capture these potentially hidden cognitive aspects. Such research would also facilitate a deeper and more nuanced examination of the nature and role of affective engagement in influencing cognitive engagement and learning, underscoring the continued calls to not abandon motivational or attitudinal variables in attempting to account for what environmental factors lead to task-based learning (see recent discussion in Dörnyei, 2019). Finally, linguistic target and task type will also be fruitful variables to examine in future research on L2 engagement given we found affective engagement especially relevant for learning one of the more arguably difficult structures (copula) on the more difficult task: open production.

Examining the measurements of cognitive and affective engagement we used may also shed light on these possible explanations of our results and elucidate the diverging findings between our study and one other study (Dao, 2017) exploring a link between engagement and learning.

Recall that Dao found that only one measurement of cognitive engagement (question idea units) predicted learning; emotional/affective engagement did not. Regarding cognitive engagement, supplementing the measure we used with one similar to Dao's (e.g. a more production-oriented measure such as target-like production of the structures examined in our study) and examining the predictive power of each individual measure with a larger data set may uncover more effects for cognitive engagement on learning. With respect to affective engagement, the different measurements between Dao (Likert-scale self-report, laugh episodes and qualitative trends including three elicited adjectives from learners, though not included in Dao's statistical analysis) and the current study (quantitative scores based on three adjectives) may also explain the differing results. Thus, future research might employ multiple measures for each dimension of engagement to assess what particular aspects of cognitive and affective engagement might predict learning. As mentioned, a retrospective measure would also provide an additional control and opportunity for learners to expand their perspectives on the data.

By exploring how engagement relates to L2 learning, the current study allowed for comparison to previous work doing the same. Importantly, in doing so, it illustrated that different measures of learner engagement, a common theme and challenge emerging in the discussion by scholars investigating the construct (e.g. Fredricks & McColskey, 2012; Philp & Duchesne, 2016; Reschly & Christenson, 2012) may account for why, in recent empirical work, different types of engagement have been found to relate to L2 learning or processes associated with L2 learning. Undoubtedly, more research exploring this topic is in order.

Conclusions and Future Directions

This study was the first to examine cognitive and affective engagement (as operationalized by Svalberg, 2009, 2012) as well as behavioral engagement (number of turns) in relationship to Spanish L2 learning in FTF and SCMC. Results demonstrate FTF interaction led to significantly higher cognitive and affective engagement as compared to SCMC. Furthermore, learners significantly improved their open oral production of vocabulary and copula as well as their guided oral production of prepositions, with FTF affective engagement significantly predicting improvement in open production of Spanish copula.

Examining the predictive power of engagement for L2 learning in two common learning settings (FTF and SCMC) is an important next step in L2 engagement research. Although exploratory in nature, our results indicate future studies of engagement must consider and report factors including learners' perceptions of and use of different communication modes, the role of the interlocutor, measures of engagement (particularly the affective and cognitive dimensions), type of linguistic target and learning measure. Research can also build upon this study with designs including longer treatment sessions to maximize learning opportunities and potentially uncover additional engagement patterns. Delayed posttests can also be implemented to examine the durational effects of a role for engagement in learning. Additionally, studies may examine longitudinally how the incorporation of tasks in intact L2 classrooms influences affective and social dispositions (Henry & Thorsen, 2019), given that engagement may be a crucial variable for understanding L2 achievement in the classroom (Dörnyei, 2019; Mercer & Dörnyei, 2020). Finally, given that only affective engagement predicted learning in this study, research can build upon the current measure of affective engagement by examining other data sources of learners' perceptions such as comments from stimulated recalls, interviews, or learning journals as recommended by other researchers (e.g. Baralt *et al.*, 2016). As a field we have advanced into more complex and holistic considerations, and this study, triangulating types of engagement, is one more demonstration of how critical this is.

Implications

Engagement is an important construct for L2 pedagogy as it may help account for the relationship between classroom behaviors and L2 learning, and for why learning outcomes may differ across contexts (Dörnyei, 2019). By examining this under-researched issue of how learner engagement looks in different interaction modes and how it may mediate learning, this study found affective engagement in a particular type of interaction (FTF) predicted the most learning, highlighting the context-dependent nature of engagement, echoing results from Baralt *et al.* (2016).

Our results are, of course, specific to the context at hand: adult, university-level L2 learners interacting FTF with an expert interlocutor carrying out a one-way information-gap task. Thus, in future efforts to utilize engagement findings to inform L2 pedagogy, research can build upon this initial attempt to link engagement and learning by targeting different age groups, curricular contexts, and learning modalities (video

SCMC, virtual gaming) and with different tasks and interlocutors. Expanding engagement research into these areas is called for by Philp and Duchesne (2016) who argue this will help lead to a developmental picture of engagement which could inform teachers' instructional decisions. That is understanding whether, how and why learners engage with certain learning tasks and how this relates to L2 acquisition can inform teachers' choices in the classroom that may in turn affect the nature and levels of engagement. Such choices include task design, selection (Baralt *et al.*, 2016; Philp & Duchesne, 2016) and sequencing, as well as student grouping; this is especially important given how research – including the present study – has found less engagement when learners interact with peers and/ or in SCMC. The relationship between factors at various levels is part and parcel of a holistic, complexity theory-informed approach to SLA (Larsen-Freeman & Cameron, 2008), but these relationships, while undoubtedly prevalent in SLA, are not well-investigated or understood – an issue which needs more attention in the future. Understanding in more detail how context mediates engagement and ultimately learning can guide teachers to preemptively encourage engagement when it is likely to be low.

Methodologically, this study largely replicated Baralt *et al.* (2016), and included additional measures for behavioral engagement. Perhaps our largest contribution to methodological advancement is the unequivocal demonstration of the myriad factors at play with engagement. For example, our study demonstrated a link between affective engagement in FTF and learning using engagement measures from Baralt *et al.* (2016) and Baralt (2014) as well as measures similar to Dao (2017), and while we are not able to fully explain this relationship, our hypothesis is that this could be due to an incomplete elicitation of cognitive engagement. Additional measures such as retrospective protocols will need to be added to future designs to uncover this. We also noticed, in the discussion comparing our results to others', that there may be an interlocutor effect at work; future research should investigate this further. Thus, our study makes a solid contribution to the importance of replication in contexts of nuanced differences, and demonstrates the need for future work to tease apart the nature of types of engagement and remaining factors at play.

Notes

(1) We would like to thank JD Seo at the Indiana University Statistical Consulting Center for his statistical insights and help with this project.

(2) An anonymous reviewer pointed out the difficulty in disentangling behavioral engagement from cognitive, affective, and social engagement, given that all dimensions of engagement entail student participation/involvement. The reviewer suggests the possibility that behavioral engagement may refer to *amount* of involvement, while other dimensions of engagement may capture the *quality* of involvement, similar to the dual focus on engagement (e.g. limited vs. elaborate) found in some research (e.g. Storch, 2008). This interesting possibility may be explored in future research as a way to refine current operationalizations of learner engagement.

(3) While not examined in our study, other factors such as task type (e.g. task complexity, see Baralt, 2010, 2013, 2014) have been shown to mediate mode effects as well as how engagement plays out in different modes and impacts attention to language (e.g. Baralt *et al.*, 2016). Thus, future research examining how engagement relates to L2 learning in different modes would do well to examine the role of task type, as well as other factors that may influence mode effects such as learning outcomes (e.g. De la Fuente, 2003; Lai & Zhao, 2006; Yilmaz, 2012).

(4) For our interpretations of effect sizes, we draw on Plonsky and Oswald's (2014: 12) SLA specific benchmarks, as well as the effect sizes found by Ziegler's (2016) meta-analysis of SCMC studies. We broadly interpret $d = 0.40$ as a small effect size, $d = 0.70$ as medium, and $d = 1.00$ as large, with reference to the domain-specific effect sizes reported in Ziegler (2016) guiding our interpretation.

(5) Effect sizes were not available for engagement measures because they cannot be calculated for continuous covariates in ANOVAs.

References

Balfanz, R., Herzog, L. and Mac Iver, D.J. (2007) Preventing student disengagement and keeping students on the graduation path in urban middle-grades schools: Early identification and effective interventions. *Educational Psychologist* 42, 223–235.

Baralt, M. (2010) Task Complexity, the Cognition Hypothesis, and Interaction in CMC and FTF Environments. Unpublished doctoral dissertation, Georgetown University, Washington, D.C.

Baralt, M. (2013) The impact of cognitive complexity on feedback efficacy during online vs. face-to-face interactive tasks. *Studies in Second Language Acquisition* 35, 689–725.

Baralt, M. (2014) Task sequencing and task complexity in traditional versus online classes. In M. Baralt, R. Gilabert and P. Robinson (eds) *Task Sequencing and Instructed Second Language Learning* (pp. 95–122). London: Bloomsbury.

Baralt, M. and Gurzynski-Weiss, L. (2011) Comparing learners' state anxiety during task-based interaction in computer-mediated and face-to-face communication. *Language Teaching Research* 15, 201–229.

Baralt, M., Gurzynski-Weiss, L. and Kim, Y. (2016) The effects of task complexity and classroom environment on learners' engagement with the language. In M. Sato and S. Ballinger (eds) *Peer Interaction and Second Language Learning: Pedagogical Potential and Research Agenda* (pp. 209–240). Amsterdam: John Benjamins.

Blake, R. (2000) Computer mediated communication: A window on L2 Spanish development. *Language Learning & Technology* 4, 120–136.

Christenson, S.L., Reschly, A.L. and Wylie, C. (eds) (2012) *Handbook of Research on Student Engagement*. New York: Springer.

Dao, P. (2017) Learner Engagement in Peer Task-based Interaction: Identifying the Effect of Interlocutor Proficiency and Task Outcome. Unpublished doctoral dissertation, Concordia University.

De Bot, K. (2015) *A History of Applied Linguistics: From 1980 to the Present*. New York: Routledge.

De la Fuente, M.J. (2002) Negotiation and oral acquisition of L2 vocabulary: The roles of input and output in receptive and productive acquisition of words. *Studies in Second Language Acquisition* 24, 81–112.

De la Fuente, M.J. (2003) Is SLA interactionist theory relevant to CALL? A study on the effects of computer-mediated interaction on L2 vocabulary acquisition. *Computer Assisted Language Learning* 16, 47–81.

Dörnyei, Z. (2019) Task motivation: What makes an L2 task engaging? In Z. Wen and M. Ahmadian (eds) *Researching L2 Task Performance and Pedagogy. In Honour of Peter Skehan* (pp. 53–66). Philadelphia, PA: John Benjamins.

Dörnyei, Z. and Kormos, J. (2000) The role of individual and social variables in oral task performance. *Language Teaching Research* 4, 275–300.

Dörnyei, Z. and Ryan, S. (2015) *The Psychology of the Language Learner Revisited*. New York: Routledge.

Fredricks, J.A., Blumenfeld, P.C. and Paris, A.H. (2004) School engagement: Potential of the concept, state of the evidence. *Review of Educational Research* 74, 59–109.

Fredricks, J.A. and McColskey, W. (2012) The measurement of student engagement: A comparative analysis of various methods and student self-report instruments. In S.L. Christenson, A.L. Reschly and C. Wylie (eds) *Handbook of Research on Student Engagement* (pp. 763–782). New York: Springer.

Geeslin, K.L. (2003) A comparison of copula choice: Native Spanish speakers and advanced Learners. *Language Learning* 53, 703–764.

Gettinger, M. and Walter, W. (2012) Classroom strategies to enhance academic engaged time. In S.L. Christenson, A.L., Reschly and C. Wylie (eds) *Handbook of Research on Student Engagement* (pp. 653–673). New York: Springer.

González-Lloret, M. and Ortega, L. (eds) (2014) *Technology-Mediated TBLT: Researching Technology and Tasks* (Vol. 6). Philadelphia, PA: John Benjamins.

Gumperz, J.J. and Berenz, N. (1993) Transcribing conversational exchanges. In J.A. Edwards and M.D. Lampert (eds) *Talking Data: Transcription and Coding in Discourse Research* (pp. 91–122). Hillsdale, NJ: Lawrence Erlbaum.

Gunterman, G. (1992) An analysis of interlanguage development over time: Part II, *ser* and *estar. Hispania* 75, 1294–1303.

Gurzynski-Weiss, L. and Baralt, M. (2014) Exploring learner perception and use of task-based interactional feedback in FTF and CMC modes. *Studies in Second Language Acquisition* 36, 1–37.

Gurzynski-Weiss, L. and Baralt, M. (2015) Does type of modified output correspond to learner noticing of feedback? A closer look in face-to-face and computer-mediated task-based interaction. *Applied Psycholinguistics* 36 (6), 1393–1420.

Gurzynski-Weiss, L., Henderson, C. and Jung, D. (2018) Examining timing and type of learner-modified output in relation to perception in face-to-face and synchronous computer-mediated chat task-based interaction. In M. Ahmadian and M.P. García Mayo (eds) *Recent Perspectives on Task-Based Language Teaching and Learning* (pp. 53–78). Berlin: de Gruyter.

Henry, A. and Thorsen, C. (2019) Weaving webs of connection: Empathy, perspective-taking, and student motivation. *Studies in Second Language Learning and Teaching* 9, 31–53.

Huddleston, R. (1984) *Introduction to the Grammar of English*. Cambridge: Cambridge University Press.

Hulstijn, J.H. and Laufer, B. (2001) Some empirical evidence for the involvement load hypothesis in vocabulary acquisition. *Language Learning* 51, 539–558.

Jackson, T.W. (2002) Enhancing self-efficacy and learning performance. *The Journal of Experimental Education* 70, 243–254.

Kim, Y. (2012) Task complexity, learning opportunities and Korean EFL learners' question development. *Studies in Second Language Acquisition* 34, 627–658.

Lafford, B. and Ryan, J. (1995) The acquisition of lexical meaning in a study abroad context: The Spanish prepositions por and para. *Hispania* 78, 528–547.

Lai, C. and Zhao, Y. (2006) Noticing and text-based chat. *Language Learning & Technology* 10, 102–120.

Lambert, C., Philp, J. and Nakamura, S. (2017) Learner-generated content and engagement in second language task performance. *Language Teaching Research* 21, 665–680.

Lantolf, J. (2012) Sociocultural theory: A dialectic approach to L2 research. In S.M. Gass and A. Mackey (eds) *The Routledge Handbook of Second Language Acquisition* (pp. 57–72). London: Routledge.

Larsen-Freeman, D. and Cameron, L. (2008) *Complex Systems and Applied Linguistics.* Oxford: Oxford University Press.

Laufer, B. and Hulstijn, J. (2001) Incidental vocabulary acquisition in a second language: The construct of task-induced involvement. *Applied Linguistics* 22, 1–26.

Leow, R.P. (1997) Attention, awareness, and foreign language behavior. *Language Learning* 47, 467–506.

Long, M.H. (1996) The role of the linguistic environment in second language acquisition. In W.C. Ritchie and T.K. Bhatia (eds) *Handbook of Second Language Acquisition* (pp. 413–468). New York: Academic Press.

Long, M.H. (2007) *Problems in SLA.* Mahwah, NJ: Erlbaum.

Loschky, L. and Bley-Vroman, R. (1993) Grammar and Task-Based Methodology. In G. Crookes and S.M. Gass (eds) *Task and Language Learning: Integrating Theory and Practice* (pp. 121–165). Clevedon: Multilingual Matters.

Mackey, A. (1999) Input, interaction, and second language development: An empirical study of question formation in ESL. *Studies in Second Language Acquisition* 21, 557–587.

Mackey, A., Abbuhl, R. and Gass, S.M. (2012) Interactionist approach. In S.M. Gass and A. Mackey (eds) *The Routledge Handbook of Second Language Acquisition* (pp. 7–23). Routledge.

McDonough, K. and Sunitham, W. (2009) Collaborative dialogue between Thai EFL learners during self-access computer activities. *TESOL Quarterly* 43, 231–254.

Mercer, S. and Dörnyei, Z. (2020) *Engaging Learners in Contemporary Classrooms.* Cambridge: Cambridge University Press.

Mosher, R. and McGowan, B. (1985) Assessing student engagement in secondary schools: Alternative conceptions, strategies of assessing, and instruments, unpublished paper, accessed 18 June 2019. http://eric.ed.gov.

Payne, J.S. and Whitney, P.J. (2002) Developing L2 oral proficiency through synchronous CMC: Output, working memory, and interlanguage development. *CALICO Journal* 20 (1), 7–32.

Philp, J. and Duchesne, S. (2016) Exploring engagement in tasks in the language classroom. *Annual Review of Applied Linguistics* 36, 50–72.

Phung, L. (2017) Task preference, affective response, and engagement in L2 use in a US university context. *Language Teaching Research* 21, 751–766.

Plonsky, L. and Oswald, F.L. (2014) How big is 'Big'? Interpreting effect sizes in L2 research. *Language Learning* 64, 878–912.

Reschly, A.L. and Christenson, S.L. (2012) Jingle, jangle, and conceptual haziness: Evolution and future directions of the engagement construct. In S.L. Christenson, A.L. Reschly and C. Wylie (eds) *Handbook of Research on Student Engagement* (pp. 3–19). New York: Springer.

Révész, A. (2011) Task complexity, focus on L2 constructions, and individual differences: A classroom-based study. *The Modern Language Journal* 95, 162–181.

Ryan, J. and Lafford, B. (1992) The acquisition of lexical meaning in a study abroad environment: *Ser y estar* and the Granada experience. *Hispania* 75, 714–722.

Salaberry, R. (2000) L2 morphosyntactic development in text-based computer-mediated communication. *Computer Assisted Language Learning* 13, 5–27

Schmidt, R. (2001) Attention. In P. Robinson (ed.) *Cognition and Second Language Instruction* (pp. 3–32). Cambridge: Cambridge University Press.

Smith, B. (2004) Computer-mediated negotiated interaction and lexical acquisition. *Studies in Second Language Acquisition* 26, 365–398.

Storch, N. (2008) Metatalk in a pair work activity: Level of engagement and implications for language development. *Language Awareness* 17, 95–114.

Storch, N. and Wigglesworth, G. (2010) Learners' processing, uptake and retention of corrective feedback on writing: Case studies. *Studies in Second Language Acquisition* 32, 303–334.

Svalberg, A.M.L. (2009) Engagement with language: Interrogating a construct. *Language Awareness* 18, 242–258.

Svalberg, A.M.L. (2012) Language awareness in language learning and teaching: A research agenda. *Language Teaching* 45, 376–388.

Swain, M. (2005) The output hypothesis: Theory and research. In E. Hinkel (ed.) *Handbook on Research in Second Language Teaching and Learning* (pp. 471–84). Mahwah, NJ: Lawrence Erlbaum.

Swain, M. (2013) The inseparability of cognition and emotion in second language learning. *Language Teaching* 46, 195–207.

Swain, M. and Lapkin, S. (1998) Interaction and second language learning: Two adolescent French immersion students working together. *The Modern Language Journal* 82, 320–337.

Warschauer, M. (1997) Comparing face-to-face and electronic communication in the second language classroom. *CALICO Journal* 13, 7–26.

Wigglesworth, G. and Storch, N. (2012) Feedback and writing development through collaboration: A sociocultural approach. In R. Manchón (ed.) *L2 Writing Development: Multiple Perspectives* (pp. 69–100). Berlin: Mouton De Gruyter

Williams, J. (2001) The effectiveness of spontaneous attention to form. *System* 29, 325–340.

Yilmaz, Y. (2012) The relative effects of explicit correction and recasts on two target structures via two communication modes. *Language Learning* 62, 1134–1169.

Ziegler, N. (2016) Synchronous computer-mediated communication and interaction: A meta-analysis. *Studies in Second Language Acquisition* 38, 553–586.

Appendix 7.1: Post-task questionnaire

A. Task Preferences

(1) How long do you think the face-to-face task took? _____ minutes

(2) How long do you think the chat task took? _____ minutes

(3) Which mode (i.e. face-to-face or via messenger) did you **prefer**?
   a) I preferred completing the task face-to-face with my partner
   b) I preferred completing the task with my partner via chat
   c) I did not prefer one mode to the other

(4) Did you feel like you **learned** more in one of the modes?
   a) I feel like I learned more completing the task via chat
   b) I feel like I learned more completing the task face-to-face
   c) I don't think I learned more in one mode versus another

(5) What were the **best and worst aspects** of completing the task **face-to-face**? Please explain in detail. _____

_____

_____

_____

_____

_____

(6) What were the **best and worst aspects** of completing the task **via chat**? Please explain in detail. _____

_____
_____
_____
_____

(7) Please choose three adjectives to describe your experience completing the task **face-to-face**:
a) _____ b) _____ c) _____

(8) Please choose three adjectives to describe your experience completing the task **via chat**:
a) _____ b) _____ c) _____

(9) What do you think we were investigating in the **face-to-face** task? Please explain.

_____
_____
_____

(10) What do you think we were investigating in the **chat** task? Please explain.

_____
_____
_____

(11) Did you learn anything from this study? _____

_____
_____
_____

(12) What is your opinion about Spanish practice in **person** and via **chat**?

_____
_____
_____

(13) How was it interacting with your partner in **face-to-face**? Please explain what you remember most from your interactions. _____

_____
_____
_____

(14) How was it interacting with your partner in **chat**? Please explain what you remember most from your interactions. _____

_____

_____

_____

_____

B. Computer Use

(1) Please indicate how much time you do each computer activity per week in English.
   a) E-mail _____ hrs/wk
   b) Chat _____ hrs/wk
   c) Social networking (Facebook, Twitter, etc.) _____ hrs/wk
   d) Word processing _____ hrs/wk
   e) Other: _____ _____ hrs/wk
(2) Please indicate how much time you do each computer activity per week in Spanish.
   a) E-mail _____ hrs/wk
   b) Chat _____ hrs/wk
   c) Social networking (Facebook, Twitter, etc.) _____ hrs/wk
   d) Word processing _____ hrs/wk
   e) Other: _____ _____ hrs/wk

C. Biographical and Background Information

(1) Participant name: _____ Net ID: _____
   @ [university name].edu
(2) Native language: _____ Dialect (if applicable): _____
(3) What year in school are you?
   Freshman   Sophomore   Junior   Senior   Graduate
(4) What is/are your current major(s)/minor(s): _____
(5) What other languages have you studied and for how many semesters?
   Language: _____ Number of semesters: _____
   Language: _____ Number of semesters: _____
   Language: _____ Number of semesters: _____
(6) Why are you taking Spanish? Please circle all reasons that apply.
   a) Career: _____
   b) Fun
   c) Speak with friend/significant other
   d) Requirement
   e) Study abroad
   f) Other: _____

(7) What classes have you taken in Spanish?

_____

_____

_____

_____

_____

(8) Have you ever lived abroad in a Spanish speaking country? If so, for what purpose, where, when and for how long? (Please include study abroad experience.)

_____

_____

_____

_____

_____

Please return the completed questionnaire to the researchers. Thank you for your participation!

Appendix 7.2: Examples of FTF and SCMC cognitive engagement

FTF

Participant:	*¿Cómo se llama esta cosa?* (motions with hands) ← **LRE, hand motion** 'How do you say this thing'
Interlocutor:	*El mostrador* 'The countertop'
Participant:	*El mostrador, si sigues el mostrador arriba de, encima de hay la cosa que si calentar pan* ← **Modified output** 'The countertop, if you follow the countertop above, above there is the thing that if to heat bread.'
Interlocutor:	*La tostadora* 'The toaster'
Participant:	*La tostadora. Eso es más derecha, derecho, del...* ← **Modified output** 'The toaster. That is more right, straight, from the...'

SCMC

Participant:	*y a la derecha del lavaplatos, pero encima/dentro del mostrador hay una baño para platos?* ← **LRE** 'And to the right of the dishwasher, but above/inside of the countertop there is a [incorrect feminine gender] bath for plates?'
Participant:	**un bano* ← **Self-correction** a bath [correct masculine gender]'
Interlocutor	*hay un fregadero, sí* there is a sink, yes'
Participant	*ok fregadero :) si* ← **Modified output** 'ok, sink :) yes'

8 Fake or Real Engagement – Looks can be Deceiving

Sarah Mercer, Kyle R. Talbot and
Isobel Kai-Hui Wang

Introduction

Every teacher wants their learners to be engaged, to be actively working on the task, emotionally invested and cognitively focused on it (Sinatra *et al.*, 2015). Students' engagement in the L2 classroom has been considered especially important for L2 use and development in instructional settings (Philp & Duchesne, 2016; Storch, 2008). However, in the age of distractions, this is becoming increasingly difficult. The question every language teacher asks is: how do I get my learners' attention and keep them focused on task?

In this chapter, we report on a two-stage study designed to investigate language learner engagement from the learner perspective. Stage 1 involved a series of five exploratory focus groups, which aimed to understand the quality and character of learner engagement, in particular, their perspectives on why and when they were engaged or not. An interesting finding in the analysis of these data revealed that learners sometimes consciously manipulate their behaviors in order to feign engagement in front of the teacher. This aspect of the data has important implications for practice and how teachers interpret learner behaviors, which may outwardly resemble engagement but may in fact be complete disengagement or acts of compliance as students enact the diligent learner role. Such behavior also threatens the validity of research approaches, which may rely strongly on observational data as a measure of engagement or at least behavioral engagement.

Consequently, Stage 2 of the study sought to better understand the 'fake' engagement of learners in tertiary-level English language classes through focused, in-depth interviews. The findings reveal the types of strategies learners employ but also their reported motives in doing so and how this varies across contexts, concentrating on notions of compliance and procedural versus substantive engagement (Nystrand & Gamoran, 1991; Shernoff, 2013). As teachers and researchers, it is imperative that we distinguish between fake and real engagement. This study provides insights into this under-researched yet incredibly important aspect of learner engagement.

Literature Review

Defining engagement

Engagement is a key factor in addressing low achievement, student boredom and high dropout rates (Fredricks, 2014), and has been demonstrated to be highly predictive of achievement-related outcomes (Fredricks *et al.*, 2004). Engagement is widely accepted as being a multidimensional construct, which comprises three main dimensions: *behavioral* (active participation), *cognitive* (thoughtful mental investment) and *affective* (willingness and emotional responses) (Fredricks *et al.*, 2004) (see also Chapter 2 by Sang & Hiver, this volume). It is argued that these three dimensions are not always simultaneously activated to the same degree (Trowler, 2010). In other words, a student may be cognitively engaged but not necessarily affectively engaged, or they may be behaviorally engaged but not deeply cognitively engaged. However, as Appleton *et al.* (2008) note, while scholars tend to agree on the multidimensionality of engagement, there remains inconsistency about which dimensions to include, although typically, there seems to be a blend of both psychological and behavioral components (Finn & Zimmer, 2012). Alternative definitions include additional components such as agentic engagement (Reeve, 2012) or social engagement (Svalberg, 2009). For the purposes of this chapter, we see engagement (and all aspects of psychology) as being fundamentally socially embedded and contextually defined. We thus conceptualize language learning engagement as having three interrelated subcomponents including cognitive, affective and behavioral (including social) elements.

The behavioral component of engagement

A defining feature of engagement is the notion that it involves *active participation* and *involvement* in certain behaviors (Mercer & Dörnyei, 2020). As Skinner *et al.* (2008: 778) explain, the 'core construct, most prototypical of engagement, is behavioral participation in the classroom.' This notion of active participation is one of the main ways engagement differs from motivation. As Reschly and Christenson (2012: 14) explain, 'motivation represents intention and engagement is action.' Skinner and Pitzer (2012) explain the importance of the activity underlying student engagement, emphasizing that without action, without engagement, it will be hard, if not impossible, for actual, meaningful learning to take place.

For a student to be engaged, Schlechty (2011: 14) writes that four components need to be present: attentiveness to the task, commitment to the task, persistence on the task even in the face of difficulties, and, finally, that the task is perceived as being meaningful and valuable. In his view, a student could be attentive to a given task and also find it meaningful, but not necessarily engaged if they lacked commitment and voluntary persistence. As he stresses, on-task behavior is not the same as engagement. Instead, he notes that there are different forms of engagement and involvement in tasks and school life. He proposes that 'authentic' engagement (as he formerly termed it) is what most educators are striving for where learners are genuinely interested, focused on task, persisting voluntarily and finding meaning and value in the task (Schlechty, 2011). However, he notes that there are other forms of classroom involvement that may at first sight be confused with engagement but which are clearly not: strategic compliance (doing what is expected or required), ritual compliance (doing the minimum required to avoid negative consequences), retreatism (causing no problems as long as not forced to comply) and rebellion (refusing to comply and actively diverting attention elsewhere) (Schlechty, 2011). In most of these scenarios, students may appear to be engaged, but, in reality, they may be thinking about another class, daydreaming, or just going through the motions to appease the teacher. This ties closely to the notion of 'studenting' (Liljedahl, 2019) which refers to the default behaviors students are involved in (e.g. figuring out how to get certain grades, 'beating the system', dealing with boredom so that it is not obvious to teachers) and the relative contribution such behaviors make to their learning.

The implication of these models and definitions is that for engagement to be 'authentic' and for it to lead to genuine, deep and meaningful learning, it needs to comprise multiple dimensions and certainly not just behavior. We need to understand how learners are psychologically thinking and feeling about their task and the degree of volition underlying their participation and commitment to the task. As Shernoff (2013: 49, emphasis in original) explains, 'highly engaged learners are just as identifiable as disengaged ones in terms of associated behavioral patterns, and yet their most distinguishing qualities are *internal*, both emotional and cognitive in nature'. In other words, appearances can be deceptive. 'Authentic' engagement involves congruence between the internal and external states and expressions of engagement. 'Fake' engagement is reflected in behaviors that are made, consciously or unconsciously, by learners to achieve an outside appearance of being attentive and on-task; however, in reality, their internal states, are not congruent and, for diverse motives, they may be complying or just merely pretending compliance.

Engagement in language learning

While the notion of engagement has been recognized as an important feature of successful language learning in a number of studies (e.g. Dincer *et al.*, 2019; Oga-Baldwin & Nakata, 2017; Philp & Duchesne, 2016; Phung, 2017; Sanaoui, 1995; Svalberg, 2009), there remains relatively limited empirical research on learners' engagement in language learning, especially when compared to the wealth and breadth of research on learner motivation. Indeed, Mercer and Dörnyei (2020: 5) believe that, 'the high level of interest in motivation has "stolen the show" and diverted attention away from engagement.' In language teaching, especially in communicative contexts, a key notion of pedagogical approaches is 'learning-by-doing,' which means that a language cannot be learned without using it – here engagement is key. To communicate, to learn the language by using it, the individual must be actively engaged in that process. Yet, given the increasing problems in keeping learners' attention and ensuring genuine on-task behavior, the construct of engagement has become more critically important to understand than ever before (Mercer & Dörnyei, 2020).

Method

Context and participants

The site of this study is an Austrian university. To recruit participants for the study, emails were sent to all students at the university who were enrolled in English language courses. The email explained that the research team was interested in speaking to students about their

Table 8.1 Focus group biodata

Focus group No.	Pseudonym	Semester of Eng. studies	Second subject
FG 1	Becky	7th	Philosophy & Psychology
	Joanna	7th	Mathematics
	Jenny	9th	Spanish
FG 2	Bill	3rd	French
	Susan	7th	Religion
	Anna	11th	German
FG 3	Jon	10th	Religion
	Claudia	12th	Literature
	Julia	3rd	History
FG 4	Lukas	9th	History
	Laura	8th	German
	Hannah	9th	German
FG 5	Lucy	5th	Italian
	Jane	7th	German
	Milena	11th	Spanish

Table 8.2 Interview biodata

Interview No.	Pseudonym	Age	Second subject	Semester of Eng. studies
Interview 1	Fion	31	Unknown	4th
Interview 2	Tina	27	Health	Unknown
Interview 3	Cathy	19	Spanish	4th
Interview 4	Niki	21	Biology	4th
Interview 5	Sam	23	Psychology	10th
Interview 6	May	31	History	3rd
Interview 7	Lisa	35	Chemistry	14th

perspectives and experiences in their English language lessons. In sum, we talked to 22 students. Fifteen of these students took part in Stage 1, which were focus groups of three students each (see Table 8.1). In Stage 2, seven additional volunteer students participated in in-depth, semi-structured interviews (see Table 8.2).

Stage 1 – Focus groups

Rationale for focus groups

Cyr (2016: 235) explains that in a focus group, '[s]pecific interactions or moments in an extended conversation may uncover surprising and unexpected reactions to a question. They may, therefore, spark new ideas about the phenomenon under consideration.' As the goal of this project was to explore the quality and character of student engagement with a specific focus on why language students were engaged or not engaged in their English language lessons, we utilized focus groups as a means to try and reveal such potentially unexpected and/or novel information.

Focus group protocol design

A focus group protocol was designed to organize each of the focus group discussions. This protocol was designed with four sections taking inspiration for the questions and prompts from survey tools and literature (Darr, 2012; Fredricks, 2014). The four sections consisted of: (1) general/contextual/school-related engagement (e.g. 'What does it feel like to be a student at this university?'); (2) engagement in English classes (e.g. 'In what situations do you fully focus your attention in class?'); (3) cognitive engagement (e.g. 'What types of activities in your English classes do you find especially interesting and why?'); and (4) Emotional engagement (e.g. 'Do your English classes usually put you in a good mood? Why/why not?'). The protocol consisted of 15 questions in total. The questions were primarily designed to be open-ended in order to explore similar engagement-related themes across all discussions.

Procedure

Five focus groups were conducted between December 2017 and January 2018. Focus groups were conducted and recorded by two members of the research team. They were transcribed by one member of the research team with content analysis in mind. Whereas some grammatical errors and normal speech markers were not transcribed, extended silences and laughter were marked when deemed significant. Each question from the protocol was printed on an individual piece of paper. The researcher would place a question in the center of the table between the student participants to allow them to discuss with minimal researcher intervention. Each focus group attended to all 15 questions.

Stage 2 – Individual interviews

Rationale for interviews

In this second stage of the study, one-to-one interviews were conducted with seven additional students to develop a more in-depth understanding of student engagement at the tertiary level but this time with a specific focus on an element which emerged from the analysis of the data collected in Stage 1, namely, the notion of 'fake engagement'.

Interview protocol design

The interview protocol was adapted from the focus group protocol, but also now focused in more depth on the issue of fake engagement. The protocol covered the following three main topics: (1) the participants' engagement within the university; (2) their engagement (fake or real) in English classes; and (3) their engagement in their university studies generally. The protocol consisted of 24 questions in total. The most substantial changes between the focus group protocol and interview protocol occurred in the second section related to these students' engagement in their English language classes. This section was expanded with a series of more focused questions about fake engagement in order to explore this topic in further detail. For example:

- Are there times when you don't feel like paying attention or concentrating in class? If so, do you know what causes you to feel that? What do you tend to do in such situations?
- Do you sometimes just pretend you are concentrating in class? If so, why and what do you do?
- Do you think your teacher can tell if you are paying attention or not? Why do you think this?

Procedure

The interviews were semi-structured and each one was approximately one hour in length. Seven interviews were conducted in English between May and July 2019. With the interviewees' permission, all the interviews were audio-recorded, and later transcribed by one member of the research team.

Data analysis

Data analysis for both stages of this study began with two members of the research team reading through the transcripts line-by-line and creating detailed memos. For the purposes of this chapter, only excerpts related to fake engagement were extracted from the larger transcripts of both data sets and put into the data management software Atlas.ti. These excerpts were coded thematically for when fake engagement occurred, why it occurred, what it looked like, its function, and how it may relate to the teacher and task. The first wave of coding was conducted by one researcher and then cross-checked by each other member of the main research team in turn.

Ethics

All participants for both stages of this study were contacted by email. To ensure that they were aware of how the study would proceed, they were provided an information and consent sheet about their involvement and how their data would be held, stored and protected. All participants signed a consent form. All data in this study were generated with explicit permission of the students. Data were anonymized at the point of transcription by removing any identifying names or markers in order to protect the students' identities.

Findings

The findings have been organized around our guiding questions: What does fake engagement look like? When and why do students fake their engagement? Why bother (or not) to fake engagement? We will address each question in turn with data extracts from the focus group and interview data.

What does fake engagement look like?

The first thing we wanted to know from a behavioral perspective is what fake engagement looks like in the language classroom and how teachers and/or researchers might recognize this. There are two main categories of findings – those concerned with the physical actions as well as the work-related actions that are both used to fake engagement.

Bodily display behavior

The students reported using a range of bodily display behaviors deliberately to 'fake' their engagement in the language classroom. These included eye movements, gesture and posture.

For example, students reported on how they used their eyes to convey engagement. For instance, the extract below from the focus group data details the interaction between Jenny and Becky about what they did when they were not engaged but still trying to display that they were actively involved:

Extract 1

Jenny:	And then you just, I don't know try to focus on a point (laughs)...
Becky:	Yeah!...
Jenny:	... near the speaker, just pretend you're listening
Becky:	I tend to, yeah, I do that.
Jenny:	There is a dot that I am looking at. (Focus group)

Interestingly, another student who took part in the same focus group mentioned that a signal of being disengaged for her was also signaled by her gaze. She explained, '[i]f I can't concentrate my eyes close and I think teachers notice (others laugh) and I'm really sorry for that'.

In the interview data, three participants explicitly mentioned that they displayed a combination of eye contact, gesture and posture to make their teachers feel that they were engaged in the class. For example, Tina explained how eye contact was a way of conveying engagement, even when off task:

> Just want to make the teacher feel that what she says is important. Make her feel that I am listening. I also nod and give her eye contact, make her feel I am listening. (Tina, individual interview)

Head movement such as nodding was also identified as another indicator of fake engagement in the class from both the focus group and individual interview data. For example, in response to the question about whether these students ever consciously faked their classroom engagement, Jon explained, 'Oh god, certainly (laughter from all). If you ever see me just sitting there like this (he starts to nod) and nodding, I'm usually just thinking about whatever'. Lukas described similar behavior, 'So I just keep nodding my head, "whoah, hmm, interesting"'. His description prompted Laura to say that this nodding behavior was normal and that, 'everyone does that'.

Three students in the interviews also reported that they pretended to be engaged, interested and concentrated in the class by nodding:

> R: ... Do you try to hide the fact you distracted?
> S :   Yes, probably, I usually like to nod (laughs) like to look at the teacher. Yes, definitely, I do hide it. (Sam, individual interview)

In addition to eye movement and gesture, posture was also used by the participants as a way of displaying their engagement in the class. One student in the focus groups, Joanna, described that for her, fake engagement involved assuming her, 'thinking pose'. Joanna later described physically getting into the pose, 'So, I just took... the very concentrated thinking and writing [pose]'. It was described as physical and embodied and something that she was able to consciously enact.

Three students in the interviews also described their 'thinking pose' as a strategy for displaying supposed concentration.

> R: Is there anything you do to make you look like you're still attending the class?
> S: Looking at the teacher, my posture as well, sit still so try to represent (laughs) myself I'm not completely away. (Sam, individual interview)

Work-related actions

Apart from body display behavior, the participants also pointed out that they performed specific work-related actions, such as note-taking and reading, to feign their engagement in the class.

Pretending to take notes was identified as one way of indicating fake engagement. For example, in the focus groups, Lucy described taking notes on a different topic to class as she was prioritizing her upcoming exam over the current course.

> Like writing notes, uh, I just did like this morning. I was studying for my exam which I have very soon...So, taking notes, taking fake notes on something else. (Lucy, focus group)

In the interviews, Fion mentioned three times that she used doodling as a useful strategy for fake engagement when she was suffering from fatigue, for instance:

> R: Do you sometimes just pretend you are concentrating in class?
> F: Yes, I'm just drawing something, e.g. circles, otherwise I fall asleep, because I was just really tried so I have to do something. I don't want to do anything which uses my brain, because I'm not listening, not hear anything what the teacher says. (Fion, individual interview)

Furthermore, Cath feigned her engagement in the class by pretending to type up notes on her laptop.

> When I am using my laptop, the teacher can't really tell what I am doing. When you open your laptop, it's like a wall between you and the teacher. Most of the time, they stand in front. They don't really know what you are doing. If you don't type anything, I think they might know that you are not doing anything. (Cath, individual interview)

The students also pretended to be active participants in the language classes by reading or appearing to work on other material. Susan explained in the focus group discussion that she was more likely to use this strategy in lectures rather than other types of instruction, such as seminars:

> In lectures, I would say yes. But then I just read other stuff and it likes I'm doing stuff for this lecture, but actually I'm just doing other homework or something. (Susan, focus group)

In addition to notetaking and doodling, evidence from responses in the individual interviews showed that four students faked their engagement by using their technology and mobile devices to read and search other information on the internet:

> You have your phone and laptop with you, if I'm not interested in the course, I might check some websites to pretend to read course-related materials. If my laptop is not with me, I'm probably sitting there, and thinking about other things or drawing something on my sheet but sometimes we have to use our laptops to write, or do some research for our course. (Niki, individual interview)

When and why do students fake their engagement?

Students reported consciously using a number of strategies to behaviorally pretend to be engaged even when they were doing or thinking about completely different things. The question we then wished to explore was when and why they faked their engagement. Four main categories emerged from the analysis: Physical conditions, the teaching style, the content of the class and a number of other facets which took attention away from the class focus.

Physical conditions

Firstly, fake engagement tended to occur under a number of physical conditions either in relation to the individual students themselves, or to the classroom. Evidence from responses in both the focus groups (5 students) and student interviews (7 students) shows that the students were likely to lose concentration and display fake engagement when they felt tired or bored, or because of their mood of the day:

> I mean sometimes you, especially those times where you are kind of like so tired, and you almost fall asleep and it's not because, well of course it's kind of boring, but it also has a lot to with having lunch before, something, or just really, really, sleepy. (Jenny, focus group)

> R: Are there any other times you don't want to pay attention to the class?
> S: Tiredness for sure, if I'm hungry, sometimes you don't know why you're annoyed. There is no real reason but some days you just do not work out. (Sam, individual interview)

In the interview data, Tina and Cath also mentioned that some of their English language classes were held in the basement of the building and they highlighted that environmental factors were likely to influence their attention and engagement, such as lighting and air quality:

R: What conditions or factors make it harder for you to pay attention in class?

T: I think the room is very important, the environment. Some classes are in the basement. It's not good.

R: Do you mean the lighting in the basement is not good?

T: Yes, the lighting, the air. (Tina, individual interview)

Teaching style

The lecture format was especially problematic for sustaining engagement and attention. It seemed to be a key reason which leads learners to enact 'fake' engagement. In Jon's words in the focus group, 'After about 30–40 minutes my concentration just peters off and then just takes some time until I can ramp it up again…90 minutes is just too long to constantly listen to class'.

In the interviews, the delivery style, in particular the amount of teacher talk and types of student involvement, were also highlighted as problematic. Fion, Tina and Sam all stated that they became disengaged in the lesson due to excessive teacher talk and passively listening to lectures:

R: So what are the moments you can't pay attention anymore? What triggers that?

I: I guess it's just really long, really long class time, not being able to be active myself, not being able to be active something. If there's no response from students, I'm more likely to switch off a little bit.

R: So very front transmission model

I: Yes, if I have to be passive, then it can make me switch off a little bit. (Sam, individual interview)

The ability to actively participate was a key issue which was also exacerbated, for example, through seating arrangements. Both Tina and Cath pointed out that setting up with rows of chairs facing forward toward the teacher limited their mobility and participation in tasks, prompting them to disengage.

R: So what conditions or factors make it easier for you to pay attention in class?

C: When we have tasks to do, when we have to talk to each other, that's really helpful. Also it's more than a lecture, you have tasks to do, sometimes we were asked to stand up and walk around, this is really helpful, and that's really wakening.

R: What conditions or factors make it harder for you to pay attention in class?

C: En…the organization of the class, just in rows, sit like in school, and the university hall where the teacher just stands in front, tells you one and a half hours about certain topics. This is very hard to concentrate. (Cath, individual interview)

Nevertheless, Sam commented in his interview that seating in rows facing the front of the class could allow students to face the teacher directly rather than other students, and therefore could force students to stay concentrated, even though this type of seating arrangement might not facilitate interaction between students:

> I think at the university how the tables form definitely makes a huge difference, because in some rooms there is a U. It can sometimes have positive sides and negative sides. If you're sitting on this side…facing other students, it happens easily that you look at them doing. It's really hard. The rows often schools use is calming, is not engaging, but again everybody facing the front, something like lectures, it's easy to focus. It depends on the setting… (Sam, individual interview)

Content

Evidence from responses in both the focus groups (three students) and individual interviews (six students) suggests that student engagement at the class level also depended on the content of the course. As Fion reported in her interview:

> **R:** Do you think if your interests also affect how you engage in the class?
> **F:** Yes, absolutely. For example, Linguistics, we have to analyze the language, how we use it. Oh my god, this is amazing. I really enjoy it. I love it. I engage a lot in the class as well, because I'm really interested in this subject. By contrast, I don't engage that much in general English classes, to be honest, because some of them are a bit boring, because I've studied English grammar since school. I know which answer is the correct one. (Fion, individual interview)

Four other interview participants also stressed that they would disengage and feign engagement when they were not personally interested in the subject or topic, especially if they felt the content was not relevant to their future life or examinations. As Fion explained, 'Sometimes if I notice the stuff I have already known or it's irrelevant to me or to the exam, then ok my mind can wander'. In the focus groups, three students also stated that they would disengage and fake engagement when they felt a course was repeating what they already knew or if they felt there was nothing to be gained:

> Yeah, but that's why I do other stuff (laughs). If you have to be there because it's mandatory but you know there is nothing you can get out, and all the colleagues to your right already do other stuff, at some point you will start to, just study, do homework or whatever, but you're not listening anymore. At least for me it's like that. (Susan, focus group)

Furthermore, in response to the question about whether they ever got so absorbed in a task in English that you didn't notice time passing by, five students who participated in the individual interviews commented that they were more likely to become absorbed when the content being taught was new, meaningful and practical:

> When the new content is introduced, I am normally very concentrated, feel time pass quickly. When the teacher teaches something I really want to know for a long time, e.g. how to write a good introduction, and how to structure an essay, that's something I want to know for a long time. I think it depends on the content. (Tina, individual interview)

Other attentional priorities

Four students from the interviews and three students from the focus groups also described some specific instances in which they had been distracted by other priorities on their attentional resources when they pretended to be actively engaged in tasks during a lesson. For example, Sam reported prioritizing a major exam over the current lesson. She pretended to pay attention to the class, but in fact she was revising for her upcoming exam:

> **R:** Can you think of any specific instances you have been distracted, not engaged while you pretended that you were, but you were doing something completely different?
>
> **S:** I had a very important exam the next day... but we were sitting in the seminar, in my head, I was revising everything. I was thinking of something completely else, but I was still in the class. So definitely, because I got very nervous about the exam, it's a really important exam. (Sam, individual interview)

In the interviews, May also stressed that studying at university while being a parent was challenging, and she found it difficult to balance between family life and academic responsibilities. Sometimes, she was mentally focusing on family issues and not the class she was sat in:

> I probably look at my schedule or maybe a paper I have to work on at the moment, or check my dates or appointments, sometimes I have to text my mum or my husband. Usually I have to do the administrative things. (May, individual interview)

In the focus groups, Susan also mentioned that other students could be a distraction. Specifically, three students in the interviews reported instances when they were distracted by other students' use of digital devices for off-task activities. As Lisa explained,

> **R:** Did you get any distractions?
>
> **L:** Yes... when you have classes in the basement, you can see all the people walking by. That can be distracting. And laptops can be distracting too, because you can always see what other students are doing on their laptops. That's not always course-related. When you sit next to them, you can see everything. That's really a distraction, because people often do other things on laptops all the time, all the time ↓

> **R:** Do you have any strategies for managing distractions?
>
> **L:** I tried to sit on the other side...But if I see other people do other things on their laptops, it can be really distracting because I just read and see what they doing. (Lisa, individual interview)

Why bother (or not) to fake engagement?

So far, our data have revealed when and why the students feigned their engagement in their English language classes and what this looks like in terms of behavior. In this final findings section, we delve deeper into the issue of why the students bothered or not to fake their engagement. There are two main drives – the first is social norms and the second is to actively and consciously want to please the teacher.

Social expectations/norms

Most of the students who participated either in the focus groups or the individual interviews did not view faking their engagement as problematic. For example, students in the focus group discussion interacted candidly about the function of what their displayed fake engagement seemingly accomplished.

> **Lucy:** So, taking notes, taking fake notes on something else.
>
> **Milena:** Why not? I think it's like, you're always responsible for your own learning and...
>
> **Jane:** ... and so you're not disrupting or anything...
>
> **Lucy:** ... no...
>
> **Milena:** ... and so why not? I mean I...
>
> **Jane:** ... saving time.
>
> **Lucy:** Trying to survive.
>
> **Milena:** I was always glad when I had a class on Monday which wasn't so difficult because then I organized my whole week like (others laugh). (focus group)

For these students, they felt it was non-disruptive and merely created time for them to catch up and to 'survive' student life by using their class time for other more pressing things. As an anonymous reviewer of this paper suggested, procedural engagement may in fact be a default feature of many academic settings where there are multiple, simultaneous competing demands for learners' attention. The students also viewed it as an act of politeness, respect and consideration for others to fake their engagement:

> I think it's a kind of polite way...You make extra effort and you show respect to the teacher and other students as well. Other students they come here to study. Although I don't care, you can't just disturb others. I think it's really impolite to sit in the class, look at your phone, and you talk to your neighbors. Everyone is working, and you distract the students and your teacher. (Fion, individual interview)

When I do that, I just do it to kind of be polite because sometimes we aren't always listening the professor will just look for eye contact, and once he has your eye contact, he won't let go (all laugh). (Lucas, focus group)

To please the teacher

Apart from politeness, the students tried to hide their disengagement because they wanted to please their teacher, although the reasons for this varied. For example, Cath explained that her teachers preferred the students to take notes while they were listening rather than sitting passively. She took fake notes simply to satisfy the teacher because she did not want to offend them – a seeming act of compliance but not one that was congruent with how she felt.

Sometimes they ask why we don't write down what they say, and they hate their students just sit so sometimes I just pretend I am writing something, even though you know these things are not useful...So you just pretend to write something down to satisfy the teachers. (Cath, individual interview)

Niki and her fellow students reported having to feign their engagement to satisfy the teacher, as the teacher constantly stressed that their classroom participation affected their grades so they faked engagement for fear of a bad grade, again merely complying under perceived pressure:

We're trying enough to satisfy the teacher. We're participating in the activities although we're not interested and we don't enjoy, because the teacher gives us a lot of pressure that we have to participate. Especially, in the class we really have to participate because we are quite small groups, she knows everyone. She always tells us that she knows exactly when we're not participating. It will influence our grade in bad ways. (Niki, individual interview)

However, Niki also explained that she would not be upset if her fake engagement was detected by her teacher. She felt that if she was asked directly, she was mature and self-confident enough to let her teacher know why she was not engaged:

I would be honest with the professor if he or she asks me whether I'm concentrating or not, I would be confident to say I'm not because it's difficult for me to concentrate, because I'm not interested in the topic, or maybe I even say that I just don't get on well with him or her, because we are all at the age we can talk about that. But I have to admit that I did experience the situation when I pretend I'm concentrating in class, but if the teacher asks me, I probably would be honest with the professor. (Niki, individual interview)

This suggests that, especially with the learners at tertiary level like those in this study, although many of these students conform to social norms and fake their engagement so as not to disturb their peers or be openly disrespectful to the teacher, if pressed, they might reveal their lack of engagement, given their age, experience and the fact they are voluntarily attending classes as university students. However, the pressure to appease the teacher, to comply and ensure a good grade were also reasons to pretend to be engaged, even though this was not necessarily the case.

Discussion

In this chapter, we have explored the notion of 'fake engagement', which refers to the behavioral actions that are deliberately enacted by the learners in order to create the impression of engagement in instances when, in fact, learners are thinking about or doing something completely different to the task at hand, or merely complying to pressures to meet teacher expectations. Our findings serve as a salutary warning about the use of observational data for the investigation of engagement (see also Chapter 5 by Zhou *et al.*, this volume). What can be observed is only part of the story and may well be deliberately misleading. Nystrand and Gamoron (1991) make the distinction between *procedural engagement* (going through the motions of school) and *substantive engagement* (a sustained commitment to and involvement with academic work). As they caution, 'It is exceedingly difficult to distinguish between procedural and substantive engagement simply by observing students or asking them what they think about in class' (Nystrand & Gamoron, 1991: 5). As noted at the outset, engagement is multidimensional and the behavioral component is a key component; however, for authentic engagement, learners need to also be emotionally and cognitively invested in the task at hand. Engagement must be conceived as both a psychological as well as behavioral construct (Finn & Zimmer, 2012).

These data also provide several warnings and lessons for educators about their practice in respect to engagement. Not only do teachers need to be cautious when interpreting learner behaviors, but it is important to reflect on the notion of compliance and the worrying implications of this for education at all levels. It appears that learners will project an image of being engaged and on-task to their teacher and peers for various reasons including social norms, respect for teacher and peers, and also fear of a bad grade. Shernoff (2013) warns against such passive compliance to the teacher as an authority figure and explains that compliance must never be confused with genuine engagement for learning. This means that fake engagement may not just be off-task as was prevalent in our data, but it may also be the kind of busyness on task in which learners are merely 'going through the motions' in order to satisfy teachers and comply to schooling norms and expectations such as in Niki's data (Shernoff, 2013). Such actions cannot be truly thought of as 'authentic engagement' either.

From our data, we conclude there are a number of key lessons to be learned in practical terms. Firstly, the physical conditions of the class (e.g. lighting, temperature etc.) and the learners' own physical well-being can impact on their ability and willingness to engage. If a student is physically or mentally uncomfortable in class, then it will be much harder for them to engage. As such, attending to the classroom environment is important as well as building in 'brain breaks' to enable students to recharge their batteries when getting tired and weary (Weslake & Christian, 2015). The second big caution in these data against the use of lecture formats of instruction. Lectures remain widely used in tertiary settings. Yet, there is ample evidence in this study and beyond (Risko *et al.*, 2012; Young *et al.*, 2009) that lectures are damaging for learner engagement and attention. Instead, a more active-form of teaching is likely to engage learners where learners are not passively listening but are involved in action – the essence of engagement. The third caution for educators is related to the notion of value and relevance of what is being learned. Expectancy-value theory (Wigfield & Eccles, 2000) emphasizes how the perceived value of an activity affects engagement. Even at tertiary level, learners appear to make decisions about the perceived value or utility of what is being presented and it may be useful for educators to make the real-world relevance of tasks explicit or deliberately encourage learners to find and make their own connections. The final practical caution from the data is that learners have lives beyond our language classes and quite simply, sometimes they may be distracted because they need time and support for other aspects of their lives. If learners are disengaged or faking their engagement, it can be valuable to find out from learners why and if they need additional support for their commitments beyond the class at hand. Given that this study was conducted with students at one Austrian university, it would be worthwhile to explore if these bodily displays and other fake engagement behaviors found in this study are similar or different in other contexts. Future studies could perhaps include students from various contexts and educational levels including also possible a cross-cultural design.

Conclusion

Fake engagement is a natural part of life and many of us will recognize ourselves in these data and can think of occasions when we have also pretended to be engaged although we were not. Bothering to fake engagement may be a marker of politeness; however, in educational contexts, we must also question the act of compliance that this represents. Although these data imply that educators may often not be aware of 'fake' engagement, if we are, we must then reflect critically to consider why learners are faking their engagement, its implications about their response to our teaching but also what it implies about the power dynamics in class. An interesting dimension to this study is that many of the behaviors evinced in the data were not specifically relevant to language learning and teaching, although this was the context for the research and focus of the questions. Rather, these are issues that can affect any educator regardless of the subject they may be teaching. In a communicative language classroom with active participatory activities, the hope is that fake engagement would be less of a problem; however, even in such contexts, the risk of students faking their engagement remains. Especially in respect to L2 learning, given the slow and incremental nature of language acquisition processes, we might argue that engagement in such settings can be particularly challenging when it is required repeatedly and over time.

In instructed second language acquisition (SLA), we have been much slower than other subject domains in empirically seeking to understand the nature of engagement in language learning and teaching contexts specifically. Now there is an urgent and somewhat belated need for a program of research to understand what factors can facilitate or inhibit language learner engagement, especially domain-specific and context-specific determinants. Research must also critically learn how to differentiate between 'authentic engagement' that leads to genuine, meaningful, deep learning and 'fake engagement', which may simply reflect compliant 'busyness' without any connection to real learning or which may be masking complete disengagement as the student focuses on something else entirely unrelated to the learning objectives of the class.

It is increasingly difficult for educators to maintain learner engagement in the face of decreasing learner attention and an increasing range of distractions (Barkley, 2010). However, engagement is perhaps one of the most desirable goals for language teaching at present as the key to actual learning progress. As such, language learning engagement needs to become a priority for researchers who must remain cautious about how they interpret any observational data – engagement must also be understood from the psychology of the learners and not just through their actions alone.

References

Appleton, J., Christenson, S. and Furlong, M. (2008) Student engagement with school: Critical conceptual and methodological issues of the construct. *Psychology in the Schools* 45 (5), 369–386.

Barkley, E.F. (2010) *Student Engagement Techniques: A Handbook for College Faculty.* San Francisco, CA: Jossey-Bass.

Cyr, J. (2016) The pitfalls and promise of focus groups as a data collection method. *Sociological Methods & Research* 45 (2), 231–259.

Darr, C.W. (2012) Measuring student engagement: The development of a scale for formative use. In S.L. Christenson, A.L. Reschly and C. Wylie (eds) *Handbook of Research on Student Engagement* (pp. 707–723). New York: Springer.

Dincer, A., Yeşilyurt, S., Noels, K. and Vargas Lascano, D. (2019) Self-determination and classroom engagement of EFL learners: A mixed-methods study of the self-system model of motivational development. *SAGE Open* 9 (2), 1–15.

Finn, J.D. and Zimmer, K.S. (2012) Student engagement: What is it? Why does it matter? In S.L. Christenson, A.L. Reschly and C. Wylie (eds) *Handbook of Research on Student Engagement* (pp. 97–131). New York: Springer.

Fredricks, J.A. (2014) *Eight Myths of Student Disengagement: Creating Classrooms of Deep Learning.* Los Angeles: Corwin.

Fredricks, J., Blumenfeld, P. and Paris, A. (2004) School engagement: Potential of the concept, state of the evidence. *Review of Educational Research* 74 (1), 59–109.

Liljedahl, P. (2019) A commentary: Accounting-of and accounting-for the engagement of teachers and teaching. In M. Hannula, G. Leder, F. Morselli, M. Vollstedt and Q. Zhang (eds) *Affect and Mathematics Education.* ICME-13 Monographs. Cham: Springer.

Mercer, S. and Dörnyei, Z. (2020) *Engaging Language Learners in Contemporary Classrooms.* Cambridge: Cambridge University Press.

Nystrand, M. and Gamoran, A. (1991) Instructional discourse, student engagement, and literature achievement. *Research in the Teaching of English* 25 (3), 261–290.

Oga-Baldwin, W.L.Q. and Nakata, Y. (2017) Engagement, gender, and motivation: A predictive model for Japanese young language learners. *System* 65, 151–163.

Philp, J. and Duchesne, S. (2016) Exploring engagement in tasks in the language classroom. *Annual Review of Applied Linguistics* 36, 50–72.

Phung, L. (2017) Task preference, affective response, and engagement in L2 use in a US university context. *Language Teaching Research* 21 (6), 751–766.

Reeve, J. (2012) A self-determination theory perspective on student engagement. In S.L. Christenson, A.L. Reschly and C. Wylie (eds) *Handbook of Research on Student Engagement* (pp. 149–172). New York: Springer.

Reschly, A.L. and Christenson, S.L. (2012) Jingle, jangle, and conceptual haziness: Evolution and future directions of the engagement construct. In S.L. Christenson, A.L. Reschly and C. Wylie (eds) *Handbook of Research on Student Engagement* (pp. 3–19). New York: Springer.

Risko, E., Anderson, N., Sarwal, A., Engelhardt, M. and Kingstone, A. (2012) Everyday attention: Variation in mind wandering and memory in a lecture. *Applied Cognitive Psychology* 26 (2), 234–242.

Sanaoui, R. (1995) Adult learners' approaches to learning vocabulary in second languages. *The Modern Language Journal* 79 (1), 15–28.

Schlechty, P. (2011) *Engaging Students: The Next Level of Working on the Work.* San Francisco: Jossey-Bass.

Shernoff, D.J. (2013) *Optimal Learning Environments to Promote Student Engagement.* New York: Springer.

Sinatra, G.M., Heddy, B.C. and Lombardi, D. (2015) The challenges of defining and measuring student engagement in science. *Educational Psychologist* 50 (1), 1–13.

Skinner, E.A., Furrer, C., Marchand, G. and Kindermann, T. (2008) Engagement and disaffection in the classroom: Part of a larger motivational dynamic? *Journal of Educational Psychology* 100 (4), 765–781.

Skinner, E.A. and Pitzer, J.R. (2012) Developmental dynamics of student engagement, coping, and everyday resilience. In S.L. Christenson, A.L. Reschly and C. Wylie (eds) *Handbook of Research on Student Engagement* (pp. 21–44). New York: Springer.

Storch, N. (2008) Metatalk in a pair work activity: Level of engagement and implications for language development. *Language Awareness* 17 (2), 95–114.

Svalberg, A.M.L. (2009) Engagement with language: Interrogating a construct. *Language Awareness* 18 (3–4), 242–258.

Trowler, V. (2010) *Student Engagement Literature Review.* York: Higher Education Academy.

Weslake, A. and Christian, B.J. (2015) Brain breaks: Help or hindrance? *Teach Collection of Christian Education* 1 (1), 38–46.

Wigfield, A. and Eccles, J.S. (2000) Expectancy–value theory of achievement motivation. *Contemporary Educational Psychology* 25 (1), 68–81.

Young, M.S., Robinson, S. and Alberts, P. (2009) Students pay attention! Combating the vigilance decrement: Combating the vigilance decrement to improve learning during lectures. *Active Learning in Higher Education* 10, 41–55.

9 The Effect of Choice on Affective Engagement: Implications for Task Design

Linh Phung, Sachiko Nakamura and Hayo Reinders

Introduction

In L2 learning, learner engagement has been recognized as 'the place where learning happens' (Svalberg, 2009: 243) and as being especially important because successful language learning requires sustained practice and use over an extended period of time (Mercer, 2019). At the core of engagement is the notion of 'energized, directed, and sustained actions' (Russell *et al.*, 2005: 225). In task-based language teaching (TBLT) in particular, there has been an increasing interest in identifying ways in which tasks can be designed and manipulated to increase learner engagement.

Conceptually, there is some consensus that engagement is a multidimensional construct consisting of behavioral, cognitive, emotional and social dimensions, which overlap and interrelate with one another (Christenson *et al.*, 2012; Philp & Duchesne, 2016). Operationally, in communicative tasks, learners can be described as engaged when they use language productively (the behavioral dimension); when there is evidence of heightened attention and involvement and persistence in achieving task goals (the cognitive dimension); when they demonstrate positive emotions and affective states, such as enjoyment and interest (the emotional dimension); and when they respond positively to peer interaction (the social dimension) (Bygate & Samuda, 2009; Egbert, 2003; Philp & Duchesne, 2016; Sato, 2017; Svalberg, 2009). This study focuses on the emotional dimension of engagement in task performance, but uses the term affective engagement to include emotions (enjoyment and anxiety) that learners experience during task performance as well as their perceptions of their own performance (focus and freedom of expression).

Aiming to increase engagement through task design and implementation, studies such as Aubrey (2017), Butler (2017), Lambert *et al.*, (2017),

Nakamura *et al.* (in press), Phung (2017) and Qiu and Lo (2017) investigated the effects of learner-generated content, choice, topic and interlocutor on learners' engagement in task performance. Perhaps unsurprisingly, these studies generally indicate that when learners have more control or choice over which tasks to perform, topics to discuss, or ideas to bring up, they are more likely to be engaged in task performance. In addition, when learners find the topics personally relevant or emotionally engaging, they are more likely to have a positive affective disposition to the task (Phung, 2017; Qiu & Lo, 2017). However, when they find the topic or task unfamiliar or perceive it as difficult or restricting, their responses to the task tend to be negative (Phung, 2017).

To investigate this further, we conducted a study in which learners were asked to complete two decision-making tasks, one with more and the other with less constrained choices. We then examined the effect of choice on the four dimensions (behavioral, cognitive, social and emotional) of task engagement (Nakamura *et al.*, in press). While that study found a positive effect of choice on engagement based on various measures of the four dimensions of engagement previously mentioned, it yielded mixed findings on emotional engagement. The participants reported having experienced higher levels of both negative (anxiety) and positive (enjoyment) emotions while being highly engaged in the task. We thus set out to conduct a further study to understand this phenomenon by (1) investigating additional affective engagement variables which were not examined in the initial study and (2) qualitatively examining the transcripts of the learners' task performance.

Choice and Engagement

Choice has been demonstrated to play a role in affecting learners' L2 engagement in tasks. A number of task-based studies have shown that when learners experience choice, in the sense of having more freedom in creating their own content for the task that they later perform, designing and playing instructional games or bringing their own proposals to a discussion, they are more likely to be engaged in performing the task (Butler, 2017; Lambert *et al.*, 2017; Phung, 2017). Butler (2017) asked Japanese children to design their own games, choose topics and decide task parameters and found that the most appealing features were challenge (various difficulty levels), storyline, fantasy and control over the progress of the game. Lambert *et al.* (2017) compared learners' engagement in narrative tasks that utilized the content from learners' actual lives and experiences versus narrative tasks with fictitious ideas and events. The study revealed that learners' behavioral, cognitive and social engagement, as measured by the amount of language production, elaboration of ideas, negotiation of meaning and backchanneling, was higher in tasks operating on the content generated by the learners than the other sets of tasks. Learners in Phung (2017) mentioned freedom to make their own choices and decisions and opportunities to create and think about their own ideas for discussion as the two main reasons for preferring one of the two tasks they performed in the study. In addition, they demonstrated a higher level of engagement in L2 use as measured by the amount of negotiation in their preferred task. These findings point to the positive role of control and/or choice in learner engagement in performing tasks.

However, not all studies investigating the effects of choice on educational outcomes, such as performance in a test after an intervention, have found positive effects (Mozgalina, 2015; Patall *et al.*, 2008). In fact, in a review of studies investigating choice, Katz and Assor (2006) suggest that choice is only motivating when the options given to learners support their needs for autonomy, competence and relatedness, three important components in self-determination theory (SDT) of motivation (Deci & Ryan, 2000). Autonomy refers to learners' need to have agency to regulate their own learning experiences and actions that align with their intrinsic interests and values. Competence refers to learners' need to have a sense of mastery and efficacy and a sense that they can influence the outcomes. Relatedness is concerned with learners' feelings of connectedness and support in their social setting (Deci & Ryan, 2000). Note that the studies cited above focused on the effect of choice on motivation, not necessarily engagement. However, it is possible that by enhancing learners' motivation, choice that supports those psychological needs is likely to move learners to active engagement (Floweray & Shraw, 2003; Mercer, 2019).

With regards to choice as a variable, Reeve *et al.* (2003) suggest that there are various types of choices and that 'action choice' (i.e. choice in work methods, pace and effort) affects self-determination and intrinsic motivation while 'options choice' (i.e. choice among mandated options) may not. In their study, participants in the action choice condition could choose what puzzle (among four, then three and then two puzzles) to solve and how much time they could spend on solving each puzzle. Participants in the options choice condition could choose among the puzzles, but were given a fixed amount of time to solve the puzzles. A control group was not given options or allowed to determine their pace of work on the puzzles. The study found that participants offered action choices reported statistically higher perceived self-determination and intrinsic motivation. This finding regarding different types of choice offers an explanation for conflicting findings regarding the effect of choice and suggests that option choices may not affect learners' experience of self-determination and intrinsic motivation to the extent that moves them to active engagement.

In this light, Nakamura *et al.* (in review) examined the effects of two levels of choice (choice among nine options given in the +constraint task or choice among options that learners themselves created in the −constraint task) on learner engagement during task performance. Nakamura *et al.*'s study is different from the Reeve *et al.* (2003) study in its focus on engagement and is similar in that the opportunity for choice in the +constraint task and –constraint task approximated options choice and action choice, respectively, in the latter study. Nakamura *et al.* found that choice had a significant effect on various measures of engagement: the number of turns (behavioral engagement), amount of negotiation and self-repair (cognitive engagement) and the number of turn overlaps (social engagement). The authors argued that these measures indicated an overall higher level of engagement in learners' performance of the –constraint task. At the same time, it yielded mixed findings on emotional engagement. Learners reported higher levels of both anxiety and enjoyment in performing the –constraint task. These findings indicate that the affective dimension of engagement and their links to choice may be more complex than they appear at first glance.

Affective Engagement

There is a consensus that research into learner engagement needs to consider the construct in its multiple dimensions: behavioral, cognitive, social and emotional. Swain (2013) argues that language learning is not only a cognitive process but an emotional one as well. However, the latter aspect has been generally neglected and needs more investigation in second language acquisition (SLA) research (Swain, 2013). In addition, Linnenbrink (2007) suggests that learners' emotions mediate the relation between motivation and engagement. Philp and Duchesne (2016) describe emotional engagement as intrinsic to, as well as constituting a facet of, engagement. These scholars all highlight the importance of emotional engagement in defining, discussing and researching engagement.

Emotional engagement in general refers to the affective nature of learners' involvement in tasks and has been defined differently in different contexts (Philp & Duchesne, 2016). Researchers have described emotional engagement in terms of learners' positive or negative emotions (enthusiasm, interest and enjoyment vs. anxiety, frustration and boredom); purposefulness, willingness and autonomy; as well as the feeling of connection to or disconnection from interlocutors during learning activities (Baralt *et al.*, 2016; Skinner *et al.*, 2009; Svalberg, 2009). This study uses the term 'affective engagement' and investigates learners' enjoyment and anxiety as well as their perceptions of focus and freedom of expression during task performance as indicators of their affective engagement. These variables were selected based on the conceptualization of emotional engagement reviewed above and their relevance in language learning as reviewed in the next sections.

Enjoyment and Anxiety

It is commonly accepted that, to be truly engaged, learners need to be emotionally invested in the task at hand instead of merely going through the motions of participating in it, reflecting a distinction that has been made by Nystrand and Gamoran (1991) between substantive engagement and procedural engagement. The importance of positive emotions such as enjoyment has been emphasized in language learning in recent years (Dewaele, 2015; Dewaele & MacIntyre, 2016). An increasing number of studies have reported positive links between enjoyment and L2 learning and performance (e.g. Dewaele *et al.*, 2018; MacIntyre & Gregersen, 2012). In describing flow, a psychological state characterized by intense focus and involvement that leads to improved engagement and performance on a task (Csikszentmihalyi, 1990), Egbert (2003) includes enjoyment as one of the characteristics of flow and includes items in her flow questionnaire to measure it. Considering the relevance of enjoyment, this study examines enjoyment as an indicator of learners' affective engagement.

Language anxiety, a feeling of tension and apprehension associated with language learning especially writing, listening and speaking, is an area that has attracted extensive research because of the complex relationship between anxiety and L2 achievement (Horwitz, 2001; MacIntyre & Gardner, 1994). Early research has found negative, neutral and even positive relationships between anxiety and L2 achievement (see Horwitz, 2001 for a review). Since then, it has been acknowledged that there are various types of anxiety with different effects on L2 performance and achievement. The situation-specific type called Foreign Language Anxiety has, in fact, been found to correlate moderately and negatively with L2 achievement as measured by course grades, teacher ratings or test scores (Horwitz, 2001). In a recent anthology on anxiety, MacIntyre (2017) describes the dynamic nature of anxiety, which interacts with other psychological processes, emotions and the specificities of the L2 situation, an insight that may direct future research.

Focused Attention

Focused or heightened attention has been an important characteristic of high engagement or flow (Egbert, 2003; Philp & Duchesne, 2016). When in flow, learners focus on the activity so intensely that they forget themselves, forget time and even forget that they are communicating in another language (Egbert, 2003). Focus is a construct of interest in this study as learners' focus during task performance may indicate a higher level of engagement (though not necessarily flow). In L2 learning, focused attention deemed beneficial for language acquisition can be of the kind directed to communicating meaning or consciously attending to and noticing language (Schmidt, 1990, 2001; Swain, 2005). Therefore, researchers investigating engagement in language learning activities see focused attention, i.e. the lack of distractions and wandering thoughts not relevant to the tasks, as an important indicator of engagement and have attempted to find evidence of it through observations or questionnaires (Aubrey, 2017; Egbert, 2003; Lambert *et al.*, 2017).

Egbert (2003) took notes of learners' behaviors during task performance using a checklist that included items relating to whether learners appeared present, looked around, checked their watch/clock, were off-task, etc. In addition, learners completed a flow questionnaire consisting of 14 Likert-scale items with three items on focus. Egbert found that, among various tasks, the task involving talking with native speakers piqued learners' curiosity and helped them to focus. In addition, they focused on both the meaning and form of the language at hand as they tried to make themselves understood, a condition argued to be conducive to language learning (e.g. Long, 1996; Schmidt, 1990; Swain, 2005). Other studies (Aubrey, 2017; Lambert *et al.*, 2017) adopted this flow questionnaire in their studies of engagement during task performance, but did not analyze the focus component of the questionnaire separately from other components in the questionnaire instrument they used or take into consideration that the rare and ephemeral state of flow might be qualitatively different from engagement, which may be more readily measured on a scale from low to high.

Self-expression

There is broad recognition in the field that communicative success and opportunities for authentic self-expression give language learners joy, satisfaction, pride and a sense of control that can affect engagement in language learning (Aubrey, 2017; Egbert, 2003; Phung, 2017; Wolf & Phung, 2019). Authentic self-expression might stem from the opportunities to interact with interlocutors who do not share the same language or culture, creating a genuine need to communicate. Aubrey (2017) investigated the effect of intercultural versus intracultural task-based interactions on learners' flow and engagement in L2 use in an English as a foreign language (EFL) context and found that intercultural contact in tasks (i.e. contact between Japanese and international students) had a significant effect on flow and the number of turns during task performance. Egbert (2003) also found that learners reported experiencing flow when they completed a task that required communication with native speakers of their target language. In addition, in a study that involved L2 learners in completing two different tasks, Phung (2017) found that learners preferred a task more when it offered them a genuine need to communicate, resulting from the differences among the participants in the study, who had different backgrounds, cultures and ideas in the discussion.

Communicative success or lack of success in English also affects learners' emotions. Wolf and Phung's (2019) study, which asked international students at a US university to report experiences with using English to listen, read, write and communicate, reported that students expressed mixed emotions toward various academic tasks and situations that required oral communication. When they experienced communicative success, they reported joy, satisfaction and pride. When they could not communicate their ideas or understand their interlocutors, they felt embarrassed and ashamed. The researchers suggested that, different from experiences with reading, writing and passive listening in English, learners' success (or lack of success) in oral communication and interactions with others greatly affected how those students felt on a daily basis. Similar experiences were reported by Haga and Reinders (forthcoming) with L2 learners experiencing strong emotions in response to negative feedback from L1 speakers. Considering these findings, the current study aimed to answer the question: Do learners report experiencing greater freedom of expression in a task with less constrained choice than in a task with more constrained choice?

Method

Participants

Twenty-four students (15 male, 9 female) majoring in engineering, science or technology at a Thai university volunteered to participate in the study. Twenty participants were in their fourth year, while two were in their third and another two were in the second year of their undergraduate studies. They were all enrolled in a semester-long academic writing course taught by the second author. Their English levels were approximately B1 or B2 on the CEFR (Common European Framework of Reference) based on their course enrollment data and the pre-course evaluation of the second author. The students had studied together in the course for two months when the study took place.

Materials

The study involved two decision-making tasks. In one, they were asked to discuss and agree on three items among the given options (+constraint). In the other, they discussed and agreed on three items among the options they themselves generated (−constraint). Specifically, working in groups of three, the learners were asked to come to an agreement on three new buildings that their university should construct to make it the number one university in the country for international students. In the +constraint task, each learner in the group was given three buildings (Learner A: counseling office, tennis court and buffet restaurant; Learner B: scholarship office, internet cafe and swimming pool; Learner C: language exchange room, sports gym and Japanese restaurant). They were then given two minutes to think about these buildings. The task involved learners in discussing these nine buildings and required them to decide on three to propose to the university. In the

−constraint task, each learner was asked to spend two minutes to come up with three buildings on their own and think about them before discussing them in their group. There was no set length of time to complete the task.

Procedure

The students were randomly assigned to eight groups of three. Four groups performed the −constraint task first while the other four groups began with the +constraint task, and three weeks later they performed the other task in order to counterbalance for performance effects. Their spoken interaction during task completion was audio-recorded. After they finished each task, learners were asked to complete a questionnaire to report their subjective responses to the tasks. The questionnaire (see Appendix 9.1) was developed by the researchers of the study based on prior research into affective responses to tasks. It used 23 six-point Likert-scale items (1 = strongly disagree, 6 = strongly agree) in six components: enjoyment (5 items), anxiety (4 items), focus (3 items), freedom of expression (4 items), task difficulty (3 items) and task familiarity (3 items). In addition, learners were asked to indicate which task they preferred and provide an explanation for their preference. Among the six questionnaire components, items measuring enjoyment (Cronbach's $\alpha = 0.85$), anxiety ($\alpha = 0.85$), focus ($\alpha = 0.75$) and task difficulty ($\alpha = 0.83$) showed acceptable internal consistency. However, items measuring freedom of expression ($\alpha = 0.56$) and task familiarity ($\alpha = 0.49$) had much lower internal consistency. These data sets were analyzed but the results were interpreted with caution. The audio-recorded interaction was transcribed by the researchers, employing the verbatim transcription method to transcribe everything produced by the students, including pauses, self-corrected/repeated words, hesitations such as 'uh' and 'um,' and the expression of emotions such as laughter.

Data analysis

Questionnaire

The average questionnaire score for each component was recorded for each learner after each task and was entered into SPSS 25 for data analysis. Descriptive statistics were generated and examined. The mean scores of task familiarity for both tasks were 4.17, indicating that learners were familiar with the content of both tasks. The mean scores of task difficulty were 3.05 and 2.92 for the −constraint and +constraint tasks, respectively, indicating a moderate level of difficulty with both tasks. These statistics reflected the researchers' intention to control learners' familiarity and difficulty with the tasks. Further analyses were conducted on the scores for enjoyment, anxiety, focus and freedom of expression. These scores were explored to see if they were distributed normally. Examination of the kurtosis and skewness scores, histograms and boxplots indicated that the data met the normality assumption. A multivariate analysis of variance (MANOVA) with post-hoc repeated measures ANOVAs was conducted on four questionnaire scores in the two conditions although the sample size was small, a limitation that will be discussed in the conclusion of the chapter. Learners' qualitative responses to the questions of which task they preferred and why were also examined to explain the findings from the questionnaire.

Transcripts

In order to examine how learners' affective engagement was manifested in the −constraint and +constraint tasks, individual learners' affective engagement scores were used to select representative transcripts. More specifically, we used the means and standard deviations of the affective scores and selected the transcripts from two groups consisting of learners with higher and lower scores on each of the affective variables (enjoyment, anxiety, focus and freedom of expression). The High Affective Engagement Group consisted of two male students (L4, L6) and one female (L5) student. The Low Affective Engagement Group consisted of two male students (L1, L3) and one female (L2) student. We closely examined these transcripts and the recording of the interactions to find incidences that best represent the manifestation of high and low affective engagement.

Results

Questionnaires

Table 9.1 displays the descriptive statistics for enjoyment, anxiety, focus and freedom of expression. On average, learners reported a higher level of enjoyment, focus, freedom of expression and anxiety in the -constraint task than the +constraint one.

MANOVA results confirmed a statistical difference in the questionnaire scores in response to the two tasks, Pillai's Trace $= 0.76$, $F(4, 20) = 15.46$, $p < 0.001$, partial eta squared $= 0.76$. Tests of within-subjects contrasts showed that learners in the −constraint condition reported a statistically higher level of enjoyment, $F(1, 23) = 10.97$, $p = 0.003$; anxiety, $F(1, 23) = 14.26$, $p < 0.001$; focus, $F(1, 23) = 52.99$, $p < 0.001$; and freedom of expression, $F(1,23) = 23.85$, $p < 0.001$. Table 9.2 shows specific inferential statistics of these six subjective responses.

The findings of these analyses indicate that learners enjoyed themselves more, but also felt more anxious doing the task with less constrained choice. In addition, they reported being more focused and experiencing greater freedom of expression during the task.

Table 9.1 Descriptive statistics for affective engagement scores

Measure	Task	Min	Max	Mean	SD
Enjoyment	−Constraint	3.00	5.80	4.64	0.74
	+Constraint	3.37	5.00	4.17	0.45
Anxiety	−Constraint	3.37	5.00	4.17	0.45
	+Constraint	1.00	4.75	3.08	1.02
Focus	−Constraint	3.33	6.00	4.90	0.77
	+Constraint	3.44	5.22	4.17	0.50
Freedom of Expression	−Constraint	3.50	6.00	4.57	0.69
	+Constraint	3.44	5.22	4.17	0.50

Note: $N = 24$.

Table 9.2 Tests of within-subjects contrasts

	F	p	Partial eta squared	Observed power
Enjoyment	10.97	0.003	0.323	0.887
Anxiety	18.97	<0.001	0.452	0.986
Focus	52.99	< 0.001	0.697	> 0.999
Expression	23.85	< 0.001	0.509	0.997

Qualitatively, in response to the questions of which task they preferred more, 15 learners indicated that they preferred the −constraint task, and nine preferred the +constraint task. All 15 learners mentioned either free expression (open ideas, my own ideas, my own opinion, etc.), enjoyment, or both as their reasons for preferring the −constraint task. Conversely, the main reasons from those who preferred the +constraint task were not having to think much in the +constraint task, not being able to come up with buildings to propose in the −constraint task or being too excited in the −constraint task. This finding was consistent with the quantitative finding that the learners' enjoyment, anxiety and freedom of expression differed in the two tasks. Learners did not comment on their focus for these tasks.

Transcript analysis

The examination of the two transcripts showed that the High Affective Engagement group reported high affective engagement scores during the −constraint task and the Low Affective Engagement Group reported low affective engagement during the +constraint task. There were noticeable differences in the two task performances that supported the differences found in their affective engagement scores (enjoyment, anxiety, focus and freedom of expression). Overall, the interaction in the +constraint task consisted of monologues from each learner explaining his/her choice and ended with a predictable decision-making process involving each learner choosing one building. Below is an excerpt that illustrates this pattern of interaction from the Low Affective Engagement Group in the +constraint task.

Excerpt 1: Interactional pattern of the Low Affective Engagement Group

L1: So I have 3 option to improve our university. The first is a counseling office for for a student who want to advise something or when they have a problem, they can come here and have a advice. The next is tennis court for student who want to exercise er they can come every time to play tennis together. And the last for me is the buffet restaurant er er for student who can eat as much as they want and anytime. So what about you?
(Learners took turns to explain their given buildings)

L1: So we have to pick up three building. From me, I offer er counseling office.

L3: For me I prefer swimming pool because we all student need to relax our body. And you?

L2: Er for me I choose language exchange room.

L1: So we got counseling office, swimming pool and language exchange room. (L3: yes) Right?

L3: Absolutely nice

L1: Okay, we are finish

With the choices given to learners in advance, time spent rehearsing the proposal of their buildings, and the predictable pattern of decision making, this group of learners might have felt *less anxious* during their task performance. However, the interaction also indicated they were *less emotionally invested*. They seemed to have chosen an 'easy' way to complete the task as can be seen in the nice and neat decision-making process at the end of the interaction.

In contrast, the interaction in the −constraint task was characterized by shorter turns, more instances where students completed each other's turns, more negotiation of meaning and more backchannels. Overall, it sounded more like a highly interactive discussion. In addition, there were more instances of laughter and giggles, especially when the reasons for their choice were directly related to their context, such as the hot weather in Thailand, the small library on campus and their university's food court nicknamed KFC. These findings were consistent with the quantitative findings of the higher levels of *enjoyment and freedom of expression* in the −constraint task. In addition, the highly interactive discussion might have been *both exhilarating and anxiety-inducing* to the learners, explaining the higher enjoyment and anxiety scores in the −constraint task. Excerpt 2 below illustrates the discussion from the High Affective Engagement Group in the −constraint task.

Excerpt 2: High Affective Engagement Group in the -constraint task

L4:   Okay so about me (**L5**: yeah) er I want more er larger er library because our campus is has very small ones so if we have more er library (**L5**: yeah) it should more like more students to come and study together. (**L6**: uhm hmm) So and next I want more er laboratory building such like a che chemistry building or maybe electronics and electrical buildings (**L5**: ah) (**L6**: uh) so we can more doing er

L5:   your major things (**L4**: yes) more subjects

L4:   Yes, something like that. (**L6**: uhm) And the last one [giggles] please building swimming pool [giggle]

L5:   Swimming pool?

L4:   Yes [giggle]

L6:   why? [giggle]

L4:   Because I think (**L5**: yeah I) everyone love to swim right [giggle] and (**L5**: yeah that's good idea) and when when

L5:   Thailand is so hot.

L4:   uhm yeah if if we have a swimming pool (**L5**: yeah) so we can do activity like hmm ah compe competition or something like that (**L5**: yeah)

(**L6**: ah) like a sport doing sport something like that (**L6**: hmm) (**L5**: uh)

It is worth noting that, different from the decision-making process in the Low Affective Engagement Group, the decision-making process in the High Affective Engagement Group in the −constraint task was longer with more turns dedicated to confirmation checks and clarification requests (Excerpt 3). These negotiation moves might have also required more *focus* from students and persistence in working with each other to achieve the task goals.

Excerpt 3: Decision making in the High Affective Engagement Group

L4:   So what about you ah you guys think we should have a

L5:   Choose three

L4:   Yeah (**L6**: three). The first one is from you. Er what what is that again? Er the communicates [giggle]
        Discussion of the first building (Omitted)

L4:   So we should go with that, right?

L6:   Yes (**L5**: yeah)

L4:   Okay so that's that's the first

L5:   yeah yeah

L4:   and how about other twos?

L5:   And then I also agree with the

L4:   Laboratory (**L6**: laboratory)

L5:   Yeah (**L6**: building)

L4:   Yeah so we have two and how about the rast..the last one? [giggle]

L6:   Hmm [**L4**: giggle] fast food, fast food restaurant. What do you think?

L4:   I think I go with the restaurant [giggle] (**L6**: restaurant)

L5:   Really?
L4:   yeah
L5:   Restaurant?

In summary, the analysis of the transcripts in a group with high affective engagement scores and a group with a low affective engagement scores showed how the −constraint task induced enjoyment, anxiety, focus and freedom of expression. Together with the quantitative results and learners' qualitative responses in the questionnaires, this transcript analysis provided evidence to the positive effect of choice on learners' affective engagement in performing communicative tasks.

Discussion

The findings from the study showed that choice in the −constraint task created a condition that induced greater enjoyment, focus and sense of free self-expression, indicating a higher level of affective engagement. The affective dimension is seen by some as intrinsic to engagement and mediates the relation between motivation and engagement (Linnenbrink, 2007; Mercer, 2019; Philp & Duchesne, 2016). In other words, high engagement in a task has to be characterized by learners' positive affective response or emotional investment as well.

However, learners also reported feeling more anxious in the −constraint task because, according to their qualitative responses, the task was too 'exciting' for them or required them to think about their own ideas. This 'excitement' might have stemmed from the faster pace of the interaction on the −constraint task as illustrated in the analysis of the transcript from the −constraint task. However, anxiety during the task did not seem to necessarily reduce enjoyment or other affective aspects of engagement. Higher anxiety, together with enjoyment and focus, could be argued to indicate overall higher affective engagement in the −constraint task, a finding consistent with Linnenbrink's (2007) suggestion that activated unpleasant affect (e.g. anxiety and anger) may lead to more intense engagement than deactivated unpleasant affect (e.g. sadness and exhaustion).

The positive effect of choice could be explained by the specific operationalization of choice in the present study as the ability to bring ideas to the discussion instead of discussing ideas that were given in the task materials. Choice in this study probably felt less like an options choice, i.e. choice among mandated options, and more like action choice because learners could determine how they would go about proposing a solution to meet the requirements of the task (Reeve et al., 2003). It also gave learners a higher level of control than when the topic and semantic content of the task were supplied to the learners. With this choice, learners felt they could actually talk about *their* ideas, express *their* opinions and share *their* own thoughts. In fact, when asked which task learners preferred, the majority (15 out of 24) said they preferred the task with less constrained choice because, to paraphrase, they could talk about their ideas, had freedom to choose what they wanted to express and felt that the ideas were theirs. The ability to express one's authentic self and ideas was particularly important in these tasks probably because they were communicative tasks in a foreign language where success in the tasks meant success in communicating ideas. This finding confirms suggestions from previous studies that learners find joy, enjoyment, satisfaction and pride in communicative success in an L2 especially when there is a genuine communicative gap (Aubrey, 2017; Egbert, 2003; Phung, 2017; Wolf & Phung, 2019). This finding is also encouraging in that even in a context where learners share the same L1 and culture, tasks with certain features can offer learners a sense of authentic self-expression more commonly found in intercultural settings.

In addition, the comments learners made regarding expressing their own ideas, opinions and thoughts were consistent with their higher rating on freedom of expression through the questionnaire and the analysis of the transcripts. This suggests that learners might have experienced a greater sense of autonomy in that they felt they could exercise their agency to carry out the discussions based on the ideas that they themselves had generated in the -constraint task. In doing so, it was possible that learners also felt a greater sense of success or competence in completing the task and communicating in English with peers. In other words, it could be argued that choice in the −constraint task supported learners' sense of autonomy and competence, important antecedents of motivation, which in turn promote active engagement (Mercer, 2019).

As previously mentioned, these data set were part of a larger study (Nakamura *et al.*, in press) that investigated the effects of choice on the four dimensions of engagement: behavioral, cognitive, social and emotional. The findings of Nakamura *et al.* (in press) relate to this study in interesting ways. Nakamura *et al.* (in press) indicated that learners in the -constraint task demonstrated a higher level of behavioral, cognitive and social engagement in the −constraint task than the +constraint task with more turns, negotiation of meaning and form, self-repairs and overlaps in their interactions. Those results indicated that interactions in the −constraint task were more conversational and spontaneous than the interactions in the +constraint task, which had longer turns that sounded like rehearsed monologues. The study suggested that learners' engagement in the two tasks was qualitatively different, and this qualitatively different experience with language use might have prompted learners to be more focused during task performance in the −constraint task. In other words, the findings from both studies suggest that choice might not have caused learners to be more focused, but that choice led to the kind of learner engagement characterized by greater focus and attention paid to communicating one's own ideas, negotiating meaning with interlocutors, choosing linguistic forms and responding to other interlocutors. It was clear that different dimensions of engagement were interrelated, and that active and heightened engagement was demonstrated when different dimensions (behavioral, cognitive, social and affective) of engagement were present, supporting widely recognized multidimensional models of learner engagement (Christenson *et al.*, 2012; Philp & Duchesne, 2016; Svalberg, 2009). The study also shows that both learners' behaviors and affective responses need to be taken into account in studying learner engagement.

Implications

While learners come to an L2 classroom with different dispositions and initial levels of motivation, which subsequently affect their engagement in language learning activities, this study indicates that teachers can develop and manipulate task conditions to encourage active engagement. One variable to consider in task design is the provision of choice over the content of tasks. Learners can be asked to generate their own ideas to be included in the task that they later perform, which is likely to encourage learners' engagement in task performance, including affective engagement. However, it is important to bear in mind that not all types or levels of choice lead to positive outcomes; action choice that offers learners greater autonomy in how to go about completing the task may be more engaging.

Furthermore, to promote learner engagement, it is important for teachers to think of engagement not only as behaviors that learners exhibit and cognitive resources they utilize, but also in terms of how they feel during task performance. Affective responses and emotions (such as enjoyment and anxiety), learners' evaluations of aspects of their performance (such as focus) and experience (such as perceived freedom of expression) are also informative for understanding engagement. Taking notes of how learners interact and asking learners how they feel on a regular basis may be helpful practices for teachers to better understand and enhance engagement among their learners.

Limitations and Future Research

We would like to acknowledge a few limitations of the study. Low Cronbach's α in items related to freedom of expression indicate some items will need further piloting and revising if they are to see use in future studies. Although the use of questionnaire items measuring freedom of expression generated interesting insights on learners' experience during task performance, due to the low internal consistency of this measure, the findings related to this measure should be interpreted with caution. Future research may also use existing questionnaires of perceived autonomy, perceived competence and perceived choice for a better understanding of learners' experience along these important constructs as initial conditions for the kind of motivation that, under the right circumstances, will move learners to more active engagement. Another limitation of the study is the small sample size of 24 affecting the reliability of the results; future research needs to conduct power analyses to determine an adequate sample size to ensure sufficient power when conducting statistical analyses in the study. However, overall, the positive findings on the effect of choice on affective engagement are encouraging for their implications for task design. Considering the importance attached to engagement in language learning activities, our recommendation is for researchers to examine other task features for their effect on learner engagement and how learner engagement is generated, maintained and interacts with other developmental processes in language learning.

References

Aubrey, S. (2017) Inter-cultural contact and flow in task-based Japanese EFL classroom. *Language Teaching Research* 21 (6), 717–734.

Baralt, M., Gurzynski-Weiss, L. and Kim, Y. (2016) The effects of task complexity and classroom environment on learners' engagement with the language. In M. Sato and S. Ballinger (eds) *Peer Interaction and Second Language Learning: Pedagogical Potential and Research Agenda* (pp. 209–240). Amsterdam: John Benjamins.

Butler, Y.G. (2017) Motivational elements of digital instructional games: A study of young L2 learners' game designs. *Language Teaching Research* 21 (6), 735–750.

Bygate, M. and Samuda, V. (2009) Creating pressure in task pedagogy: The joint roles of field, purpose and engagement within the interaction approach. In A. Mackey and C. Polio (eds) *Multiple Perspectives on Interaction: Second Language Research in Honor of Susan M. Gass* (pp. 90–116). New York: Routledge.

Christenson, S.L., Reschly, A.L. and Wylie, C. (eds) (2012) *Handbook of Research on Student Engagement*. New York: Springer.

Csikszentmihalyi, M. (1990) *Flow: The Psychology of Optimal Experience*. New York: Harper Perennial.

Deci, E.L. and Ryan, R.M. (2000) The 'what' and 'why' of goal pursuits: Human needs and the self-determination of behavior. *Psychological Inquiry* 11, 227–268.

Dewaele, J.-M. (2015) On emotions in foreign language learning and use. *The Language Teacher* 39 (3), 13–15.

Dewaele, J.-M., Witney, J., Saito, K. and Dewaele, L. (2018) Foreign language enjoyment and anxiety: The effect of teacher and learner variables. *Language Teaching Research* 22 (6), 676–697.

Dewaele, J-M. and MacIntyre, P.D. (2016) Foreign language enjoyment and foreign language classroom anxiety. The right and left feet of FL learning. In P.D. MacIntyre, T. Gregersen and S. Mercer (eds) *Positive Psychology in SLA* (pp. 215–236). Bristol: Multilingual Matters.

Egbert, J. (2003) A study of flow theory in the foreign language classroom. *The Modern Language Journal* 87 (4), 499–518.

Floweray, T. and Shraw, G. (2003) Effect of choice on cognitive and affective engagement. *The Journal of Educational Research* 96 (4), 207–215.

Haga, E. and Reinders, H. (in review) ESL learners' emotional responses to out-of-class feedback on their language.

Horwitz, E.K. (2001) Language anxiety and achievement. *Annual Review of Applied Linguistics* 21, 112–126.

Katz, I. and Assor, A. (2006) When choice motivates and when it does not. *Educational Psychology Review* 19, 429–442.

Lambert, C., Philp, J. and Nakamura, S. (2017) Learner-generated content and engagement in second language task performance. *Language Teaching Research* 21 (6), 655–766.

Linnenbrink, E.A. (2007) The role of affect in student learning: A multidimensional approach to considering the interaction of affect, motivation, and engagement. In P.A. Schutz and R. Pekrun (eds) *Emotion in Education* (pp. 107–124). Boston, MA: Elsevier.

Long, M. (1996) The role of the linguistic environment in second language acquisition. In W. Ritchie and T. Bhatia (eds) *Handbook of Second Language Acquisition* (pp. 413–468). San Diego, CA: Academic Press.

MacIntyre, P.D. (2017) An overview of language anxiety research and trends in its development. In C. Gkonou, M. Daubney and J.-M. Dewaele (eds) *New Insights into Language Anxiety: Theory, Research and Educational Implications* (pp. 11–30). Bristol: Multilingual Matters.

MacIntyre, P.D. and Gardner, R. (1994) The subtle effects of induced anxiety on cognitive processing in the second language. *Language Learning* 44, 283–305.

MacIntyre, P.D. and Gregersen, T. (2012) Emotions that facilitate language learning: The positive- broadening power of the imagination. *Studies in Second Language Learning and Teaching* 2, 193–213.

Mercer, S. (2019) Language learner engagement: Setting the scene. In X. Gao, C. Davison and C. Leung (eds) *International Handbook of English Language Teaching*. Cham: Springer.

Mozgalina, A. (2015) More or less choice? The influence of choice on task motivation and task engagement. *System* 49, 120–132.

Nakamura, S., Phung, L. and Reinders, H. (in press) The effect of learner choice on L2 task engagement. *Studies in Second Language Acquisition*.

Nystrand, M. and Gamoran, A. (1991) Instructional discourse, student engagement, and literature achievement. *Research in the Teaching of English* 25 (3), 261–290.

Patall, E.A., Cooper, H. and Robinson, J.C. (2008) The effects of choice on intrinsic motivation and related outcomes: A meta-analysis of research findings. *Psychological Bulletin* 134, 270–300.

Philp, J. and Duchesne, S. (2016) Exploring engagement in tasks in the language classroom. *Annual Review of Applied Linguistics* 36, 50–72.

Phung, L. (2017) Task preference, affective response, and engagement in L2 use in a US university context. *Language Teaching Research* 21 (6), 751–766.

Qui, X. and Lo, Y.Y. (2017) Content familiarity, task repetition and Chinese EFL learners' engagement in second language use. *Language Teaching Research* 21 (6), 681–698.

Reeve, J., Nix, G. and Hamm, D. (2003) The experience of self-determination in intrinsic motivation and the conundrum of choice. *Journal of Educational Psychology* 95, 375–392.

Russell, V.J., Ainley, M. and Frydenberg, E. (2005) Student motivation and engagement. *Schooling Issues Digest* 2, 1–11.

Sato, M. (2017) Interaction mindsets, interactional behaviors, and L2 development: An affective-social-cognitive model. *Language Learning* 67 (2), 249–283.

Schmidt, R. (1990) The role of consciousness in second language learning. *Applied Linguistics* 11 (2), 129–58.

Skinner, E.A., Kindermann, T.A. and Furrer, C.J. (2009) A motivational perspective on engagement and disaffection: Conceptualization and assessment of children's behavioral and emotional participation in academic activities in the classroom. *Educational and Psychological Measurement* 69 (3), 493–525.

Svalberg, A. (2009) Engagement with language: Interrogating the construct. *Language Awareness* 18 (3–4), 242–258.

Swain, M. (2005) The output hypothesis: Theory and research. In E. Hinkel (ed.) *Handbook on Research in Second Language Teaching and Learning* (pp. 471–484). Mahwah, NJ: Erlbaum.

Swain, M. (2013) The inseparability of cognition and emotion in second language learning. *Language Teaching* 46 (2), 195–207

Wolf, D. and Phung, L. (2019) Studying in the United States: Language learning challenges, strategies, and support services. *Journal of International Students* 9 (1), 211–224.

Appendix 9.1

Questionnaire

Enjoyment

E1. I enjoyed doing this task.
E2. Doing the task was fun.
E3. I thought the task was enjoyable.
E4. This task was interesting.
E5. This task was boring. R

Focus

F1. I paid attention to what my classmates said.
F2. When doing this task, I thought about other things that were *un*related to the task. R
F3. I was focused on doing the task.

Freedom of expression

FE1. This task allowed me to express my own ideas.
FE2. I could make decisions about what to say and when to say it.
FE3. I had a choice in what to propose.
FE4. I felt restricted in expressing my ideas. R

Task difficulty

TD1. I found the task difficult.
TD2. Doing this task was difficult.
TD3. Doing this task was easy. R
TD4. I found the task easy. R

Task familiarity

TF1. I was *un*familiar with the content of the task. R
TF2. The content of the task was familiar to me.
TF3. I had prior knowledge about the content of the task.

Task anxiety

TA1. Doing this task made me nervous.
TA2. I was anxious while doing this task.
TA3. I got tense while doing this task.
TA4. Doing this task made me feel anxious.

[After they have completed the two tasks]
Which task did you enjoy more?
TG (You were given 3 building options on your handout)
LG (You needed to come up with 3 buildings by yourself)
Why?

10 How Ideal Classmates Priming Increases EFL Classroom Prosocial Engagement

Tetsuya Fukuda, Yoshifumi Fukada, Joseph Falout and Tim Murphey

Introduction

Encouraging students to imagine possible ideal classmates has been hypothesized to prime prosocial engagement with actual classmates in second language (L2) classrooms, particularly for classrooms in which student silence, resistance and demotivation stand as problems to classroom group dynamics and personal academic achievement. This hypothesis has not yet been tested in a rigorously designed study until now. For this study, we specifically conceptualized prosocial peer learning support as a type of engagement in which students' perceptions of their mutually constructive participation matter to them in their academic achievement. University English as a foreign language (EFL) communication classrooms were randomly assigned to either ideal classmates or future selves priming conditions. Depending on the condition, students individually expressed their imagined EFL-related ideal classmates or future selves. The students then self-reported their own past, present and future EFL motivations at the beginning and end of one semester, while also relating the levels of their classmates' and their own prosocial learning behaviors. Qualitative analyses of open-ended comments from students helped explain their subjective experiences of student–student prosocial engagement, while quantitative analyses explored the degree to which ideal classmates priming influenced prosocial peer learning support and its relationship to individual-level motivation.

The Genesis of Ideal Classmates

Student silence, resistance and demotivation can stand in the way of good classroom group dynamics and personal achievement in spite of well-conceived and well-implemented lesson plans. Especially where student passivity, disinterest and unwillingness to engage prevail, Murphey *et al.* (2014) presented a way of greeting all students in the classroom with peer-generated ideas that can help unfocused and inattentive students gain focus and involvement in the classroom, turn boredom into interest and make apathy and avoidance of learning dissolve into purposeful and willing participation. King's (2013a, 2013b) observational study illustrates the problem with over 900 students attending 30 separate English classrooms, 13 of which were for students majoring in English-related fields, situated in nine universities across Japan. From over 48 hours of observation, the percentage breakdowns showed students passively listening to the teacher at 37% of the time, listening to other students at 8%, conversing in pair or group talk at 7%, being disengaged from learning (primarily chatting in the L1 raucously, using mobile phones and sleeping) at 20% and initiating talk in the L2 at 0.04%. King's (2013a, 2013b) classifications of the salient reasons for student silence include:

- *Disengagement* – Appearance of **boredom, apathy** and **inattention** on the part of students. Students seem to be allowed to disengage perhaps because teachers feel there is nothing else they can do; when students **give up** on classroom activities, teachers seem to **give up** on trying to engage students. Perhaps teacher **helplessness** is thus a related problem.
- *Confusion* – Students do not receive clear instructions, scaffolding, or time to cognitively process and understand what they are expected to do for speaking activities. Depending on the degree of confusion, it **distracts** students temporarily or **prevents** them from full participation. Sometimes students fake being confused to **avoid** engaging in interactive activities.
- *Hypersensitivity to others* – A prevalent **reluctance** or even **fear** in this cultural context of being judged negatively by others. As a result of poor performance or speaking mistakes in front of others, students commonly feel **shame** and **self-blame. Refusing** to engage can be a defense mechanism for avoiding embarrassment and the prolonged attention of others.
- *Salient cliques* – The dark side of group dynamics when the students together turn on the teacher to cooperatively engage through passive aggression in **resistance** to classroom participation. One or more cohesive cliques can team up to **oppose** the teacher or **pressure** others to not raise their hands, not answer the teacher and **not properly or wholeheartedly** do activities.

Markers of disengagement have been put into bold text above to highlight and readily match up with the motivational components of Skinner and

Table 10.1 Motivational components of engagement and disaffection in the classroom

	Engagement	Disaffection
Behavior	Action initiation, effort, persistence, intensity, focus, involvement	Passivity, giving up, half-hearted, unfocused, inattentive, distracted
Emotion	Enthusiasm, interest, enjoyment, satisfaction, pride, vitality	Boredom, disinterest, frustration, worry, shame, self-blame
Cognition	Purposeful, goal strivings, willing participation, preference for challenge, follow-through, care	Helpless, unwilling, opposition, avoidance, apathy, pressured

Note: Adapted from Skinner and Pitzer (2012: 25).

Pitzer's (2012) notion of *disaffection*, which is their term for disengagement, in Table 10.1. These researchers proposed that initial motivation can play out in *constructive participation* – or engagement – in prosocial societal institutions, school academics and extracurricular activities and classroom learning activities. In this multilevel model of motivational dynamics, Skinner and Pitzer (2012) postulate that engagement or disaffection at any level can make or break healthy human development as well as academic and personal achievement. For maintaining motivation and its tangible outcome of engagement, human connectivity reigns paramount.

Since motivation and engagement at first glance may seem to be overlapping concepts, some researchers have attempted to articulate their distinctions. For instance, 'motivation is considered to be intent and engagement as action' (Reschly & Christenson, 2012: 14), and 'motivation refers to the underlying sources of energy, purpose and durability, whereas engagement refers to their visible manifestation' (Skinner & Pitzer, 2012: 22). Additionally, concepts of engagement are becoming more nuanced and domain-specific, such as with academic engagement, affective engagement, cognitive engagement and social engagement (Finn & Zimmer, 2012).

One theory of learner motivation explicitly conceptualized as having an integral connection to the learner's social environment is a framework called *present communities of imagining* (e.g. Falout *et al.*, 2013; Fukada *et al.*, 2017). Chosen for the present study, the framework comprises *three mind–time frames of motivation*, which students carry into any classroom situation and which potentially affect their engagement, specifically their lived and imagined *past, present* and *future self-concepts* in relation to L2 learning. The past mind–time frame centers upon the *antecedent conditions of the learner*, or the emotional baggage that influences the way a student tackles learning a subject, for better or worse (Falout, 2016). The present mind–time frame encompasses in-class and out-of-class time, effort and heart put into learning alongside the expected return on the *investment* (Norton & McKinney, 2011). The future mind–time frame contains not only the notion of an individual's *ideal* future in relation to the subject of study, as anchored into Dörnyei's (2009) *L2 motivational self-system*, but opens up to wider possibilities of the future self-concept, and especially a *probable* or *expected* future self, as described in *possible selves theory* (Markus & Nurius, 1986).

A survey of the literature regarding the effects from peers on motivation (Juvonen *et al.*, 2012) gives the general conclusion that the greater and deeper the friendships students have in school, the more they become involved in academic and extracurricular pursuits. The key aspect that makes a difference is not necessarily the number of friends, but the personal closeness and mutual care felt between students. One study (Wentzel, 1994) found that the greater the respect for each other's feelings shared among classmates and the greater the concern students had of their classmates' academic well-being, the more they valued and followed their teacher's requests and classroom rules. For this chapter we introduce a type of engagement termed *prosocial peer learning support*. Prosocial peer learning support alludes to the ready resource in the classroom for promoting social engagement – the students themselves. Prosocial peer learning support incorporates students' perceptions of constructive participation in L2 learning. More specifically, prosocial peer learning support focuses upon students' perceptions of how much they are helping each other to learn better and more enjoyably, with separate directional components from self to others and others to self.

In theorizing that social engagement creates an ecology of learning, ideal classmates priming was developed as a socio-motivational process that helps orientate students' minds to engage more with each other and to support each other in ways that they themselves can specify (Murphey *et al.*, 2014). The ideal classmates priming procedures start with the prompt: 'Please describe a group of classmates that you could learn English well with. What would you all do to help each other learn better and more enjoyably?' Individual students' responses are collected anonymously and compiled together by class, and these whole-class response sheets are redistributed back to their respective whole-class groups, which is a part of the procedure termed as *looping back* the responses.

We hypothesized that after students read and reflect upon each other's ideas for learning better and more enjoyably together, they would then have a chance to enact these ideas as the semester progresses. It is further hypothesized that with minimal reminders thereafter, ideal classmates priming will help not only to increase their *metacognitive awareness* of how to engage each other in prosocial learning behaviors (Davis, 2018), but also to prime them to actually do so. The present study experimentally investigates whether or not these simple procedures show any effects by the end of the semester by asking: *Does ideal classmates priming increase EFL students' personal motivation and prosocial engagement? And if so, to what degree and how?*

Method

Participants

To assess the impact of Ideal Classmates Priming (ICP) on students' three mind–time frames of motivation as well as on their Prosocial Peer Learning Support (PPLS, pronounced *people's*) engagement, we set up two randomized treatment groups: an ICP group and a Future Selves Priming (FSP) group. Both groups actually represented almost a dozen separate courses, with each class undergoing only one of the two treatments. Of the 21 required or elective English communication courses offered by three of the four authors of this chapter at three private universities in the Kanto region in Japan, 11 classes were randomly assigned to the ICP group with the other 10 classes to the FSP group. The two treatment groups were divided equally among the English courses at the three universities by coin toss. Some students in the English courses were assumed to meet or learn together in other academic classes and subjects. All of the English courses at the three universities consisted of 15 weeks of lessons. The students studied together for 90 minutes in each lesson once a week. The data were collected for two years, 2017 and 2018. In total, 237 students (124 in 2017; 113 in 2018) were in the ICP group and 177 students (67 in 2017; 110 in 2018) were in the FSP group.

Priming treatments

At the beginning of the semester (week 1 or 2), an open-ended question was asked to each group. Students in ICP classes were given the prompt: 'Please describe a group of classmates that you could learn English well with. What would you all do to help each other learn better and more enjoyably?' Students in FSP classes were given the prompt: 'Please describe a future you using English. What would you be doing with your English in future situations?'

In addition to the priming treatments, activities were offered that related to either the ideal classmates or future selves of the students, depending on the treatment group. The activities varied by class and author. For example, in classes with one of the authors, students in rotating pairs discussed their ideal classmates or future selves, depending on the assigned treatment, through pictures they had drawn themselves. Then later in the semester, selected pictures were presented to the whole class in a projected slideshow as an introductory example of a focus-on-form activity. In another example, for future selves treatment classes with another author, a 10-year class reunion activity was offered, in which students imagined they were 10 years older and enacted an imaginary class reunion. The students' imaginations were stimulated by three questions; 'What is your job?' 'Where are you living?' and 'Do you use English at work or in private?' The students then conversed in English while pretending to be at the venue of their class reunion.

Instruments

Both qualitative and quantitative data from the two treatment groups were collected by administering pre-, mid- and post-surveys at the beginning, middle and end of the 15-week semester. The qualitative data were collected in one year (2018) in three sets of questions. The first data set was on students' ideal classmates or future selves images, which came from the pre-survey (pre-Q19). The second set came from the mid-survey, which had the open-ended question, Q5: 'In what new ways are your classmates helping you to learn and enjoy English in the last few weeks?' Lastly, the third data set was on effects of PPLS engagement on the students' English learning within the classroom by asking in the post-survey the open-ended question, post-Q19: 'Please describe any changes you have made during this semester in your behavior or attitudes toward your classmates. What influences do you think these changes may have had on your classmates, relationships in and out of class, and your English learning?'

The quantitative data were collected over two years (2017 and 2018) using 6-point Likert scale question items with 1 indicating 'Not at all' and 6 indicating 'Yes, very much.' Pre- and post-surveys measured three mind–time frames of motivation using 18 items (e.g. Falout *et al.*, 2013; Fukada *et al.*, 2017). The mid- and post-surveys measured PPLS engagement with four items: Q1. My classmates are helping me to learn English; Q2. I am helping my classmates to learn English; Q3. My classmates are helping me to enjoy English; and Q4. I am helping my classmates to enjoy English.

Data analysis

Qualitatively, open coding of the data explored the qualities of students' ideal classmates or future selves images (based on pre-Q19 data), and their different ways of engagement in student–student prosocial English-learning (based on Q5 data), and also the effects of PPLS engagement on their English-learning within the classroom (based on post-Q19 data). The students' responses were placed in an Excel sheet, repeatedly read and then coded by each semantic segment without a preset coding frame. The coding results and the wording of the codes were reviewed and discussed among us authors before the coding results were finalized. The number of semantic segments categorized into each code helped to gain insight into the tendencies of the types of self-reported PPLS engagement and their qualitative impact on learning.

Quantitatively, questionnaires went through validation steps of checking for internal consistency with Cronbach's alpha and conducting an exploratory factor analysis. Afterwards, the ICP group and the FSP group

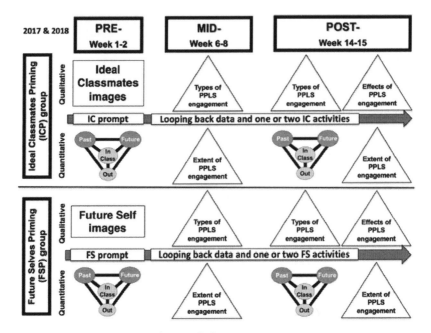

Figure 10.1 Representation of research design

were compared in terms of changes and degrees of English-learning motivations as well as their PPLS engagement. Figure 10.1 is a visual representation of the research design.

Results of Qualitative Data Analyses

Ideal classmates and future selves images

The students' ideal classmates and future selves images were gathered through the respective prompts. As for their ideal classmates images, some students responded in few words, such as 'Many many smile' (Student 33) and 'Talk each other' (Student 30), while other students commented longer, describing in more detail how their ideal classmates could engage with others: 'People good at English are teaching others. And people doesn't good at English are talking English many times and not be shy.' (Student 130); 'Even if grammar is wrong, it is important to try using English without being shy. It is necessary for a friend not to make fun of it even if he uses wrong English. And Teach each other.' (Student 243).

The FSP group related different types of future selves images. Some were related to their hobbies: 'I want to talk many people in pc game.' (Student 202); 'I'm playing baseball with foreign friends.' (Student 197), and their everyday life: '日常的な会話 (Everyday conversation)' (Student 108); 'to teach how to get to the place' (Student 95); and work: 'I using

English in job to send the mail for another country …' (Student 103); '仕事をする仲間に外国人がいて英語でコミュニケーションをとる (I will have foreign co-workers and communicate with them in English)' (Student 185). Since most of the participants were students of science, technology, engineering and mathematics, their future selves images related to engineering or science-related jobs: 'I have a dream to become a scientist. I think there will be opportunities to present in English in conference. If I don't speak English in the future, I can't talk to other scientists from all of the world.' (Student 325); 'I want to be a robot engineer in the future. I would like to help elderly people around the world by using my robot. I will work abroad to study robot engineering. I will discuss the new ideas of robot with foreign people in English. I will enjoy talking with my friends who live in foreign countries.' (Student 330).

Different types of PPLS engagement

From the open-coding of the qualitative data collected by Q5 both in mid- and post-surveys in 2018, students had reported eight (seven positive and one negative) different types of PPLS engagement. Table 10.2 shows selected sample comments for each category of engagement. Note that many individuals pointed out more than one type of PPLS engagement.

Comparison of the two treatment groups' PPLS engagement

For further analysis, we compared the parts of comments that could be categorized into each type of PPLS engagement. Compared to the FSP group, the ICP group were more likely among their own group to report five types of PPLS engagement (types 2, 3, 4, 6 and 7) in the mid-survey, while the FSP group more often mentioned four types of PPLS engagement (types 1, 3, 4 and 6) in the post-survey (Table 10.3). Additionally, the FSP group more often reported a type of negative PPLS engagement, 'Not having much support from my classmates,' both in mid- and post-surveys, although the number of comments was small (see type 8 column of data in Table 10.3).

Additionally, since Q5 was asked both in the mid- and post-surveys, results from each treatment group were compared to figure out how the types of PPLS engagement for each group had changed throughout the semester. The ICP group resulted in having more intense positive feelings in three types of PPLS engagement (types 1, 3 and 5), while the FSP group also did in three other types of PPLS engagement (types 3, 4 and 6) throughout the semester. However, their feelings on negative PPLS engagement were also strengthened for both groups, and more so for the ICP group than the FSP group (see the last two rows of data in Table 10.3).

Overall, the reactions or emotions expressed by the two treatment groups were comparable. Based on the qualitative data analysis, we

Table 10.2 Types of PPLS engagement and student comments

	Positive or negative	Type	Comments (participant number)
1	Positive	Trying communicating in English [Not speaking Japanese] inside or outside the classroom	I tried to talk in English as much as possible. (9) They talk with me in English. (7)
2	Positive	Creating friendly atmosphere which promotes each other's English communication	making good atmosphere to enjoy this period (138) funny joke and positive English. (158)
3	Positive	Support completing class activities	My classmates help me to explain what to do in class activity. (247) My classmates adviced me How to make a good speech. (190)
4	Positive	Teaching English [even when not directly related to task] in or out of class	When I cannot understand the thing that the teacher told us, my classmates teach about it. (322) When I can not understand a word, my classmates teach me the word meaning in English. (302)
5	Positive	Metacognitive suggestions or advice for homework and tests	2 weeks ago, I took a test. I prepared for the test with my classmates and had a good time. (308) We both talk about homework after school that is good experience. (86)
6	Positive	Sharing information/ideas with me [in English]	Suggest that I should watch an English movie. (320) We share English songs which we like. (312)
7	Positive	Inspiring me	刺激を与えてくれる [Inspiring me] (293)
8	Negative	Not having much support from my classmates	Nothing (295) I have few chance. (307)

concluded that we cannot judge which treatment, ICP or FSP, was more effective in promoting students' PPLS engagement. However, the ICP group utilized the second type of PPLS engagement (creating a friendly atmosphere which promotes each other's English communication) more than the FSP group both in mid- and post-surveys (mid-survey: ICP = 33.85%, FS = 26.92%; post-survey: ICP = 32.37%, FSP = 19.85%). Also, we found possible strength of FSP in promoting students' TL communication: The FSP group was found to utilize the first type of PPLS engagement (trying communicating in English (Not speaking Japanese) inside or outside the classroom) more than the ICP group in both of the surveys (mid-survey: ICP = 28.46%, FSP = 33.65%; post-survey: ICP = 30.94%, FSP = 33.09%). Chi-square tests for independence between the two groups in the post-survey indicated that, while we were not able to recognize statistical significance in the first type of PPLS engagement (1. Trying communicating in English), the ICP group reported utilizing

Table 10.3 Types of PPLS engagement reported in response to Q5 (In what new ways are your classmates helping you to learn and enjoy English in the last few weeks?)

		1. Trying communicating in English (Not speaking Japanese) inside or outside the classroom (Positive)	2. Creating friendly atmosphere which promotes each other's English communication (Positive)	3. Support completing class activities (Positive)	4. Teaching English (even when not directly related to task) in or out of class (Positive)	5. Metacognitive suggestions or advice for homework and tests (Positive)	6. Sharing information/ideas with me (in English) (Positive)	7. Inspiring me (Positive)	8. Not having much support from my classmates (Negative)	9. Others (Not specific comments) (Negative)	Total
Mid-survey											
Ideal classmates	n	37	44	6	21	4	9	1	1	7	130
	%	28.46	33.85	4.62	16.15	3.08	6.92	0.77	0.77	5.38	100.00
Future selves	n	35	28	4	11	9	6	0	4	7	104
	%	33.65	26.92	3.85	10.58	8.65	5.77	0.00	3.85	6.73	100.00
Post-survey											
Ideal classmates	n	43	45	8	21	9	6	0	4	3	139
	%	30.94	32.37	5.76	15.11	6.47	4.32	0.00	2.88	2.16	100.00
Future selves	n	45	27	9	21	7	13	0	6	8	136
	%	33.09	19.85	6.62	15.44	5.15	9.56	0.00	4.41	5.88	100.00
Post–Mid surveys											
*Ideal Classmates Diff. of %		(+2.47)	(−1.47)	+1.14	(−1.05)	+3.40	(−2.61)	(−0.77)	2.11	(−3.22)	
*Future L2 selves Diff. of %		(−0.57)	(−7.07)	+2.77	+4.86	(−3.51)	+3.79	0.00	0.57	(−0.85)	

Note: About differences between the post- and mid-surveys, results with higher % in post-surveys were written with a positive sign (+), and those with lower % in post-surveys were written with a negative sign (−).

the second type of PPLS engagement (2. Creating friendly atmosphere) significantly more than the FSP group, χ^2 (1, $n = 275$) = 11.94, $p = 0.001$, $phi = 0.21$.

Effects on PPLS engagement between ICP and FSP treatment groups

We also qualitatively explored the effect of PPLS engagement on students' own learning within the classroom by analyzing the students' responses to post-Q19, which was asked in the post-survey at the end of the semester. Through open-coding of the comments, we found many positive and some negative effects on classroom-learning (see Table 10.4). These coding results show that PPLS engagement helped promote positive group dynamics within the classrooms overall, although some students were demotivated by or had no positive impact from their classmates. Furthermore, by counting the number of parts of student comments that were categorized into each type of effect, we found the ICP group were more likely to report the positive effects of (1), (3), (8), (11) and (12), while the FSP group were more likely among their own group to report the positive effects of (4), (5), (7), (9), (10) and (13). However, the ICP group more often reported the negative effects of (2), (6) and (14).

Results of Quantitative Data Analyses

In this section, three statistical analyses are discussed and their results are presented: validation of the questionnaires; comparison of the two groups in terms of improvement in motivation and engagement (Comparison 1); and comparison of the two groups in terms of the relationship between motivational change across one semester and end-of-semester engagement (Comparison 2). The statistical analyses were conducted with SPSS Version 25 (IBM, 2017).

Validation of the questionnaires

To measure levels of motivation and engagement, we employed the three mind–time frames of motivation questionnaire and the PPLS engagement questionnaire. The questionnaires went through validation processes with an internal consistency test and an exploratory factor analysis (EFA). The motivation questionnaire initially consisted of 18 items, and the engagement questionnaire consisted of four items.

We tested the internal consistency of the two large factors, namely three mind–time frames of motivation and PPLS engagement, and both alphas were > 0.90. According to Pallant (2016), the minimum acceptable value of alpha is 0.70, thus the two questionnaires were found to be internally consistent. The internal consistency of the four

Table 10.4 Effects on PPLS engagement reported in response to post-Q19 (Please describe any changes you have made during this semester in your behavior or attitudes toward your classmates. What influences do you think these changes may have had on your classmates, relationships in and out of class and your English learning?)

Post-Q19		1. Opportunities of communicating in English increased within the classroom / My classmates speak English more actively (Positive)	2. Less opportuni-ties of speaking English. (Negative)	3. We got more along with each other / Friendly atmosphere increased within the classroom. (Positive)	4. Ss / I became more supportive. (Positive)	5. My English-learning motivation was strengthened. (Positive)	6. I was demotivated. (Negative)	7. I became able to enjoy learning or speaking English. (Positive)	8. I became more active in communicating in English with others. (Positive)	9. My English (comm.) skills improved. (Positive)	10. I became more confident in speaking English. (Positive)	11. I had a different perception toward English (-using) or new insights. (Positive)	12. I became more active in learning or using English outside the classroom (with my classmates). (Positive)	13. I was inspired by my classmates. (Positive)	14. No / Not much change (in my or our behavior / English). (Negative)	15. Others (positive comments but not specific) (Positive)	Total
IC																	
	n	11	3	31	5	9	3	12	32	3	2	5	6	2	18	3	145
	%	7.59	2.07	21.38	3.45	6.21	2.07	8.28	22.07	2.07	1.38	3.45	4.14	1.38	12.41	2.07	100.00
FS																	
	n	10	1	32	8	16	1	19	29	15	4	3	2	5	14	4	163
	%	6.13	0.61	19.63	4.91	9.82	0.61	11.66	17.79	9.20	2.45	1.84	1.23	3.07	8.59	2.45	100.00
Diff. b/w the 2		+1.45	+1.46	+1.75	-1.46	-3.61	+1.46	-3.38	+4.28	-7.13	-1.07	+1.61	+2.91	-1.69	+3.82	-0.39	

Note: About differences between the two groups, the values for when the ideal classmates group had higher % were written with a positive sign (+), while values for when the future selves group had higher % were written with a negative sign (–).

Table 10.5 Results of the exploratory factor analysis on the motivation survey

Item	Past self	Present in-class	Present out-of-class	Future self	Communality
1. I enjoyed learning English in class in the past.	**0.85**				0.77
2. I enjoyed learning English out of class in the past.	**0.72**				0.65
3. Even if English had not been a compulsory subject, I would have chosen to study it in the past.	**0.68**				0.61
4. I was confident in learning English in the past.	**0.65**				0.59
5. I regularly use English in class with my classmates this semester.		**0.85**			0.79
6. Even if the teacher were not close to me, or could not hear me, I still speak English with my classmates in class this semester.		**0.82**			0.76
7.* In this class, my classmates and I support each others' English learning reciprocally.		**0.66**	**0.42**		0.58
8.* In this class, my classmates and I talk about our English-related future careers.			**0.70**		0.63
9. Outside of this class, I make an effort to speak more English with my classmates.			**0.76**		0.63
10. Outside of this class, my classmates and I support each other's English learning reciprocally.			**0.79**		0.66
11. Outside of this class, my classmates and I talk about our English-related future careers.			**0.80**		0.77
12. Outside of this class, I make an effort to speak more English with other people (friends, teachers, family, etc.).			**0.72**		0.68
13. Outside of this class, other people (friends, teachers, family, etc.) and I support each other's English learning reciprocally.			**0.72**		0.66

(Continued)

Table 10.5 *Continued*

		Factor			
Item	Past self	Present in-class	Present out-of-class	Future self	Communality
14.* Outside of this class, other people (friends, teachers, family, etc.) and I talk about our English-related future careers.		0.69		0.43	0.69
15. I think I will use English in my daily life in the future.				0.78	0.72
16. I think I will get a job using my English abilities in the future.				0.85	0.81
17. I can imagine belonging to a group of friends who use English in the future.				0.80	0.80
18. I can imagine belonging to a group of professionals who use English in a job in the future.				0.82	0.81

Note: * indicates items eliminated from correlational analyses following EFA results.

components in motivation, namely *past self, present in-class invest-ment, present out-of-class investment* and *future self,* ranged from 0.73 to 0.91. When each item was examined for its contribution to internal consistency, almost all the items were contributing, but Item 8 was found to be contributing negatively to the *in-class present* component. If Item 8 were deleted, the consistency would rise from 0.73 to 0.76. Thus, at this stage, it was decided to look at Item 8 carefully in the fol-lowing analyses.

The dimensionality of the 18 items in motivation was analyzed using EFA. Table 10.5 shows the factor loadings when calculated with the threshold of 0.40. Of the four items in *present in-class investment* (Items 5–8), Item 7 loaded both on the *present in-class investment* factor and the *present out-of-class investment* factor. Also, Item 8, which was found to be negatively contributing to internal consistency, loaded on the *out-of-class* factor. In addition, of the six items in the *present out-of-class invest-ment* component (Items 9–14), Item 14 loaded on the *future self* factor, too. Following these results of EFA, it was decided that Items 7, 8 and 14 would be excluded in the subsequent analyses. As a result, the internal consistency of the motivation survey became 0.88, and that of the four components became 0.78, 0.78, 0.86 and 0.90 respectively. The results suggest that four underlying factors, namely *past self, present in class, present out of class* and *future self,* can reliably form a larger factor of *three mind–time frames of motivation.*

Table 10.6 Means of motivation pre, motivation post and engagement in two groups

	Motivation pre-survey	Motivation post-survey	PPLS engagement post-survey
ICP Group	3.21	3.62	4.20
FSP Group	3.43	3.84	4.27

Comparison 1

After validating the questionnaires, the ICP group and the FSP group were compared in two ways: motivational change across one semester and end-semester level of PPLS engagement. In addition, correlations between motivation and engagement were examined.

Table 10.6 shows the means of the three mind–time frames of motivation levels at the beginning (pre-survey) and at the end (post-survey) of the semester and the PPLS engagement levels among the students in two groups. Two paired samples t-tests were conducted to evaluate the impact of the intervention on students' motivation level. In the ICP group, there was a statistically significant increase in their motivation level from pre-survey ($M = 3.21$, $SD = 0.81$) to post-survey ($M = 3.62$, $SD = 0.87$), $t(236) = -8.18$, $p < 0.001$ (two-tailed). The mean increase in the motivation level was 0.41 with a 95% confidence interval ranging from -0.50 to -0.31. The eta squared statistic (-0.48) indicated a medium effect size. In the FSP group, there was also a statistically significant increase in their motivation level from pre-survey ($M = 3.43$, $SD = 0.85$) to post-survey ($M = 3.84$, $SD = 0.86$), $t(176) = -6.54$, $p < 0.001$ (two-tailed). The mean increase in the motivation level was 0.41 with a 95% confidence interval ranging from -0.53 to -0.29. The eta squared statistic (-0.48) indicated a medium effect size.

To compare the engagement levels for the ICP group and the FSP group, an independent-samples t-test was conducted. There was no significant difference in the engagement level for the ICP group ($M = 4.20$, $SD = 0.98$) and the FSP group ($M = 4.27$, $SD = 0.97$), $t(410) = -0.75$, $p = 0.454$ (two-tailed). The mean difference was 0.07 with a 95% confidence interval ranging from -0.26 to 0.12. The effect size was small (eta squared $= 0.07$).

Next, Spearman correlations were calculated between the motivation level and the engagement level. For the entire data set including both treatment groups, the overall correlation between three mind–time frames of motivation pre-survey and PPLS engagement post-survey was 0.33, and that between the motivation post-survey and PPLS engagement post-survey was 0.43. Thus, both relationships were considered to be moderately correlated. As indicated in Table 10.7, the correlations in each group were also found to be moderate, ranging from 0.32 to 0.48. All correlation coefficients were statistically significant at $p < 0.001$. In other words, it can be said for both groups that the more engaged students were in prosocial ways, the more

Table 10.7 Spearman correlations between motivation and engagement

	Engagement post-survey
Motivation pre-survey	
ICP Group (n = 235)	0.32*
FSP Group (n = 177)	0.36*
Motivation post-survey	
ICP Group (n = 235)	0.48*
FSP Group (n = 177)	0.37*

* $p < 0.001$
($N = 412$)

motivated they were, and vice versa. In sum, students in both treatment groups became more engaged in studying English by the end of the semester, and their motivation and PPLS engagement were related.

Comparison 2

The two groups were also compared in terms of the relationship between motivational change and end-of-semester PPLS engagement. As discussed in the previous section, both groups were found to have motivational increases. Also, their final motivational levels were found to relate moderately to their PPLS engagement levels, which themselves were found to be similar between the two groups. In these last two aspects, we expected to find a difference between the groups.

Correlation coefficients were computed between the motivational change and PPLS engagement levels in each group. In the ICP group, the correlation coefficient was 0.16 with statistical significance ($p = 0.013$), while in the FSP group, the correlation coefficient was 0.04, and it was statistically insignificant. Figure 10.2 shows the scatter plots of students in the ICP group. The correlation between the motivational change and PPLS engagement of the ICP group is not large, but it is significant. This relationship was not found in the FSP group. This result indicates that ICP may promote students' motivations and engagement in a way that brings about their co-development. In other words, the ideal classmates intervention could be helping the three mind–time frames of motivation and PPLS engagement to grow at a closer pace together or more in harmony with each other.

Discussion and Conclusion

Both initial motivation and subsequent engagement appear to be lacking in Japanese tertiary education, the setting of this study. This is particularly the case as it has been observed that students are often bored during English classes, afraid of peer judgement and interaction, and confused

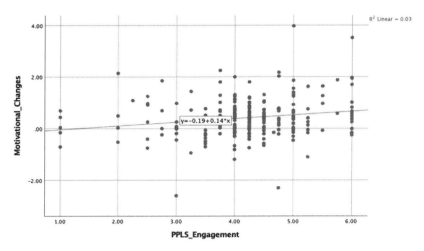

Figure 10.2 Plots indicating the relationship between motivational change and PPLS engagement in the ideal classmates group

about how to engage each other in conversation (King, 2013a, 2013b). Our study randomly placed whole classes into either of two priming treatments, sharing each other's ideal classmates or their future selves, to test whether the ICP can have a discernable effect on learners' three mind–time frames of motivation and their resulting PPLS engagement. Both treatments appeared to boost personal motivation and peer engagement through creating mutual understanding and closer personal relationships during class time, as summarized in Table 10.8. Students in both conditions reported positive feelings of increased friendliness among their classmates while making or taking greater opportunities to speak English together, with minimal reports of negative feelings such as demotivation.

The most salient result in the open-ended descriptions about how students were assisting each other in class was that the ICP group reported more than the FSP group the intentional efforts of peers in making a friendly, safe and buoyant environment in which to practice speaking English. By tapping into the emotional and behavioral aspects of

Table 10.8 Summary of findings

Qualitative	Quantitative
Undetectable as to which treatment promotes students' engagement more.	Both groups improved three-mind time frames of motivation at the same rate.
ICP may promote creating a friendly and safe atmosphere more.	Both groups report the same levels of prosocial engagement.
FSP may promote communicating in English more.	ICP may more likely foster a closer or harmonious development between an individual's motivational growth and the group's prosocial engagement.

motivation, this can reduce feelings of social hypersensitivity and fear of negative judgement of others. Meanwhile, the FSP group reported at a slightly higher rate than the ICP group with relation to sustained speaking in English inside and outside the classroom. Perhaps they were able to stay on-task with using the target language because of a heightened awareness of the mutual long-term goal of being able to speak English, which can be attached to the cognitive aspects of motivation. Based on this difference, we can infer different ways of boosting personal motivation and peer engagement between the ICP and FSP groups, as highlighted in Table 10.9.

The interconnectivity between the increase of personal motivation and peer engagement did not appear to be affected to the same extent in the two groups. Although the interconnectivity was very small in both ICP and FSP groups, only for the ICP group did there arise a statistically significant inter-correlation between the increase of personal motivational growth and peer engagement, as represented in Figure 10.3. This association suggests that the ICP helps inspire the kind of peer engagement that interfaces deeply with personal motivation. This means that ICP could increase EFL prosocial engagement in a way that taps into individual students' personal motivation.

While the FSP and the ICP both performed well, the ICP seems to offer a better fit for enhancing in-class prosocial engagement in the present. The implications are that teachers may be able to encourage more motivation and engagement in classes by having students share their ideal classmates. The bigger implication is that humans in general may have ecological pro-social tendencies but need explicit guidance and focus, along with time and opportunities, to put motivational intentions into visible actions. Much within educational and assessment systems worldwide isolates and indi-vidualizes students, placing them into direct competition with each other, which discourages them from bonding socially and cooperating academi-cally. Such educational practices incur an unwise disregard of the funda-mental need of human connectivity for healthy motivations and engagement in learning and living (Skinner & Pitzer, 2012).

Both treatments in this study are designed to help students make meaning-ful connections together about and through their L2 learning. Although both

Table 10.9 Ways of boosting personal motivation and peer engagement

ICP	FSP
Mutual preferences among classmates for how to care for each other's L2 learning becomes identifiable.	Mutual goals among classmates for future L2 use can become more identifiable.
Mutual preferences and requests for helpful classroom learning behaviors becomes highlighted.	Non-mutual goals can become more appreciated and respected.
New ideas for how to help others learn can be inspiring, so new ways to assist peers can be tried out.	Different goals can be communicable, so new goals and perhaps greater aspirations can spread across the classroom social network.

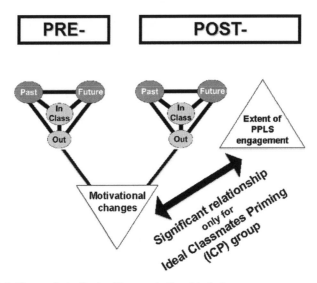

Figure 10.3 The statistically significant relationship between peer engagement and growth in personal motivation recognized only in ICP group

have their advantages, the ICP has an added advantage because when sharing ideal classmates images, there is a built-in focus on the *how-to* of giving help in peer-assisted English learning in the present moment; whereas in looping back answers to the FSP, there is a built-in focus on the *what* of using English in a far off future. Thus, the key difference seems to be that the ICP provides students with *how-to* information in an immediate situation in which they can practice it. For example, if smiling at a conversational partner is said by class-mates to be advantageous in learning, students can put it to the test right there in class. Such declarative knowledge, if practiced, becomes procedural knowl-edge. In other words, the *how-to* of ideal classmates becomes the *know-how* in a practical way. For students who feel stuck, the *how-to* gives them pathways thinking and agency thinking, which means they have hope (Snyder *et al.*, 1999). Thus, cognitive, emotional and behavioral components of engagement (Skinner & Pitzer, 2012) appear to be more deeply interconnected and acti-vated by motivation with the ICP. In contrast, there is no *how-to* information built into sharing future selves images, nor is there an immediate and actual situation available to put these future selves into practice, other than perhaps what could be imagined. Students can imagine becoming globe-trotting busi-nesspeople giving board meeting talks in English, but few are the practical ways of putting the actual required skills of future selves to the test in the classroom. The ICP readily increases chances for metacognition and peer engagement, handing a visceral boost to underlying personal motivation in reciprocation of others' raised motivations. Further increases to motivation can be gotten whenever there is a peer available to put the *how-to* into practice. This kind of motivation is therefore sustainable through peer networks inside and outside the classroom. Students can use their *know-how* to greet each other with peer-tested ideas that can help unfocused and inattentive peers gain focus and involvement, turn boredom into interest and make apathy and avoidance of learning dissolve into purposeful and willing participation.

References

Davis, W. (2018) Raising metacognitive awareness using ideal classmates. In J. Mynard and I. Brady (eds) *Stretching Boundaries. Papers from the Third International Psychology of Language Learning Conference, Tokyo, Japan, 7–10 June, 2018* (pp. 79–81). International Association of the Psychology of Language Learning (IAPLL).

Dörnyei, Z. (2009) The L2 motivational self system. In Z. Dörnyei and E. Ushioda (eds) *Motivation, Language Identity and the L2 Self* (pp. 9–42). Bristol: Multilingual Matters.

Falout, J. (2016) Past selves: Emerging motivational guides across temporal contexts. In J. King (ed.) *The Dynamic Interplay Between Context and the Language Learner* (pp. 47–65). Basingstoke: Palgrave Macmillan.

Falout, J., Fukada, Y., Murphey, T. and Fukuda, T. (2013) What's working in Japan? Present communities of imagining. In M.T. Apple, D. Da Silva and T. Fellner (eds) *Language Learning Motivation in Japan* (pp. 245–267). Bristol: Multilingual Matters.

Finn, J.D. and Zimmer, K.S. (2012) Student engagement: What is it? Why does it matter? In S.L. Christenson, A.L. Reschly and C. Wylie (eds) *Handbook of Research on Student Engagement* (pp. 97–131). New York: Springer.

Fukada, Y., Murphey, T., Falout, J. and Fukuda, T. (2017) Essential motivational group dynamics: A 3-year panel study. In R. Breeze and C.S. Guinda (eds) *Essential Competencies for English-Medium University Teaching* (pp. 249–266). Basel: Springer.

IBM. IBM SPSS statistics for Macintosh, Version 25.0 [computer software]. Armon, NY: IBM.

Juvonen, J., Espinoza, G. and Knifsend, C. (2012) The role of peer relationships in student academic and extracurricular engagement. In S.L. Christenson, A.L. Reschly and C. Wylie (eds) *Handbook of Research on Student Engagement* (pp. 387–401). New York: Springer.

King, J. (2013a) *Silence in the Second Language Classroom*. Basingstoke: Palgrave Macmillan.

King, J. (2013b) Silence in the second language classrooms of Japanese universities. *Applied Linguistics* 34 (3), 325–343.

Markus, H. and Nurius, P. (1986) Possible selves. *American Psychologist* 41 (9), 954–969.

Murphey, T., Falout, J., Fukuda, T. and Fukada, Y. (2014) Socio-dynamic motivating through idealizing classmates. *System* 45, 242–253.

Norton, B. and McKinney, C. (2011) An identity approach to second language acquisition. *Alternative Approaches to Second Language Acquisition* (pp. 73–94). New York: Routledge.

Pallant, J. (2016) *SPSS Survival Manual* (6th edn). Maidenhead: McGraw-Hill Education.

Reschly, A.L. and Christenson, S.L. (2012) Jingle, jangle, and conceptual haziness: Evolution and future directions of the engagement construct. In S.L. Christenson, A.L. Reschly and C. Wylie (eds) *Handbook of Research on Student Engagement* (pp. 3–19). New York: Springer.

Skinner, E.A. and Pitzer, J.R. (2012) Developmental dynamics of student engagement, coping, and everyday resilience. In S.L. Christenson, A.L. Reschly and C. Wylie (eds) *Handbook of Research on Student Engagement* (pp. 21–44). New York: Springer.

Snyder, C.R., Michael, S.T. and Cheavens, J.S. (1999) Hope as a psychotherapeutic foundation of common factors, placebos, and expectancies. In M.A. Hubble, B.L. Duncan and S.D. Miller (eds) *The Heart and Soul of Change: What Works in Therapy* (pp. 179–200). Washington, DC: American Psychological Association.

Wentzel, K.R. (1994) Relations of social goal pursuit to social acceptance, classroom behavior, and perceived social support. *Journal of Educational Psychology* 86 (2), 173–182.

11 Engagement and Immersion in Virtual Reality Narratives

Nicole Mills

Introduction

At the *New Images Festival* in Paris in June 2019, artists, filmmakers and media specialists convened to discuss new formats of reality, virtual worlds and the power of immersive content. Vicki Dobbs Beck, an executive at Lucas films' ILMxLAB, discussed how we can move from storytelling to story living through the power of presence in immersive technologies. Zillah Watson, the editorial lead for digital storytelling projects at the British Broadcasting Corporation (BBC), further discussed how virtual worlds enhance traditional journalism by allowing users to feel as if they are 'living' experiences. Associated with experiential events, Sarah Ellis, the director of digital development at the Royal Shakespeare Company, illustrated how immersive content allows theater enthusiasts to go places that they could not go before by blending the digital and real worlds. Access to new and novel locations are also of interest to media creators and artists such as Hsien-Chien Huang, who described how artists can now create virtual worlds and invite audiences to 'walk' into their art. Finally, Roel Amit, the head of digital and multimedia at the museum and exhibit hall the Grand Palais, claimed that immersive technologies are creating a 'new design of attention.' The emergence of immersive content is clearly raising questions in diverse fields about how we can design experiences to engage participants and involve audiences.

In the field of foreign language education, Walker and White (2013) state that emerging technologies are also transforming the teaching of language and culture in powerful ways. Through the expansion of traditional classroom boundaries, virtual environments have the potential to create meaningful opportunities for cultural and linguistic immersion. Depending on the instructional design, learners can complete tasks, receive scaffolded support, interact with virtual objects or people, and exercise some form of control within immersive worlds. Thus, the exploratory nature of virtual environments has the potential to develop 'heightened and sustained engagement in learning' (Brill & Park, 2008: 74). If instructors thoughtfully align carefully constructed goals with sound pedagogy, immersion and engagement can become 'intrinsically linked' (Allcoat & Von Muhlenen, 2018: 1).

Virtual reality (VR) is an immersive technology that 'provides the user with a highly responsive and fully immersive experience of a constructed virtual environment that is both visual and auditory' (Schott & Marshall, 2018: 843). In this 360-degree multidimensional space, learners experience a deeply contextualized, real-world environment in multiple sensory modalities. Scholars suggest that learners create deep connections with course content, alter their perceptions and attitudes and learn complex information in immersive contexts (Liu *et al.*, 2017). This chapter describes the development of a Paris Narrative VR project for beginning French language students in which four Parisians from different backgrounds recorded their personal, social, and professional lives with a VR camera. Each Parisian VR narrative allows language learners to vividly experience Parisian life in visual, auditory and sensory modalities.

In contrast to many other contributions in this volume, this chapter is not empirical but instead showcases how this deeply contextualized and culturally immersive platform and its accompanying teaching materials target the cognitive, behavioral, emotional and social dimensions of engagement (Philp & Duchesne, 2016). As such, this chapter will showcase the potential future of engagement in the L2 classroom in a theory meets practice approach. First, the chapter will highlight the theoretical and research-based foundations of the Paris VR narrative project and then turn to practical implementations that aim to foster student engagement through instructional design. Future research implications regarding research design and data elicitation will follow.

Immersion in Virtual Environments

Immersion in digital environments is a 'mediated, simulated experience that involves the willing suspension of disbelief' (Dede *et al.*, 2017: 4). It is 'the subjective experience of being in one place environment, even when one is physically situated in another' (Witmer & Singer, 1998: 225). Virtual immersion can motivate learners through the illusion of *presence,* or the perceived participation in the experiences of another reality (Sadowski & Stanney, 2002). Powerful immersion and place illusion occur when immersion takes place on several levels: sensory, actional, social, psychological and symbolic/narrative (Dede *et al.*, 2017). Learners can experience *sensory immersion* through visual, audio and sensory stimuli in head-mounted, three-dimensional displays. To achieve *actional immersion,* learners initiate actions that spark consequences within the virtual environments, thus motivating learners and focusing their attention.

Participation in social interactions can absorb students in *social immersion* and give them the impression that they are part of the virtual world, whereas immersive contexts with strong, real-world narratives can trigger *symbolic/narrative immersion* by deepening the intellectual nature of the experience. *Psychological immersion* is the 'mental state of being completely absorbed or engaged in something' (Dede *et al.*, 2017: 3) and can happen when sensory, actional, social and symbolic/narrative immersion unite in digital environments.

Scholars suggest that the use of virtual reality can ease the transfer of knowledge, deepen understanding and empathy, and change the ways students experience material (Dede *et al.*, 2017). While immersed in a simulated experience, participants can turn and move around as they would in the real world which makes participants feel that their actions are closely connected to the VR experience. This type of embodiment and sensorimotor engagement in immersive reality can lead to the implicit learning of complex information, sometimes beyond what is possible in reality (Johnson-Glenburg, 2017; Slater, 2017). For example, individuals can implicitly learn motor tasks using VR experiences (Bailenson *et al.*, 2008). Other research suggests that VR can allow individuals to simulate realistic scenarios and participate (peripherally) in authentic communities of practice (Krämer, 2017). Klinger *et al.* (2005), for instance, found that individuals were able to implicitly confront social anxiety through simulated small-talk conversations in VR.

Dede (2009) states that immersion in educational multi-user virtual environments can enhance learner engagement. In the middle school science education program *River City,* for example, students take on the role of scientists immersed in a simulated 19th-century city and are charged with the task of determining why the inhabitants are falling ill. They interact with digital avatars, manipulate artifacts, explore the context and collaboratively use their problem-solving skills to hypothesize causes for illness and propose evidence-based solutions. Clark *et al.* (2006) claim that students were deeply engaged in this immersive curriculum because of its actional and symbolic immersion characteristics. Engagement measures included pre-and post-implementation surveys and focus groups about students' attendance at school (which increased) and teachers' perceptions of student motivation and disruptive behavior (which decreased). Their research findings further suggest that students were more engaged in this immersive environment than in a similar paper-based curriculum with laboratory experiments. Iqbal *et al.* (2010) indicate that experiential learning occurs in immersive environments like *River City* because learners interact 'in a graphical, immersive, and embodied context' (2010: 3201). To design for engaged learning, they conclude that virtual environments (similar to other engagement-driven learning design environments) should be authentic, experiential, inquiry-based, and game-like and the instructional design should facilitate collaboration and social interaction.

Flow

Whereas psychological *immersion* is a mental state of being absorbed in an environment, *flow* describes an intrinsically enjoyable and rewarding mental state when a person is completely immersed in an activity. Csikszentmihalyi (2014a) outlines several conditions that encompass the flow experience. With clear goals and immediate feedback, individuals experiencing 'flow' are so deeply involved, concentrated and focused on an activity that their actions become spontaneous and automatic. This feeling of deep concentration leads to a sense of control, a lack of self-consciousness and the impression that anything is possible. Participants in flow do not feel separated from their performed actions, but instead entirely present and embodied within the experience. As such, time either passes faster or slower. This intense concentration leads individuals to feel as if they are transcended outside the reality and routine of everyday life. Csikszentmihalyi states: When the concentration reaches a certain point, people begin to feel the condition that often is described as 'ecstatic.' Ecstasy sounds like a very mystical term, and it can be that, but in its original Greek sense, ecstasy simply meant 'to stand to the side' or 'to step to the side.' The experience of standing to the side is that you are not a part of the routine of everyday life anymore (2014a: 134). This perceived transcendence leads individuals 'in flow' to feel as if they are participating peripherally in the activity – looking from the outside in.

To achieve flow in educational contexts, Csikszentmihalyi (2014b) states that instructional design should intrigue students with rewarding and personally meaningful content. Although this idealized state can be difficult to attain (if even attainable) in language classrooms, Egbert (2003) claims that appropriate task design may facilitate flow in language learning contexts. For example, she encourages the design of teaching materials that encourage self-discovery and a process orientation. Opportunities to experience control and freedom within the learning activity, yet clearly understand the goals, rules and structure of the task can further encourage flow experiences. By incorporating a certain degree of structured ritual through clear instructions and predictability in lesson design, learners' attention can be focused (a key feature of engaged learning). Furthermore, a range of levels within the challenges allows students to participate meaningfully and purposefully at their own level (or slightly above). Students are further motivated if connections are made to students' existing knowledge. Collaboration among learners then helps build a sense of community among diverse learners (Csikszentmihalyi, 2014b).

In the field of foreign language education, Egbert posits that there are four essential conditions of flow in FL learning tasks:

(a) there is a balance between challenge and skills that arouses the participants' will to explore;
(b) the participant perceives that his or her attention is focused;

(c)   the participant finds the task intrinsically interesting or authentic (and will repeat it); and

(d)   The participant perceives a sense of control. (2003: 502)

Through the interaction of challenge, attention, intrinsic interest, and perceived control, Egbert suggests that optimal language learning may occur. Recognizing the importance of mindful attention to carefully structured input in second language acquisition, Egbert further suggests that both unintentional focus and targeted noticing should be key elements of flow experiences in FL learning contexts. Egbert further describes how enjoyment and playfulness, conditions described in flow theory, are also highlighted in studies of language play research in second language acquisition (Cook, 2000).

Engagement

Characteristics of flow, including interest, mindful attention and a sense of control, may all be present during immersion in VR environments. Although separate constructs, flow has been described as the 'ultimate in engagement' (Philp & Duchesne, 2016: 59) and reflects the experience of being deeply immersed in an enjoyable activity. *Engagement*, however, refers to a range of interactions with learning experiences – from the optimal to the less optimal. Optimal engagement occurs when students are focused, persistent, on task, challenged, curious and involved (Christenson *et al.*, 2012; Oga-Baldwin & Nakata, 2017). Engagement has often been described as a multifaceted construct with interrelated and interdependent characteristics (Boekaerts, 2016; Eccles, 2016). Although there has been a lack of consensus among scholars regarding its multidimensional features, scholars generally agree that engagement includes three major components: behavioral (action), affective (feeling) and cognitive (thinking) (Mercer, 2019). Philp and Duchesne (2016) believe that engagement includes four dimensions: cognitive, behavioral, emotional and social. I review these briefly to add coherence to my description of this project.

Cognitive engagement occurs when students make connections, justify arguments, reason, exchange ideas, answer questions and solve problems. Indicators of cognitive engagement are the use of questions, connectors such as 'because,' or phrases that express opinions ('I think'), examples ('in particular'), or conflicting viewpoints ('it is argued that') (Philp & Duchesne, 2016). When students are then asked to notice or observe phenomena followed by thoughtful reflection, cognitive engagement develops (Svalberg, 2009).

Behavioral engagement happens when students pay attention, focus, participate, extend effort and persist during classroom tasks. Instructional tasks that provide clear instructions, establish explicit objectives, and break down complex tasks into accessible steps focus students' attention and strengthen behavioral engagement (Philp & Duchesne, 2016).

Social engagement takes place when students interact, explain ideas, collaborate and participate in group work. When students engage socially with peers who listen attentively to their ideas, they enjoy the activity, spend more time on task (like behavioral engagement), and feel supported and positively encouraged (Philp & Duchesne, 2016). Instructors socially engage students by providing clear feedback and praise, respecting opinions and soliciting student input (Gettinger & Walter, 2012).

Emotional engagement occurs when learners experience a strong interest, connection and excitement toward a task. An emotionally engaged student finds pleasure in the learning experience and feels that the topic is valuable, meaningful and inherently interesting. Teaching materials that allow learners to discover, explore and make choices based on their own interests provide the autonomy necessary to establish emotional engagement (Lam *et al.*, 2012).

Course Description

Goals of the Paris VR narrative project within the beginning French II course were to immerse students in culturally relevant VR experiences and target the social, cognitive, emotional and behavioral dimensions of engagement. The design of the course, entitled 'Paris in Virtual Reality,' is framed within a global simulation curriculum and asks students to adopt a French or francophone identity and immerse themselves in a simulation of life in the 11th *arrondissement* of Paris. They live virtually with their fellow classmates in a building in the 11th *arrondissement* near *La Place de la République* and write chapters of their lives in their memoirs. Through interactive writing assignments and in-class role-plays, they co-develop a storyline with their fellow 'neighbors' while exploring various facets of Parisian culture. The virtual world and real world come together in this course by exploring Parisian culture through themes such as architecture, art, music and graffiti in the various Parisian quarters and current events such as COVID-19 in Paris and the Yellow Vest movement. Through the course materials, students become familiar with various products of Parisian culture including housing, historical sites, films, authors, musicians and artists. They also learn about the daily life of Parisians including the diversity of routines, leisure activities and social practices. Through virtual reality experiences, interactions with native speakers, and the exploration of various texts and media forms (i.e. photos, art and film), the goals of the course are to develop students' understanding of the diversity of Parisian life while engaging students in interpersonal communication and the interpretation and production of language in written and oral forms. Through the course materials, students learn to speak and write in the past, present and future tenses, make suggestions, express emotions, express opinions, extend, accept and refuse invitations, give advice, and express hypothetical situations. In addition to the four interactive writing assignments, assessment includes chapter quizzes, daily homework including grammar and vocabulary exercises, conversations with native speakers using the Talk Abroad platform (one per chapter), and a final written and oral exam.

College students enrolled in the Beginning French II course at Harvard University have typically taken one semester of Beginning French or have less than two years of high school French. Placement in the course is confirmed through a university placement exam. Each section of the course has a maximum of 17 students and the course is three days per week (1-hour 15-minute sessions). The department typically offers five to six sections of the course in the Spring and one section in the Fall. The course curriculum is taught by various instructors, with coordinator supervision and oversight. Since the project's development in 2018, all students enrolled in the course participate in the Paris VR immersive experiences. All VR experiences take place in the students' assigned classroom.

Paris VR Narrative Project

Narratives and stories have long been recognized as efficient tools for language learning and teaching as they establish context and encourage connected discourse (Ryan & Irie, 2014). Hiver *et al.* (2019: 88) state that, 'people create meaning and purpose through the construction of life stories'. Dörnyei and Ryan (2015) introduced a narrative-based model for the psychology of language learner that centralizes the role of the L2 learner's life stories and identity. In his description of this model, Dörnyei (2017: 87) states that it focuses on 'the dynamic development of real people in real contexts'. In the field of VR, media specialists are similarly exploring how we can use immersive technologies such as VR to expand storytelling platforms and deepen intellectual engagement through *narrative immersion* (Dede *et al.*, 2017). Watson (2019) states that VR content should provide participants with unique and distinctive stories that they would not be able to experience the same way in any other medium.

For this course, four different Parisians who live in and around *La Place de la République* were hired to document and share the stories of their lives with a 360 VR camera. These real people in real contexts constructed their life stories in VR with the end goal of creating narrative identities that inspire and motivate L2 learners. The four characters were Aude, Benoît, Youssef and Lee. Aude was a talkative, social, and friendly 23-year-old woman who worked as a waitress near the Champs-Elysées. She lived alone in a small studio and regularly visited her family of French and English origins in the suburbs outside of Paris. Benoît was a creative, free-spirited 25-year-old magician/actor/singer-songwriter and tour guide of hidden Paris. He was born in La Réunion and his family of Spanish and

French origins lived in a small town in the Pyrenees. Youssef was a 33-year old filmmaker from Tunisia who came to France at the age of 17 to study film. He lived with his girlfriend in the 11th *arrondissement*. Lee was an 11-year-old who lived with his parents and younger brother. He was a curious and intelligent young boy with interests in books, tennis and biking.

By showcasing the lives of four Parisians with different careers, ethnicities and backgrounds who live and experience the same space, the representation of Parisian culture becomes rich, nuanced and deeply contextualized. The goal of the VR documentation was to give students the opportunity to 'live' the stories of diverse Parisians through virtual immersion. They could see not only the architecture and cultural landmarks but participate peripherally in experiences that were unexplored and unexpected. The four Parisians provided virtual access to certain encounters that students may never come across during a visit or long-term stay in Paris. Students were invited to intimate conversations among close friends during a late afternoon *apéro*, house parties with twenty-something French students, or visits to off-the-grid Parisian locations. Whereas students traditionally explore Parisian culture through film clips, interviews and photos, the goals of the Paris VR project were to immerse students in real-world Paris in authentic ways though visual, auditory, and sensory stimuli. Targeted goals include (1) motivating, engaging and awakening enthusiasm in students; (2) providing students with active learning experiences through virtual exploration and interaction; and (3) deepening their knowledge of culture and authentic language use.

The four dimensions of engagement (Philp & Duchesne, 2016) will be highlighted in brackets throughout the description of the VR program and instructional design. Although the targeted (and most salient) dimensions of engagement are often highlighted separately throughout the following description in brackets, it is important to recall that engagement is a multidimensional construct with interrelated and interdependent characteristics. Several dimensions of engagement may be happening simultaneously. Furthermore, although this example showcases the interplay of the various dimensions of engagement within a Paris VR project for beginning French students, general design principles for a pedagogy of engagement (applied to various instructional contexts) will follow.

The 360 footage from the four participants was carefully reviewed, selected and later edited using Wonda VR 360 editing software under the guidance of Rus Gant, the Director of the university's visualization lab and Arnaud Dressen, CEO of Wonda VR. To begin the VR experience, the learner enters a digitally constructed immersive map of Paris with *La Place de la République* highlighted at the center. As the learner turns their head and looks around the Parisian map, he sees the profile photos of four Parisians. Using an eye-gaze interface, the learner can select a photo to get more personal information about the character (i.e. age, profession, likes and dislikes, origin, etc.) The learner can then choose to *lancer le film* (begin the film) or look at the character's weekly agenda to get more detailed information about their life. The weekly agenda includes the character's authentic daily schedule with several links to short 3–5-minute VR extracts. Students may select and view the short VR segments, or they may instead choose to be immersed in the extended story of one of the four Parisians without interruption [emotional engagement]. If the students choose to start the film, the VR experience begins with the character's introduction through voiceover narration. This introduction is transcribed for reference. Titles then introduce the context, location and time of each new scene within the story (see Figure 11.1). At any point within the experience, the learner can decide to watch a scene again, advance to a different scene of greater interest, or return to the character's agenda to make a new selection [emotional engagement]. At the end of the extended immersive experience, the character concludes their story with a transcribed voiceover farewell (see Figure 11.1).

Within the program, there are a variety of support and interactive features to scaffold the learner experience [behavioral engagement]. Narrative voice-over was added to VR segments with less conversation exchange. Because an affordance of the VR experience is the ability to observe complex cultural phenomena, consistent subtitles are not included as they could divert students' attention from careful observation within the 3D environment. To provide support for those who needed or preferred additional scaffolding, students have the option to turn the transcribed narration on or off depending on their comprehension level [emotional engagement/cognitive engagement]. Intermittent subtitles are also included in certain scenes to provide the beginning level students with a general understanding of the conversation topic.

Figure 11.1 Structure of La République

Figure 11.2 Interactive character selection

In selected scenes, learners can make choices within the immersive experience [emotional engagement]. At Aude's birthday party in her studio apartment, for example, learners can choose to immerse themselves in the ambiance of the 'party' experience and feel as if they are socializing and mingling among party guests as they dance beside them. If learners want to get more information about the guests, they can select the targeted pin above the guest using an eye-gaze interface. The party then pauses, and Aude provides a narrated description of the party guest with transcribed voice-over for scaffolded support (see Figure 11.2).

In another scene, students have the option to explore and interact with objects in Benoît's apartment [emotional engagement/social engagement]. If learners want to learn more information about the story behind the poster, book or computer in his apartment, for example, they can select the object using an eye-gaze interface. After they select the object, they can hear Benoît narrate the humorous story of the computer that he had the good fortune of picking up off the street as an irritated girlfriend threw her boyfriend's belongings out the window. If they select the poster, they can hear Benoît passionately describe his acting role in a theatrical performance of Shakespeare (see Figure 11.3). The voiceover narration is also transcribed and visually made available to students.

Engagement Through Instructional Design

Fredricks *et al.* (2016) suggest that engagement is malleable and highly contextual. The interrelated dimensions of engagement may be influenced by the classroom environment, course design and instructional practices (Oga-Baldwin & Nakata, 2017). Engagement can be enhanced if the instructional design intrigues students with meaningful content. The Paris VR narrative project aims to spark students' interest in Parisian culture. Targeted goals of the unit entitled *Qu'est-ce que ça veut dire être Parisien?* (What does it mean to be Parisian?) are to explore students' preconceptions

Figure 11.3 Interactive object selection

of Parisian culture and to challenge or confirm preconceptions through VR exploration, discussion and analysis of Parisian life. On the first day of the unit, students are asked to write down and discuss their answers to the question 'What does it mean to be Parisian?' [cognitive and social engagement] (see Table 11.1). The goal of this initial question is to elicit students' existing knowledge, preconceptions and perceptions of Parisian culture. When students are asked to justify arguments and make connections by expressing opinions with supporting examples, such as with this sample prompt, students may become cognitively and socially engaged (Svalberg, 2009).

Following this class discussion, the instructor describes the Paris VR narrative project. The instructor explains that four Parisians who live in and around *La Place de la République* documented their lives with 360 cameras over the course of two months. The instructor describes how, during each day of the unit, students immerse themselves in the storied life of a different Parisian in VR. On the final day, the students take part in a comparative discussion and analysis of the four narratives and synthesize their understanding of Parisian life.

Table 11.1 What does it mean to be Parisian?

In your opinion, what does it mean to be Parisian? [open-ended response]

- What are key products of Parisian culture? (i.e. buildings, architecture, theater, food, etc.)
- What do you know about the cultural practices of Parisians? (social interactions, behaviors, how do they interact in varied situations, etc.?)
- How would you describe the attitudes, values, beliefs, and worldview of Parisians?

Note: Translated from French.

Before beginning the VR experience, the students are given a brief 5-minute introduction to the structure of *La République* in English. Using Figure 11.1 as a reference, the instructor explains how to navigate the program using the agenda, eye-gaze interface and main menu. The goal is to establish clarity and focus students' attention by clearly laying out the goals, rules and structure of the VR experience [behavioral engagement]. Instructions as to how to fit the headset, control volume, and raise their hand to flag technical difficulties are also provided. Students are encouraged to take personal control of the experience by re-watching intriguing scenes and skipping less-appealing segments [emotional engagement]. Because a certain degree of structured ritual focuses students' attention and maximizes participation (Csikszentmihalyi, 2014a), the instructional materials that accompany each character's VR experience are divided into four distinct phases: (1) Pre-viewing; (2) Immersive Viewing; (3) Focused Viewing; and (4) Analysis. Students refer to the instructional tasks on separate handouts.

Phase 1: Pre-viewing

In the pre-viewing phase, students receive an image of the character's weekly agenda in a supporting handout. Students are asked to read the weekly agenda, make predictions about the character's identity, and hypothesize the VR narrative content (see Figure 11.4). Predictions spark curiosity and further engage and intrigue students in the content that will follow [emotional engagement].

Discussion questions aim to activate students' prior knowledge and schemata [cognitive engagement]. Examples include: Who is this character? What is his personality like? How does he spend his time? (see Table 11.2). Students discuss predictions with a partner and the class de-briefs in a large group discussion [social engagement].

Figure 11.4 Character agenda

Table 11.2 Sample pre-viewing task

Look at the agenda of this Parisian whose name is Lee. Imagine…
• Who is Lee? What is his personality like?
• With whom do you think he spends the most of his time? His family? His friends? Explain.
• Where do you think he spends his time? At the house? Outside?
• How does he spend his time? Doing his homework? Having fun?
Questions created by Emily Epperson & Emma Zitzow-Childs

Note: Translated from French.

The next pre-viewing task presents the character's transcribed introduction. Students further hypothesize the character's identity [cognitive engagement] and discuss the questions in pairs and follow-up large group discussion [social engagement]. Sample questions include: Where, how and with whom does he spend his time? In your opinion, what is his personality like?

Phase 2: Immersive viewing

Recall that emotional engagement occurs when learners feels that the topic is valuable, meaningful, and interesting. Tasks that are perceived as relevant and authentic create intrinsically motivating experiences for students. Furthermore, the visual, audio and sensory stimuli found in VR experiences can foster sensory immersion, embodiment and a sense of presence in the experiences of another reality (Dede *et al.*, 2017; Sadowski & Stanney, 2002). As such, in the immersive viewing phase, students read three reflection questions [cognitive engagement] and then immerse themselves in the character's authentic world for 15 minutes [emotional engagement/behavioral engagement]. Sample instructions include: 'Now we will meet Benoît! Before beginning the virtual experience, here are some questions to keep in mind…' (translated from French). This phase includes a few generalized questions about the character's personality, background, relationships with others, or identity. For Benoît, sample questions include: Describe Benoît. What can you say about his professional life? What can you say about his social life? (translated from French). Emotional engagement is enhanced by allowing learners to discover, explore, and make choices (Lam *et al.*, 2012). In this phase, students are given the autonomy to independently discover and explore the VR narrative and advance or re-watch sections as desired [emotional engagement]. After the immersion phase, students discuss the guiding questions with a partner. During the large group discussion, instructors further engage students by soliciting student opinions, offering feedback, and encouraging and praising students for their contributions [social engagement]. To focus students' attention, the task includes instructions

Table 11.3 Sample immersive viewing task

I.   During the viewing

Now we are going to meet Benoît!

Before entering the VR experience, here are a few questions to keep in mind:

- What is Benoît' like? Describe his life.
- Where does Benoît work? How would you describe his professional life?
- What are Benoît's friends like? What can you say about his social life?

[Instructions: Choose *Benoît* and click *lancer le film*. The entire series of VR film clips for Benoît lasts approximately 16 minutes, but you can click the arrow button to move to the next segment (or return to the previous segment) if you wish. We will ask you to immerse yourself in Benoît's life for approximately 15 minutes.]

Discussion with your partner.

Guiding Questions created by Elsa Cazeneuve

Note: Translated from French.

in English to clarify how to navigate the VR program [behavioral engagement]. A VR headset icon similarly alerts students that the task incorporates VR viewing (see Table 11.3).

Phase 3: Focused viewing

During the focused viewing phase, students re-watch selected short clips with targeted comprehension and observation questions. Students are not yet asked to analyze, but rather observe the clips to gather facts and information. This data collection phase focuses students' attention by breaking down the complex immersive experience into focused viewing of shorter VR clips curated by theme [behavioral engagement]. Recall that students' attention is focused and behavioral engagement occurs when complex tasks are broken down into accessible steps (Philp & Duchesne, 2016). Like phase two, VR headset icons alert VR viewing and instructions in English ensure clarity regarding navigation. The shorter clips are accessed via the agenda.

For Youssef's VR experience, the class is divided into three groups of three to four students. During phase three, each group is asked to explore one facet of Youssef's life: personal identity, professional identity, or social identity (see Table 11.4). Each group watches two VR clips curated according to the three themes. Students read the guiding questions and then re-watch the selected VR clips [cognitive engagement]. After watching the selected clips, students discuss the data collection questions with their small group. Each group then presents their observations of Youssef's personal, professional or social identity to the class [social engagement/behavioral engagement/cognitive engagement]. The instructor then guides

Table 11.4 Sample focused viewing task

[Instructions : We will divide the class into three groups. Group one will watch the *L'identité privée* clips. Group two will watch the *L'identité professionnelle* clips. Group three will watch the *L'identité sociale* clips. Choose *Youssef* and click on his *agenda*. You will then discuss the questions below with your group.]

Group 3: Social Identity

1.   Café Rue Saint-Maur

- Where are Youssef and his two friends? What are they doing? Describe the place and surroundings, drinks, etc.

- How are they dressed?

2.   Anniversaire de Jeanne

- When does the party take place?

- Describe the apartment: the colors, the furniture.

- Describe the atmosphere: what do the invited guests do? What do they hear? What do they drink?

- How are they dressed?

- What is Youssef doing?

Task and questions created by Grégoire Menu

Note: Instructions were originally in English. Other tasks and questions are translated from French.

students to compare the various facets of Youssef's life in a large group discussion by providing feedback, guiding questions and supportive commentary in phase four [social engagement].

Phase 4: Analysis

Using the collected data from the focused viewing phase, students are asked to make hypotheses and analyze the broader (cultural) context. Thoughtful discussion questions, sometimes accompanied by thought-provoking citations, allow students to think critically about their observations from phases two and three. Questions encourage students to make connections, reason, and justify arguments. Supporting prompts such as 'I think that…' or 'I find that…' encourage students to express opinions. Sample phrases that express example ('for example') or conflicting viewpoints ('in contrast') offer students scaffolded support to engage in a thoughtful discussion with their peers [cognitive and social engagement]. Small vocabulary boxes are sometimes provided to help students articulate their ideas with clarity. In the case of Benoît, students discuss and explore characteristics of his artist lifestyle in phase three. In phase four, students discuss whether they believe that Benoît's daily life corresponds

Table 11.5 Sample analysis questions

Discussion and Analysis
1.   Does Benoit's daily life correspond to your understanding of the life of an artist in Paris in 2018? Why or why not?
I am surprised that…
I am shocked that…   + subjunctive
It is strange that…
I think that…
I find that…   + indicative
For example…
In contrast…
Questions and prompts created by Elsa Cazeneuve

Note: Translated from French.

to their preconceptions of a Parisian artist in 2019 (see Table 11.5). With partners, and later in a large group discussion guided by the instructor, students analyze the larger context and participate in a thoughtful discussion of their opinions [cognitive and social engagement].

Synthesis

On the last day of the unit, there is a culminating class discussion in which students synthesize the knowledge gained from the four Parisian VR narratives [cognitive and social engagement]. Students participate in a comparative discussion of the diverse Parisian narratives with the support of a PowerPoint presentation and handout. There is no VR immersion during the final synthesis discussion. Instead, students engage in a comparative analysis by comparing the homes, social encounters and daily routines of the diverse Parisians. For example, in one task, the class looks at photos of the apartments of Benoît, Lee and Youssef and describes the similarities and differences in the furniture, objects, style and organization. Sample phrases that encourage students to express opinions ('I thought that…') or preconceptions ('I had the impression that') are included within the discussion prompt [cognitive engagement]. Students are then asked to return to their initial clichés about Parisians and to discuss which stereotypes have been confirmed or challenged through the VR experiences, observations and discussions [cognitive engagement]. They discuss how where one lives may or may not influence his/her identity and whether their definition of what it means to be Parisian has become more complex (see Table 11.6). The final class session oscillates between pair and large group discussion with teacher guidance [social engagement].

Table 11.6 Synthesis discussion

Parisian identity reimagined?

Do you remember the clichés that you had about Parisians and Parisian life? What conceptions did you have about Parisians?

- I had the impression that…
- I thought that…

You have seen and discovered a lot this week! Keeping all of this in mind, what is your understanding of Parisian identity now?

- Did your definition become simpler or more complex?
- Do you need to be born in Paris to be Parisian? Do you need to live there all your life?
- What exactly does it mean to be Parisian?

Use examples from the videos, class sessions, etc.

Discussion questions created by Madeleine Wolf

Note: Translated from French.

Pedagogy of Engagement

To design for engaged learning, Iqbal *et al.* (2010) claim that virtual environments should be authentic, experiential, inquiry-based and game-like and the instructional design should foster social interaction. This narrative-based immersive platform and its accompanying teaching materials aim to target engagement through experiential and inquiry-based encounters with real Parisian stories. Although instructors may not always engage students simultaneously in all four dimensions, instructional design should aim for the interplay of the multiple dimensions of engagement. The first step toward student engagement should happen in reflective instructional design. Although applied to a VR unit, this four-phase approach toward engagement could be applied to other instructional contexts incorporating different text types (broadly defined from written, to audio, to audio-visual) (see Kern, 2000).

Several key principles should guide engagement-driven pedagogy. General principles include clear and explicit instructions (using icons, bolding and title headings), predictability in lesson structure, and carefully scaffolded tasks to focus students' attention. Contextualized lessons with compelling themes and complex tasks should be broken down into simple, accessible steps. Each stage of the lesson should be interspersed with small and large group discussions with teacher feedback and guidance.

Phase one of this engagement-driven model aims to target cognitive and social engagement through a preparatory phase in which students discuss predictions and hypotheses about content. Discussion of diverse predictions spark student interest and entices their curiosity about the content that follows, thus targeting cognitive, social and emotional engagement. Phase two of this model encourages autonomy and exploration. This stage gives students' agency to discover and explore the 'text(s)' (broadly defined). Open-ended questions that encourage divergent responses allow students to engage in discovery and enlarge their locus of control. Small and large group discussion of these discoveries further entice students' interest by opening their eyes to material in the text that they may not have identified. All four dimensions of engagement (cognitive, social, emotional and behavioral) may be targeted during this phase. By re-visiting, re-reading, or re-observing targeted shorter segments or elements of the text(s) and highlighting observed phenomena during phase three, students may focus their attention on salient features, thus targeting the cognitive, behavioral and social dimensions. Phase four's discussion and analysis of collected data from phase three emphasize both cognitive and social engagement. At this stage, students may engage in synthesis, comparison and application in small and large group discussion. Vocabulary support accompanied by carefully guided prompts help scaffold the expression of opinions (i.e. 'I think that…') and the support of arguments (i.e. 'for instance…').

This four-phase engagement-driven model could be repeated over several days. Each day could potentially explore a different text type (i.e. song, memoir, painting, etc.) showcasing diverse perspectives on the same theme or topic. Cognitive and social engagement could be further enhanced through the development of carefully scaffolded reflection questions that encourage students to compare, analyze and synthesize the multiple texts' perspectives or representations.

Future Research Directions

Following engagement-driven design on the lesson, unit, and/or curricular levels, evaluation should follow to assess the efficacy of engagement-driven instructional planning. As we move forward with research today, it is important to measure learner engagement with a specificity that corresponds to the learning task(s). Context appropriate measures (see also Chapter 5 by Zhou et al., this volume) that closely align with the instructional design provide the specificity needed to assess the efficacy of the intervention (Mills, 2014). Future directions for the Paris narrative VR project, for example, include data collection to assess the relationship between learner engagement and this engagement-driven instructional design. Future research could include measuring behavioral, social, cognitive and emotional engagement survey items that align with the four phases of the Paris VR narrative instructional design: (1) pre-viewing; (2) immersive viewing; (3) focused viewing; and (4) analysis. Table 11.7 includes a sample engagement item from the *Engagement Versus Disaffection with Learning Measure* (Skinner et al., 2009) that has been adapted to align with the instructional design of the Paris VR project. Because Svalberg (2017) claims that perceived value of a pedagogical task

Table 11.7 Sample adapted engagement items aligned with Paris VR intervention

Sample Behavioral Engagement Items

I pay attention in this class.

Phase 1: When I looked at the character's agenda, I paid close attention.

Phase 2: When I did the extended 15-minute immersion of the character's life in VR, I paid attention to various facets of his life.

Phase 3: When I watched the shorter VR videos, I paid attention to targeted information

Phase 4: When I discussed and analyzed the VR experiences, I paid attention to my classmates' and teachers' comments

Note: Original item from the 'Engagement Versus Disaffection with Learning Measure' (Skinner *et al.*, 2009) is in italics. The additional items listed below are adapted to the Paris VR narrative context. The original survey includes Likert-type scales with responses from 1 (strongly disagree) to 7 (strongly agree).

may predict willingness to engage in a learning experience, a pre-test survey could collect information about student demographics and their attitudes toward VR in the L2 classroom. In a post-test, students could complete the entire adapted engagement survey to further understand students' perceived engagement during the four phases of instruction. Similar approaches to the adaptation of engagement items could be replicated in other contexts and for different task formats.

To supplement the survey data, video recordings and transcriptions of discussions from the five-day unit could be coded for evidence of the various dimensions of engagement. Students could be observed during VR immersion for indications of behavioral and emotional engagement via gestures, body movements, or expressions. Criteria for identifying engagement from Svalberg (2009) and Philp and Duchesne (2016) could be referenced for coding (see Table 11.8). Researchers could be open to overlapping coding to capture the various dimensions of engagement during each phase of instruction.

Next, semi-structured interviews could be conducted for further information about students' perceived engagement during each phase of the learning experience. Regarding emotional engagement, for example, interview questions could include: Were you excited and intrigued by the

Table 11.8 Criteria for identifying engagement (adapted from Svalberg (2009) and Philp & Duchesne, 2016)

Cognitive engagement: reasoning, inducting, making hypotheses, comparing, inferring, drawing conclusions

Social engagement: being socially supportive, interacting, negotiating, scaffolding, initiating

Emotional engagement: exclaiming, laughing, talking, showing waves of excitement, leaning forward, moving closer

Behavioral engagement: being on task, focusing, paying attention, putting forth effort, persisting immersive VR experiences? Why or why not? Which aspects of the VR experiences intrigued you? With reference to cognitive engagement, sample interview questions include: Did you engage in thoughtful analysis of Parisian culture? Why or why not? Which topics and tasks led you to think critically about Parisian culture? Although these recommended evaluation procedures target the Paris VR narrative project, these suggested approaches to evaluation could be adapted to different text types and instructional contexts.

Conclusion

Beck (2019) states that what we do today in the field of VR storytelling is incredibly important for what the field will do tomorrow. The same could be said for the VR experiences and other media designed for foreign language education contexts of the future. Experimentation in instructional design (grounded in scholarly research in engagement) will be an important starting point. If we carefully design teaching materials aligned with engagement theory and research, immersion and engagement have the potential to inform each other and become 'intrinsically linked' (Allcoat & Von Muhlenen, 2018: 1). Instructional design that models this kind of theory-meets-practice orientation can establish an important foundation for the measurement and analysis of learner engagement in the L2 classroom. Data collection and analysis can then provide constructive information to further refine and enhance the instructional materials toward optimal engagement. Without a theory-meets-practice orientation, however, VR and other future emerging technologies with great potential could quickly become 'fun' classroom frills that lose their pedagogical appeal among second language acquisition (SLA) scholars and practitioners. Instead, interactive, narrative-driven immersive experiences with thoughtful attention to engaged instructional design, will allow our foreign language learners to go from simply learning about a language and culture to 'living' and critically engaging with the language and culture in the classroom.

Acknowledgments

I express sincere gratitude to the collaborators on the Paris VR narrative project, Rus Gant and Chris Dede (Harvard University) and Arnaud Dressen and Florian Pannetier (Wonda VR), and to the *Harvard Initiative for Learning and Teaching* for their support of this project. I would also like to thank the French 11 teaching team (Elsa Cazeneuve, Emily Epperson, Grégoire Menu, Madeleine Wolf, Emma Zitzow-Childs) for their innovative pedagogical contributions. A special acknowledgement to *ABL Connect* for their recognition of our project with Harvard's Teaching Innovator Award.

References

Allcoat, D. and Von Muhlenen, A. (2018) Learning in virtual reality: Effects on performance, emotion, and engagement. *Research in Learning Technology* 26, 1–13.

Bailenson, J., Patel, K., Nielsen, A., Bajscy, R., Jung, S.-H. and Kurillo, G. (2008) The effect of interactivity on learning physical actions in virtual reality. *Media Psychology* 11 (3), 354–376.

Beck, V.D. (2019) Star Wars: Step inside our stories. Paper presented at the New Images Festival. Paris, France.

Boekaerts, M. (2016) Engagement as an inherent aspect of the learning process. *Learning and Instruction* 43, 76–83.

Brill, J.M. and Park, Y. (2008) Facilitating engaged learning in the interaction age taking a pedagogically-disciplined approach to innovation with emergent technologies. *International Journal of Teaching and Learning in Higher Education* 20 (1), 70–78.

Christenson, S., Reschly, A. and Wylie, C. (eds) (2012) *Handbook of Research on Student Engagement*. New York: Springer.

Clark, J., Dede, C., Ketelhut, D.J. and Nelson, B. (2006) A design-based research strategy to promote scalability for educational innovations. *Educational Technology* 46 (3), 27–36.

Cook, G. (2000) *Language Play, Language Learning*. Oxford: Oxford University Press.

Csikszentmihalyi, M. (2014a) Flow and education. In M. Csikszentmihalyi (ed.) *Applications of Flow in Human Development: The Collected Works of M. Csikszentmihalyi* (pp. 129–147). Dordrecht: Springer.

Csikszentmihalyi, M. (2014b) Intrinsic motivation and effective teaching. In M. Csikszentmihalyi (ed.) *Applications of Flow in Human Development: The Collected Works of M. Csikszentmihalyi* (pp. 173–186). Dordrecht: Springer.

Dede, C. (2009) Immersive interfaces for engagement and learning. *Science* 323 (5910), 66–69.

Dede, C. Jacobsen, J. and Richards, J. (2017) Introduction: Virtual, augmented, and mixed realities in education. In D. Liu, C. Dede, R. Huang and J. Richards (eds) *Virtual, Augmented, and Mixed Realities in Education* (pp. 1–18). Singapore: Springer.

Dörnyei, Z. (2017) Conceptualizing L2 learner characteristics in a complex, dynamic world. In L. Ortega and Z. Han (eds) *Complexity Theory and Language Development: In Celebration of Diane Larsen-Freeman* (pp. 79–96). Amsterdam: John Benjamins.

Dörnyei, Z. and Ryan, S. (2015) *The Psychology of the Language Learner Revisited*. New York: Routledge.

Eccles, J.S. (2016) Engagement: Where to next? *Learning and Instruction* 43, 71–75.

Egbert, J. (2003) A study of flow theory in language learning contexts. *The Modern Language Journal* 87 (4), 499–518.

Fredricks, J.A., Wang, M., Schall, J., Hofkens, T., Parr, A. and Snug, H. (2016) Using quantitative methods to develop a measure of math and science engagement. *Learning and Instruction* 43, 1–4.

Gettinger, M. and Walter, M.J. (2012) Classroom strategies to enhance academic engaged time. In S.L. Christenson, A.L. Reschly and C. Wylie (eds) *Handbook of Research on Student Engagement* (pp. 653–673). New York: Springer.

Hiver, P., Obando, G., Sang, Y., Tahmouresi, S., Zhou, A. and Zhou, Y. (2019) Reframing the L2 learning experience as narrative reconstructions of classroom learning. *Studies in Second Language Learning and Teaching* 9 (1), 83–116.

Iqbal, A., Kankaanranta, P. and Neittaanmaki, M. (2010) Engaging learners through virtual worlds. *Procedia-Social and Behavioral Sciences* 2 (2), 3198–3205.

Johnson-Glenburg, M.C. (2017) Embodied education in mixed and mediated realities. In D. Liu, C. Dede, R. Huang and J. Richards (eds) *Virtual, Augmented, and Mixed Realities in Education* (pp. 193–218). Singapore: Springer.

Kern, R. (2000) *Literacy and Language Teaching.* Oxford: Oxford University Press.

Klinger, E., Bouchard, S., Légeron, P., Roy, S., Lauer, F., Chemin, I. and Nugues, P. (2005) Virtual reality therapy versus cognitive behavior therapy for social phobia: A preliminary controlled study. *CyberPsychology & Behavior* 8, 76–88.

Krämer, N.C. (2017) The immersive power of social interaction. In D. Liu, C. Dede, R. Huang and J. Richards (eds) *Virtual, Augmented, and Mixed Realities in Education* (pp. 55–70). Singapore: Springer.

Lam, S., Wong, B.P.H., Yang, H. and Liu, Y. (2012) Understanding engagement in a contextual model. In S.L. Christenson, A.L. Reschly and C. Wylie (eds) *Handbook of Research on Student Engagement* (pp. 403–420). New York: Springer.

Liu, D., Dede, C., Huang, R. and Richards, J. (2017) *Virtual, Augmented, and Mixed Realities in Education.* Singapore: Springer.

Mercer, S. (2019) Language learner engagement: Setting the Scene. In X. Gao, C. Davison and C. Leung (eds) *International Handbook of English Language Teaching.* Cham: Springer.

Mills, N. (2014) Self-efficacy in second language acquisition. In S. Mercer and M. Williams (eds) *Multiple Perspectives on the Self in SLA* (pp. 6–19). Bristol: Multilingual Matters.

Oga-Baldwin, W.L.Q. and Nakata, Y. (2017) Engagement, gender, and motivation: A predictive model for Japanese young language learners. *System* 65, 151–163.

Philp, J. and Duchesne, S. (2016) Exploring engagement in tasks in the language classroom. *Annual Review of Applied Linguistics* 36, 50–72.

Ryan, S. and Irie, K. (2014) Imagined and possible selves: Stories we tell ourselves about ourselves. In S. Mercer and M. Williams (eds) *Multiple Perspectives on the Self in SLA* (pp. 109–123). Bristol: Multilingual Matters.

Sadowski, W. and Stanney, K. (2002) Presence in virtual environments. In K. Stanney (ed.) *Human Factors and Ergonomics. Handbook of Virtual Environments: Design, Implementation, and Applications* (pp. 791–806). Mahwah, NJ: Lawrence Erlbaum.

Schott, C. and Marshall, S. (2018) Virtual reality and situated experiential education: A conceptualization and exploratory trial. *Journal of Computer Assisted Learning* 34, 843–852.

Skinner, E.A., Kindermann, T.A. and Furrer, C.J. (2009) A motivational perspective on engagement and disaffectation: Conceptualization and assessment of children's behavioral and emotional participation in academic activities in the classroom. *Educational and Psychological Measurement* 69 (3), 493–525.

Slater, M. (2017) Implicit learning through embodiment in immersive virtual reality. In D. Liu, C. Dede, R. Huang and J. Richards (eds) *Virtual, Augmented, and Mixed Realities in Education* (pp. 19–34). Singapore: Springer.

Svalberg, A.M.L. (2009) Engagement with language: Interrogating a construct. *Language Awareness* 18 (3-4), 242–258.

Walker, A. and White, G. (2013) *Technology Enhanced Language Learning. Connecting Theory and Practice.* Oxford: Oxford University Press.

Watson, Z. (2019) Winning wider audiences. Paper presented at the New Images Festival. Paris, France.

Witmer, B.G. and Singer, M.J. (1998) Measuring presence in virtual environments: A Presence questionnaire. *Presence: Teleoperators and Virtual Environments* 7, 225–240.

12 Engagement Growth in Language Learning Classrooms: A Latent Growth Analysis of Engagement in Japanese Elementary Schools

W.L. Quint Oga-Baldwin and Luke K. Fryer

Introduction

The many facets of engagement make it a topic of specific importance for language education. As a theoretical construct (though not a grand theory in and of itself; Fredricks *et al.*, 2004), engagement represents the actions learners take to further their learning. The latter qualification provides an important key; actions which simply comply with external pressure or 'go through the motions' of classwork cannot be engagement as they do not further real learning. Engagement is represented by specific actions which promote learning, and each aspect has specific indicators and possibilities for measurement (Oga-Baldwin, 2019). Behaviorally, learners might sit up, look at the speaker, take notes, or speak out in the target language. Emotionally, they may smile, laugh and enjoy using the target language in class. Cognitively, they think about what they want to say, commit target words to memory and connect language patterns to previous learning. These constructs, behavioral, cognitive and emotional engagement, form the middle, mediating point between learners' prior attitudes, experiences and abilities and their outcome learning and achievement (Oga-Baldwin, 2019).

With the emergence of engagement as a topic in language learning research (Mercer, 2019), new methods for investigating and interpreting this construct (see also Chapter 5 by Zhou *et al.*, this volume) are necessary. Recognizing the dynamic nature of engagement as an individual difference variable, we sought to demonstrate how this construct grows over time during young learners' first two years of exposure to learning a new language.

Engagement in language education

Engagement is now one of the trending topics in both general education and language education. The existence of the present volume in the reader's hands and other educational psychology volumes (see Christenson *et al.*, 2012), as well as recent commentary (Mercer, 2019), indicates that it is a clear topic of interest to the field of language learning (see also Chapter 2 by Sang & Hiver, this volume). Engagement interacts with many environmental and intra-individual factors (Lam *et al.*, 2012), and is a useful and necessary, though not sufficient, construct for explaining learning (Oga-Baldwin, 2019).

Engagement is student action, thought and emotion, measured in or close to the moment it happens, much as in Dörnyei's (2000) actional phase of the learning process. It is not a trait, but a highly variable state. Importantly, this point of action arises at the interaction of the local environment, the person's prior experiences, and their existing attitudes (including motivation). It then reciprocally predicts the valence of those later attitudes (Jang *et al.*, 2016; Oga-Baldwin, 2019; Reeve & Lee, 2014); positive engagement is likely to indicate positive motivation and affect for the task in the future, while disengagement predicts an unwillingness to do that task again. When the environment facilitates behavior, cognition and emotion, learners will continue to feel motivated. When circumstances prevent them from acting, feeling and thinking, learners' motivation will gradually diminish. This point differentiates engagement from motivation. Where motivation exists as an exclusively internal feeling, engagement is the external expression of that motivation. A model of the relationships between motivation, engagement and other constructs is presented in Figure 12.1.

Other concepts like flow (Csikszentmihalyi, 2003), the experience of optimal exertion toward an optimal challenge, may be considered a special case of engagement, but not all engagement reaches flow. Similarly, Svalberg's (2009) conception of engagement with language is likely another special case; how learners think about and socially make use of language in response to their linguistic needs is a relevant issue in learning a language. It is also quite difficult to capture, measure, and categorize along the conceptualizations of emotional, behavioral, and cognitive engagement. Like Mercer (2019), we recognize that Svalberg's (2009, 2017) social engagement is again a special case of the more basic cognitive, behavioral, and emotional aspects of interaction, with social engagement both facilitated by and facilitating the root elements of behavior, cognition and emotion. The key element here is the impact of engagement on attitudes and learning.

Our definition of engagement as action, thought and emotion follows the corollary definitions of behavioral engagement, cognitive engagement

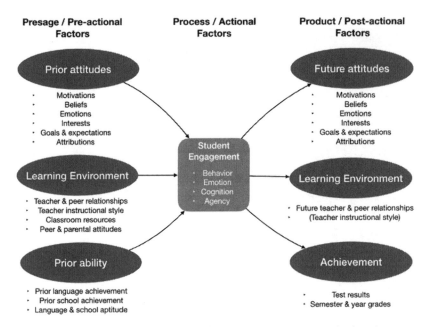

Presage / Pre-actional Factors	Process / Actional Factors	Product / Post-actional Factors

Prior attitudes

- Motivations
- Beliefs
- Emotions
- Interests
- Goals & expectations
- Attributions

Student Engagement

- Behavior
- Emotion
- Cognition
- Agency

Future attitudes

- Motivations
- Beliefs
- Emotions
- Interests
- Goals & expectations
- Attributions

Learning Environment

- Teacher & peer relationships
- Teacher instructional style
- Classroom resources
- Peer & parental attitudes

Learning Environment

- Future teacher & peer relationships
- (Teacher instructional style)

Prior ability

- Prior language achievement
- Prior school achievement
- Language & school aptitude

Achievement

- Test results
- Semester & year grades

Figure 12.1 A model of the relationships between engagement and other classroom variables (from Oga-Baldwin, 2019)

and emotional engagement. While other definitions, instrumentations and applications exist (Christenson *et al.*, 2012) these facets of the construct appear to be the most widely and commonly used. Behavioral engagement is seen in the visible actions that learners take in class, including tracking the speaker, nodding in agreement, taking notes, and all other signs of visibly paying attention (Lemov, 2014). Emotional engagement may be found when students connect with material emotionally, feeling joy, interest, excitement, satisfaction or other generally positive affect during learning tasks. While this does not scratch the surface of all possible emotions during language learning (Shao *et al.*, 2019), it does cover a range of facilitative emotions that can help memory and learning (Pekrun, 2006). Finally, cognitive engagement is represented by the ways learners connect old knowledge with new, focus on and memorize the material, plan their language use and attempt to understand what a speaker tells them. By focusing their limited, voluntary, selective and conscious attention (Willingham, 2009) on processing the new language, learners can encode the language into long-term memory. As interrelated pieces of the whole, these three aspects of engagement can be treated as three separate latent variables, or as subcomponents of a larger whole. Depending on the focus of the research such as a specific aspect of the L2 class (behavior, emotion or cognition), researchers can flexibly look at these as suits the purposes of their study.

Empirical studies using facets of engagement to measure activity in language learning settings have shown support for the hypothesized relationship between engagement and observable behavior and learning. As noted, engagement and motivation are indeed similar but still quite different phenomena; motivation exists solely within the individual, while engagement is expressed in the world. Butler and Lee (2006) found that measurement of behavioral engagement (then titled on-task behavior) was best and most accurately measured by self-report directly after the task in question. Following this procedure, Oga-Baldwin and Nakata (2017) measured elementary school students' in-class engagement directly after their language classes, and found that these ratings predicted students' attitudes at the end of the semester. Higher engagement predicted more self-determined autonomous motivation, and was consistent with observer triangulation. This pattern was repeated in a larger follow up study which controlled for prior attitudes and abilities (Oga-Baldwin et al., 2017). In this study, motivation and engagement both predicted students' achievement. In a later study, Stroud (2017) measured a small sample of university students' engagement with discussion tasks, indicating that the group who were instructed to pay more attention to their performance with a tracking system were slightly more consistently engaged. Studies have measured other aspects of engagement using tracking systems, such as how students interact with and feel about their language performance throughout the course of a learning task (MacIntyre, 2012). Recent work has emphasized how the intention to act can indirectly predict learning through other motivational variables (Hiver & Al-Hoorie, 2020), though intention is slightly different from our conception of engagement as recognized retrospectively (Oga-Baldwin, 2019). All these studies used either a limited conception of engagement focused only on behavior (see Butler & Lee, 2006; MacIntyre, 2012; Stroud, 2017), used cross-sectional intention to act as a proxy for actual effort expended (Hiver & Al-Hoorie, 2020), or used a more aggregated latent variable that did not separate the different facets of engagement (behavioral, cognitive, emotional) to investigate the different effects of each type (Oga-Baldwin & Nakata, 2017; Oga-Baldwin et al., 2017).

Thus, the dynamic nature of engagement has yet to be demonstrated through large-scale longitudinal investigation. Though researchers have shown engagement as a construct recognizable to observers and teachers (Oga-Baldwin et al., 2017), no work has shown the differential trajectories of the facets of engagement in response to the learning environment. Better knowledge of how each of these facets interact and predict one another can give a clearer picture of how learning happens in real-world contexts.

Elementary foreign language studies in Japan

Foreign language learning in Japanese elementary schools is a relatively new area of research and study. It was only required as a field of study from 2011 (MEXT, 2008), and then became recognized as a testable subject in 2020 (MEXT, 2017). Given this, teachers in elementary schools have received relatively little training to teach the foreign language (Fennelly & Luxton, 2011), and the few specialist teachers available are not always employed to the best of their abilities (Nakao *et al.*, 2019). Under this paradigm, languages are taught most often as foreign language experiences (Kang & Crandall, 2014), designed to improve students' enjoyment of the language, rather than as skill oriented foreign language classes. While these classes in some senses resemble instructed language classes (Butler, 2015), they do not carry many of the same features, such as standard achievement assessment or can-do style success criteria (MEXT, 2008). Teaching generally focuses on meaning-focused input primarily using instructed listening and speaking task and simplified interaction tasks (Nation & Newton, 2009).

Given that elementary schools in Japan are generally nurturing venues (Cave, 2007), this approach toward foreign language teaching is largely congruent with the general focus on well-being (Oga-Baldwin & Nakata, 2014). Under this paradigm of instruction, elementary foreign language classes are designed to promote experiential learning through game-like instruction. Teachers are instructed to help students experience the 'joy of communication' (MEXT, 2008) for the express purpose of improving long term learning attitudes.

Language education in this setting is thus meant to be behaviorally and emotionally engaging, with the hope that this leads to cognitive engagement as well. By providing learners with an engaging learning environment, the explicit goal of this policy is to improve students' love of learning and 'international understanding,' the latter of which is primarily concerned with a basic understanding of the practices and conventions of other countries. In short, the designers of the program sought to provide humanistic instruction and increase students' positive affect for the language, but without specific linguistic or academic benchmarks (Fennelly & Luxton, 2011). In this setting, a stronger understanding of how engagement develops over the course of students' studies is necessary to empirically demonstrate the validity of this program of instruction.

Gender in language learning

Another important point regarding language education involves the role of gender. Girls show a consistent motivational advantage in general educational settings (Meece *et al.*, 2006). Women worldwide generally outperform men in language learning (Education First, 2019). Henry (2009) demonstrated that Swedish secondary school girls had a more positive attitude than boys toward new language communities. In Japanese elementary school, girls have shown higher intrinsic motivation, interest in foreign countries and enjoyment compared with boys (Carreira, 2011). These differences may come from different societal models of male and female attitudes toward languages (Chaffee *et al.*, 2020), thus resulting in differences in patterns of engagement (Oga-Baldwin & Nakata, 2017).

Aims

The current study pursued three research questions related to the development and change of engagement during English language learning class at Japanese elementary school. Does students' engagement grow across two years of English classes (RQ1)? What is the relationship between initial engagement and potential growth (RQ2)? What is the role of gender within both initial engagement and its growth (RQ3)?

Method

We note here that parts of the larger data set have been published in other venues (Oga Baldwin & Fryer, 2018; Oga-Baldwin et al., 2017), but this is the first usage of these 5 points of data to measure changes in engagement over time.

Participants

Four-hundred and seventy-seven students (female $n = 237$; starting age 10–11 years, final age 12–13 years) in 16 classes in five schools participated in this study for the full two years. Participants were administered surveys and data were tracked using assigned identification numbers. The schools were all from the same rural–suburban municipal school district in western Japan. Permission for data collection was granted by the Fukuoka University of Education ethics board. The local board of education, school leaders and cooperating teachers all volunteered for the research project. Parents and guardians were notified of the research and its scope through communication from the schools, and were allowed to withdraw at any time. No children refused or requested to withdrawal from the study.

As in most elementary English classes in Japan, two teachers led each weekly class: a native English-speaking teacher and the students' homeroom teacher, a native speaker of Japanese. Classroom activities included games, songs and chants. We did not explicitly investigate any interventions or implement specific procedures, and by default classes followed the Ministry-approved curriculum (MEXT, 2012).

Instruments

Following the example set by prior studies (Jang et al., 2012; Reeve & Lee, 2014), scales measuring students' behavioral, cognitive and emotional engagement were created. Items were created through focus groups with students and teachers (Oga-Baldwin & Nakata, 2015, 2017). Students responded to the survey immediately following their foreign language classes five times between June 2013 and March 2015, roughly 4 months between each survey. Survey items measured students' engagement in the class they had just completed, using the item anchor 'In today's foreign language activities class ...'. Surveys were administered directly following class to achieve the most accurate self-assessments (Butler & Lee, 2006). This scale showed acceptable internal reliability at each time point (Cronbach's alpha = 0.72 – 0.86; Nunnally & Bernstein, 1994). Details of these surveys' development and testing have been previously published (Oga-Baldwin *et al.*, 2017; Oga-Baldwin, 2019). The 11 items are presented in Appendix 12.1.

Analyses

Analysis of the current study's data began with the calculation of means, reliability and bivariate correlations. Prior research with this data set had already established acceptable convergent and discriminant validity through Confirmatory Factor Analysis (Oga-Baldwin & Nakata, 2014b), indicating the best model fit for a three-factor solution predicted by a higher-order general latent variable factor. After these initial analyses, latent growth curve (LGC) analyses were undertaken in two steps (using M*plus* 8.0, Muthén & Muthén, 1998–2017). Initially, all three LGCs were calculated together and allowed to covary freely. After ascertaining acceptable fit and reviewing the inter-correlations, gender was included as a predictor for a second LGC model test. Based on the regular four month gap between each of the five data points included in the LGCs, the slopes were set at 0, 1, 2, 3 and 4 respectively.

Fit of LGC models was assessed based on multiple fit indices (Curran *et al.*, 2010). Acceptable fit for LGCs was determined based on the following cut-off criteria: $0.9 <$ comparative fit index (CFI), $0.9 <$ Tucker–Lewis index (TLI), $0.08 >$ standardized root mean square residual (SRMR) (Hu & Bentler, 1999), $0.08 >$ root mean square error of approximation (RMSEA) (Browne & Cudeck, 1992).

Results

Descriptive results

Descriptive statistics and correlations are presented in Table 12.1. Students indicated generally high engagement, as is often the case with samples of elementary school students (Spinath & Steinmayr, 2008). Zero-order correlations were generally strong and statistically significant (all correlations $p < 0.001$, correlation range 0.18–0.71), but none strong enough to suggest strong multicollinearity ($r < 0.8$, Tabachnick & Fidell, 2007).

Latent growth curve results

The latent growth curve results are presented in three steps. First the fit for the three LGCs tested together, allowed to freely covary, will be

Table 12.1 Zero-order correlations and descriptive statistics

	1	2	3	4	5	6	7	8	9	10	11	12	13	14	15
1. Emotional T1															
2. Behavioral T1	0.68														
3. Cognitive T1	0.68	0.65													
4. Emotional T2	0.45	0.32	0.36												
5. Behavioral T2	0.36	0.43	0.37	0.58											
6. Cognitive T2	0.33	0.34	0.38	0.55	0.59										
7. Emotional T3	0.67	0.45	0.46	0.37	0.34	0.28									
8. Behavioral T3	0.50	0.51	0.44	0.31	0.45	0.29	0.72								
9. Cognitive T3	0.47	0.43	0.50	0.35	0.40	0.41	0.67	0.69							
10. Emotional T4	0.49	0.35	0.37	0.29	0.30	0.23	0.57	0.46	0.45						
11. Behavioral T4	0.39	0.42	0.32	0.27	0.37	0.24	0.49	0.52	0.43	0.70					
12. Cognitive T4	0.40	0.37	0.40	0.30	0.43	0.39	0.49	0.50	0.52	0.71	0.68				
13. Emotional T5	0.44	0.27	0.25	0.23	0.25	0.18	0.48	0.35	0.35	0.57	0.46	0.42			
14. Behavioral T5	0.35	0.35	0.24	0.21	0.33	0.21	0.39	0.42	0.32	0.47	0.55	0.44	0.69		
15. Cognitive T5	0.30	0.28	0.22	0.24	0.36	0.31	0.38	0.38	0.39	0.43	0.52	0.49	0.60	0.70	
Mean	3.91	4.17	3.60	4.00	4.16	3.60	3.91	4.05	3.70	3.96	4.21	3.85	3.93	4.21	3.94
SD	0.93	0.78	0.93	0.88	0.79	0.92	0.90	0.78	0.81	0.90	0.73	0.85	0.87	0.75	0.84
95% CI	[3.82, 3.99]	[4.10, 4.24]	[3.52, 3.69]	[3.91, 4.08]	[4.09, 4.23]	[3.51, 3.68]	[3.82, 3.99]	[3.98, 4.13]	[3.62, 3.77]	[3.88, 4.04]	[4.14, 4.27]	[3.78, 3.93]	[3.85, 4.01]	[4.14, 4.27]	[3.87, 4.02]
Cronbach's alpha	0.83	0.72	0.78	0.81	0.78	0.76	0.86	0.74	0.77	0.86	0.72	0.79	0.84	0.77	0.79

Note: All correlations significant at $p < 0.001$.

Table 12.2 Mean intercepts, slopes and standard errors

	Unstandardized value	SE	SD	95% CI	p-value
Cognitive intercept	3.60	0.06	1.20	[3.49, 3.71]	0.001
Cognitive slope	0.10	0.02	0.37	[.07, .13]	0.001
Behavioral intercept	4.20	0.05	1.07	[4.10, 4.30]	0.001
Behavioral slope	0.001	0.01	0.31	[-.03, .03]	0.929
Emotional intercept	3.90	0.06	1.24	[3.80, 4.01]	0.001
Emotional slope	0.01	0.02	0.33	[-.02, .04]	0.513

reviewed. The growth curves intercepts and slopes will be presented followed by the relationship between the three LGCs. Finally, the fit and ßs for the second LGC model, which includes the role of gender as a predictor of engagement intercept and slope, will be reviewed.

Fit for the LGCs met the criteria outlined: $(x^2[df] = 266.6$ [78], $p < 0.001$ CFI $= 0.96$, TLI $= 0.94$, RMSEA $= 0.071$ (CI 90% $= 0.06$–0.08), SRMR $= 0.076$. The average intercept $(M = 3.60)$ and slope $(M = 0.10)$ for cognitive engagement were both statistically significant $(p < 0.001)$. For both behavioral $(M_{intercept} = 4.20$ and $M_{slope} = 0.001)$ and emotional $(M_{intercept} = 3.90$ and $M_{slope} = 0.01)$, only the intercept was significant $(p < 0.05)$. Table 12.2 presents the intercepts, slopes and standard errors as provided by M*plus*.

The average intercepts and slopes for all three types of engagement were significantly related $(p < 0.01$; SEs $= 0.039$–0.92). In the interest of brevity and substance, only the significant $(p < 0.05)$ intercepts and slopes will be reviewed here; non-significant slopes indicate a lack of growth, and therefore will not provide information of interest. The growth of cognitive engagement was negatively related to all three average intercepts $(r_{cog} = -0.55$, $r_{behav} = -0.31$, $r_{emot} = -0.33)$ which are the initial starting points for the curves. This suggests that students starting at the beginning of the two years with lower engagement are more likely to increase. The average intercepts for each form of engagement were all strongly correlated $(r = 0.80$–0.87) as we would expect from these closely related variables. Figure 12.2 displays the estimated growth for each time point, with relevant slopes presented in Table 12.3.

Fit for the same LGCs, which included gender as a predictor for the intercept and slope, met the criteria outlined: $(x^2[df] = 279$ [87], $p < 0.001$ CFI $= 0.95$, TLI $= 0.94$, RMSEA $= 0.069$ (CI 90% $= 0.06$–0.08), SRMR $= 0.073$. Gender (Female $= 0$, Male $= 1$) was a significant $(p < 0.05)$ predictor for behavioral engagement growth $(ß = -0.07)$. This relationship indicates that girls were more likely to report increasing behavioral engagement in learning a new language across the two years researched. Descriptive statistics for boys and girls for each data point are presented in Table 12.4.

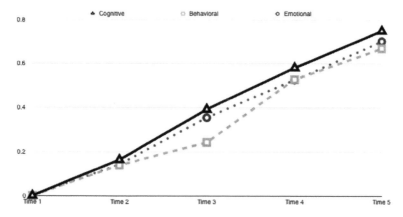

Figure 12.2 Growth slopes of each engagement variable at each time point

Table 12.3 Slopes for each time point

	Time 1	Time 2	Time 3	Time 4	Time 5
Cognitive	0	0.164	0.392	0.581	0.749
Behavioral	0	0.139	0.243	0.528	0.669
Engagement	0	0.143	0.355	0.526	0.701

Table 12.4 Gender means, standard deviations, standard errors and confidence intervals

	Female				Male			
Variable	Mean	SD	SE	95% CI	Mean	SD	SE	95% CI
Emotional T1	3.84	0.96	0.06	[3.71, 3.96]	3.98	0.91	0.06	[3.86, 4.10]
Behavioral T1	4.19	0.73	0.05	[4.10, 4.29]	4.16	0.83	0.05	[4.05, 4.26]
Cognitive T1	3.62	0.92	0.06	[3.50, 3.74]	3.59	0.94	0.06	[3.47, 3.71]
Emotional T2	4.02	0.84	0.06	[3.91, 4.13]	3.97	0.92	0.06	[3.85, 4.09]
Behavioral T2	4.22	0.75	0.05	[4.12, 4.32]	4.10	0.83	0.05	[3.99, 4.21]
Cognitive T2	3.65	0.88	0.06	[3.54, 3.76]	3.54	0.96	0.06	[3.42, 3.67]
Emotional T3	3.83	0.90	0.06	[3.71, 3.95]	3.98	0.90	0.06	[3.87, 4.10]
Behavioral T3	4.09	0.73	0.05	[3.99, 4.19]	4.02	0.83	0.06	[3.91, 4.13]
Cognitive T3	3.70	0.81	0.05	[3.60, 3.81]	3.69	0.82	0.05	[3.59, 3.80]
Emotional T4	3.92	0.90	0.06	[3.80, 4.03]	4.01	0.90	0.06	[3.89, 4.12]
Behavioral T4	4.19	0.72	0.05	[4.09, 4.28]	4.23	0.74	0.05	[4.14, 4.33]
Cognitive T4	3.89	0.80	0.05	[3.79, 4.00]	3.82	0.89	0.06	[3.70, 3.93]
Emotional T5	3.88	0.87	0.06	[3.77, 3.99]	3.98	0.87	0.06	[3.87, 4.09]
Behavioral T5	4.17	0.77	0.05	[4.08, 4.27]	4.24	0.73	0.05	[4.15, 4.33]
Cognitive T5	3.91	0.87	0.06	[3.80, 4.02]	3.98	0.81	0.05	[3.87, 4.08]

Discussion

Overview

The current study was an initial foray into understanding longitudinal engagement experiences during foreign language classes at Japanese elementary schools. LGCs for self-reported cognitive, behavioral and emotional engagement were estimated to determine whether/how student engagement might change across two years of classes. Gender was then included as a potential predictor of both intercept and slope to assess whether female and male students experienced their environments differently.

Significant ($p < 0.05$) growth was observed only for cognitive engagement in English classes (RQ1). Students beginning with lower initial engagement reported greater growth in engagement (all three types) across the study (RQ2). Female students reported stronger growth in engagement (behavioral only) than male students across the study (RQ3).

Implications for theory

Theoretically, the growth of cognitive engagement indicates that students reported increasing their cognitive use of the foreign language over the course of two years. This would follow logic, as students became more experienced with the language during this time, and thus felt they could effectively process more complicated thoughts and ideas. More importantly, given the generally high correlations between behavioral, emotional, and cognitive engagement, these results indicate that the interplay between the three factors has a facilitative role, each promoting and supporting the others. Thus, by engaging behavior and emotions during language learning, cognitive engagement might also increase; all three factors can be modeled as predicted by a more general latent factor (Oga-Baldwin & Nakata, 2014b), and therefore movement in one may indicate a more general positive trend. This is heartening, as increased cognitive engagement theoretically has a positive relationship with learning (Oga-Baldwin, 2019), and may be connected to further intention to expend effort. Though research has not explicitly connected intended effort and cognitive engagement, just as prior achievement can predict the intention to learn (Hiver & Al-Hoorie, 2020), increased cognitive engagement might increase intention and motivation (Oga-Baldwin & Nakata, 2017).

Students with lower beginning engagement had the greatest room to grow. By giving special focus to these students, making the classroom a place where less initially interested students can interact and actively use the language, teachers can offer the greatest chance of improvement, including in the quality of motivation (Oga-Baldwin *et al.*, 2017). This further supports the idea that continued engagement provides a mechanism for the development of positive motivational outcomes (Oga-Baldwin & Fryer, 2018; Reeve & Lee, 2014).

As in previous similar samples, girls were more engaged than boys (Oga-Baldwin & Nakata, 2017). This may reflect Japanese ideas regarding foreign language and gender roles, where male students feel less comfortable with language learning, or could be symptomatic of the larger trend where female students outperform males both generally and in language learning (Chaffee *et al.*, 2020; Meece *et al.*, 2006). Recognizing that engagement in language learning emerges from the complex interaction between the person and the environment (Oga-Baldwin, 2019), boys show lower engagement in response to the same classroom stimuli, indicating that intrapersonal attitudinal variables are the most likely key individual difference here. In short, though boys and girls are experiencing quite similar classroom environments, boys' identities and orientations appear to be more associated with lower engagement.

Implications for practice

Practically speaking, teachers in foreign language experience classes need to engage students' emotions and behavior to a high degree, and this may help to promote students' feelings of active language use. Learners who enjoy classes more and actively participate in learning games are more likely to develop stronger memories of the language focus in each game. Neuroscientific evidence supports this implication; emotions and memory are linked in the brain (Willingham, 2009), meaning that learners who are more emotionally engaged are likely to also become more cognitively engaged.

For elementary foreign language classes, these results indicate that the focus on games as a teaching method are likely to improve student learning and ability. This runs counter to commentary which states that game activities may not be enough to promote learning (Otsu, 2004) – young learners who engage in foreign language games are more likely to report cognitive growth as well. By focusing classes on these games, teachers in this study successfully engaged their learners on all three fronts across two years, but most importantly, learners' cognitive engagement improved over this time. While the degree of actual learning was not assessed through external performance measures in the current study, previous work (Oga-Baldwin *et al.*, 2017) on a related data set has found a small but meaningful effect on teacher-assigned grades.

As early as elementary school, boys are showing poorer attitudes toward learning foreign languages. Teachers hoping to correct for this should be aware that gender roles and stereotyping (Chaffee *et al.*, 2020) may be at work even at this early age, and make efforts to include male linguistic role models for students. Male teachers might act as proximal models to support students in speaking the language (Oga-Baldwin & Nakata, 2013), and thereby improve their behavioral engagement with the language.

Limitations and Future Directions

Though other parts of the current data set were externally triangulated (Oga-Baldwin *et al.*, 2017), we do not currently have a covariate which may be used to triangulate these curves. Given that engagement should theoretically have observable outcomes (Oga-Baldwin, 2019), this represents a limitation to the current data set. Given that summative testing was not implemented as a part of course of study (MEXT, 2008) and has always been viewed with a critical eye as a part of public elementary education (Cave, 2007; Oga-Baldwin & Fryer, 2019), achievement tests were also not a feasible covariate. The self-reported nature of the current data also should be noted. Though not without advantages and accuracy, self-report has notable shortcomings as well (Dinsmore & Fryer, 2020). Future studies should triangulate self-reported cognitive engagement with other measures of cognition, including eye-tracking, and electroencephalogram. As retention and development of language ability can also be recognized as a sign of cognition, regular use of language achievement measures may provide further triangulation.

Given our findings regarding gender differences, it is also important that large- and small-scale interventions aimed at supporting male students' engagement be undertaken. Boys operate at a disadvantage for both motivation and achievement in languages (Oga-Baldwin & Nakata, 2017; Education First, 2019). Critically, these efforts need to be paired with careful measurement to ensure that the effects of such research can be meaningfully assessed.

On a final note for future work in this area, the present study can best be extended by undertaking similar longitudinal studies across both early and later stages of secondary school. Japan, like much of Pacific-Asia, has a reputation for rigorous, often test-driven secondary education (Oga-Baldwin & Fryer, 2019). This is an approach which can result in disengagement and lower long-term interest in academia (Fryer, 2019; Jang *et al.*, 2016; Sakai & Kikuchi, 2009). Similar to this study, we recommend a large-scale approach, across multiple institutions to ensure reasonable external validity.

Conclusion

Two conclusions can be drawn from this study. The first is that the national program (MEXT, 2008, 2017) for elementary school foreign language education is resulting in students experiencing increasing cognitive engagement in language learning. This is good news for Japan and reflects recent person-centered findings from our program of research (Oga-Baldwin & Fryer, 2018). The second conclusion is that the benefits to students' engagement do not appear to be evenly shared by male and female students. While this is not a local problem, it will need a local solution. Any attempt at addressing this issue will need to be carefully assessed to ensure potential solutions are sustainable and useful across institutions.

While the Japanese foreign language experience is unique in some ways, the general structure of classes focusing on input and interaction (Nation & Newton, 2009) offer a window into other low-stakes instructional settings. More generally for language education settings, whether they are community language experiences for children or more formal school based second or foreign language classes, the interrelated nature of engagement indicates the importance of behavior and emotion for improving cognition during language classes. For teachers wishing to improve students' language learning, a focus on behavior, emotion and cognition in class might offer a visible measure of student progress and learning.

References

Browne, M. and Cudeck, R. (1992) Alternative ways of assessing model fit. *Sociological Methods & Research* 21, 230–258.

Butler, Y.G. (2015) English language education among young learners in East Asia: A review of current research (2004–2014). *Language Teaching* 48 (3), 303–342.

Butler, Y.G. and Lee, J. (2006) On-task versus off-task self-assessments among Korean elementary school students studying English. *The Modern Language Journal* 90 (4), 506–518.

Carreira, J.M. (2011) Relationship between motivation for learning EFL and intrinsic motivation for learning in general among Japanese elementary school students. System 39 (1), 90–102.

Cave, P. (2007) *Primary School in Japan: Self, Individuality and Learning in Elementary Education*. New York: Routledge.

Chaffee, K.E., Lou, N.M., Noels, K.A. and Katz, J.W. (2020) Why don't 'real men' learn languages? Masculinity threat and gender ideology suppress men's language learning motivation. *Group Processes & Intergroup Relations* 23, 301–318.

Christenson, S.L., Reschly, A.L. and Wylie, C. (eds) (2012) *Handbook of Research on Student Engagement*. New York: Springer.

Csikszentmihalyi, M. (2003) *Flow*. London: Rider.

Curran, P.J., Obeidat, K. and Losardo, D. (2010) Twelve frequently asked questions about growth curve modeling. *Journal of Cognition and Development* 11 (2), 121–136.

Dinsmore, D. and Fryer, L.K. (2020) Self-report data: Promises and pitfalls. *Frontline Learning Research*.

Dörnyei, Z. (2000) Motivation in action: Toward a process-oriented conceptualisation of student motivation. *British Journal of Educational Psychology* 70, 519–538.

Education First (2019) EF English Proficiency Index 2019. Available from: http://www.ef.co.uk/epi/

Fennelly, M. and Luxton, R. (2011) Are they ready? On the verge of compulsory English, elementary school teachers lack confidence. *The Language Teacher* 35 (2), 19–24.

Fredricks, J., Blumenfeld, P. and Paris, A. (2004) School engagement: Potential of the concept, state of the evidence. *Review of Educational Research* 74 (1), 59–109.

Fryer, L.K. (2019) Getting interested in learning a language: Developing a sustainable source of engagement. *System* 86, 102–120.

Henry, A. (2009). Gender differences in compulsory school pupils' L2 self-concepts: A longitudinal study. *System* 37, 177–193.

Hiver, P. and Al-Hoorie, A.H. (2020) Reexamining the role of vision in second language motivation: A preregistered conceptual replication of You, Dörnyei, and Csizér (2016). *Language Learning* 70 (1), 48–102.

Hu, L.T. and Bentler, P.M. (1999) Cutoff criteria for fit indexes in covariance structure analysis: Conventional criteria versus new alternatives. *Structural Equation Modeling* 6, 1–55.

Jang, H., Kim, E.J. and Reeve, J. (2012) Longitudinal test of self-determination theory's motivation mediation model in a naturally occurring classroom context. *Journal of Educational Psychology* 104 (4), 1175–1188.

Jang, H., Kim, E.J. and Reeve, J. (2016) Why students become more engaged or more disengaged during the semester: A self-determination theory dual-process model. *Learning and Instruction* 43, 27–38.

Kang, J.S. and Crandall, J. (2013) *Teaching Young Learners English*. New York: Heinle Cengage.

Kang, J.S. and Crandall, J. (2014) *Teaching Young Learners English: From Theory to Practice*. New York: Heinle.

Lam, S.F., Wong, B.P.H., Yang, H. and Liu, Y. (2012) Understanding student engagement with a contextual model. In S.L. Christenson, A.L. Reschly and C. Wylie (eds) *Handbook of Research on Student Engagement* (pp. 403–420). New York: Springer.

Lemov, D. (2014) *Teach Like a Champion 2.0*. San Francisco, CA: Jossey-Bass.

MacIntyre, P.D. (2012) The idiodynamic method: A closer look at the dynamics of communication traits. *Communication Research Reports* 29 (4), 361–367.

Meece, J.L., Glienke, B.B. and Burg, S. (2006) Gender and motivation. *Journal of School Psychology* 44, 351–373.

Mercer, S. (2019) Language learner engagement: Setting the scene. In X. Gao (ed.) *Second Handbook of English Language Teaching* (pp. 1–19). New York: Springer.

MEXT (2008) *Explanatory commentary for the elementary school curriculum guidelines: Foreign language activities*. Retrieved 8/26/10 from http://www.mext.go.jp/component/a_menu/education/micro_detail/__icsFiles/afieldfile/2009/06/16/12349 31_012.pdf.

MEXT (2012) *Hi, Friends! 1*. Tokyo: Kyouiku Shuppan.

MEXT (2017) *Explanatory commentary for the elementary school curriculum guidelines: Foreign Language*. Retrieved August 2, 2018, from http://www.mext.go.jp/component/a_menu/education/micro_detail/__icsFiles/afieldfile/2018/05/07/13870 18_10_1.pdf

Muthén, L.K. and Muthén, B.O. (1998–2017) *Mplus User's Guide* (7th edn). Los Angeles, CA: Muthén & Muthén.

Nakao, K., Oga-Baldwin, W.L.Q. and Fryer, L.K. (2019) Expanding Japanese elementary school English education: Native and nonnative speaking team-teachers' perspectives on team-teaching quality. *The Bulletin of the Graduate School of Education of Waseda University* 29, 17–31.

Nation, I.S.P. and Newton, J. (2009) *Teaching Listening and Speaking*. New York: Routledge.

Nunnally, J.C. and Bernstein, I.H. (1994) *Psychometric Theory* (3rd edn). New York: McGraw-Hill.

Oga-Baldwin, W.L.Q. (2019) Acting, thinking, feeling, making: The engagement process in language education. *System* 86, 102–128.

Oga-Baldwin, W.L.Q. and Fryer, L.K. (2018) Schools can improve motivational quality: Profile transitions across early foreign language learning experiences. *Motivation and Emotion* 52 (3), 527–545.

Oga-Baldwin, W.L.Q. and Fryer, L.K. (2019) Growing up in the walled garden: Motivation, engagement, and the Japanese educational experience. In G.A.D. Liem and S. Tan (eds) *Student Motivation, Engagement, and Growth: Asian Insights*. New York: Routledge.

Oga-Baldwin, W.L.Q. and Nakata, Y. (2013) Native vs. non-native teachers: Who is the real model for Japanese elementary school pupils? *The Journal of Asia TEFL* 10 (2), 91–113.

Oga-Baldwin, W.L.Q. and Nakata, Y. (2014a) Supplementing the elementary foreign language course of study with a self-determination framework. *International Journal of Curriculum Development and Practice* 16 (1), 13–26.

Oga-Baldwin, W.L.Q. and Nakata, Y. (2014b) Assessing engagement in upper elementary foreign language classes. Poster presented at the *International Conference on Motivational Dynamics and Second Language Acquisition*, August 29, 2014. University of Nottingham, UK.

Oga-Baldwin, W.L.Q., Nakata, Y., Parker, P. and Ryan, R.M. (2017) Motivating young language learners: A longitudinal model of self-determined motivation in elementary school foreign language classes. *Contemporary Educational Psychology* 49, 140–150.

Otsu, Y. (2004) *Is Elementary School English Necessary?* Tokyo: Keio Gijuku Daigaku Shuppan Kai.

Pekrun, R. (2006) The control-value theory of achievement emotions: Assumptions, corollaries, and implications for educational research and practice. *Educational Psychology Review* 18 (4), 315–341.

Reeve, J. and Lee, W. (2014) Students' classroom engagement produces longitudinal changes in classroom motivation. *Journal of Educational Psychology* 106 (2), 527–540.

Reschly, A.L. and Christenson, S.L. (2012) Jingle, jangle, and conceptual haziness: Evolution and future directions of the engagement construct. In S.L. Christenson, A.L. Reschly and C. Wylie (eds) *Handbook of Research on Student Engagement* (pp. 3–19). New York: Springer.

Sakai, H. and Kikuchi, K. (2009) An analysis of demotivators in the EFL classroom. *System* 37 (1), 57–69.

Shao, K., Pekrun, R. and Nicholson, L. (2019) Emotions in classroom language learning: What has been done and what can be learned? *System* 86, 102–121.

Spinath, B. and Steinmayr, B. (2008) Longitudinal analysis of intrinsic motivation and competence beliefs: Is there a relation over time? *Child Development* 79, 1555–1569.

Stroud, R. (2017) Second language group discussion Participation: A closer examination of 'barriers' and 'boosts'. *Proceedings of the International Conference on Education and Learning* (ICEL) 1, 40–56.

Svalberg, A.M.L. (2009) Engagement with language: Interrogating a construct. *Language Awareness* 18 (3–4), 242–258.

Svalberg, A.M.L. (2017) Researching language engagement: Current trends and future directions. *Language Awareness* 27 (1–2), 21–39.

Tabachnick, B.G. and Fidell, L.S. (2007) *Using Multivariate Statistics* (5th edn). Needham Heights, MA: Allyn & Bacon.

Willingham, D.T. (2009) *Why Don't Students Like School?* San Francisco, CA: Jossey-Bass.

Appendix 12.1

Behavioral engagement

    I participated in today's class activities
    I paid attention to my teacher today
    I listened very carefully in class

Emotional engagement

    I felt good in class today
    I enjoyed today's classroom activities
    I was interested in today's class
    Today's class was fun

Cognitive engagement
I expressed myself using English
I thought about what I wanted to say
I thought about what other people were saying in English
I tried to comprehend my teacher's English

13 Modeling the Relations Between Foreign Language Engagement, Emotions, Grit and Reading Achievement

Gholam Hassan Khajavy

Introduction

As language teachers, we might have seen different behaviors from our students in the class. While some students are actively involved in the class, answer teachers' questions and do their homework, other students might not be interested in the classroom activities, daydream while sitting in the class and do not pay attention to what is going on in the class. One possible reason for these different behaviors might be that the first group is engaged in the classroom activities, while the second group is not. Therefore, a better understanding of engagement can help us to involve all students in the class (Cleary & Zimmerman, 2012; Mercer, 2019; Philp & Duchesne, 2016).

Engagement has been linked to many positive learning outcomes (Fredricks *et al.*, 2016; Schlenker *et al.*, 2013; Wang & Fredricks, 2014; Wang & Holcombe, 2010). Although engagement has some domain-general characteristics such as psychophysiological arousal, attention and meta-cognitive awareness, domain-specific aspects of engagement can provide us with a deeper insight about the domain (Sinatra *et al.*, 2015). Considering this, while many studies have been devoted to examining engagement in science, technology, engineering and mathematics (STEM), research on engagement in second language acquisition (SLA) has not received much attention among the researchers of this field (see Mercer, 2019; Oga-Baldwin & Fryer, 2018; Philp & Duchesne, 2016). Given the importance of engagement in academic success, exploring this construct within the domain of SLA would be important to shed more light on its role within this field. Therefore, in this study, I aim to broaden the nomological network of second/foreign (L2) engagement by examining its relation to L2-specific variables including L2 reading comprehension, L2 grit and L2 emotions. As previous research has indicated that emotions (Linnenbrink-Garcia *et al.*, 2011; Ouweneel *et al.*, 2011) and grit (Hodge *et al.*, 2018) are related to engagement, I tested these relations within the L2 context. Before that, a review of these constructs and their relations with engagement is presented.

Engagement

There is some agreement on the multifaceted nature of engagement (see also Chapter 2 by Sang & Hiver, this volume). The most common multidimensional conceptualization of engagement is what Fredricks *et al.* (2004) proposed including behavioral, cognitive and emotional (or affective) engagement. Behavioral engagement refers to students' involvement in their own learning and classroom activities and is measured based on participation, persistence, effort, attention and absence of disruptive behavior (Fredricks *et al.*, 2016). Cognitive engagement is defined as psychological investment by trying to understand complex ideas, self-regulating, exerting effort for solving challenging tasks and using deep learning strategies (Fredricks *et al.*, 2016; Sinatra *et al.*, 2015). Emotional engagement refers to students' positive and negative reactions to the subject area, peers and teachers, as well as their valuing of and interest in the subject (Fredricks *et al.*, 2016). Social engagement is an additional aspect of engagement (e.g. Finn & Zimmer, 2012; Linnenbrink-Garcia & Pekrun, 2011), which refers to social interaction with peers and teachers, collaborative learning, sharing ideas and maintaining the relationships in the class (Fredricks *et al.*, 2016). In this study, I use this typology for conceptualizing L2 engagement.

Another point, which is important to understand about engagement, is its domain-specificity (Wang *et al.*, 2016). This means that engagement varies based on the context and subjects (Sinatra *et al.*, 2015) and this necessitates different models of engagement (Shernoff *et al.*, 2016). Although there are some domain-general aspects of engagement, we cannot rule out the domain-specific characteristics of engagement which can deepen our understanding of engagement within specific contexts (Sinatra *et al.*, 2015). It is also argued that the scale which measures engagement should be developed based on the specific characteristics of the subject (Wang *et al.*, 2016). For example, Wang *et al.* (2016) developed separate scales to measure engagement in math and science classes.

Considering the domain-specificity of engagement, some studies have investigated engagement in L2 classrooms. As one of the pioneering researchers who examined engagement in language classrooms, Svalberg (2009, 2018) introduced the model of engagement with language (EWL) through which learners develop language awareness. Svalberg (2009: 244) considers EWL to be cognitive, social, and affective 'in which the learner is the agent and the language is the object'. Moreover, Svalberg (2018) explains that engagement can have other definitions in SLA literature. One of them is how Ellis (2010) uses the term engagement as *engagement with corrective feedback* which refers to the way learners respond to corrective feedback. Svalberg (2018) considers engagement with corrective feedback as a subcategory of EWL. Another conceptualization of engagement in SLA literature is *task engagement* which is learner's involvement with linguistic data and she states that, while it is different from EWL, it can facilitate EWL.

In addition to Svalberg (2009, 2018), Philp and Duchesne (2016) conceptualized engagement in task-based language teaching. They referred to engagement as a multidimensional construct including cognitive, affective, social and behavioral aspects. Some indicators were also defined to measure each of these aspects (see Lambert *et al.*, 2017; Philp & Duchesne, 2016; Phung, 2017). The number of words, the number of turns, and the amount of time spent on completing a task were considered as indicators of behavioral engagement. The number of clauses which expand the semantic content of the narrative such as suggestions and opinions as well as the number of moves related to the negotiation of meaning such as corrective feedback and confirmation checks were measures of cognitive engagement. The number of backchannels, overlaps, and turn completions has been considered as measures of social engagement.

Emotional engagement refers to learners' emotional involvement and is assessed based on 'subjective impressions that learners experience during the performance of a task' and is reported in questionnaires or stimulated-recall interviews (Lambert *et al.*, 2017: 5).

What can be inferred from the above-mentioned studies on task engagement in SLA is that these studies mainly focused on linguistic aspects of engagement in which counting different grammatical and lexical features is considered as an indicator of engagement. However, considering the definition of engagement in the field of education, psychological aspects of engagement were not taken into account in these studies. There are still very few studies examining engagement in SLA based on its psychological definition (for exceptions see Dincer *et al.*, 2019; Hamedi *et al.*, 2019; Oga-Baldwin & Fryer, 2018; Oga-Baldwin & Nakata, 2017). Dincer *et al.* (2019) examined the role of basic psychological needs in engagement and the role of engagement in achievement and absenteeism among Turkish EFL (English as a foreign language) learners. It should be noted that, in this study, in addition to behavioral, cognitive and emotional engagement, researchers measured agentic engagement which refers to learners' active contribution to their learning such as offering input, asking questions, seeking clarification and talking about their interests. Their findings indicated that basic psychological needs were positive predictors of all engagement subscales. Only emotional and agentic engagement were predictors of achievement, while cognitive engagement was the only predictor of absenteeism. Hamedi *et al.* (2019) examined the role of reading emotions and reading engagement in reading comprehension and found that while anxiety and boredom had negative relations with reading engagement components, enjoyment had a positive relation with them. Moreover, L2 engagement and its subscales (cognitive, behavioral and emotional) were positive predictors of reading comprehension. Using a person-centered analytical strategy (latent profile analysis and latent profile transition analysis), Oga-Baldwin and Fryer (2018) investigated Japanese EFL learners' motivation and engagement. The results of their study revealed that engagement was associated with more autonomous motivation. Oga-Baldwin and Nakata (2017) found that engagement was a positive predictor of intrinsic motivation and a negative predictor of extrinsic motivation. Moreover, males had less engagement than females in the language classroom. Given that only a handful of studies have focused on psychological aspects of engagement in the language classroom, it is notable that they return some support for the notion that L2 engagement is an influential factor in language learning classrooms.

Emotions

Research on emotions in the field of education and SLA has been of interest to many researchers (Dewaele, 2019; Khajavy *et al.*, 2018; Li *et al.*, 2019). Emotions can be generally classified into positive and negative ones. In the field of SLA, most research has been devoted to examining one emotion, namely anxiety (Alrabai, 2015; Khodadady & Khajavy, 2013; Teimouri *et al.*, 2019). Moreover, as anxiety which occurs in the language classroom is specific to this context, it has been called L2 anxiety (Horwitz *et al.*, 1986; MacIntyre, 1999). It has been defined as 'the worry and negative emotional reaction aroused when learning or using a second language' (MacIntyre, 1999: 27). Many studies have examined the role of L2 anxiety in L2 outcomes such as L2 achievement (see Teimouri *et al.*, 2019 for a review) and willingness to communicate (WTC) (Khajavy *et al.*, 2018; Peng & Woodrow, 2010). However, with the emergence of positive psychology, more attention has been directed toward positive emotions besides negative ones. According to MacIntyre and Mercer (2014), one of the main concepts of positive psychology is the distinction between positive and negative emotions. They stated that 'differentiating positive and negative emotions leads to a more nuanced understanding of how they affect L2 learning and communication' (MacIntyre & Mercer, 2014: 162). Therefore, to have a better understanding of the role of emotions in SLA, positive emotions should also be examined alongside negative ones (MacIntyre *et al.*, 2019).

Following this, several studies have been conducted to investigate how L2 anxiety and L2 enjoyment can jointly affect L2 outcomes. For example, Dewaele *et al.* (2018) found that while students with higher levels of L2 enjoyment had more positive attitudes toward the foreign language and their teacher, had more L2 use, and spent more time on speaking, students with higher levels of L2 anxiety had less positive attitudes toward the foreign language. Khajavy *et al.* (2018) examined the role of L2 anxiety, L2 enjoyment and classroom environment in WTC using multilevel structural equation modeling. The results of their study indicated that at the individual level, L2 enjoyment was positively related to L2 WTC, whereas L2 anxiety had a negative relationship with it. At the class level, while L2 enjoyment was a positive predictor of WTC, the effect of anxiety was not significant. This finding showed the positive effect of enjoyment on WTC is even more important than the negative effect of L2 anxiety. Other studies have also supported the positive role of L2 enjoyment and the negative role of L2 anxiety on self-perceived and actual FL achievement (Jiang & Dewaele, 2019; Jin & Zhang, 2018; Li *et al.*, 2019). All these studies show that enjoyment is an important factor which should be examined alongside anxiety in SLA studies.

Concerning the important role of emotions in engagement, Boekaerts (2016) recommends engagement researchers to investigate the role of discrete positive and negative emotions on students' engagement. She further explains that emotions can be like sparks that ignite the process of engagement or can extinguish the fire. Moreover, based on Fredrickson's (2001) broaden-and-build theory, positive emotions are likely to increase engagement. One reason for this relation is that positive emotions encourage individuals to get involved in specific tasks (Ouweneel *et al.*, 2011). This means positive emotions can 'broaden the scopes of attention, cognition, and action, widening the array of percepts, thoughts, and actions' (Fredrickson & Branigan, 2005: 315). Several empirical studies have supported the assumption that positive emotions are related to higher engagement, while negative emotions were related to lower engagement (Linnenbrink-Garcia *et al.*, 2011; Ouweneel *et al.*, 2011; Reschly *et al.*, 2008). However, as mentioned by Boekaerts (2016), most of these studies relied on general positive or negative affect, without focusing on discrete emotions. Therefore, I believe that examining the specific role of anxiety and enjoyment in engagement within the context of SLA can provide a more nuanced understanding about the links between emotions and engagement.

Grit

As a rather new non-cognitive construct introduced by Duckworth and colleagues (Duckworth *et al.*, 2007: 1087), grit refers to 'perseverance and passion for long-term goals'. It has been widely examined by many researchers in the field of education. Grit has been found to be a significant predictor of positive academic outcomes such as academic achievement (Akos & Kretchmar, 2017; Wolters & Hussain, 2015). Grit is conceptualized as a higher-order construct which has two lower-order components, perseverance of effort and consistency of interest. Perseverance of effort refers to individuals' tendency to work hard in order to achieve long-term goals even in the face of obstacles and setbacks. Consistency of interest refers to individuals' tendency to sustain their interest in achieving their goals over time. To measure grit, two well-known scales have been used: the Grit Scale (Duckworth *et al.*, 2007) and the Short Grit Scale (Duckworth & Quinn, 2009). Researchers studying grit treat it in different ways. For example, while some researchers rely on total grit score (Duckworth & Quinn, 2009; Luthans *et al.*, 2019), others examine the two subscales separately (Steinmayr *et al.*, 2018; Wolters & Hussain, 2015). Using a total grit score can pose some problems as the subscales might show different relations with achievement. This is true as many studies which have investigated the links between grit subscales and achievement have reported that only perseverance was significantly related to achievement. Therefore, it is recommended that it would be better to examine the two constructs separately.

Another point which has recently been examined is the domain-specific nature of grit. While grit has been operationalized as a general personality trait which is common for all long-term goals, it can also be specific for different domains. This means that it might be possible for a person to be gritty in their academic life, but not gritty in their personal relations (Duckworth & Quinn, 2009). Such an assumption was supported by two recent studies (Cormier *et al.*, 2019; Schmidt *et al.*, 2019) which found that domain-specific grit is different from domain-general grit and that grit might be different for each subject. Therefore, it is recommended that a domain-specific measurement of grit might reveal a clearer picture of how the construct functions.

In the field of SLA, very few studies have investigated grit. For example, Yamashita (2018) found mixed findings of negative, positive and no relations between domain-general grit and language achievement. Teimouri *et al.* (2020) developed an L2-specific grit scale. The results of their study showed no relation or very weak relations between domain-general grit and different language achievement measures, while L2-specific grit had stronger relations with language achievement measures and all of them were significant. Khajavy *et al.* (in press) also found no relation between general grit components and L2 achievement.

Concerning the relationship between grit and engagement, some studies have found a positive role for grit in engagement within academic contexts. For example, Hodge *et al.* (2018) found a positive relation between general grit and general engagement in their model. Muenks *et al.* (2018) also reported a positive relation between behavioral engagement with the interest and effort subscales of grit.

It is worth mentioning that there are some controversies concerning the effectiveness of grit in educational contexts (Credé *et al.*, 2017). While some studies reported positive links between grit or its subscales and positive academic outcomes (Hodge *et al.*, 2018), there are also studies which did not find any significant relation between grit and different positive academic outcomes (Usher *et al.*, 2019). According to Credé *et al.* (2017), there are different reasons for such inconclusive findings such as measurement of grit, nature of the task and the moderating role of other individual differences variables. Therefore, it is necessary to consider that the relation between grit and other variables might vary in different contexts and domains and further research is needed to examine the role of grit in language learning classrooms.

The present study

Given the above-mentioned literature about engagement and its relations with achievement, emotions, and grit, I hypothesized a path model in which L2 grit and L2 emotions are related to L2 engagement. Moreover, it was hypothesized that all these variables are related to L2 reading comprehension. The proposed path model[1] can be seen in Figure 13.1.

Method

Participants

The participants in the study were 125 undergraduate students (69.6% female) of teaching English as a foreign language (TEFL) program at the University of Bojnord, Iran. Students' age range was from 18 to 45 with a mean of 21.27 (SD = 2.97). Participants rated their English proficiency as pre-intermediate (12.2%), intermediate (48.7%), upper-intermediate (27.4%) and advanced (11.7%). Most participants (76.4%) reported that Persian was their native language, followed by Kurdish (14.3%) and Turkish (9.3%).

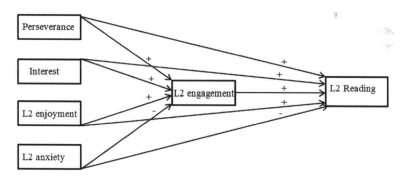

Figure 13.1 The proposed path analysis model

Instrumentation

All questionnaires were answered on a six-point Likert type scale ranging from 1 (strongly disagree) to 6 (strongly agree).

L2 grit

To assess L2 grit, nine items from Teimouri *et al.* (2020) were used. This scale measures both perseverance of effort (5 items, e.g. 'I am a diligent English language learner') and consistency of interest (4 items, e.g. 'I think I have lost my interest in learning English', a reversed item).

L2 emotions

In this study, I measured two types of emotions, L2 anxiety and L2 enjoyment. Six items from Khodadady and Khajavy (2013, adapted from Horwitz *et al.*, 1986) were used for assessing L2 anxiety (e.g. 'I start to panic when I have to speak without preparation in English class'). Moreover, three items from Khajavy *et al.* (2018) were utilized for measuring L2 enjoyment (e.g. 'I enjoy speaking English').

L2 engagement

To assess engagement within the L2 context, I modified Wang *et al.*'s (2016) engagement scale which was designed and developed for measuring engagement in math and science classes. As a result, a 22-item scale was developed to assess L2 engagement. Consistent with its original scale, it measures four dimensions of engagement including behavioral (4 items, e.g. 'I put effort into learning English'), cognitive (6 items, e.g. 'When I learn a new grammatical structure, I think about how to use it in a sentence'), emotional (6 items, e.g. 'I feel good when I am learning English'), and social aspects (6 items, e.g. 'I try to work with others who can help me in English').

L2 reading comprehension

In order to assess L2 reading comprehension, an IELTS reading comprehension test including 13 items was used. The types of questions were true/false/not given and summary completion. One score was assigned for each correct answer making the maximum possible score of 13.

Data analysis

All the analyses were conducted using SPSS and AMOS software. To examine the relations between variables, correlations and path analysis were used. To have a better interpretation for the findings, I used effect size measures (Plonsky & Oswald, 2014). For correlations, I used field-specific effect sizes as $r = 0.25$, $r = 0.40$, and $r = 0.60$ which represent small, medium and large effect sizes, respectively. Before testing the path analysis, confirmatory factor analysis (CFA) was run for each construct. The fit of the path model and CFAs was assessed based on goodness-of-fit indices. In this study, I used comparative fit index (CFI), root mean square error of approximation (RMSEA), and standardized root mean square residual (SRMR). To have a fit model, CFI should be above 0.90, and RMSEA and SRMR should be less than 0.08 (Hu & Bentler, 1999; Marsh *et al.*, 2004).

Results

Confirmatory factor analysis

The measurement model of each construct was assessed using CFA. Goodness-of-fit indices for all tested models can be seen in Table 13.1. First, the factor structure of engagement scale was examined. Two competing models were tested for engagement, (a) a four-factor correlated model and (b) a second-order model in which the four factors of engagement formed a higher-order construct. As Table 13.1 indicates, the second-order model showed a better fit than the four-factor model suggesting that L2 engagement is consisted of four distinct factors which form a higher-order construct, i.e. L2 engagement. CFA was also conducted for emotions and grit and both models indicated good fit to the data (see Table 13.1).

Descriptive statistics and correlations

Table 13.2 summarizes descriptive statistics including mean, standard deviation, skewness and kurtosis as well as the reliability of the variables. Considering the normality of the scales, all skewness and kurtosis values are within the range of −2 and +2 which confirms the normal distribution of the data. As Table 13.2 indicates, given the possible range of the data (between 1 to 6), all four types of L2 engagement have means above the midpoint (3.5) which shows that learners were engaged cognitively, behaviorally, socially, and emotionally in their L2 classes. Correlations among all variables can be seen in Table 13.3.

Path analysis

In order to examine the relations among L2 emotions, L2 grit, L2 engagement and L2 reading comprehension, I tested a path model (see

Table 13.1 Goodness of fit indices for the measurement models

	χ^2	df	CFI	TLI	RMSEA	SRMR
Four-correlated factor model of engagement	325.49	189	.87	.85	.08	.07
Second-order factor model of engagement	311.75	191	.92	.91	.07	.07
L2 emotions model	33.61	25	.97	.96	.05	.05
L2 grit model	48.85	24	.95	.93	.08	.06

Table 13.2 Descriptive statistics and reliability estimates of the variables

	M	SD	Skewness	Kurtosis	Cronbach's α
Perseverance	4.35	0.89	−0.46	0.62	0.82
Interest	4.75	1.12	−0.80	0.02	0.85
Anxiety	3.21	1.10	0.22	−0.70	0.80
Enjoyment	5.10	0.77	−1.02	1.42	0.68
Cognitive	4.21	0.73	−0.70	0.43	0.73
Behavioral	4.59	0.84	−0.65	0.84	0.77
Social	4.67	0.76	−0.66	0.63	0.71
Emotional	5.12	0.79	−1.12	1.39	0.83
L2 engagement	4.63	0.66	−0.82	0.67	0.81
L2 reading	6.77	2.57	−0.33	−0.14	0.73

Table 13.3 Correlations among all variables

	1	2	3	4	5	6	7	8	9
1. Perseverance	1.00								
2. Interest	0.48**	1.00							
3. Anxiety	−0.26**	−0.27**	1.00						
4. Enjoyment	0.51**	0.38**	−0.22**	1.00					
5. Cognitive	0.65**	0.52**	−0.28**	0.36**	1.00				
6. Behavioral	0.69**	0.54**	−0.21*	0.29**	0.80**	1.00			
7. Social	0.38**	0.47**	0.01	0.27**	0.52**	0.57**	1.00		
8. Emotional	0.50**	0.61**	−0.19	0.40**	0.63**	0.67**	0.65**	1.00	
9. Engagement	0.70**	0.64**	−0.29**	0.45**	0.87**	0.91**	0.81**	0.88**	1.00
10. Reading	0.41**	0.25*	−0.43**	0.16	0.55**	0.57**	0.29**	0.36**	0.55**

Note: * $p < 0.05$, ** $p < 0.01$

Figure 13.1). Based on this model, L2 grit and L2 emotions are predictors of L2 engagement and L2 reading comprehension. Moreover, L2 engagement is a predictor of L2 reading comprehension. The final model can be seen in Figure 13.2. Goodness of fit indices showed that the model fitted the data adequately ($\chi^2 = 40.05$, $df = 3$, $p < 0.001$, CFI = 0.95, RMSEA = 0.07, SRMR = 0.06).

The model accounted for 62% of the variance in L2 engagement. Both of grit components including interest ($\beta = 0.36$, $p < 0.001$) and perseverance ($\beta = 0.45$, $p < 0.05$) positively predicted L2 engagement. Moreover, among the two emotions, enjoyment positively predicted L2 engagement ($\beta = 0.19$, $p < 0.05$). Anxiety was not a significant predictor of L2 engagement.

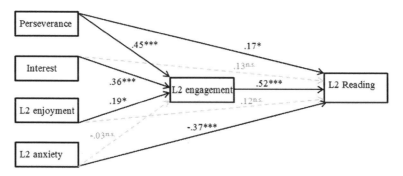

Figure 13.2 The final path analysis model

I also examined the role of L2 emotions, L2 grit and L2 engagement in L2 reading comprehension. The model accounted for 48% of the variance in L2 reading comprehension. L2 engagement was a positive predictor of L2 reading comprehension ($\beta = 0.52$, $p < 0.05$). Moreover, anxiety was a negative predictor ($\beta = -0.37$, $p < 0.05$) and perseverance ($\beta = 0.17$, $p < 0.05$) was a positive predictor of L2 reading comprehension. We also performed bootstrapped mediation analysis to see whether L2 engagement mediates the relation between emotions and L2 reading as well as the relation between grit and L2 reading. The bias-corrected bootstrap confidence interval showed that L2 engagement mediated the relationship between perseverance and L2 reading ($\beta = 0.23$, $p < 0.05$, CI = 0.43–0.96), interest and L2 reading ($\beta = 0.19$, $p < 0.05$, CI = 0.18–.77), and L2 enjoyment and L2 reading ($\beta = 0.10$, $p < 0.05$, CI = 0.14–.52).

Discussion

The purpose of this study was to examine the relations among L2 engagement, L2 grit, L2 emotions and L2 reading comprehension. A path model was proposed to examine these relations. The results of both correlation and path analysis indicated significant relations between L2 grit components and L2 emotions with L2 engagement. Among the correlations, I found that both perseverance and interest had large relations with L2 engagement. Results of path analysis also showed that among the L2 grit components, both perseverance and interest were positive predictors of L2 engagement. Considering the relations found between grit and L2 engagement, it can be understood that L2 grit plays an important role in engaging students in the language classrooms. These findings imply that students who try hard to learn English and do not disappoint while facing challenges in learning English are more engaged in learning English. Moreover, students' consistent interest in learning English affects their thinking, acting, feeling and socializing in the language classroom.

The positive role of grit and its components in predicting engagement has been already confirmed in previous studies (e.g. Hodge *et al.*, 2018).

For L2 emotions, small and medium correlations were obtained for the relations between anxiety and enjoyment with L2 engagement, respectively. Results of path analysis further indicated that L2 enjoyment was a positive predictor of L2 engagement. Therefore, students' enjoyment of their L2 learning increases their engagement in the language classrooms. L2 anxiety was not a significant predictor of L2 engagement. The positive link between enjoyment and engagement in the language classrooms confirms Fredrickson's (2001) broaden-and-build theory that positive emotions increase engagement due to involving individuals with the task. Moreover, findings of this study are in line with previous studies (Hamedi *et al.*, 2019; Linnenbrink-Garcia *et al.*, 2011; Ouweneel *et al.*, 2011; Reschly *et al.*, 2008). Furthermore, although anxiety was a significant negative predictor of engagement in Hamedi *et al.*'s (2019) study, it can be understood that the regression weights were much lower in comparison with those of enjoyment as predictor of engagement. Therefore, emotions are like sparks of fire that can ignite or put off the engagement process (Boekaerts, 2016). Considering the role of enjoyment as an L2 emotion and both L2 grit components as concurrent predictors of L2 engagement, it can be implied that L2 grit components might be more relevant to L2 engagement.

The impact of L2 engagement on L2 reading comprehension was also examined while the role of L2 emotions and L2 grit was taken into account. Results of correlation indicated that L2 engagement had medium relation with L2 reading comprehension Moreover, both perseverance and interest had medium and small correlations with L2 reading. In addition, L2 anxiety had a medium negative correlation with L2 reading. Path analysis showed L2 engagement was a positive predictor of L2 reading. In addition to L2 engagement, L2 anxiety was a negative predictor and perseverance was a positive predictor of L2 reading comprehension. Among these three significant predictors of L2 reading, L2 engagement was the strongest predictor showing the importance of L2 engagement in L2 reading. Taking these findings together, it can be inferred that when students are engaged in the L2 classroom activities and put effort into learning an L2, they would be more successful in achieving higher grades in reading comprehension. Previous studies have also shown that engagement can predict reading comprehension (Hamedi *et al.*, 2019) and course grades in math and science (Baroody *et al.*, 2016; Wang *et al.*, 2016). Given that L2 engagement could predict L2 reading comprehension when L2 grit and L2 emotions are also included in the model implies that L2 engagement has its own unique variance in reading comprehension and should be considered as a factor in teaching this skill.

In addition to the direct link between L2 engagement and L2 reading, findings indicated that L2 engagement acts as a mediator for the relations between L2 enjoyment-L2 reading, perseverance-L2 reading and interest-L2 reading. Furthermore, although L2 enjoyment and interest were not directly related to

L2 reading, they were indirectly related to it through L2 engagement. This means that interest in language learning and enjoying the classroom activities are related to higher engagement in the language classroom which in turn is linked with better performance in L2 reading comprehension.

Conclusion

The findings of this study deepen our understanding of the role of engagement in language learning classrooms. First, I examined the role of L2 grit components and L2 emotions (L2 anxiety and L2 enjoyment) in L2 engagement. Both L2 grit dimensions and L2 enjoyment could predict L2 engagement but with different predictive powers. Among these predictors, L2 grit dimensions had stronger predictive power implying that improving L2 grit can enhance L2 engagement which can lead to better achievement (reading comprehension in this study) in the language classrooms. Moreover, I examined the simultaneous role of L2 emotions, L2 grit and L2 engagement in predicting reading comprehension and found the negative role of L2 anxiety and the positive role of L2 engagement and perseverance, while L2 engagement was the strongest predictor of L2 reading implying that L2 engagement has a significant role in reading comprehension and possibly other L2 outcomes such as speaking, listening and writing. In addition, L2 engagement functioned as a mediator which linked perseverance, interest, and L2 enjoyment to reading comprehension.

Pedagogical implications

The results of this study suggest several pedagogical implications. As previous research in the field of education has shown that engagement can be enhanced (e.g. Gil-Doménech & Berbegal-Mirabent, 2019; Han & Finkelstein, 2013), it can also be enhanced in the language classroom to improve reading comprehension. Given the stronger role of L2 engagement in L2 reading in comparison with emotions and grit, teachers should create conditions to engage their students in the language classrooms. To engage L2 learners, teachers should use interesting and challenging tasks (Oga-Baldwin & Nakata, 2017) and provide a supportive classroom environment (Shernoff et al., 2016). Moreover, based on the findings of this study, L2 grit can have an influential impact on students' L2 engagement. Therefore, teachers should help their students to become grittier by encouraging them to continue their efforts in learning English and not to give up easily even if they face challenges. Teachers should also keep their students interested in learning English by showing them the tangible benefits of learning English. In addition to grit, L2 emotions also are related to students' L2 engagement. Therefore, providing a joyful environment in which students can enjoy learning English can also foster students' L2 engagement (Khajavy et al., 2018).

Limitations and Suggestions for Further Research

There were some limitations in the present study which can be addressed in future research. First, I relied on a small sample from a university in Iran. Therefore, the results cannot be generalized to other settings. Second, the L2 engagement scale was developed based on a scale which was intended to measure engagement in math and science classes (Wang *et al.*, 2016). Although I modified the items to measure engagement in the language classrooms, future research is needed to use qualitative methods such as interview and observation to capture more detailed and specific characteristics of engagement in the language classroom and then to develop a scale based on the themes extracted in the qualitative phase. Third, in this study, I focused on psychological aspects of L2 engagement. However, linguistic aspects in which L2 engagement is measured based on linguistic aspects of the spoken and written text were not used. Future studies can investigate how psychological aspects of L2 engagement can be related to its linguistic dimensions and both measures combined. Fourth, I only focused on reading comprehension in this study and the role of L2 engagement in other skills should be examined in future studies. Fifth, I examined L2 engagement which measures engagement in the L2 classroom generally without considering its specificity for different language skills. This means that an L2 learner might be engaged for speaking tasks and not for reading tasks. Therefore, further research is needed to test whether L2 engagement is a domain-specific construct. Finally, this study relied on questionnaires and examined the relations among variables. Further research is needed to use interventions to improve different types of L2 engagement in the language classrooms.

Note

(1) As Bollen and Pearl (2013) caution, 'researchers do not derive causal relations from an SEM. Rather, the SEM represents and relies upon the causal assumptions of the researcher. These assumptions derive from the research design, prior studies, scientific knowledge, logical arguments, temporal priorities and other evidence that the researcher can marshal in support of them. The credibility of the SEM depends on the credibility of the causal assumptions in each application.'

References

Akos, P. and Kretchmar, J. (2017) Investigating grit at a non-cognitive predictor of college success. *The Review of Higher Education* 40 (2), 163–186.

Alrabai, F. (2015) The influence of teachers' anxiety-reducing strategies on learners' foreign language anxiety. *Innovation in Language Learning and Teaching* 9 (2), 163–190.

Baroody, A.E., Rimm-Kaufman, S.E., Larsen, R.A. and Curby, T.W. (2016) A multimethod approach for describing the contributions of student engagement on fifth grade students' social competence and achievement in mathematics. *Learning and Individual Differences* 48, 54–60.

Boekaerts, M. (2016) Engagement as an inherent aspect of the learning process. *Learning and Instruction* 43, 76–83.

Bollen, K.A. and Pearl, J. (2013) Eight myths about causality and structural equation models. In S.L. Morgan (ed.) *Handbook of Causal Analysis for Social Research* (pp. 301–328). New York: Springer.

Cleary, T.J. and Zimmerman, B.J. (2012) A cyclical self-regulatory account of student engagement: Theoretical foundations and applications. In S.L. Christenson, A.L. Reschly and C. Wylie (eds) *Handbook of Research on Student Engagement* (pp. 237–258). New York: Springer.

Cormier, D.L., Dunn, J.G. and Dunn, J.C. (2019) Examining the domain specificity of grit. *Personality and Individual Differences* 139, 349–354.

Credé, M., Tynan, M.C. and Harms, P.D. (2017) Much ado about grit: A meta-analytic synthesis of the grit literature. *Journal of Personality and social Psychology* 113 (3), 492–511.

Dewaele, J.M. (2019) When elephants fly: The lift-off of emotion research in applied linguistics. *The Modern Language Journal* 103 (2), 533–536.

Dewaele, J.M., Witney, J., Saito, K. and Dewaele, L. (2018) Foreign language enjoyment and anxiety: The effect of teacher and learner variables. *Language Teaching Research* 22 (6), 676–697.

Dincer, A., Yeşilyurt, S., Noels, K.A. and Vargas Lascano, D.I. (2019) Self-determination and classroom engagement of EFL learners: A mixed-methods study of the self-system model of motivational development. *SAGE Open* 9 (2), 1–15.

Duckworth, A.L., Peterson, C., Matthews, M.D. and Kelly, D.R. (2007) Grit: Perseverance and passion for long-term goals. *Journal of Personality and Social Psychology* 92 (6), 1087–1101.

Duckworth, A.L. and Quinn, P.D. (2009) Development and validation of the Short Grit Scale (GRIT–S). *Journal of Personality Assessment* 91 (2), 166–174.

Ellis, R. (2010) A framework for investigating oral and written corrective feedback. *Studies in Second Language Acquisition* 32, 335–349.

Finn, J.D., and Zimmer, K. (2012) Student engagement: What is it? Why does it matter? In S.L. Christenson, A.L. Reschly and C. Wylie (eds) *Handbook of Research on Student Engagement* (pp. 97–131). New York: Springer.

Fredricks, J.A., Blumenfeld, P.C. and Paris, A.H. (2004) School engagement: Potential of the concept, state of the evidence. *Review of Educational Research* 74 (1), 59–109.

Fredricks, J.A., Filsecker, M. and Lawson, M.A. (2016) Student engagement, context, and adjustment: Addressing definitional, measurement, and methodological issues. *Learning and Instruction* 43, 1–4.

Fredrickson, B.L. (2001) The role of positive emotions in positive psychology: The broaden-and-build theory of positive emotions. *American Psychologist* 56 (3), 218–226.

Fredrickson, B.L. and Branigan, C. (2005) Positive emotions broaden the scope of attention and thought-action repertoires. *Cognition & Emotion* 19 (3), 313–332.

Gil-Doménech, D. and Berbegal-Mirabent, J. (2019) Stimulating students' engagement in mathematics courses in non-STEM academic programmes: A game-based learning. *Innovations in Education and Teaching International* 56 (1), 57–65.

Hamedi, S.M., Pishghadam, R. and Fadardi, J.S. (2019) The contribution of reading emotions to reading comprehension: The mediating effect of reading engagement using a structural equation modeling approach. *Educational Research for Policy and Practice*. Advance Online Access. doi:10.1007/s10671-019-09256-3

Han, J.H. and Finkelstein, A. (2013) Understanding the effects of professors' pedagogical development with Clicker Assessment and Feedback technologies and the impact on students' engagement and learning in higher education. *Computers & Education* 65, 64–76.

Hodge, B., Wright, B. and Bennett, P. (2018) The role of grit in determining engagement and academic outcomes for university students. *Research in Higher Education* 59, 448–460.

Horwitz, E.K., Horwitz, M.B. and Cope, J. (1986) Foreign language classroom anxiety. *The Modern Language Journal* 70, 125–132.

Hu, L.T. and Bentler, P.M. (1999) Cutoff criteria for fit indexes in covariance structure analysis: Conventional criteria versus new alternatives. *Structural Equation Modeling: A Multidisciplinary Journal* 6 (1), 1–55.

Jiang, Y. and Dewaele, J.M. (2019) How unique is the foreign language classroom enjoyment and anxiety of Chinese EFL learners? *System* 82, 13–25.

Jin, Y. and Zhang, L.J. (2018) The dimensions of foreign language classroom enjoyment and their effect on foreign language achievement. *International Journal of Bilingual Education and Bilingualism*. Advance Online Access. doi:10.1080/13670050.2018.1526253

Khajavy, G.H., MacIntyre, P.D. and Barabadi, E. (2018) Role of the emotions and classroom environment in willingness to communicate: Applying doubly latent multilevel analysis in second language acquisition research. *Studies in Second Language Acquisition* 40 (3), 605–624.

Khajavy, G.H., MacIntyre, P.D. and Hariri, J. (in press) A closer look at grit and language mindset as predictors of foreign language achievement. *Studies in Second Language Acquisition*.

Khodadady, E. and Khajavy, G.H. (2013) Exploring the role of anxiety and motivation in foreign language achievement: A structural equation modeling approach. *Porta Linguarum* 20, 269–286.

Lambert, C., Philp, J. and Nakamura, S. (2017) Learner-generated content and engagement in second language task performance. *Language Teaching Research* 21 (6), 665–680.

Li, C., Dewaele, J.M. and Jiang, G. (2019) The complex relationship between classroom emotions and EFL achievement in China. *Applied Linguistics Review*. Advance Online Access. doi:10.1515/applirev-2018-0043

Linnenbrink-Garcia, L. and Pekrun, R. (2011) Students' emotions and academic engagement: Introduction to the special issue. *Contemporary Educational Psychology* 36 (1), 1–3.

Linnenbrink-Garcia, L., Rogat, T.K. and Koskey, K.L. (2011) Affect and engagement during small group instruction. *Contemporary Educational Psychology* 36 (1), 13–24.

Luthans, K.W., Luthans, B.C. and Chaffin, T.D. (2019) Refining grit in academic performance: The mediational role of psychological capital. *Journal of Management Education* 43 (1), 35–61.

MacIntyre, P.D. (1999) Language anxiety: A review of literature for language teachers. In D.J. Young (ed.) *Affect in Foreign Language and Second Language Learning* (pp. 24–43). New York: McGraw Hill Companies.

MacIntyre, P.D. and Mercer, S. (2014) Introducing positive psychology to SLA. *Studies in Second Language Learning and Teaching* 4 (2), 153–172.

MacIntyre, P.D., Gregersen, T. and Mercer, S. (2019) Setting an agenda for positive psychology in SLA: Theory, practice, and research. *The Modern Language Journal* 103 (1), 262–274.

Marsh, H.W., Hau, K.T. and Wen, Z. (2004) In search of golden rules: Comment on hypothesis-testing approaches to setting cutoff values for fit indexes and dangers in overgeneralizing Hu and Bentler's (1999) findings. *Structural Equation Modeling: A Multidisciplinary Journal* 11 (3), 320–341.

Mercer, S. (2019) Language learner engagement: Setting the scene. In X. Gao (ed.) *Second Handbook of English Language Teaching* (pp. 1–19). Cham: Springer.

Muenks, K., Yang, J.S. and Wigfield, A. (2018) Associations between grit, motivation, and achievement in high school students. *Motivation Science* 4 (2), 158–176.

Oga-Baldwin, W.L.Q. and Fryer, L.K. (2018) Schools can improve motivational quality: Profile transitions across early foreign language learning experiences. *Motivation and Emotion* 42 (4), 527–545.

Oga-Baldwin, W.L.Q. and Nakata, Y. (2017) Engagement, gender, and motivation: A predictive model for Japanese young language learners. *System* 65, 151–163.

Ouweneel, E., Le Blanc, P.M. and Schaufeli, W.B. (2011) Flourishing students: A longitudinal study on positive emotions, personal resources, and study engagement. *The
Journal of Positive Psychology* 6 (2), 142–153.

Peng, J.E. and Woodrow, L. (2010) Willingness to communicate in English: A model in
the Chinese EFL classroom context. *Language Learning* 60 (4), 834–876.

Philp, J. and Duchesne, S. (2016) Exploring engagement in tasks in the language classroom. *Annual Review of Applied Linguistics* 36, 50–72.

Phung, L. (2017) Task preference, affective response, and engagement in L2 use in a US
university context. *Language Teaching Research* 21 (6), 751–766.

Plonsky, L. and Oswald, F.L. (2014) How big is 'big'? Interpreting effect sizes in L2
research. *Language Learning* 64 (4), 878–912.

Reschly, A.L., Huebner, E.S., Appleton, J.J. and Antaramian, S. (2008) Engagement as
flourishing: The contribution of positive emotions and coping to adolescents' engagement at school and with learning. *Psychology in the Schools* 45 (5), 419–431.

Schlenker, B.R., Schlenker, P.A. and Schlenker, K.A. (2013) Antecedents of academic
engagement and the implications for college grades. *Learning and Individual
Differences* 27, 75–81.

Schmidt, F.T.C., Fleckenstein, J., Retelsdorf, J., Eskreis-Winkler, L. and Möller, J. (2019)
Measuring grit: A German validation and a domain-specific approach to grit.
European Journal of Psychological Assessment 35 (3), 436–447.

Shernoff, D.J., Kelly, S., Tonks, S.M., Anderson, B., Cavanagh, R.F., Sinha, S. and Abdi,
B. (2016) Student engagement as a function of environmental complexity in high
school classrooms. *Learning and Instruction* 43, 52–60.

Sinatra, G.M., Heddy, B.C. and Lombardi, D. (2015) The challenges of defining and
measuring student engagement in science. *Educational Psychologist* 50, 1–13.

Steinmayr, R., Weidinger, A.F. and Wigfield, A. (2018) Does students' grit predict their
school achievement above and beyond their personality, motivation, and engagement?. *Contemporary Educational Psychology* 53, 106–122.

Svalberg, A.M.L. (2009) Engagement with language: Interrogating a construct. *Language
Awareness* 18 (3–4), 242–258.

Svalberg, A.M.L. (2018) Researching language engagement; current trends and future
directions. *Language Awareness* 27 (1–2), 21–39.

Teimouri, Y., Goetze, J. and Plonsky, L. (2019) Second language anxiety and achievement:
A meta-analysis. *Studies in Second Language Acquisition* 41, 363–387.

Teimouri, Y., Plonsky, L. and Tabandeh, F. (2020) L2 Grit: Passion and perseverance for
second-language learning. *Language Teaching Research*. Advance online access.
https://doi.org/10.1177%2F1362168820921895

Usher, E.L., Li, C.R., Butz, A.R. and Rojas, J.P. (2019) Perseverant grit and self-efficacy:
Are both essential for children's academic success? *Journal of Educational Psychology*
111 (5), 877–902.

Wang, M.T. and Fredricks, J.A. (2014) The reciprocal links between school engagement,
youth problem behaviors, and school dropout during adolescence. *Child Development*
85 (2), 722–737.

Wang, M.T., Fredricks, J.A., Ye, F., Hofkens, T.L. and Linn, J.S. (2016) The math and
science engagement scales: Scale development, validation, and psychometric properties. *Learning and Instruction* 43, 16–26.

Wang, M.T. and Holcombe, R. (2010) Adolescents' perceptions of school environment,
engagement, and academic achievement in middle school. *American Educational
Research Journal* 47 (3), 633–662.

Wolters, C.A. and Hussain, M. (2015) Investigating grit and its relations with college
students' self-regulated learning and academic achievement. *Metacognition and
Learning* 10 (3), 293–311.

Yamashita, T. (2018) Grit and second language acquisition: Can passion and perseverance
predict performance in Japanese language learning? Unpublished PhD thesis,
University of Massachusetts.

Appendix 13.1

L2 engagement items

Behavioral engagement

I put effort into learning English.
I keep trying English even if it is hard.
I talk about learning English outside of class.
I don't participate in English class activities.*

Cognitive engagement

I do my English homework very well and make sure that it's right.
When I learn a new grammatical structure, I think about different ways to use in a sentence.
I try to connect what I am learning in my English classes to things I have learned before.
I would rather be told the answer of a grammatical or vocabulary question than have to do the work*.
I don't think that hard when I am doing work for my English class.*

Emotional engagement

I feel good when I am in English class.
I often feel frustrated in English class.
I don't want to be in English class.*
I don't care about learning English.*
I often feel down when I am in English class.
I enjoy learning new things about English.

Social engagement

I try to understand other people's ideas in English class.
I try to work with others who can help me in English.
I try to help others who are struggling in English.
I prefer to learn English alone not with others.*
When working with others in English class, I don't share ideas.*
I don't like working with classmates.*

L2 grit items

Perseverance

I will not allow anything to stop me from my progress in learning English.
I am a diligent English language learner.
Now that I have decided to learn English, nothing can prevent me from reaching this goal.
When it comes to English, I am a hard-working learner.
I put much time and effort into improving my English language weaknesses.

Interest

I think I have lost my interest in learning English.*

I have been obsessed with learning English in the past but later lost interest.*

My interests in learning English change from year to year.*

I am not as interested in learning English as I used to be.*

L2 emotions items

Anxiety

I don't feel safe when I speak English in the class.

I become nervous when I don't understand all the words that my English teacher says.

I get nervous when I don't understand what a teacher says in English.

In the English class, I feel shy to answer the questions voluntarily.

I feel anxious when I speak English in the language classroom.

I can feel my heart pounding when I'm going to be called on in language class.

Enjoyment

I enjoy speaking English.

I enjoy the challenge of learning English.

I have a good feeling that I got what I what from my English classes.

* reverse-coded items.

14 Conceptualizing Willingness to Engage in L2 Learning beyond the Classroom

Isobel Kai-Hui Wang and Sarah Mercer

Introduction

Increasing numbers of people are learning languages 'beyond the classroom' (Benson & Reinders, 2011). This refers to language learning which takes place outside of more traditional, more formalized classroom contexts such as when individuals learn languages at home, privately, in social groups, or in online communities. Such contexts are increasingly becoming a key setting for contemporary language learning due in part to the burgeoning of online resources and mobile technologies (Richards, 2015). Although the notion that language learning is restricted to or even largely located within formalized contexts has weakened, research in contexts outside of formalized learning settings remains relatively limited (Lai & Zheng, 2018; Reinders & Benson, 2017).

One key feature of language learning contexts beyond the classroom is that learners typically need to be especially proactive in order to fully exploit the affordances they offer. Paradoxically, they may also find themselves overwhelmed with options if they lack the metacognitive knowledge or guidance of a teacher to know best how to effectively approach their learning. As such, perhaps even more so than in traditional learning contexts, success in language learning beyond the classroom depends largely on the actions, investment, and engagement of the learner themselves and their own self-directed actions (Cadd, 2015; Stanley, 2015; Wang, 2018). For these reasons, language learning beyond the classroom may represent an especially interesting set of contexts for understanding learner engagement, what affects it and how it develops.

In this chapter, we explore data from a six-month longitudinal study based on a series of semi-structured interviews and learning journals of a beginner learner of German, who was learning independently outside of any formalized learning classes. We explore her data to show the role of an antecedent state in which the learner is willing to engage before actual active engagement in a language learning or use activity. Inspired by the pyramid model of willingness to communicate (WTC) (MacIntyre *et al.*, 1998) and the notion of willingness to participate (WTP) (Kubanyiova & Yue, 2019; Sert, 2015), we outline a model of willingness to engage (WTE) emerging from our analysis of the data. The model comprises individual, social and contextual variables, which interact together to describe and explain the learner's state prior to actual engagement in opportunities for L2 learning and use beyond the classroom. We argue that this notion of WTE is helpful for both formalized language learning contexts as well as learning beyond the classroom. It is hoped that the notion of WTE can contribute to understanding how teachers and learners can increase the likelihood that language learning opportunities (in class and beyond) are capitalized upon. The chapter concludes with an agenda for understanding learner engagement in L2 learning beyond the classroom and a consideration of the practical implications of this model of WTE.

Literature Review

Defining engagement

There are various theoretical models, which seek to define and explain engagement (see Chapter 2 by Sang & Hiver, this volume), and it is widely agreed that engagement should be conceptualized as a multidimensional construct. The most common framework sees engagement as comprising behavioral, cognitive and affective dimensions which may be activated to differing degrees at any one time (Fredricks *et al.*, 2004). It is important to note that for genuine engagement, a learner ideally needs to be engaged on all three dimensions (see Chapter 8 by Mercer *et al.*, this volume). For example, merely being busy but not cognitively or affectively engaged in the task at hand is less likely to lead to long-term, meaningful learning. There is, therefore, a qualitative dimension to engagement which is reflected in the different facets of engagement coming together. This means that a more meaningful form of engagement is when a learner is active on task and is truly thinking about the task at hand, being challenged in their existing competencies to an appropriate degree, and positively enjoying and being interested in the action being undertaken. In other words, meaningful engagement that is likely to lead to learning will involve more than just action – it involves thinking and feeling about the task too (Skinner & Pitzer, 2012).

Another popular model proposed by Reeve (2012) added agentic engagement (i.e. proactive, intentional and constructive attempts to enrich the learning activity) to highlight the active role learners play in the learning process. Mercer (2012) also argued that agency is tightly connected to engagement and she suggests that, 'learners' success in embracing lan-guage learning opportunities within and beyond the classroom depends primarily on their agency and engagement, which stem from what they think, feel and do' (Mercer, 2015: 1). Indeed, a key feature of the concept of engagement is 'actual involvement or participation in learning' (Gettinger & Walter, 2012: 658).

In language learning specifically, Svalberg (2009: 246) has also added the dimension of social engagement with language, which she defines as 'the behavioral readiness to interact' (a state) or 'initiating and maintain-ing interaction' (a process). As with other chapters in this volume, we have thus concluded that engagement centers around the notion of action and this distinguishes it from the related construct of motivation which is con-cerned with the intention to act (Dincer, 2014; Reschly & Christenson, 2012; Russell *et al.*, 2005). In contrast, engagement describes the active process of interacting cognitively, affectively and behaviorally with affor-dances or opportunities to use or learn the language. We distinguish engagement from the antecedent states which may contribute to engage-ment, such as feeling motivated or feeling confident, but which do not reflect actual engagement itself.

Willingness to engage (WTE)

Based on our examination of the literature, we felt an important dis-tinction could be made between the states contributing to engagement and the act or process of actually engaging in language learning or use. In this section, we outline our rationale for making this distinction and explain the theoretical underpinnings of our line of thinking. To do this, we pro-pose the notion of WTE as a way of understanding the antecedent state that precedes active engagement on a task.

In the literature on engagement, a number of factors are known to contribute to engagement, and these are typically divided into individual differences (intra-personal factors) and contextual factors (including interpersonal relationships as well as environmental factors). For example, research has shown that self-efficacy (Appleton *et al.*, 2008; Caraway *et al.*, 2003; Linnenbrink & Pintrich, 2003), self-regulation abilities (Moyer, 2014; Wolters & Taylor, 2012) and facilitative emotions (Linnenbrink & Pintrich, 2004; Linnenbrink-Garcia & Pekrun, 2011; Linnenbrink-Garcia *et al.*, 2011; Pekrun & Linnenbrink-Garcia, 2012) are positively linked with student engagement. The nature of learning con-texts has also been found to be influential for the development of learner engagement (Pianta *et al.*, 2012; Shernoff, 2013), in particular, the rela-tionship between teacher and student (Mikami *et al.*, 2011; Roorda *et al.*, 2011).

Perhaps the most commonly used model for understanding how engagement develops is based on 'self-determination theory' (SDT) (Deci

& Ryan, 1985; Ryan & Deci, 2017). This framework states that a learner's engagement can be fostered by meeting three fundamental needs: the need for competence, autonomy and relatedness (Reeve, 2012). This means a learner needs to feel able to do the task they are being asked to do (competence). They need to feel that they are able to influence their own learning actions and hold a degree of responsibility for their outcomes (autonomy). Finally, they need to feel a sense of security and positive connection to those people connected with their learning experiences. This perspective suggests that these states contribute to a learner's willingness to engage and mirror the fact that a large body of research has utilized the SDT framework to understand learner motivation (Brooks & Young, 2011; Cerasoli & Ford, 2014), which we are proposing is part of the antecedent states contributing to a learner's WTE. Reeve (2012) proposes that the classroom context can be designed to meet these needs for competence, autonomy and a sense of belonging, and thereby foster the conditions for engagement. Importantly, he suggests that the actions and engagement of the learners change the nature of the context which can further influence engagement. In other words, learner engagement and contextual affordances for learning are in a reciprocal relationship. An example of this would be how the manner in which learners work or collaborate with peers affects the nature of group dynamics and classroom atmosphere, which, in turn, can further enhance learners' willingness to engage with others and the learning task. Together, the research literature implies that learner engagement can be affected by both individual traits and psychological states as well as by social and contextual variables including the reciprocal consequences of learners' own acts of engagement, whereby a form of success breeds further success.

In sum, the literature already indicates that learners' active engagement in a task is more (or less) likely depending on the interaction of various psychological and contextual factors. We have referred to this dynamic emergent state as WTE and have drawn on two key constructs in second language acquisition (SLA) for inspiration: WTC (MacIntyre et al., 1998) and WTP (Kubanyiova & Yue, 2019; Sert, 2015). MacIntyre et al. (1998: 547) defined WTC as 'a readiness to enter into discourse at a particular time with a specific person or persons, using a L2' Their model of WTC consists of a range of linguistic, communicative and psychological variables, including intergroup climate, personality, communicative competence, social situation, intergroup attitudes, L2 self-confidence, motivation and desire to communicate. The authors described how WTC emerges from the interactions between these variables, and they suggest that WTC is an important antecedent of actual L2 communication. Similarly, Kubanyiova and Yue (2019) examined the notion of WTP which they argue is a crucial antecedent of participation in classroom discourse. They conceptualize WTP as a capacity emerging from communication rather than a pre-existing capacity that individuals possess.

Inspired by these two constructs and the literature on factors contributing to engagement, we suggest WTE reflects the dynamic antecedent state prior to actual engagement – the actual action. We hypothesize that WTE emerges from the interaction of intrapersonal (motivational, cognitive and affective) and social or contextual factors. It is important in our understanding to distinguish between motivation and engagement. We suggest that motivation is just one of the facets that contributes toward a learner being willing to engage with an affordance for learning. However, there are other components that also play a role including the design or character of the task or language opportunity, the learner's interest in a topic, their physiological state at a moment in time (how tired, well, or energetic they feel), and the degree of social support, among other factors. In other words, multiple facets come together and create a dynamic state that emerges from the interaction of all these components – a resultant emergent state, which we have termed WTE. This emergent state is dynamic and can change from moment-to-moment (temporal dynamism) or situation-to-situation (contextual dynamism), thereby affecting how willing a learner is to engage.

To explore WTE in practice, we decided to examine data in an under-examined context for which engagement is critically important, namely, independent language learning beyond the classroom. Given our understanding of WTE as being dynamic and context-sensitive, we want a situated, exploratory design that would allow us to better appreciate the interaction of the intrapersonal and social–contextual factors leading to this emergent state across different timescales and levels of granularity.

Language learning beyond the classroom

The range of affordances available outside the classroom to support language learning have exploded in the past decades and now include online chat rooms, self-access centers, digital games, apps, listening logs, online resources, social media and internet television (Richards, 2014). These opportunities provide language learners the chance to explore, practice and develop their target language competences without structured or formalized support. However, such non-classroom settings also demand that language learners exercise their agency to direct their attention and actively engage with the opportunities available (Moyer, 2014; Wang, 2018). What this means is that making positive use of the affordances available for language use and learning depends on learner agency and engagement with those affordances. To date, however, the limited research on engagement in SLA has focused almost exclusively on language learning and use in L2 classrooms (e.g. Ellis, 2005; Henry & Thorsen, 2018; Philp & Duchesne, 2016; Phung, 2017; Platt & Brooks, 2002; Storch, 2008) with only a few exceptions considering language learner engagement in online communities (Akbari et al., 2016; Wach, 2013; Yang, 2011).

In order to describe and understand the diverse opportunities for learning a language beyond a classroom, Benson (2011) has proposed a comprehensive framework which comprises four main dimensions, which we use below to describe the context of language learning in this study:

- *location*, referring to a wide range of non-classroom settings where learners can autonomously carry out activities to develop their knowledge of a subject or where they can engage in language activities to supplement other types of learning;
- *formality*, referring to the degree to which learning is linked to formal qualifications offered by educational institutions;
- *pedagogy*, referring to the role and types of teaching involved in language learning, such as self-instructed and non-instructed or instructed language learning;
- *locus of control*, referring to who makes the decisions about learning and teaching, such as self-directed and autonomous compared with other-directed language learning.

This framework is useful for understanding the character of language learning activities beyond the classroom as each context and learner profile will be different (Reinders & Benson, 2017). In our study, the language learning context can be characterized as settings which are part of daily life but not formalized learning contexts, an informal style of learning and not linked to any qualifications, and are all self-directed using a range of tools available online or in the immediate context where the target language is spoken in daily life.

The Study

Participant and context

The study was carried out with the first author of this article, Wang, as the participant. Having moved recently to Austria, Wang has now started studying German (the local language) as her third foreign language and she had no prior knowledge of the language. Her L1 is Chinese, she has professional-level proficiency in English (i.e. C1), and limited proficiency in Japanese (i.e. A2) according to the European Common Framework of Reference. She has considerable experience of studying and living in other countries, including ten years in the UK. She has specialized in vocabulary learning strategies and cross-cultural adaptation, so she had a heightened awareness of how to strategize in order to maximize language learning and intercultural experiences.

Although she is living in a German-speaking context, English is used as the major language of communication in her workplace. Her self-reported main motivation for studying German is to be able to respond to everyday situations and be socially integrated into the local community.

Unlike English and Japanese, which she had learned in formal instructional settings, at the time when these data were generated, she had no formal opportunities to learn German. However, she chose to find and employ a personal tutor (a German-language instructor from an Austrian university) with whom she had two one-to-one sessions using a coursebook called *Netzwerk Neu A1*. Each session lasted approximately one hour. The first session focused on the pronunciation of the German alphabet and a brief introduction to the German grammar. The second session focused on the formal and informal greetings in German. Both sessions occurred in April 2019, in the second month of her German learning journey.

Research design
Collaborative autoethnography

This study took a collaborative autoethnographic (CAE) approach which is 'simultaneously collaborative, autobiographical, and ethnographic' (Chang *et al.*, 2013: 17). In collaborative autoethnography, different co-researchers work collectively to contribute to their data collection process, interpret and analyze their data. Chang *et al.* (2013) explain that CAE is emerging as a flexible, pragmatic application of the autoethnographic approach to qualitative inquiry and each research team can make their decisions about the extent of collaboration according to the unique needs of the team. There is no rigid format in terms of when and how researchers should share their research responsibilities. Collaboration can be done partially or fully. For example, not all researchers need to generate autobiographical data, but they could contribute to different stages in the research process, such as data collection and analysis. In particular, both professional and personal rapport between researchers tends to enrich individual's stories and allows the researchers to explore the phenomena together.

In this study, data were collected through autoethnographic narrative interviews based on Wang's experiences of learning German through journals she kept. Her co-researcher, Mercer, was an expert in both language learner and teacher psychology. She conducted the semi-structured interviews at regular points to support Wang in exploring her psychological and social experiences of learning German.

Data collection procedures

The data collection for this project lasted for four months, between 1 March 2019 and 31 July 2019 in Austria, and the data were generated from three semi-structured interviews and 15 learning journal entries. The first interview was held shortly after Wang arrived in Austria. The aim of this interview was to reflect on her past language learning experiences, language learning approaches, motivation for learning German, goals, expectations and concerns about learning the target language.

Table 14.1 Interview data

Interview #	Dates of the interviews	Length of each interview	Word count
1st interview	2019-03-29	41 minutes	3122 words
2nd interview	2019-05-02	45 minutes	3320 words
3rd interview	2019-07-03	65 minutes	4900 words

Another two interviews were carried out in May 2019 and July 2019, and the interview questions were mainly used to explore Wang's experiences of learning German beyond the classroom, her perception of factors influencing her engagement and her strategies for learning German. Each of the interviews lasted approximately 60 minutes, and was digitally recorded and transcribed for content analysis. The dates of the interviews, length of each interview and size of word count for each interview are presented in the Table 14.1.

In addition, Wang kept regular learner journals between March 2019 and July 2019, and a total of 15 journal entries were collected. Mostly, she kept a diary every week and sometimes every two weeks. Learner journals/diaries are a valuable research tool for uncovering psychological processes and changes in second language learning, generating rich contextual information and enabling the participant to self-reflect (Gkonou, 2013; Oxford, 2011). Wang also used journals as a learning tool to record her own learning processes. Although no fixed guidelines were used for the journal entries, focal themes were agreed upon with the co-researcher and included:

- past language learning experiences;
- opportunities and contextual constraints for engaging with German;
- situations of being willing to engage with German;
- situations of being unwilling to engage with German;
- the joys and worries of engaging with German (affect);
- strategies for learning German.

Wang also included photographs to supplement her written texts and represent how she used different affordances as well as her feelings and emotions involved in the learning process. The journals were mainly written in English but also included some key German words she had learned. The journal data created a corpus of 7159 words.

Data analysis

Using the qualitative data analysis software Atlas.ti, the data were analyzed inductively, and the analysis process involved the identification of emerging themes and patterns for conceptualizing WTE, characteristics of WTE and how various factors contribute to the emergence of WTE. The first wave of coding was conducted by one researcher and a list of relevant codes was prepared. Next, the coding list as well as the interview and diary excerpts were discussed with the co-researcher together. The second wave of coding was refined and expanded in light of the research team discussion. The final wave of coding was used to group themes and codes together into superordinate categories with a view to understanding when, why and how she engaged with language learning and use opportunities.

Findings

The findings presented below will examine the nature of WTE. WTE is defined as a readiness to engage with the target language and language learning opportunities and as the antecedent state prior to active engagement in a specific language learning/use context. In both the interviews and diaries, Wang repeatedly showed a willingness to engage with the target language (i.e. German) beyond the classroom, 82 instances in total.

Firstly, the social context is critical in WTE – without opportunities to engage with, use or learn the language, then WTE would remain potentially unfulfilled. Having moved to a German-speaking country, the milieu of everyday life provided Wang with numerous opportunities to see, hear, use and practice German (e.g. words on the street, public transport, advertising, etc.). However, her willingness to utilize these opportunities also depended on her beliefs about language learning. It is this interaction of her mental attitudes and the opportunities that generates an affordance. It is not the opportunity alone that creates WTE but how the individual perceives those opportunities. Based on her past experiences, Wang had a strong belief that it was more enjoyable to learn and practice a foreign language through communication rather than studying language explicitly alone. In addition, she perceived the local people in Austria as being kind and hospitable, which further contributed to her desire to become socially integrated into the local community.

> I really like people here. They are very friendly. They like to talk to you...
> My neighbors often invite me to have a coffee or have a drink together
> during the weekend... When you talk to their language, I think I could get
> closer to them, and get to know them better. (Interview, 29 March 2019)

However, her willingness to interact with local people alone was not sufficient for the emergence of WTE in day-to-day conversations with native speakers. In the extract below, Wang compared her complete novice status in German with her English proficiency, and concluded that she did not have sufficient knowledge and skills to communicate with local people in German at any level. As a result, she was reluctant to engage in daily conversations to practice the language and so she chose not to engage with locals in this way, despite this being her reported usual preferred mode of learning. In other words, her WTE was dependent on her self-efficacy as well as the social context including whom she was speaking to.

> When I went to England, I already had a great deal of knowledge about English grammar and vocabulary etc. So I found that it was useful to develop my English through interacting with local people, and communicating with native speakers. But learning German is different since I have very very little knowledge of it. I did learn some German words, but still found it very difficult to produce the language for daily conversations. I think I'm more willing to teach my mum rather than interacting with native speakers at the moment. When I taught what I had learned to her, I felt that I really achieved something in German and enjoyed the experience (Interview, 02 May 2019)

Wang is more willing to teach her Mum than interact with local people. She was happier to see herself as a teacher but was reluctant to position herself in communication situations while feeling such a low sense of communicative competence. In this instance, her mum, who spoke absolutely no German, represented a better affordance for practicing the language than local L1 speakers of German and created a more enjoyable experience of language use. Wang described social comparisons in the verbal interaction, in this case, with native speakers of German and her mum, leading to different senses of competence. The data highlighted the situated nature of WTE which emerged through the interplay of her strong beliefs about language learning through communication, perceived self-efficacy, positive emotional states and specific social contextual variables such as the nature of the interlocutor. It is possible to see that her WTE emerges and is dynamic depending on the interaction of all these intrapersonal and social components.

Wang stated in the interview that she was sociable and outgoing. As a result of her extensive intercultural experience, she felt that she was quick to adapt to new situations, making good use of whatever resources are available and responding sensitively to contextual opportunities. It would seem that her past experiences of language learning use and engagement provided her a schema to draw on and generated confidence and creativity in the present. For instance, she realized that her workplace afforded opportunities for learning German, including authentic materials and social interaction with her local colleagues.

> Learning German actually can take place anytime and anywhere. My workplace is a great place to develop my German and build work-related vocabulary, e.g. drucken 'to print' and Unterschrift 'signature'. I like to talk to my colleagues and offer my help. If I don't know any words in German and have any questions understanding German, I'm also never afraid to ask for their help. (Interview, 02 May 2019)

Wang actively participated in conversations with her local colleagues and was also open to different ways of developing her vocabulary knowledge. In the extract below, it is possible to see how she had a small sense of success when she used cognates in English to work out the meaning of words and a sense of positive pride about her success. She then capitalized on this by using photographs as an additional strategy for learning and remembering the words.

> When we talked about something about recycling, my colleagues all said 'karte' and 'papier'. I guessed that they meant 'card' and 'paper', because the German words sounded very similar to the English words. I checked my guesses with them. They all confirmed. I was quite proud of myself at that time, because that was the first time when I was able to understand a few words when people were talking in German. I was very willing to do more things to remember these two words. To help me remember them, I also took several pictures of the things related to the words to remind me of the words and the situation when I heard.

(Diary, 23 April 2019)

Throughout the data, her interactions and support from colleagues play a notable role in helping raise her willingness to engage in learning German, including in aspects of grammar:

> I felt most willing to engage in learning German, even a bit of grammar, during these two months. I am so glad that my colleagues have become my German 'teachers'. They created a very relaxed and positive atmosphere where I'm not afraid to make mistakes and ask questions. They have labelled all the objects in the office in German. I hope that I will be able to recognize and remember all the office-related words by the next

month. They added the article (die 'female', der 'male', and das 'neutral') to each word. When I'm not sure any of the words on stickers, I can always ask or check with them. Now when I use/see them, it also reminds me how they are called in German, as well as their spelling. I also try to pronounce them a few times and remember them.

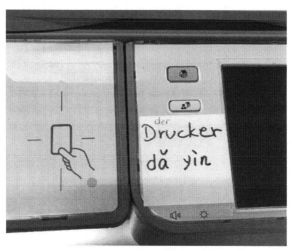

(Diary, 14 June 2019)

This data extract shows how her willingness to engage with the language emerges from her perception of the social context including her relationships to her colleagues and positive learning atmosphere at work, her emotional states as well as her cognitions about how to learn, especially her strategic knowledge. Her high WTE in German learning in the workplace appears to result from a complex combination of her previous language learning experiences, her enduring personality characteristics, her affective reactions and a variety of contextual variables (e.g. atmosphere and opportunities for learning at work), as well as her future learning goals (i.e. being able to master work-related vocabulary for pragmatic reasons); all of these came together to lead her to actually engage in vocabulary learning. These data point to both the situated and temporal nature of WTE incorporating perceptions of the past and present as well as visions for the future.

In understanding Wang's WTE, it is also worth noting that she recorded 17 instances when she was not willing to engage with German. Interestingly, the focus of her lack of WTE centered largely on aspects of language learning related to structured German grammar. As Wang was not attending any formal classes during this time (no courses were available), she actively found herself a private one-to-one tutor to work with in order to make greater progress than merely continuing to work alone.

May [one-to-one German tutor] briefly taught me some important grammar. 1) der, die, das – Gender of Nouns in German; 2) Four Cases. Oh my god! I realized that those are the things I am struggling with a lot! I felt scared to start the grammar. I need to do lots of extra work to understand them and practice using them!!!! (Diary, 29 April 2019)

Before Wang's one-to-one tutor introduced the German grammar, especially the concept of the four cases and noun genders, she had no prior knowledge of the grammar. The diary entry (29 April, 2019) revealed her sense of fear and a lack of self-confidence, coupled with her belief that she was going to have to invest more effort and work hard at this to be able to master it. She further noted in the diary entry (19 July, 2019), this belief about difficulty, her lack of self-efficacy and subsequent anxiety all lead to her avoiding engaging with German grammar.

When May taught me about the four cases, I found it very difficult to understand and remember, and felt confused too. Instead of learning the grammar, during these two months, I quite get into vocabulary. (Diary, 19 July 2019)

In contrast to the grammar, the data indicate that she was generally more willing learn German vocabulary:

I didn't really enjoy learning and remembering English vocabulary in the past. I don't know why I'm really willing to learn vocabulary now, maybe because I live here and experience the words in my everyday life, maybe because of my colleagues. I really enjoy learning vocabulary now. I am also tracking my progress so that makes me more willing to engage in the learning process. Every two or three days, I like to reflect on what I have learned. I'm able to know what I have achieved and what I need to work on more. (Interview, 19 July 2019)

Here we can see that Wang's past learning experience, future learning goals, metacognitive sense of progress, her affective enjoyment and social factors such as the context of daily language and positive social relationships with colleagues all appear to interact together. Interestingly, she compares her experiences now in German with her previous experiences of learning English vocabulary. Indeed, she frequently compares her current language learning experiences with previous experiences and this acts as an important frame of reference for her (see also Hiver *et al.*, 2019). She noted how being surrounded by the language meant she was consistently presented with meaningful opportunities to build vocabulary. She also reported her strategic behavior to monitor her own progress and thereby gained a sense of achievement as well as valuable information for formulating future goals. This self-regulatory frame forms a backdrop to her WTE and to her engaging with specific vocabulary learning and use opportunities as they arose or when she actively searched out or created such opportunities. Yet, here we can see she remains unwilling to engage with any grammar-related learning, preferring instead to prioritize vocabulary for which she had a personal link, a metacognitive knowledge of strategies, and a greater sense of progress and immediate relevance.

Drawing on the cases above, we can see that Wang's WTE is influenced by her personal interests and overriding intrinsic desire to want to be able to communicate in the language in the country she now lives in (the motivational aspect); a metacognitive knowledge of how to learn, a sense of progress and clear goals as well as a sense of efficacy (the cognitive aspect); her emotions – the positive sense of enjoyment furthering her WTE, especially vocabulary, and her anxiety holding her back from engaging (the affective aspect); relationships with colleagues and her Mum that are positive (the social aspect); affordances for language learning beyond the classroom such as sessions with a tutor, road signs to read, language in the environment, input from colleagues etc. (the contextual aspect); and, finally, a use of diverse strategies for learning the language, and actively searching out opportunities to practice and use the language in ways that suit her, also rejecting options that she is unwilling to engage with (the behavioral aspect). From these data, we have conceptualized WTE as a higher-order construct which appears to be a *conglomerate* of motivational, cognitive, affective, social, contextual and behavioral factors. We see these factors as interacting in dynamic ways which lead to the emergence of WTE which is antecedent to her actual active engagement in terms of behaviors but is also reciprocally affected by them.

Discussion

In these data, we propose the concept of WTE (Willingness to Engage) which we see as a dynamic emergent state that precedes actual learner engagement, which itself is characterized by action. The data suggest the interrelation of a number of factors which contribute to WTE including cognitive, affective, motivational, social and behavioral factors. Figure 14.1 shows a summary of the factors that emerged from this study. Although for illustrative purposes, we have separated these into categories, we see them as interacting parts of an emergent state. In some ways, this resonates with and expands on the work which outlines some of the determinants of engagement (e.g. Christenson *et al.*, 2012; Moyer, 2014; Pekrun & Linnenbrink-Garcia, 2012) and which we outlined briefly in earlier sections. Obviously, the factors we list here indicate those salient in Wang's data and are not meant to suggest a comprehensive list of factors but rather indicate the types of things that can contribute to WTE and which appeared to do so for this particular learner in this setting.

The construct of WTE is part of a more holistic view of engagement which recognizes that there are certain psychological and social–contextual factors which interact together prior to actual engagement and which make engagement more or less likely for a specific individual at a particular moment in time. We find this distinction between actual engagement and the antecedent state useful in teasing apart the processes and constructs which interact on different timescales. The future antecedent states

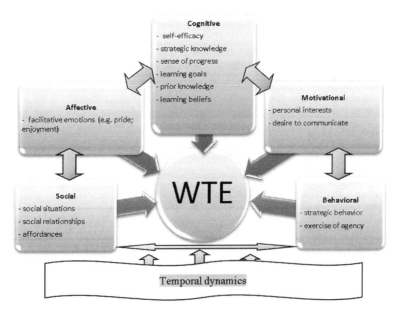

Figure 14.1 A summary of contributory components to Wang's WTE in German beyond the classroom

of WTE are affected by the individual's ongoing experiences of engagement and, as such, actual engagement and WTE are reciprocally connected. We have found that the construct of WTE reflects well the phenomenological reality of learners' social–psychological state preceding active engagement. WTE is intended to capture the complexity and dynamism of the factors interacting to contribute to this emergent state. Its emergent character helps us to appreciate that WTE is likely to vary across individuals in terms of the relative importance of diverse factors, the contributory components and the relationships and interaction between the diverse components. Further research is needed to explore the viability of this construct across diverse learners with regard to not only individuals but also groups in terms of age, proficiency and contexts of learning as well as across time.

We felt that the distinction between the action of engagement and the antecedent state facilitating or inhibiting actual engagement was an important one to make for research, theory and practice. In terms of research and theory, this distinction has consequences for whether engagement on task is being examined (action) or whether the situated social–psychological state for the learner prior to engagement is the focus. We believe that they feed into each other but they are not the same thing. A challenge for research and conceptual work has been how to tease apart factors such as interest and motivation from engagement. In our view, these are vital components of WTE but not a guarantee of actual engagement which is the action on task – in itself an actional process that has cognitive, affective and behavioral dimensions. However, these on-task dimensions of engagement are also not the same as the kinds of cognitive, affective and contextual factors which can contribute toward a learner being fundamentally willing to engage. Again, a high degree of WTE makes engagement more likely but is not in and of itself a guarantee of engagement. This distinction between WTE and actual engagement has temporal as well as definitional distinctions and may help further clarify the distinction between engagement (action), WTE (the antecedent social–psychological state prior to engagement) and motivation (the intention to act which can contribute to WTE or can also refer to a longer timeframe of intended actions and goals).

Indeed, a notable issue for us is the distribution of these factors on different timescales and the temporality of the model. Some aspects, such as beliefs and interests, are relatively enduring over time. Several factors such as beliefs or metacognitive knowledge of strategies stem from past experiences, and there is evidence of the role of future goals in determining the focus of the learner's WTE. In parallels with the pyramid model of WTC, it can be seen how some of these factors are more immediately tied to the action of engagement and some are more distal in their connection but still play an active role in the moment. Further research is needed to better understand the interaction of these factors on different timescales as well as the temporal character of WTE and its dynamism over time.

Another related key characteristic to reflect upon concerns how WTE is affected by the learner's ongoing experiences and interpretations of moments of engagement. These data imply a kind of spiral of positive engagement, whereby WTE, which results in successful and positive engagement, seems likely to further strengthen and enhance WTE, or in the case of unsuccessful experiences of engagement, risk leading to lower levels of WTE. Research is needed to examine whether WTE and perceived experiences of engagement relate in a way in which potentially the WTE-rich get richer and the WTE-poor get poorer, as has been suggested for engagement more generally (cf. Skinner & Belmont, 1993).

Finally, in mainstream education research, researchers have tended to rely on experimental designs and employ quantitative analysis to make generalizations about students' engagement or the relations between learner engagement and academic achievement. These designs have shed very little light on the complex interplay of individual learner characteristics and a range of psychological, social and temporal factors that can have an impact on learners' actual engagement. For this reason, this type of in-depth qualitative investigation appears to play an important role in complementing the quantitative research designs in understanding some of the complexity and dynamism over time and place of engagement as it is lived by an individual.

Implications for practice

A valuable insight from these data is an understanding of some of the factors that contribute toward creating the kind of state in which learners are more (or less) likely to engage with language learning and use opportunities. For teachers, this implies that it is not only possible to work on promoting engaging tasks, but further creating the requisite conditions for engagement in class and beyond is likely to foster WTE thereby making engagement more likely, although there can never be a guarantee (see also Mercer & Dörnyei, 2020). Ultimately, learners may have the optimal conditions, resources and psychological state to engage but still choose to exercise their agency by not engaging in an opportunity or with a particular resource. That remains the joy and the challenge of language education working with complex, unique humans.

An interesting dimension to this work on WTE in this setting is the potential connection between out-of-school learning opportunities and in-class learning. Shernoff (2013) also highlights the potential reciprocal link between extracurricular activities and in-school tasks. He proposes the potential for a cycle of positive engagement growth. In the language learning context, this could imply that helping students to strengthen their engagement with language beyond the classroom is likely to feed into higher engagement with language learning opportunities in class and vice versa.

While working or studying abroad, language learners may have a limited amount of time for learning the target language and receive insufficient meaningful input in the classroom. As the results of this study suggest, out-of-class experiences have the potential to provide rich affordances for language learning and use with which language learners engage. However, even experienced language learners such as Wang, who are well aware of how to strategize in order to maximize language learning, may struggle to generate and sustain their engagement in out-of-class activities. Understanding WTE may be one way in which teachers or tutors or self-directed learners can be helped in preparing for their out-of-class learning (see also Nunan & Richards, 2015).

Conclusion

In this chapter, we have proposed a new construct which we feel may play a valuable role in understanding the nature of learner engagement. In our definitions of terms, we have stressed the action component of engagement which is reflected in the active ways a learner cognitively, affectively and behaviorally engages with language learning and use opportunities. However, we also note that a number of factors come together prior to actual action and make a learner more or less likely to engage. This antecedent state is dynamic and comprises diverse components including cognitive, affective, motivational, social and behavioral states. From their interaction, which we predict will be highly individual and contextually bound, emerges a state which we have termed WTE, drawing on insights from WTC (MacIntyre *et al.*, 1998) and WTP (Kubanyiova & Yue, 2019; Sert, 2015). This is our first attempt at distinguishing the action of engagement and the social–psychological antecedent state, while acknowledging their likely reciprocal relationship. We hope our chapter will inspire discussion and debate as well as prove useful for practice. We are aware of the limited nature of our data in terms of the range of contexts, individuals and timeframe covered. Further research is needed to critically examine this notion and construct, in order to explore to what extent the distinction between WTE and engagement may be useful for both researchers and practitioners.

References

Akbari, E., Naderi, A., Simons, R.J. and Pilot, A. (2016) Student engagement and foreign language learning through online social networks. *Asian-Pacific Journal of Second and Foreign Language Education* 1 (4), 1–22.

Appleton, J.J., Christenson, S.L. and Furlong, M.J. (2008) Student engagement with school: Critical conceptual and methodological issues of the construct. *Psychology in the Schools* 45, 369–386.

Benson, P. (2011) Language learning and teaching beyond the classroom: An introduction to the field. In P. Benson and H. Reinders (eds) *Beyond the Language Classroom* (pp. 7–17). London: Palgrave Macmillan.

Benson, P. and Reinders, H. (eds) (2011) *Beyond the Language Classroom*. Basingstoke: Palgrave Macmillan

Brooks, C.F. and Young, S.L. (2011) Are choice-making opportunities needed in the classroom? Using self-determination theory to consider student motivation and learner empowerment. *International Journal of Teaching and Learning in Higher Education* 23, 48–59.

Cadd, M. (2015) Increasing the linguistic and cultural benefits of study abroad. In D. Nunan and J. Richards (eds) *Language Learning beyond the Classroom* (pp. 244–252). New York: Routledge.

Caraway, K., Tucker, C.M., Reinke, W.M. and Hall, C. (2003) Self-efficacy, goal orientation, and fear of failure as predictors of school engagement in high school students. *Psychology in the Schools* 40, 417–427.

Cerasoli, P. and Ford, M. (2014) Intrinsic motivation, performance, and the mediating role of mastery goal orientation: A test of self-determination theory. *The Journal of Psychology* 148 (3), 267–286.

Chang, H., Ngunjiri, F.W. and Hernandez, K.C. (2013) *Collaborative Autoethnography*. Walnut Creek: Left Coast Press.

Christenson, S.L., Reschly, A.L. and Wylie, C. (eds) (2012) *Handbook of Research on Student Engagement*. New York: Springer.

Deci, E.L. and Ryan, R.M. (1985) *Intrinsic Motivation and Self-Determination in Human Behavior*. New York: Plenum.

Dincer, A. (2014) Antecedents and Outcomes of Self-determined Engagement in Turkish EFL Classrooms: A Mixed Method Approach (Unpublished doctoral thesis). Erzurum: Ataturk University.

Ellis, R. (2005) Principles of instructed language learning. *System* 33, 209–224.

Fredricks, J., Blumenfeld, P. and Paris, A. (2004) School engagement: Potential of the concept, state of the evidence. *Review of Educational Research* 74 (1), 59–109.

Gettinger, M. and Walter, M. (2012) Classroom strategies to enhance academic engaged time. In S.L. Christenson, A.L. Reschly and C. Wylie (eds) *Handbook of Research on Student Engagement* (pp. 653–673). New York: Springer.

Gkonou, C. (2013) A diary study on the causes of English language classroom anxiety. *International Journal of English Studies* 13, 51–68.

Henry, A. and Thorsen, C. (2018) Disaffection and agentic engagement: 'Redesigning' activities to enable authentic self-expression. *Language Teaching Research*. Advance Online Access. doi:10.1177/1362168818795976

Hiver, P., Obando, G., Sang, Y., Tahmouresi, S., Zhou, A. and Zhou, Y. (2019) Reframing the L2 learning experience as narrative reconstructions of classroom learning. *Studies in Second Language Learning and Teaching* 9 (1), 85–118.

Kubanyiova, M. and Yue, Z (2019) Willingness to communicate in L2: Persons' emerging capacity to participate in acts of meaning making with one another. *Journal for the Psychology of Language Learning* 1, 42–66.

Lai, C. and Zheng, D. (2018) Self-directed use of mobile devices for language learning beyond the classroom. *ReCALL: An International Journal on Technologies and Language Learning* 30 (3), 299–318.

Linnenbrink, E.A. and Pintrich, P.R. (2003) The role of self-efficacy beliefs in student engagement and learning in the classroom. *Reading & Writing Quarterly* 19, 119–137.

Linnenbrink, E.A. and Pintrich, P.R. (2004) Role of affect in cognitive processing in academic contexts. In D.Y. Dai and R.J. Sternberg (eds) *Motivation, Emotion, and Cognition: Integrative Perspectives on Intellectual Functioning and Development* (pp. 57–87). Mahwah, NJ: Lawrence Erlbaum.

Linnenbrink-Garcia, L. and Pekrun, R. (2011) Students' emotions and academic engagement: Introduction to the special issue. *Contemporary Educational Psychology* 36, 1–3.

Linnenbrink-Garcia, L., Rogat, T.M. and Koskey, K.L. (2011) Affect and engagement during small group instruction. *Contemporary Educational Psychology* 36, 13–24.

MacIntyre, P.D., Clément, R., Dörnyei, Z. and Noels, K. (1998) Conceptualizing willingness to communicate in a L2: A situated model of confidence and affiliation. *The Modern Language Journal* 82, 545–562.

Mikami, A.Y., Gregory, A., Allen, J.P., Pianta, R.C. and Lun, J. (2011) Effects of a teacher professional development intervention on peer relationships in secondary classrooms. *School Psychology Review* 40, 367–385.

Mercer, S. (2012) The complexity of learner agency. *Apples–Journal of Applied Language Studies* 6 (2), 41–59.

Mercer, S. (2015) Learner agency and engagement: Believing you can, wanting to and knowing how to. *Humanising Language Teaching* 17 (4), 1–19.

Mercer, S. and Dörnyei, Z. (2020) *Engaging Language Learners in Contemporary Classrooms*. Cambridge: Cambridge University Press.

Moyer, A. (2014) Exceptional outcomes in L2 phonology: The critical factors of learner engagement and self-regulation. *Applied Linguistics* 35, 418–440.

Nunan, D. and Richards, J. (eds) (2015) *Language Learning beyond the Classroom*. New York: Routledge.

Oxford, R.L. (2011) *Teaching and Researching Language Learning Strategies*. Harlow: Pearson Longman.

Pekrun, R. and Linnenbrink-Garcia, L. (2012) Academic emotions and student engagement. In S.L. Christenson, A.L. Reschly and C. Wylie (eds) *Handbook of Research on Student Engagement* (pp. 259–282). New York: Springer.

Philp, J. and Duchesne, S. (2016) Exploring engagement in tasks in the language classroom. *Annual Review of Applied Linguistics* 36, 50–72.

Phung, L. (2017) Task preference, affective response, and engagement in L2 use in a US university context. *Language Teaching Research* 21 (6), 751–766.

Pianta, R.C., Hamre, B.K. and Allen, J.P. (2012) Teacher-student relationships and engagement: Conceptualizing, measuring, and improving the capacity of classroom interactions. In S.L. Christenson, A.L. Reschly and C. Wylie (eds) *Handbook of Research on Student Engagement* (pp. 365–386). New York: Springer

Platt, E. and Brooks, F. B. (2002) Task engagement: A turning point in foreign language development. *Language Learning* 52, 365–400.

Reeve, J. (2012) A self-determination theory perspective on student engagement. In S.L. Christenson, A.L. Reschly and C. Wylie (eds) *Handbook of Research on Student Engagement* (pp. 149–172). New York: Springer.

Reinders, H. and Benson, P. (2017) Research agenda: Language learning beyond the classroom. *Language Teaching* 50 (4), 561–578.

Reschly, A.L. and Christenson, S.L. (2012) Jingle, jangle, and conceptual haziness: Evolution and future directions of the engagement construct. In S.L. Christenson, A.L. Reschly and C. Wylie (eds) *Handbook of Research on Student Engagement* (pp. 3–19). New York: Springer.

Richards, J.C. (2015) The changing face of language learning: Learning beyond the classroom. *RELC Journal* 46 (1), 5–22.

Roorda, D.L., Koomen, H.M.Y., Spilt, J.L. and Oort, F.J. (2011) The influence of affective teacher-student relationships on students' school engagement and achievement: A meta-analytic approach. *Review of Educational Research* 81, 493–529.

Russell, V.J., Ainley, M. and Frydenberg, E. (2005) *Schooling Issues Digest: Student Motivation and Engagement.* Australian Department of Education, Employment and Workplace Relations.

Ryan, R.M. and Deci, E. L. (2017) *Self-Determination Theory: Basic Psychological Needs in Motivation, Development, and Wellness.* New York: Guilford.

Sert, O. (2015) *Social Interaction and L2 Classroom Discourse.* Edinburgh: Edinburgh University Press.

Shernoff, D.J. (2013) *Optimal Learning Environments to Promote Student Engagement.* New York: Springer.

Skinner, E.A. and Pitzer, J.R. (2012) Developmental dynamics of student engagement, coping, and everyday resilience. In S.L. Christenson, A.L. Reschly and C. Wylie (eds) *Handbook of Research on Student Engagement* (pp. 21–44). New York: Springer.

Stanley, P. (2015) Talking to strangers: Learning Spanish by using it. In D. Nunan and J. Richards (eds) *Language Learning Beyond the Classroom* (pp. 244–252). New York: Routledge.

Storch, N. (2008) Metatalk in a pair work activity: Level of engagement and implications for language development. *Language Awareness* 17 (2), 95–114.

Svalberg, A. (2009) Engagement with language: Interrogating a construct. *Language Awareness* 18 (3-4), 242–258.

Wach, A. (2013) Polish teenage students' willingness to engage in on-line intercultural interactions. *Intercultural Education* 24 (4), 374–381.

Wang, I. K.-H. (2018) *Learning Vocabulary Strategically in a Study Abroad Context.* Basingstoke: Palgrave Macmillan.

Wolters, C. and Taylor, D. (2012) A self-regulated learning perspective on student engagement. In S.L. Christenson, A.L. Reschly and C. Wylie (eds) *Handbook of Research on Student Engagement* (pp. 635–652). New York: Springer.

Yang, Y-F. (2011) Engaging students in an online situated language learning environment. *Computer Assisted Language Learning* 24 (2), 181–198.

15 Engagement: The Active Verb between the Curriculum and Learning[1]

Phil Hiver, Sarah Mercer and Ali H. Al-Hoorie

Lessons Learned

As we explained in our introduction, sorting out terminological and measurement issues was one of the main challenges contributors to this volume have tackled. It has led to some further questions as well as lessons for us editors in the process of assembling this collection of papers and situating the study of engagement in the field. Concerning definitions of engagement, many studies in this collection have drawn a sharp distinction between motivation and engagement. Motivation relates closely to the intent and desire a learner has in relation to an outcome or process – as it does to one's underlying goal(s). Engagement is best described as the active manifestation of the learner's motivation in their more overt and tangible efforts – i.e. their pursuits and practices – while learning. As Svalberg summarizes in her contribution to this volume, 'motivation research is... concerned with what drives behavior while engagement research tends to focus on the behavior itself' (Chapter 3: pp. 38–55). Going forward, we feel this distinction will remain essential for continued work in the field to establish clear aims regarding the focal point of research – learners' proactive behavior in learning (engagement) or the underlying intent or force that gives behavior its energy and direction (motivation), or indeed the dynamic interface between such precursors and learners' subsequent engagement.

The contributions to this collection also showcase a productive variety of models, frameworks and operational definitions for L2 engagement. Several drew on Svalberg's (2009, 2012) L2-specific model of engaging with language (EWL), others found a more domain-general approach from educational psychology to be congruent with their designs and data, and a handful adopted a hybrid approach investigating domain-specific categories within the parameters of their thematic area of the L2 classroom. Studies with a focus on particular components or categories of engagement (cognitive, emotional, behavioral, social) examined the role of one or more of these components or categories of engagement on students' in-class task performance (Phung *et al.*, Chapter 9), overall achievement (Khajavy, Chapter 13), or finer-grained indices of task-based learning (Carver *et al.*, Chapter 7). Some contributions also examined developmental changes of engagement in the instructed L2 setting (Oga-Baldwin & Fryer, Chapter 12), and stressed the importance of social–contextual influences on how engagement might emerge (Mills, Chapter 11; Wang & Mercer, Chapter 14), what forms engagement may take (Mercer *et al.*, Chapter 8) and the interconnectedness of the environment and various dimensions of learner engagement (Sulis & Philp, Chapter 6).

Another challenge many contributors have grappled with relates to the action dimension of engagement: that is, if all engagement is the behavioral manifestation of one's desire to participate, how can we disentangle cognitive, affective and social dimensions of engagement from the behavioral dimension? One way of dealing with this dilemma explored by Sang and Hiver in their chapter (Chapter 2) and taken up in the designs of many other chapters is this: given the realization that human action is multidimensional, if engagement is to be substantive and lead to genuinely meaningful learning, it needs to comprise multiple interconnected dimensions. This is one of the more fundamental lessons from assembling the current collection, that engagement is by its very nature a complex construct (or as Zhou *et al.* propose a 'meta-construct'). Such a complex view of engagement also fits well with earlier work, such as Baralt *et al.* (2016), showing that learners' experiences of involvement in instructed L2 classrooms can impact their affective engagement, in turn priming and further shaping their cognitive, behavioral and social engagement (or indeed disengagement).

Recent work that suggests *what* learners do is also a function of *who* they are allows us to extend this further and add that learners' engagement is the behavioral manifestation of their agency (Larsen-Freeman, 2019; Mercer, 2012). In a sense, engagement could be seen as an important way that learners actively position themselves in L2 classroom settings and enact their social and personal identities. One learner might position themselves as being detached and aloof, while another might position themselves as being a reliable participant in the ecology of the classroom. That is, engagement in the L2 classroom may represent learners' choice to exercise (or not exercise) their capacity to act and to deploy (or not deploy) their semiotic resources in such opportunities for language use and learning. This reflects aspects of the notion of *agentic* engagement, which Reeve (2012: 151) posits is a learner's 'proactive, intentional, and constructive contribution [to] the learning activity'. From this perspective, the role of engaging L2 pedagogy or classroom instruction would be to optimize the conditions for learners to realize such agency. No doubt, there remains much more to explore on this topic, and as Larsen-Freeman reminds us (2019: 65) 'agency is interpellated from [an]…interaction of factors internal and external to the system, persisting only through their constant interaction with each other.'

Another related message from these combined contributions is the emphasis on situational factors in both engagement and disengagement. Beyond such truisms that language learning takes place in social–cultural contexts and that language use fulfills important social–interactive functions, engagement for language learning can be thought of as emergent in context and situationally contingent. Contributions to this volume show that rich affordances are available for language learning and use beyond formal classroom settings and, therefore, that the relevance of engagement extends to these diverse contexts (Mills, Chapter 11; Wang & Mercer, Chapter 14). It is also clear when probing the complex and interdependent nature of the learning environment and engagement that L2 classrooms are a meaningful setting in which authentic and sustainable forms of engagement can and do occur (Oga-Baldwin & Fryer, Chapter 12; Sulis & Philp, Chapter 6). Out of such an ecological perspective, new and previously unexplored facets of engagement also arise – as with Fukuda et al.'s chapter (Chapter 10) exploring *prosocial* engagement. The potential that the multiplicative effects of learners' prosocial engagement can have lies in individuals coming together and actively creating an ecology of learning beyond the individual. Together these authors advance an intriguing idea, namely, that engagement is inseparable from context precisely because it is mutually constructive of the environment and its affordances. This is fully consonant with current thinking on how learners 'subjectively make meaning out of their experiences and their contexts, while in turn influencing and being influenced by them' (Mercer, 2018: 8).

Why Does Engagement Matter?

First, we take the position that triggering and sustaining engagement is an important process and a desired outcome of L2 education. Language learning, for many learners, is much more than a simple transactional process. It requires substantial devotion of physical and psychological energy and resources, but, equally, it has the potential to contribute in important ways to learners' self-fulfillment and wellbeing (MacIntyre et al., 2019). Many of the contributions in this collection point out that L2 learning is a meaningful participatory process through which learners both make sense of and engage with the world more broadly. There is a high level of individual and temporal variability across learners' L2 engagement, but there are also salient 'Matthew effects' (i.e. positive feedback loops), whereby being engaged in opportunities for language learning and use results in positive effects for future engagement and language learning. Not only does academic engagement benefit the immediate class and subject at hand, but over time (to underscore the issue of temporality) it has a transversal effect: it contributes to other forms of engagement in diverse settings and can position learners for positive long-term benefits in life beyond the immediate instructional settings. By orienting around such processes of initiating and developing learners' engagement, language education might find a balanced focus on helping learners' to forge their own personally significant and meaningful purpose for learning and for acting in the world along with developing more conventional language knowledge, skills and competencies (cf. Larsen-Freeman, 2019).

Secondly, engagement is an essential part of the motivation-achievement cycle of L2 development/learning, in both direct and indirect ways. In many of the chapters in this volume, there is an explicit awareness that in order to increase learners' L2 development, we must increase learners' engagement. This signals that engagement behaviors are essential to learning and L2 development. As Skinner and Pitzer (2012: 23) explain, 'engagement is the active verb between the curriculum and actual learning.' What is more implicit, given the definitions contributors have aligned themselves with, is that one way of increasing engagement is to target learners' motivation. In order to increase motivation, it may be necessary to target the conditions and practices known to have a beneficial impact on such motivation in instructed settings (e.g. psychological need satisfaction, productive goal-orientations, expectancies for success, etc.). This is the notion behind the novel concept of willingness to engage (WTE) introduced in Wang and Mercer's chapter. Regardless of the specific focus of these contributions, there is an understanding that the engaging L2 classroom fulfills fundamental individual needs 'to feel secure and respected, be active and autonomous, experience success, feel competent and have control over the outcome of a learning task or situation, be related to others, [and] understand the meaning and value of the effort demanded' (Janosz, 2012: 699).

Finally, as this collection shows, engagement is responsive to teachers' and peers' practices, and to contextual factors and design elements. Future work on L2 engagement, whether it privileges an exploratory or experimental paradigm, will no doubt build on this collection in understanding what works, for whom, in which contexts, and under which conditions (see also Byrnes, 2019). The studies reported on by our contributors have identified many aspects of the classroom learning environment that are important conditions for engagement. These include, among others, the quality of student–teacher relationships, the supportiveness of peers, the instructional approach and the course design, the mode of interaction and the nature of task–content. In a fortuitous example of the coming together of the psychological and the social, many aspects of learners' psychology tie into these contextual affordances to generate engagement. This complex interplay allows for the possibility of improving engagement and positively influencing learners' L2 development. Engagement research, we would argue, must account for these interdependencies between the environment (including the teacher and tasks), the learner and engagement.

These ideas and others are also laid out as research agendas in several of the contributions in Part 1 of this volume (Han & Gao, Chapter 4; Sang & Hiver, Chapter 2; Svalberg, Chapter 3).

Looking Forward

We turn now to looking ahead and imagining ways that research will continue to build on this collection in the coming years. Two related ways that come to mind are taking a more person-centered view of engagement and bridging the study of the process of language learning and the individual learner.

One of the hallmarks of engagement research, including many studies in this collection, is to examine isolated aspects of learners' engagement, pooled across participants. These studies provide a valuable understanding of the nature and function of the various dimensions of engagement and their separate role in learners' development, particularly at the aggregate level. Readers will hopefully appreciate the considerable variation in the level of granularity at which engagement is studied in the contributions to this collection. Some examine engagement within a specific content area, or in a specific learning task – though looking specifically at individuals' momentary states of engagement remains for future work. Others examine engagement at a much larger level of granularity, over longer windows of time. These operational and design choices in L2 engagement research can have an important impact on the research-practice interface that results from academic or practitioner-led research on the topic. There may be levels of granularity that represent the more proximal processes specific to momentary language learning such as those involved in particular learning tasks (e.g. attention, processing, retrieval, reconstruction). Scoping out and capturing general profiles in L2 engagement or the tendencies and developmental patterns of groups of learners can also highlight where teacher practice is likely to have the most immediate and sustained impact, with a view to influencing positive downstream effects in student learning behavior and development.

When considering the unit of analysis for L2 engagement research, the level of granularity can be fine-tuned through appropriate choices of the agent (the individual student vs. a group), the task (individual L2 tasks vs. a course of learning), and the time (a momentary timescale vs. an ongoing developmental timescale) (Symonds *et al.*, 2019). Yet, as recent advances in psychology of language learning research affirm, the learner is at the center of all processes of learning (e.g. Lowie & Verspoor, 2019). Engagement in the language classroom cannot truly be understood if it ignores the highly individual nature of that process of engaging. Individuals engage in language learning in real time and in individual ways (see also Larsen-Freeman, 2015a). A complementary approach to group-based research on L2 engagement research is, therefore, to adopt a person-centered approach that tries to better capture the multidimensionality and diversity of learners' engagement rather than isolating specific aspects of engagement more broadly conceived. As Molenaar (2004) proposes, 'real psychological processes,' to which we would add engagement in the language classroom, 'are heterogenous in... extreme ways' (Molenaar, 2004: 204), and this heterogeneity can go undetected if research designs are not sensitive to the person-specific aspects of learner engagement (see e.g. Hiver & Al-Hoorie, 2020).

As will be clear from the studies in this collection, engagement research straddles the psychology of language learning (PLL) as well as instructed second language acquisition (ISLA). ISLA is a subfield of applied linguistics focused on the effectiveness of classroom pedagogy (Sato & Loewen, 2019) whose research aims to understand how systematically manipulating the mechanisms of learning and the conditions under which they occur enables or facilitates learners' development in instructional settings (Kang *et al.*, 2019). By experimentally examining transferable pedagogical interventions in instructional settings (e.g. DeKeyser & Prieto Botana, 2019; Polat *et al.*, 2020; Samuda *et al.*, 2018), ISLA research has contributed to growing evidence that the type and quality of instruction matters and is directly implicated in learners' routes of progress, rates of learning and levels of ultimate attainment. PLL is a subfield of psychology focused on dimensions related to language learners and teachers (Dörnyei & Ryan, 2015) whose research aims are to understand the mind and behavior of those involved in language learning, including how individual characteristics result in variation among learners and ultimately exert a direct or indirect impact on learning outcomes (Dörnyei, 2009; Mercer & Ryan, 2016). Engagement offers a unique space where these two domains come together, particularly as work on this topic has a strong pedagogical orientation.

PLL is of interest to practitioners, researchers and theorists alike (e.g. Gregersen & Mercer, 2021; Li *et al.*, 2021). While many such topical areas or constructs from PLL are linked to questions in language learning, L2 engagement strikes us a construct with formidable potential and currency for crossover work that addresses questions occupying both ISLA and PLL scholars. This issue of having one area of research examining processes of language learning and their relation to language pedagogy, and another independent area of research focused on how and why individuals experience differential levels of success, has resulted in what Larsen-Freeman (2018: 59) refers to as a 'bifurcation of research efforts.' We feel that one productive way forward would be to undertake research that studies the relationship *between* the process of language learning and the individual learner. The fact that most of the empirical chapters in this collection speak to issues in ISLA as well as PLL is evidence that L2 engagement research is a thematic area with exciting potential to 'reunit[e] the major streams of research in the field of SLD, bringing together an understanding of learning and learner' (Larsen-Freeman, 2015b: 12). We anticipate that continued work on this important topic will in time bring the two subfields into closer dialogue with each other, and build areas of mutual concern and shared relevance, as the study of L2 learning and the L2 learner converge.

Working with the authors of these papers has been a gratifying and learning experience for each of us co-editors. We extend our appreciation to each of the contributors for embarking on this journey with us, and share their common conviction that engagement is one of the more promising means for understanding language learners' experiences and achievements both within and beyond language classrooms. To our readers, we would like to advance a call to action. It is our hope that this volume triggers greater conversation and sparks further research that will broaden our theoretical, empirical and practical understandings of engagement as it is enacted in the language learning domain. As the contributions to this volume show, further work is needed with learners of diverse languages, at all ages and levels of proficiency, from varied social and cultural contexts as well as in settings within and beyond formal instructional settings. It is clear that L2 engagement research has only begun to blossom, and we hope this volume will advance the quantity and quality of work, opening up new avenues of research that will lead to a richer, more informative and more diverse range of studies into language learner engagement.

Note

(1) We have borrowed this phrasing from Skinner and Pitzer (2012).

References

Baralt, M., Gurzynski-Weiss, L. and Kim, Y. (2016) Engagement with language: How examining learners' affective and social engagement explains successful learner-generated attention to form. In M. Sato and S. Ballinger (eds) *Peer Interaction and Second Language Learning: Pedagogical Potential and Research Agenda* (pp. 209–240). Amsterdam: John Benjamins.

Byrnes, H. (2019) Affirming the context of instructed SLA: The potential of curricular thinking. *Language Teaching Research* 23 (4), 514–532.

DeKeyser, R. and Prieto Botana, G. (eds) (2019) *Doing SLA Research with Implications for the Classroom: Reconciling Methodological Demands and Pedagogical Applicability*. Philadelphia, PA: John Benjamins.

Dörnyei, Z. (2009) Individual differences: Interplay of learner characteristics and learning environment. *Language Learning* 59, 230–248.

Dörnyei, Z. and Ryan, S. (2015) *The Psychology of the Language Learner Revisited*. New York: Routledge.

Gregersen, T. and Mercer, S. (eds) (2021) *Routledge Handbook of the Psychology of Language Learning*. New York: Routledge.

Hiver, P. and Al-Hoorie, A. H. (2020) *Research Methods for Complexity Theory in Applied Linguistics*. Bristol: Multilingual Matters.

Janosz, M. (2012) Outcomes of engagement and engagement as an outcome: Some consensus, divergences, and unanswered questions. In S.L. Christenson, A.L. Reschly and C. Wylie (eds) *Handbook of Research on Student Engagement* (pp. 695–703). New York: Springer.

Kang, E.K., Sok, S. and Han, Z.-H. (2019) Thirty-five years of ISLA on form-focused instruction: A meta-analysis. *Language Teaching Research* 23, 428–453.

Larsen-Freeman, D. (2015a) Saying what we mean: Making a case for 'language acquisition' to become 'language development'. *Language Teaching* 48, 491–505.

Larsen-Freeman, D. (2015b) Ten 'lessons' from complex dynamic systems theory: What is on offer. In Z. Dörnyei, P.D. MacIntyre and A. Henry (eds) *Motivational Dynamics in Language Learning* (pp. 11–19). Bristol: Multilingual Matters.

Larsen-Freeman, D. (2018) Looking ahead: Future directions in, and future research into, second language acquisition. *Foreign Language Annals* 51, 55–72.

Larsen-Freeman, D. (2019) On language learner agency: A complex dynamic systems theory perspective. *The Modern Language Journal* 103(s), 61–79.2

Li, S., Hiver, P. and Papi, M. (eds) (2021) *Routledge Handbook of Second Language Acquisition and Individual Differences*. New York: Routledge.

Lowie, W. and Verspoor, M. (2019) Individual differences and the ergodicity problem. *Language Learning* 69 (s1), 184–206.

MacIntyre, P.D., Gregersen, T. and Mercer, S. (2019) Setting an agenda for positive psychology in SLA: Theory, practice, and research. *The Modern Language Journal* 103, 262–274.

Mercer, S. (2012) The complexity of learner agency. *Apples–Journal of Applied Language Studies* 6, 41–59.

Mercer, S. (2018) Psychology for language learning: Spare a thought for the teacher. *Language Teaching* 51, 504–525.

Mercer, S. and Ryan, S. (2016) Stretching the boundaries: Language learning psychology. *Palgrave Communications* 2, 16031. doi:10.1057/palcomms.2016.31

Molenaar, P.C.M. (2004) A manifesto on psychology as idiographic science: Bringing the person back into scientific psychology, this time forever. *Measurement: Interdisciplinary Research and Perspectives* 2, 201–218.

Polat, N., Gregersen, T. and MacIntyre, P.D. (eds) (2020) *Research-driven Pedagogy: Implications of L2A Theory and Research for the Teaching of Language Skills*. New York: Routledge.

Reeve, J. (2012) A self-determination theory perspective on student engagement. In S.L. Christenson, A.L. Reschly and C. Wylie (eds) *Handbook of Research on Student Engagement* (pp. 149–172). New York: Springer.

Samuda, V., Van den Branden, K. and Bygate, M. (eds) (2018) *TBLT as a Researched Pedagogy*. Philadelphia, PA: John Benjamins.

Sato, M. and Loewen, S. (eds) (2019) *Evidence-based Second Language Pedagogy*. New York: Routledge.

Skinner, E.A. and Pitzer, J.R. (2012) Developmental dynamics of student engagement, coping, and everyday resilience. In S.L. Christenson, A.L. Reschly and C. Wylie (eds) *Handbook of Research on Student Engagement* (pp. 21–44). New York: Springer.

Svalberg, A.M.L. (2009) Engagement with language: Interrogating a construct. *Language Awareness* 18, 242–258.

Svalberg, A.M.L. (2012) Language awareness in language learning and teaching: A research agenda. *Language Teaching* 45, 376–388.

Symonds, J., Kaplan, A., Upadyaya, K., Salmela-Aro, K., Skinner, E.A. and Eccles, J.S. (2019) Momentary student engagement as a dynamic developmental system. *PsyArXiv*. doi:10.31234/osf.io/fuy7p.

Index

Abbuhl 138
Abdi 13, 96, 119, 257
ability 49, 56, 64, 81, 84, 90, 103, 109, 111, 114, 115, 117, 120, 123, 153, 159, 175, 176, 210, 235, 236
abroad 137, 138, 141, 142, 189, 208, 276, 277, 279
absenteeism 243, 244
accuracy 56, 80, 121, 236
achievement 4, 12, 24, 32–34, 63, 73, 77, 93, 95, 104, 118, 120, 123, 134, 144, 161, 162, 167, 179, 182–84, 224, 227, 228, 234, 236, 239, 241, 243–47, 253, 254, 256, 257, 272, 275, 279, 281, 283
action 1–4, 8, 10, 18, 19, 21, 25, 28, 29, 32, 37, 70, 76–78, 102, 103, 111, 144, 159, 165, 166, 175, 177, 184, 206, 225, 237, 245, 261, 262, 264, 273–77, 281, 286
activity 2, 13, 18, 25, 27–29, 32, 33, 39, 52, 54, 60, 71, 75–77, 79, 85, 86, 97, 105, 111, 112, 114, 115, 119, 139, 141, 144, 159, 161, 167, 174, 186, 190, 205–7, 226, 261, 279, 281
affiliation 24, 89, 278
affordance 8, 11, 44–47, 49–51, 74, 210, 260, 262–64, 267–69, 273, 276, 282, 283
agency 35, 45, 53, 57, 58, 165, 176, 200, 219, 261, 262, 264, 276, 278, 281, 287
Ahmadian 137
Ahn 42, 44, 45, 48, 52, 53
Ainley 27, 28, 33, 34, 38, 44, 52, 119, 179, 279
Akbari 264, 277
Akos 246, 254
Alberts 162
Al-Hoorie 1, 8, 13, 31, 35, 69, 72, 75, 80, 85, 90–93, 95, 118, 227, 234, 237, 280, 285, 286
Aljaafreh 59, 71
Allcoat 203, 221, 222

Allen 13, 278, 279
Almutairi 38, 54
Alrabai 244, 254
Ames 35
Anderson 13, 20, 33, 48, 50, 52, 76, 82–84, 93, 96, 119, 161, 257
Andrzejewski 72
ANOVA 131, 136, 171
Antaramian 257
antecedent 11, 19, 26, 29, 72, 176, 184, 257, 261–64, 268, 273–77
anticipation 22, 27
anxiety 22, 47, 60, 62, 70, 77, 92, 103, 110, 116, 118, 123, 124, 136, 163, 164, 166, 167, 170–73, 175, 177–79, 181, 204, 244, 245, 248, 250–57, 259, 272, 273, 278
apathy 183, 184, 201
Appel 71
Apple 201
Appleton 3, 12, 75, 83, 93, 144, 160, 257, 262, 277
apprehension 167
Arabic 54, 125
Archambault 4, 12
Askham 40, 41, 46, 50, 52, 54
assessment 32, 36, 54, 60, 71, 73, 74, 86, 94, 96, 97, 112, 116, 126–28, 179, 199, 208, 223, 228, 255, 257
Assor 165, 179
attendance 29, 76, 130, 204
attention 2, 4–8, 12, 13, 17, 20, 21, 27–30, 32, 33, 35, 38, 40–42, 51, 52, 54, 56–59, 63, 64, 75, 77, 78, 83, 87–91, 93, 97, 102, 113, 117, 120, 121, 123, 124, 126, 127, 132, 135, 136, 138, 139, 143–48, 152, 153, 155, 156, 159–63, 167, 176, 180, 183, 202, 203, 205–7, 210, 213–15, 218–21, 226, 227, 239, 241, 242, 244, 245, 255, 264, 284, 286

attitude 22, 28, 40, 43, 46, 53, 57, 62, 64, 65, 88, 89, 91–94, 104, 121–23, 133, 187, 193, 203, 212, 220, 224, 225, 227, 228, 235, 245, 263, 268
Aubrey 163, 167, 168, 176, 178
authentic 10, 19, 91, 95, 114, 116, 145, 158, 160, 168, 176, 204, 206, 209, 210, 214, 218, 269, 278, 282
autoethnography 266, 277
autonomy 22, 40, 43, 54, 66, 72, 78, 88, 103, 116, 118, 165, 166, 176–78, 207, 214, 218, 227, 244, 263, 265, 283
avatars 204
avoidance 53, 66, 183, 184, 201
awareness 5, 13, 23, 31, 36, 37, 42, 45, 46, 51–54, 59, 78, 95, 97, 119, 121, 124, 138, 139, 161, 180, 185, 199, 201, 223, 239, 241, 243, 257, 265, 279, 283, 287
Azkarai 87, 94

Bailenson 204, 222
Bajscy 222
Balfanz 120, 136
Ballinger 12, 24, 33, 35, 36, 52, 93, 94, 103, 114, 117, 119, 136, 178, 286
Banaji 94, 96
Bandura 92, 93
Barabadi 118, 256
Baralt 6, 12, 21, 22, 33, 42, 44, 52, 77, 81, 84, 87, 89, 93, 102, 117, 121–24, 126–30, 132, 134–37, 166, 178, 281, 286
Barbosa 97
Barbour 42, 53
Barkley 4, 12, 160
Baroody 252, 254
Barrett 61, 71
Barron 34
Basturkmen 119
Batstone 72, 118
Beckner 44, 52
behavioral engagement 5, 11, 20, 21, 24, 42, 61, 62, 77, 79, 83, 87, 88, 97, 102, 108, 115, 120, 123–25, 127, 128, 130, 133, 135, 143, 166, 206, 207, 210, 213–15, 220, 225–27, 232, 235, 239, 242, 243, 246, 258
beliefs 30, 34, 57, 59, 64–66, 69, 72, 121, 212, 239, 268, 269, 275, 278
Belmont 275

Bennett 255
Benson 260, 265, 277, 279
Bentler 230, 237, 249, 256
Berbegal-Mirabent 253, 255
Berenz 127, 137
Bernstein 230, 238
Beymer 96
Bhatia 138, 179
bias 81, 83, 84, 128, 251
Bieg 95
biological 90, 92
Birenbaum 94
Bitchener 58, 69, 71
bivariate 230
Blackledge 35
Blake 125, 136
Bley-Vroman 125, 138
Blumenfeld 12, 34, 72, 137, 161, 237, 255, 277
Blythe 52
Boekaerts 206, 222, 245, 252, 255
Bollen 254, 255
bootstrap 251
boredom 22, 39, 60, 103, 144, 145, 166, 183, 184, 201, 244
Bouchard 223
Bourdieu 25, 33
Bowles 59, 73
Brady 201
Branigan 245, 255
Braun 107, 117
Breeze 201
Brill 203, 222

Cadd 260, 277
Cameron 19, 31, 35, 45, 53, 135, 138
Canada 25, 74
capacity 13, 23, 27, 64, 67, 263, 278, 279, 281
Caraway 262, 277
Carless 51, 52
Carreira 228, 237
Carton 119
Carver 9, 120, 281
case study 11, 62, 69, 72, 74
causal 87, 254, 255
Cavalcanti 57, 71
Cavanagh 13, 96, 119, 257
Cazeneuve 215, 217, 221
CEFR 169
Cerasoli 263, 277

Chaffee 228, 235, 237
Chaffin 256
Chang 72, 266, 277
Chase 4, 12
chat 42, 109, 114, 137, 139–41, 264
Cheavens 201
Chemin 223
Chinese 36, 47, 63, 69, 72–74, 95, 179, 256, 257, 265
Choi 114, 117
choice 6, 10, 19, 25, 32, 82, 96, 126, 135, 137, 163–66, 169, 171, 173, 175–80, 207, 211, 214, 281, 284
Christenson 1–3, 8, 12, 13, 19, 20, 22, 31–36, 38, 54, 73, 75–77, 79, 85, 93–97, 102, 117–20, 133, 136–38, 144, 160, 161, 163, 177, 178, 184, 201, 206, 222, 223, 225, 226, 237–39, 255, 262, 273, 277–79, 286, 287
Christian 159, 161
Christiansen 52
Clark 204, 222
Clarke 21, 22, 34, 77, 95, 103, 107, 117, 118
classification 40, 42, 49, 61, 183, 244
Cleary 103, 117, 241, 255
Clément 104, 114, 118, 278
coefficient 196, 197
cognition 3, 6, 12, 13, 33, 35, 53, 54, 61, 92, 97, 120, 123, 136, 138, 139, 180, 184, 225, 226, 236, 237, 245, 255, 278
cognitive engagement 11, 21, 22, 29, 34, 42, 44, 46, 47, 59–61, 72, 74, 77, 79, 83, 85, 87, 89, 95, 98, 102, 111–13, 115, 116, 118, 121–24, 127, 129, 130, 132, 133, 135, 142, 147, 166, 184, 206, 210, 213–15, 217, 220, 221, 225, 226, 228, 232, 234–36, 240, 242–44, 258
Cohen 57, 59, 69, 71
collaboration 10, 22, 38, 40, 42, 44, 46, 47, 49, 51, 54, 55, 81, 95, 103, 107, 114, 118, 121, 138, 139, 204, 205, 207, 242, 263, 266, 277
commitment 18, 20, 26, 29, 32, 63, 109, 144, 145, 158
communication 3, 8, 9, 20, 22, 29, 39, 43, 45, 48–53, 73, 77, 96, 104, 114, 116, 118, 120, 122–25, 127, 128, 130–32, 134, 136, 138, 139, 146, 160, 163, 168, 169, 175, 176, 182, 186, 189–91, 207, 228, 229, 238, 244, 256, 257, 261, 263, 265, 268, 269, 273, 278
community 2, 4, 24–26, 28, 31, 60, 72, 75–78, 89, 108, 184, 201, 204, 205, 228, 237, 260, 264, 265, 268
competence 28, 34, 43, 54, 56, 62, 103, 109, 112, 116, 118, 165, 176, 178, 239, 254, 263, 264, 269
complexity 1, 3, 7, 9, 12, 13, 33, 35, 53, 59, 63, 68–70, 72, 73, 80, 95, 96, 101, 103, 114, 116, 119, 121, 122, 135–38, 178, 222, 257, 274, 275, 278, 286, 287
component 1–3, 5, 19, 20, 49, 85, 90, 94, 102, 103, 119, 120, 124, 144, 158, 165, 168, 170, 183, 184, 195, 200, 206, 238, 244, 246, 250–53, 264, 269, 274, 276, 280, 281
comprehension 11, 97, 210, 215, 242, 244, 247–55
computer 9, 71, 120–22, 124, 136–39, 141, 201, 211, 223, 279
computer mediated communication 9, 136–38
concentration 17, 103, 111, 115, 143, 148, 151–53, 157, 205
confirmatory factor analysis 230, 248, 249
Connell 36, 103, 118, 119
Conner 95
Conrad 57, 68, 71
consciousness 8, 9, 39, 45, 53, 54, 85, 92, 143, 145, 150–52, 156, 167, 179
context 1–3, 5, 6, 9–11, 19, 22, 23, 25, 29–32, 35, 36, 42, 44, 47, 49, 51, 54, 57, 58, 60–64, 66–78, 80–86, 89, 91, 94, 105, 106, 114, 118–20, 122, 124, 130, 134, 135, 137, 138, 143, 146, 147, 159–61, 166, 168, 173, 176, 179, 183, 201, 203–6, 208–11, 216–23, 227, 238, 242, 244–48, 255, 257, 260–65, 267–69, 271–79, 282, 283, 286
control 27, 59, 73, 91, 93, 133, 164, 165, 168, 170, 175, 202, 205, 206, 213, 219, 239, 265, 283
Cook 206, 222
Cooper 179
Cope 256
Cormier 246, 255
Coughlan 60, 71
covariate 136, 230, 236, 237, 256
Craik 59, 72

Crandall 228, 238
creativity 32, 128, 208, 269
Credé 247, 255
Croft 52
Crookes 26, 33, 138
Csikszentmihalyi 86, 94, 96, 103, 111, 118, 167, 178, 205, 213, 237
Csizér 93, 237
Cudeck 230, 237
culture 2, 4, 6, 7, 10, 25, 26, 33, 42, 57, 105, 168, 176, 183, 202, 203, 207, 209–12, 216, 221, 277, 286
Cummins 26, 33
Cunningham 94, 96
Curby 254
Curran 230, 237
curriculum 1, 134, 204, 207, 208, 219, 229, 238, 280, 283, 286
Cyr 147, 160

Dai 35, 65, 278
Dao 24, 25, 34, 78, 89, 94, 124, 127, 128, 133, 135, 136
Darr 147, 160
Dasgupta 92, 94
Da Silva 201
data 9, 10, 24, 30, 42, 45, 52, 58, 59, 68, 76, 79–87, 89–91, 104–10, 113–16, 128, 133, 134, 137, 143, 148–50, 152, 156, 158–60, 169–71, 176, 186–89, 192, 196, 203, 215, 216, 219–21, 229, 230, 232, 235–37, 243, 248–50, 260, 261, 264, 266, 267, 269–73, 275–77, 280
Daubney 179
Davis 60, 72, 185, 201
Davison 179, 223
de Bot 122, 136
Deci 165, 178, 262, 263, 277, 279
declarative 42, 50, 200
Dede 203, 204, 208, 214, 221–23
De Groot 103, 119
DeKeyser 285, 286
De la Fuente 45, 51, 54, 124, 125, 136
demotivation 182, 183, 192, 198, 239
design 7, 10, 11, 24, 25, 32, 44, 52, 68, 70, 79, 80, 83, 90, 93, 118, 125, 127, 134, 135, 147, 148, 159, 163, 164, 177, 178, 188, 202–5, 207, 209, 211, 218, 219, 221, 223, 254, 264, 266, 275, 280, 281, 283–85

development 2, 3, 5, 10, 12, 13, 17, 24, 25, 27, 28, 30–36, 38, 48, 49, 51–54, 56, 60, 70, 71, 73, 74, 76, 79, 82, 89, 93, 95–97, 102, 103, 111, 112, 116, 118–21, 123–25, 130, 135–39, 143, 160, 161, 178, 179, 184, 198, 201–3, 208, 219, 222, 229, 230, 234, 236–39, 255, 257, 262, 278, 279, 281, 283–85, 287
Dewaele 73, 104, 114, 118, 167, 178, 179, 244, 245, 255, 256
dialogue 38, 47, 48, 55, 87, 105, 121, 138, 286
diary 86, 267, 268, 270–72, 278
digital 10, 155, 178, 202–4, 209, 264, 267
Dincer 145, 160, 243, 255, 262, 277
Dinsmore 236, 237
DiPerna 97
disaffection 22, 36, 54, 95, 96, 119, 161, 184, 219, 220, 278
discourse 6, 36, 73, 77, 84, 89, 93, 106, 137, 161, 179, 208, 263, 279
disengagement 3, 4, 10–12, 20, 22, 31, 32, 44, 60, 66, 69, 70, 75, 81, 84, 95, 97, 114, 136, 143, 145, 150, 153, 154, 157, 159–61, 183, 184, 225, 236, 238, 281, 282
disinterest 10, 183, 184
diversity 1, 2, 7, 9, 11, 31, 35, 70, 71, 78, 83, 145, 202, 205, 207, 209, 217–19, 265, 273, 274, 276, 282, 283, 285, 286
Dobao 87, 94
Dochy 94
Dörnyei 4, 6, 12, 13, 17, 21, 24, 27, 34, 43, 53, 83, 87, 88, 94, 102, 103, 118, 120, 122, 123, 127, 130, 133, 134, 137, 138, 144, 146, 161, 185, 201, 208, 222, 225, 237, 276, 278, 285–87
Doughty 97
Douglass 52
Duchesne 4–6, 13, 17, 18, 20–23, 36, 39, 42, 54, 75–78, 87–89, 96, 101–3, 115, 118, 120, 122–24, 132, 133, 135, 138, 143, 145, 161, 163, 166, 167, 175, 177, 179, 203, 206, 207, 209, 215, 220, 223, 241, 243, 257, 264, 278
Duckworth 245, 246, 255
Duff 60, 71
Duncan 201
Dunn 255
Durik 28, 34

dyad 42, 48, 51
dynamic 3, 7–9, 13, 18, 27, 32, 33, 35, 36, 44, 53, 54, 64, 67, 68, 73, 85, 90, 91, 96, 97, 106, 113, 115, 119, 121, 122, 125, 159, 161, 167, 182–84, 192, 201, 208, 222, 224, 227, 238, 239, 263, 264, 269, 273–76, 279, 280, 287

Eccles 79, 94, 159, 162, 206, 222, 287
Eckerth 45, 49, 53
ecological 10, 64, 72, 74, 86, 96, 130, 185, 199, 281, 282
Edmondson 118
Edwards 137
efficacy 136, 165, 219, 273
effort 4, 17, 18, 20, 21, 27, 30, 32, 47, 60–62, 65, 66, 77, 83, 86–88, 103, 104, 106, 109, 110, 112, 113, 115, 116, 120, 132, 156, 165, 184, 194, 206, 220, 227, 234, 242, 246, 248, 252, 258, 272, 283
Egbert 163, 167, 168, 176, 178, 205, 206, 222
Ellis 5, 12, 38, 44, 45, 49–53, 56, 58, 60–64, 72, 202, 243, 255, 264, 277
emergent 25, 32, 44, 60, 107, 129, 202, 222, 224, 244, 263, 264, 267, 268, 273, 274, 282
emic 68
emotional engagement 10, 22, 77, 82, 84, 88, 89, 97, 104, 110, 112, 124, 147, 164, 166, 207, 210, 211, 213, 214, 218–20, 224, 226, 229, 234, 239, 242, 243, 258
emotions 10, 11, 17, 22, 23, 36, 44, 61–63, 65, 66, 69–75, 77, 92, 95, 96, 118, 163, 164, 166–70, 177–79, 189, 208, 226, 234, 235, 239, 241, 242, 244, 245, 247–53, 255–57, 259, 262, 267, 273, 278
Engagement With Language 5, 8, 13, 20, 23, 33, 37–54, 78, 84, 93, 97, 117, 119, 122, 139, 161, 180, 223, 225, 239, 242, 243, 257, 262, 276, 279, 280, 286, 287
engaging 4, 8, 13, 26, 31–33, 37, 40, 61, 64, 111, 114, 120, 121, 132, 137, 138, 154, 161, 164, 177, 183, 207, 209, 221, 222, 228, 234, 251, 262, 267, 272, 273, 276, 278–81, 283, 284
enjoyment 22, 27, 73, 77, 103, 104, 107, 110–13, 115, 116, 118, 163, 164, 166,

167, 170–73, 175–78, 180, 184, 206, 228, 244, 245, 248, 250–53, 255, 256, 259, 272, 273
Ennis 118
enthusiasm 7, 22, 27, 32, 39, 77, 103, 116, 166, 184, 209
environment 1, 2, 9, 10, 12, 13, 19, 20, 23, 28, 29, 36, 39, 48, 52, 82, 85, 86, 101–5, 107, 108, 110, 114–19, 136, 138, 153, 159, 178, 179, 184, 198, 203–5, 210, 211, 225, 227, 228, 235, 245, 253, 256, 257, 273, 279, 281–83, 286
Eskreis-Winkler 257
Espinoza 201
Evanovich 34
executive function 27
experience sampling method 85, 86, 95
exploratory factor analysis 187, 192, 194, 195
eye-tracking 236

Facebook 91, 141
Fadardi 255
Fallu 12
Falout 10, 182, 184, 187, 201
familiarity 24, 36, 94, 111, 112, 123, 129, 130, 170, 179, 180
feedback 8, 23, 29, 32, 53, 56–74, 77, 82, 88, 95, 105, 109, 115–17, 121, 122, 126, 127, 129, 132, 136, 137, 139, 169, 179, 205, 207, 214, 216, 218, 243, 255, 282
Feldman Farb 35
Fellner 201
Fennelly 228, 237
Ferris 56–58, 68, 69, 71, 72
Fidell 230, 239
Filsecker 94, 118, 255
Finkelstein 253, 255
Finn 1, 12, 21, 34, 76, 84, 94, 144, 158, 161, 184, 201, 242, 255
Fleckenstein 257
flow 85, 94, 96, 111, 118, 167, 168, 178, 205, 206, 222, 225, 237
Folger 94
form-focused 38, 45, 47–51, 54, 64, 287
Fotos 45, 48, 50, 53
francophone 105, 207

Fredricks 1, 3, 4, 12, 19, 22, 34, 60–62, 72, 75, 77, 79, 80, 82–84, 89, 94, 95, 97, 102, 118, 120, 128, 133, 137, 144, 147, 161, 211, 222, 224, 237, 241, 242, 255, 257, 261, 277
Fredrickson 245, 252, 255
French 9, 13, 47, 51, 101, 104, 105, 107, 110–14, 125, 139, 146, 203, 207–9, 212, 214–18, 221
frustration 22, 63, 98, 103, 166, 184, 258
Frydenberg 119, 179, 279
Fryer 10, 11, 28, 34, 224, 229, 234, 236–38, 241, 243, 244, 256, 281, 282
Fukada 10, 182, 184, 187, 201
Fukuda 10, 78, 182, 201, 282
Funayama 96
Furlong 12, 93, 160, 277
Furrer 24, 34, 36, 54, 96, 119, 161, 179, 223

Gable 86, 96
Gamoran 19, 36, 63, 73, 143, 161, 167, 179
Gao 8, 35, 56, 96, 118, 179, 223, 238, 256, 284
Garcia 33, 83, 94, 278
García Mayo 87, 94, 137
Gardner 28, 34, 43, 53, 167, 179
Gass 33, 94, 117, 138, 178
Gatenby 94, 96
Geeslin 126, 137
Geldhof 12
generalizability 69, 81, 82, 84, 85, 130, 275
German 11, 49, 146, 257, 260, 265–72, 274
gesture 87, 149, 150, 220
Gettinger 21, 34, 77, 88, 94, 123, 137, 207, 222, 262, 278
Gilabert 136
Gil-Doménech 253, 255
Ginns 13
Gkonou 179, 267, 278
Glanville 79, 95
Glienke 238
glossing 126
goal 2, 19, 21, 24–26, 28, 29, 32, 34, 39, 53, 57–59, 68, 94, 96, 103, 112, 116, 117, 147, 160, 163, 174, 178, 184, 199, 201, 203, 205, 207–9, 211–13, 228,

245, 246, 255, 258, 266, 271–73, 275, 277, 280, 283
Goetz 61, 72, 73, 86, 95
Goetze 257
Goldstein 57, 58, 64, 68, 71, 72
González-Lloret 130, 137
goodness-of-fit 248, 249
Gore 94, 96
grades 102, 145, 157, 167, 235, 252, 257
grammar 40, 42, 43, 46–51, 53, 54, 72, 74, 105, 137, 138, 154, 188, 208, 266, 269–72
granularity 6, 7, 78, 90, 264, 284
Greene 74
Greenwald 94
Gregersen 73, 167, 178, 179, 256, 285–87
Gregory 278
Griffiths 4, 12
grit 11, 241, 242, 245–58
group 5, 9, 22, 28, 40, 41, 55, 66, 80, 86, 95, 106–9, 113–18, 146–54, 156, 157, 165, 169–75, 182, 183, 185–90, 192, 193, 195–201, 207, 213–19, 227, 237, 239, 241, 256, 263, 268, 278, 284
growth 11, 12, 198–200, 224, 229, 230, 232–35, 237, 238, 276
Guinda 201
Gumperz 127, 137
Gunnar 118
Gunterman 126, 137
Gurzynski-Weiss 9, 12, 33, 52, 93, 117, 120, 124, 126, 127, 132, 136, 137, 178, 286
Guthrie 97

Haag 72
Haga 169, 179
Hall 72, 95, 153, 202, 277
Hamedi 243, 244, 252, 255
Hamm 179
Han 8, 38, 53, 56, 60, 62–69, 72, 73, 82, 85, 95, 222, 253, 255, 284, 287
Handley 60, 61, 72
Hannula 161
Hansen 52
Harackiewicz 27, 28, 30, 34, 35
Harbour 33, 34
Hariri 256
Harms 255

Hiver 1, 7, 8, 13, 17, 31, 35, 43, 60, 69, 72, 75, 76, 79–82, 85, 92, 95, 111, 118, 144, 208, 222, 225, 227, 234, 237, 242, 261, 272, 278, 280, 281, 284–87
Hodge 242, 246, 247, 252, 255
Hodgen 3, 13
Hodgkinson 22, 35, 77, 96
Hofkens 76, 79, 95, 97, 257
Holcombe 241, 257

instructed second language acquisition 56, 160, 285
intention 1, 4, 8, 18, 29, 39, 65, 102, 144, 170, 184, 199, 227, 234, 262, 275, 280
interaction 5, 6, 9, 10, 12, 13, 20, 23, 26, 28–30, 33–36, 38–40, 42–44, 49–52, 54, 58, 59, 64, 71–73, 76–78, 81, 84, 87, 89, 93–96, 103, 113, 115–17, 119–34, 136–39, 150, 154, 163, 170, 172, 173, 175, 178, 179, 197, 204, 206, 209, 218, 222, 223, 225, 228, 235, 237, 242, 262–64, 268, 269, 274, 275, 277, 279, 281–83, 286
interview 9, 45, 46, 50, 51, 58, 61, 68, 70, 76, 80, 82, 84, 85, 89, 106–8, 110, 111, 113, 116, 128, 134, 143, 147–57, 209, 220, 221, 243, 254, 260, 266–69, 272

Kang 228, 238, 285, 287
Kankaanranta 222
Kaplan 287
Katz 165, 179, 237
Kearney 42, 44, 48, 53
Kelly 13, 96, 119, 255, 257
Kern 218, 223
Ketelhut 222
Khajavy 11, 104, 114, 118, 241, 244–46, 248, 253, 256, 281
Khatib 50, 53
Khodadady 244, 248, 256
Kikuchi 236, 239
Kindermann 36, 54, 96, 119, 161, 179, 223
King 54, 67, 73, 183, 198, 201
Kinginger 26, 35
Kingstone 161
Klanda 97
Klinger 204, 223
Knifsend 201

knowledge 5, 7, 20, 23, 25, 27, 28, 33, 36, 37, 40, 42, 46, 47, 49, 50, 53, 54, 59, 64, 67–69, 71, 78, 94, 105, 180, 200, 204, 205, 209, 212, 213, 217, 226, 227, 254, 260, 265, 268, 269, 271–73, 275, 283
Koomen 279
Korean 35, 42, 45, 137, 237
Kormos 6, 12, 17, 21, 24, 34, 35, 87, 88, 94, 102, 118, 123, 127, 137
Koskey 95, 256, 278
Kowal 87, 95
Krämer 204, 223
Krapp 26, 35, 36
Krashen 49, 53
Krause 60, 73
Kretchmar 246, 254
Krog 86, 95
Kroll 71
Kubanyiova 261, 263, 277, 278
Kubiak 86, 95
Kurdish 247
Kurillo 222

Lafford 126, 137, 138
Lai 124, 130, 136, 137, 260, 278
Lam 95, 207, 214, 223, 225, 238
Lamb 93
Lambert 24, 25, 35, 77, 78, 81, 84, 87–89, 95, 102, 118, 123, 124, 127, 137, 163, 164, 167, 168, 179, 243, 256
Lampert 137
Lane 118
language acquisition 3–5, 25, 35, 51, 53, 56, 71, 72, 74, 80, 96, 97, 118, 122, 136–39, 160, 166, 167, 179, 201, 206, 221, 223, 239, 241, 255–57, 263, 285, 287
language-related episodes 5, 38, 47, 48, 59, 84, 87, 94, 102, 121, 122, 124, 127, 132, 142
Lantolf 59, 71, 74, 122, 138
Lapkin 5, 13, 38, 47, 54, 55, 59, 61, 69, 73, 121, 139
Larios 64, 73
Larsen-Freeman 19, 31, 35, 44, 45, 52, 53, 73, 135, 138, 222, 281, 283–87
latent growth curve 230, 232, 234
Lauer 223
Laufer 125, 137, 138
Lavonen 96

Lawson 18, 35, 76, 94, 95, 118, 255
Lebiere 52
Le Blanc 257
Leder 161
Lee 57, 64, 73, 208, 209, 214, 217, 225, 227, 229, 230, 234, 237, 239
Legatto 69, 73
Légeron 223
Lemov 226, 238
Leow 121, 138
Lerner 12
Leung 179, 223
Liem 238
Liljedahl 145, 161
Lilles 12
Linn 97, 257
Linnenbrink-Garcia 23, 34, 36, 61, 63, 73, 77, 78, 92, 95, 96, 166, 175, 179, 242, 245, 252, 256, 262, 273, 278
Lippman 118
listening 22, 29, 42, 46, 48, 91, 105, 113, 150, 151, 153, 154, 157, 159, 167, 169, 183, 228, 238, 253, 264
literacy 64, 72, 223
Lockhart 59, 72
Loewen 285, 287
Lohman 35
Lombardi 13, 96, 161, 257
longitudinal 3, 10, 11, 13, 34, 69, 82, 227, 234, 236–39, 257, 260
Long 48, 49, 51, 53, 121, 124, 138, 168, 179
Losardo 237
Loschky 125, 138
Lou 237
Lowie 284, 287
Lun 278
Luthans 246, 256
Luxton 228, 237

MacIntyre 28, 34, 43, 53, 69, 70, 73, 92, 96, 104, 114, 118, 167, 178, 179, 227, 238, 244, 256, 261, 263, 277, 278, 282, 287
Mac Iver 136
Mackey 33, 35, 94, 96, 114, 117, 118, 121, 124, 138, 178
Maehr 24, 35
Mahatmya 21, 35
Mahfoodh 63, 69, 73
Malmberg 95

Manca 91, 96
Manchón 139
Manion 71
MANOVA 171
Mansell 74
Marchand 119, 161
Markus 185, 201
Marsh 249, 256
Marshall 203, 223
Martin 2, 13, 102, 118
Matjasko 35
Matthews 255
McColskey 22, 34, 79, 80, 83, 84, 89, 94, 128, 133, 137
McCrae 97
McDonough 24, 34, 35, 121, 129, 138
McGowan 120, 138
McKinney 185, 201
meaning-focused 8, 38, 39, 47–51, 228
measurement 7, 8, 11, 31, 34, 36, 37, 54, 76, 79, 80, 83, 84, 86, 87, 90, 93–96, 118, 133, 137, 180, 221, 223, 224, 227, 236, 246, 247, 249, 255, 280, 287
Meece 228, 235, 238
Mehl 95
Menzies 102, 118
Mercer 1, 4, 9, 11, 13, 18, 19, 22–24, 28, 32, 35, 43, 45, 51, 53, 73, 75, 77, 84, 96, 134, 138, 143, 144, 146, 161, 163, 165, 175, 176, 178, 179, 206, 223–25, 238, 241, 244, 256, 260–62, 266, 276, 278, 280–83, 285–87
meta-analysis 35, 95, 103, 136, 139, 179, 255, 257, 279, 287
metacognitive 60, 95, 185, 190, 191, 200, 201, 257, 260, 272, 273, 275
metalanguage 47, 51, 64, 88
methods 10, 53, 68–71, 73, 79, 80, 83–86, 89, 92, 93, 104, 125, 146, 169, 170, 186, 224, 229, 235, 238, 247, 254, 255, 277
Michael 201
Mikami 262, 278
Millar 72
Miller 201
Mills 10, 202, 219, 223, 281, 282
mindsets 103, 114, 179, 256
Minn 35
mode 9, 24, 94, 121–25, 127–31, 134, 136, 137, 139, 203, 268, 283
Moeller 96

Molenaar 285, 287
Möller 257
Moore 118
Moranski 24, 35, 37
Morgan 255
Morrison 71
Morselli 161
Mosher 120, 138
motivation 1, 2, 6–8, 10, 13, 18–20,
  25–30, 32–37, 39, 43, 53, 57, 60, 64,
  69, 74, 75, 92–94, 102, 103, 105–7,
  109–12, 118, 119, 127, 137, 144, 146,
  161, 162, 165, 166, 175–79, 182,
  184–87, 192, 194–201, 204, 222,
  223, 225, 227, 228, 234, 236–39,
  244, 256, 257, 262–66, 274, 275,
  277–80, 283
Moyer 262, 264, 273, 278
Mozgalina 165, 179
Muenks 246, 256
Muir 43, 53, 118
multilingual 33, 35, 36, 53, 71–73, 95,
  138, 178, 179, 201, 223, 286, 287
Murphey 10, 182, 183, 185, 201
Murphy 64, 73
Muthén 230, 238
Mynard 201

Naderi 277
Nakamura 10, 35, 95, 118, 137, 163–66,
  176, 179, 256
Nakao 228, 238
Nakata 145, 161, 206, 211, 223, 227–30,
  234–36, 238, 239, 243, 244, 253, 256
narratives 57, 64, 95, 202, 204, 208,
  212, 217
Nation 228, 237, 238
Neittaanmaki 222
Nelson 222
Newton 228, 237, 238
Nicholson 239
Nielsen 222
Nikouee 50, 53
Nix 179
Noels 118, 160, 237, 255, 278
non-linear 63, 67
non-verbal 22, 48, 77, 87, 93, 129
Norton 18, 25, 26, 30, 35, 36, 185, 201
noticing 38, 41, 45, 49, 55, 58, 59, 62,
  73, 121, 137, 167, 206
Nugues 223

Nunan 276–79
Nunnally 230, 238
Nurius 185, 201
Nystrand 19, 36, 63, 73, 143, 158, 161,
  167, 179

Oakes 118
Obeidat 237
observational 21, 58, 59, 76,
  80–84, 86, 87, 106–9, 116, 128,
  143, 158, 160, 167, 183, 210,
  215–17, 254
Oga-Baldwin 4, 10, 11, 13, 101, 118,
  145, 161, 206, 211, 223–30, 234–36,
  238, 239, 241, 243, 244, 253, 256,
  281, 282
Oliver 96
Oort 279
Ortega 69, 73, 130, 137, 222
Oswald 136, 138, 248, 257
Otsu 235, 239
outcomes 4, 9, 11, 30, 31, 56, 75–77,
  95, 97, 102, 103, 120, 121, 123–25,
  134, 136, 144, 165, 177, 179, 234, 236,
  241, 244–47, 253, 255, 263, 277, 278,
  285, 286
out-of-class 11, 179, 184, 195, 276
output 24, 39, 45, 48, 54, 58, 88, 121,
  127, 136–39, 142, 180
Ouweneel 242, 245, 252, 257
Oxford 59, 73, 278
O'Connor 96

Pagani 12
Pallant 192, 201
Papi 95, 285, 287
Papworth 13
Park 203, 222
Parker 239
Parr 94, 222
Passeron 25, 33
Patall 165, 179
Patel 222
Patrick 115, 118, 119
Pavlenko 35
Payne 124, 138
Pearl 254, 255
pedagogy 3, 10, 12, 33, 35, 43, 51, 52,
  93, 94, 117, 119, 134, 136, 137, 146,
  178, 203, 209, 218, 219, 221, 253, 255,
  265, 281, 285–87

peer 2, 5, 9, 10, 12, 19, 22–24, 29, 32–36,
    39, 43, 46, 52, 62, 65, 71, 74, 77, 87,
    89, 90, 93, 94, 102–5, 107, 108, 110,
    111, 113–17, 119, 121–24, 129, 130,
    135, 136, 157, 158, 163, 176, 178, 182,
    185, 186, 197–201, 207, 216, 242, 263,
    278, 283, 286
Pekrun 23, 36, 61, 63, 70, 72, 73, 77,
    92, 96, 179, 226, 239, 242, 256, 262,
    273, 278
Peng 244, 257
Perenchevich 97
Perry 73
perseverance 245, 246, 248, 250–53, 255,
    257, 258
Persian 247
persistence 4, 32, 44, 77, 80, 88, 102,
    103, 107, 116, 144, 145, 163, 174,
    184, 242
Peterson 255
Phelps 91, 96
Philp 4–6, 9, 13, 17, 18, 20–23, 35, 36,
    38, 39, 42, 54, 75–78, 87–89, 95, 96,
    101–3, 114, 115, 118–20, 122–24, 132,
    133, 135, 137, 138, 143, 145, 161, 163,
    166, 167, 175, 177, 179, 203, 206, 207,
    209, 215, 220, 223, 241, 243, 256, 257,
    264, 278, 281, 282
Phung 10, 19, 24, 25, 36, 77, 123, 124,
    127, 128, 138, 145, 161, 163, 164, 168,
    176, 179, 180, 243, 257, 264, 278, 281
Pianta 2, 13, 262, 278, 279
Pilot 277
Pintrich 83, 94, 103, 119, 262, 278
Pishghadam 255
Pitzer 1, 13, 18, 36, 38, 54, 75, 77, 97,
    144, 161, 184, 199–201, 261, 279, 283,
    286, 287
Platt 17, 24, 36, 39, 54, 87, 96, 264, 279
Plonsky 136, 138, 248, 257
Poirier 72
Polat 285, 287
policy 4, 31, 33–35, 37, 75, 95, 228, 255
Polio 33, 59, 61, 74, 94, 117, 178
Potowski 26, 36
practitioner 3, 4, 6, 7, 12, 52, 70, 75,
    114, 221, 277, 285
Pratt 52
Prieto Botana 285, 286
priming 10, 48, 182, 185, 186, 198, 281
Priniski 34

Prior 63, 73
private speech 22, 29, 48, 77, 87
proactive 11, 19, 29, 107, 260, 261,
    280, 281
proficiency 6, 25, 29, 34, 57, 59, 64, 69,
    103, 105, 110, 112, 116, 136, 138, 237,
    247, 265, 268, 274, 286
prosocial 10, 89, 182, 184–87, 196, 198,
    199, 282
psychology of language learning 92,
    201, 278, 284–86
psychometric 76, 79, 81, 83, 86, 97,
    238, 257

Qin 52
Qiu 25, 36
qualitative 19, 29, 56, 61, 64, 70, 73, 74,
    79, 81, 83, 84, 90, 94, 117, 133, 171,
    175, 182, 187–89, 198, 254, 261, 266,
    267, 275
quantitative 57, 58, 69, 70, 73, 79, 81,
    83, 90, 91, 133, 172, 173, 175, 182,
    187, 192, 198, 222, 275
questionnaire 42, 57, 70, 80, 81, 83, 89,
    94, 124, 127–29, 139, 142, 167, 168,
    170, 171, 175–78, 180, 187, 192, 196,
    223, 243, 248, 254
Quinn 246, 255

Ranieri 91, 96
Rasch 93
Raye 94
reading 11, 57, 80, 91, 97, 105, 149, 151,
    169, 241, 242, 244, 247–55, 278
real-time 81–83, 85, 91
Rebuschat 5, 13, 53
reconstruction 45, 48, 49, 55,
    121, 284
Reeve 18, 19, 21–23, 36, 144, 161, 165,
    175, 179, 225, 229, 234, 238, 239, 261,
    263, 279, 281, 287
reformulations 55, 59
Reinders 10, 163, 169, 179, 260, 265,
    277, 279
Reinke 277
Reis 86, 96
relational 23, 26, 29, 72, 78, 89
reliability 31, 76, 83, 178, 230,
    249, 250
Renninger 19, 20, 26–28, 30, 35, 36
replication 127, 135, 220, 237

Reschly 1–3, 8, 12, 13, 19, 20, 22, 32–36, 53, 54, 73, 75–77, 79, 85, 93–96, 102, 117–20, 133, 136–38, 144, 160, 161, 178, 184, 201, 206, 222, 223, 237–39, 245, 252, 255, 257, 262, 277–79, 286, 287

Retelsdorf 257

Révész 121, 138

Richards 222, 223, 260, 264, 276–79

Rieber 119

Rimm-Kaufman 254

Risko 159, 161

Ritchie 138, 179

RMSEA 230, 232, 249, 250

Roca de Larios 64, 73

Rogat 95, 256, 278

Rojas 257

Roorda 262, 279

Rosenberg 96

Rotgans 28, 36

Rowe 61, 74

Roy 223

Rubin 71

Russell 102, 119, 163, 179, 262, 279

Ruzek 13, 76, 79, 95, 119

Ryan 43, 54, 93, 115, 118–20, 126, 137, 138, 165, 178, 208, 222, 223, 239, 263, 277, 279, 285–87

Sachs 59, 61, 74

Sadowski 203, 214, 223

Saito 57, 74, 178, 255

Sakai 236, 239

Salaberry 124, 138

Salih 52

Salmela-Aro 82, 86, 96, 287

sampling 11, 69, 76, 80–83, 85, 86, 89, 95, 117, 171, 178, 196, 227, 230, 235, 254

Samuda 18, 21, 33, 78, 87, 88, 94, 102, 117, 163, 178, 285, 287

Sanaoui 145, 161

Sarwal 161

Sato 12, 24, 33, 35, 36, 52, 93, 94, 103, 114, 117, 119, 136, 163, 178, 179, 285–87

Sawyer 35

scaffolding 40, 44, 47, 59, 114, 123, 183, 202, 210, 211, 216, 218–20

Schall 94, 222

Schaufeli 257

Schiefele 25, 36

Schlechty 144, 145, 161

Schlenker 241, 257

Schmidt 5, 13, 27, 28, 33, 36, 38, 54, 59, 82, 86, 95, 96, 121, 138, 167, 168, 179, 246, 257

Schneider 96

Schoenemann 52

Schott 203, 223

Schunk 34

Schutz 179

Scott 45, 51, 54

Seedhaus 38, 54

self-concept 26, 184, 185, 237

self-confidence 105, 118, 263, 272

self-determination theory 27, 36, 54, 161, 165, 238, 262, 277, 279, 287

self-efficacy 32, 66, 74, 93, 137, 223, 257, 262, 268, 269, 272, 277, 278

self-regulation 34, 59, 65, 73, 77, 81, 91, 95, 103, 119, 242, 257, 262, 278, 279

self-report 24, 34, 59, 76, 80, 81, 83, 84, 86, 89, 91, 92, 94, 133, 137, 182, 187, 227, 234, 236, 237, 265

Senna 72

Serroul 43, 53

Sert 261, 263, 277, 279

Shao 226, 239

Shapiro 97

Shernoff 2, 9, 13, 32, 36, 82, 86, 96, 101–3, 114, 116, 119, 143, 145, 158, 161, 242, 253, 257, 262, 276, 279

Shiffman 86, 96

Shraw 165, 178

Shutz 95

Sidhwa 12

Simons 277

Sinatra 3, 13, 75, 80, 96, 143, 161, 241, 242, 257

Singer 203, 223

Sinha 13, 72, 119, 257

Skehan 55, 137

skills 33, 111, 113, 116, 200, 204, 205, 228, 252, 254, 268, 283, 287

Skilton-Sylvester 26, 36

Skinner 1, 13, 18, 22, 24, 28, 32, 34, 36, 38, 39, 54, 75, 77, 96, 97, 102, 103, 119, 144, 161, 166, 179, 183, 184, 199–201, 219, 220, 223, 261, 275, 279, 283, 286, 287

Skutnabb-Kangas 33

Skype 127
Slater 204, 223
Smith 34, 124, 138
Snug 94, 222
Snyder 200, 201
Sobocinski 95
social engagement 5, 20–24, 29, 33, 42,
   44, 47, 52, 79, 81, 84, 89, 93, 106,
   107, 115, 117, 123, 124, 129, 135,
   144, 164, 166, 176, 184, 185, 207,
   211–20, 225, 242, 243, 258, 262,
   281, 286
Sok 287
Spanish 9, 30, 35, 37, 42, 51, 101, 120,
   123, 125–27, 129, 133, 134, 136, 137,
   140–42, 146, 147, 208, 279
speaking 21, 46, 108, 112–14, 129,
   142, 146, 167, 183, 190, 191, 198,
   199, 228, 235, 238, 245, 248, 253,
   254, 259, 268
Spicer 96
Spilt 279
Spinath 230, 239
Sroufe 118
Stanley 260, 279
Stanney 203, 214, 223
Steinmayr 230, 239, 246, 257
Sternberg 35, 278
stimulated recall 51, 85, 89, 132,
   134, 243
Stone 96
Storch 5, 13, 23, 36, 38, 45, 47–49, 51,
   54, 56, 58, 59, 64, 71, 74, 87, 89, 97,
   102, 119, 121, 122, 132, 135, 139, 143,
   161, 264, 279
strategies 33, 34, 57, 59, 60, 62, 65, 66,
   71, 73, 77, 94, 118, 132, 137, 138, 143,
   151, 152, 156, 180, 222, 242, 244, 254,
   265, 267, 270, 272, 273, 275, 278
Stroud 227, 239
Sulis 9, 77, 101, 281, 282
Sunitham 121, 129, 138
surveys 37, 57, 58, 61, 80, 81, 83, 84, 89,
   147, 185, 190, 191, 194, 195, 204, 219,
   220, 229, 230
Svalberg 4, 5, 8, 13, 20–24, 28, 37–42,
   44, 46, 50, 52, 54, 78, 84, 87–89, 97,
   102, 103, 119, 122, 123, 127, 133, 139,
   144, 145, 161, 163, 166, 177, 180, 206,
   212, 219, 220, 223, 225, 239, 242, 243,
   257, 262, 279, 280, 284, 287

Swain 5, 13, 38, 44, 47, 54, 55, 87,
   89, 95, 97, 121, 123, 132, 139,
   166–68, 180
Swedish 228
Sweigart 34
Symonds 284, 287

Tabachnick 230, 239
Tabandeh 257
Taboala 97
Taguchi 83, 94
Tahmouresi 95, 222, 278
Talbot 9, 143
Tan 238
task-based 9, 24, 38, 48, 50–54, 78, 81,
   84, 94, 120, 126, 131, 133, 136–38,
   163, 164, 168, 178, 243, 281, 287
Tauer 34
Taylor 262, 279
Teimouri 244, 246, 248, 257
temporal 8, 27, 32, 56, 61, 67, 90, 201,
   254, 264, 271, 275, 282
Terrell 49, 53
text 27, 28, 33, 42, 45, 48, 49, 52, 57, 58,
   62, 65, 66, 68, 71, 93, 105, 121, 124,
   137, 138, 155, 183, 207, 218, 219, 221,
   254, 267
Thai 138, 169
think-aloud 59, 73
Thornbury 45, 55
Thorsen 77, 87, 89, 95, 120, 130, 134,
   137, 264, 278
Tikly 52
timescale 2, 3, 11, 53, 264, 273,
   275, 284
Titz 73
Tonks 13, 96, 119, 257
Toohey 26, 30, 36
Torres-Guzman 33
Toth 24, 35, 37
transcripts 42, 68, 107, 128, 137, 149,
   164, 170–72, 175, 176, 220
treatment 10, 126, 127, 134, 186, 187,
   189, 190, 192, 196–99
Trowler 144, 161
Truscott 56, 72, 74
Tucker 277
Turkish 243, 247, 277
turn-taking 88, 127
Twitter 141
Tynan 255

Upadyaya 287
Usher 247, 257
Ushioda 53, 201
utility 27–29, 31, 34, 44, 159

validity 76, 83, 86, 105, 106, 122, 130, 143, 228, 230, 236
Van den Branden 287
van Lier 64, 74
Vargas Lascano 160, 255
variable 2, 11, 12, 19, 34, 35, 44, 59, 72, 94, 102, 118, 122, 128, 131, 133, 134, 137, 164–66, 171, 177, 178, 225–27, 230, 232, 233, 235, 242, 247–50, 254, 255, 261, 263, 269, 271
verbal reports 58, 68, 70, 71
Verspoor 284, 287
video recording 43, 84, 220
Vitta 13, 95
vocabulary 9, 50, 125, 126, 130–32, 134, 136–38, 161, 208, 216, 219, 258, 265, 269, 271–73, 279
Vollstedt 161
Volpe 83, 97
von muhlenen 203, 221, 222
Vygotsky 111, 114, 115, 119

Wach 264, 279
Wagner 37
Walker 60, 74, 202, 223
Walter 21, 34, 77, 88, 94, 119, 123, 137, 207, 222, 262, 278
Wang 9, 11, 19, 43, 79, 81, 94, 97, 143, 222, 241, 242, 248, 252, 254, 257, 260, 264–69, 271–74, 276, 279, 281–83
Warren 12
Warschauer 124, 139
Weidinger 257
well-being 110, 117, 159, 185, 228, 282
Wellborn 18, 36, 37, 103, 118, 119
Wen 137, 256
Wenden 71
Wentzel 36, 119, 185, 201
Weslake 159, 161
Whitney 124, 138
Wigfield 36, 80, 84, 97, 119, 159, 162, 256, 257

Wigglesworth 59, 64, 74, 121, 132, 139
Wildhagen 79, 95
Williams 27, 37, 59, 74, 97, 121, 139, 223
Willingham 226, 235
willingness to communicate 43, 73, 104, 118, 244, 245, 256, 257, 261, 263, 275, 277, 278
willingness to engage 11, 43, 44, 46, 159, 220, 260–64, 267–77, 279, 283
willingness to participate 261, 263, 277
Witmer 203, 223
Witney 178, 255
Wolters 246, 257, 262, 279
Wong 95, 223, 238
Wood 74
Woodrow 244, 257
Wright 255
writing 53, 56, 57, 60–62, 66, 68–74, 91, 95, 105, 111, 121, 139, 151, 157, 167, 169, 207, 208, 253, 278
written corrective feedback 8, 53, 56–59, 61–64, 67, 69–74, 82, 85, 95, 255
Wylie 3, 12, 13, 33–36, 53, 54, 73, 94–97, 117–19, 136–38, 160, 161, 178, 201, 206, 222, 223, 237–39, 255, 277–79, 287

Yamashita 246, 257
Yang 223, 238, 256, 264, 279
Yazzie-Mintz 22, 37
Yeşilyurt 160, 255
Yilmaz 124, 136, 139
Yue 261, 263, 277, 278

Zembylas 95
Zhang 56, 60, 62, 64, 65, 69, 74, 161, 245, 256
Zhao 124, 130, 136, 137
Zheng 56, 64, 69, 74, 260, 278
Zhou 69, 74
Ziegler 124, 136, 139
Zillah 202
Zimmer 1, 12, 21, 34, 144, 158, 161, 184, 201, 242, 255
Zimmerman 34, 103, 117, 241, 255
ZPD 60, 111, 114